Normal School

# NATIONAL EPICS

# NATIONAL EPICS

BY

KATE MILNER RABB

FIFTH EDITION

CHICAGO
A. C. McCLURG & CO.
1915

W. F. HALL PRINTING COMPANY, CHICAGO

TO

MY MOTHER.

# PREFACE.

THIS volume is intended for an introduction to the study of the epics. While the simplicity and directness of the epic style seem to make such a book unnecessary, the fact that to many persons of literary tastes some of these great poems are inaccessible, and that to many more the pleasure of exploring for themselves " the realms of gold " is rendered impossible by the cares of business, has seemed sufficient excuse for its being. Though the beauty of the original is of necessity lost in a condensation of this kind, an endeavor has been made to preserve the characteristic epithets, and to retain what Mr. Arnold called " the simple truth about the matter of the poem." It is believed that the sketch prefacing each story, giving briefly the length, versification, and history of the poem, will have its value to those readers who have not access to the epics, and that the selections following the story, each recounting a complete incident, will give a better idea of the epic than could be formed from passages scattered through the text.

The epic originated among tribes of barbarians, who deified departed heroes and recited legends in praise of their deeds. As the hymn developed, the chorus and strophe were dropped, and the narrative only was preserved. The word "epic" was used simply to distinguish the narrative poem, which was recited, from the lyric, which was sung, and from the dramatic, which was acted.

As the nation passed from childhood to youth, the legends of the hero that each wandering minstrel had changed to suit his fancy, were collected and fused into one by some great poet, who by his power of unification made this written epic his own.

This is the origin of the Hindu epics, the "Iliad" and the "Odyssey," the "Kalevala," the "Shah-Nameh," "Beowulf," the "Nibelungen Lied," the "Cid," and the "Song of Roland."

The conditions for the production of the primitive epic exist but once in a nation's growth. Its later epics must be written on subjects of national importance, chosen by the poet, who arranges and embellishes his material according to the rules of the primitive epic. To this class belong the "Æneid," the "Jerusalem Delivered," and the "Lusiad." Dante's poem is broader, for it is the epic of mediæval Christianity. Milton likewise sought "higher argument" than

> "Wars, hitherto the only argument
> Heroic deemed,"

and crystallized the religious beliefs of his time in "Paradise Lost."

The characteristics both of the primitive and the modern epic are their uniform metre, simplicity of construction, concentration of action into a short time, and the use of episode and dialogue. The main difference lies in the impersonality of the primitive epic, whose author has so skillfully hidden himself behind his work that, as some one has said of Homer, "his heroes are immortal, but his own existence is doubtful."

Although the historical events chronicled in the epics have in every case been so distorted by the fancy of the poets that they cannot be accepted as history, the epics are storehouses of information concerning ancient manners and customs, religious beliefs, forms of government, treatment of women, and habits of feeling.

Constructed upon the noblest principles of art, and pervaded by the eternal calm of the immortals, these poems have an especial value to us, who have scarcely yet realized that poetry is an art, and are feverish from the unrest of our time. If by the help of this volume any reader be enabled to find a portion of the wisdom that is hidden in these mines, its purpose will have been accomplished.

My thanks are due to Mr. John A. Wilstach for the use of selections from his translation of the "Divine Comedy;" to Prof. J. M. Crawford, for the use of selections from his translation of the "Kalevala;" to Henry Holt & Co., for the use of selections from Rabillon's translation of "La Chanson de Roland;" to Roberts Brothers, for the use of selections from Edwin Arnold's "Indian Idylls;" to Prof. J. C. Hall, for the use of selections from his translation of "Beowulf;" and to A. C. Armstrong & Son, for the use of selections from Conington's Translation of the "Æneid." The selections from the "Iliad" and the "Odyssey" are used with the permission of and by special arrangement with Houghton, Mifflin & Co., publishers of Bryant's translations of the "Iliad" and the "Odyssey." Special thanks are due to Miss Eliza G. Browning of the Public Library of Indianapolis, to Miss Florence Hughes of the Library of Indiana University, and to Miss Charity Dye, of Indianapolis.

K. M. R.

INDIANAPOLIS, IND., September, 1896.

# CONTENTS.

# SELECTIONS.

## THE RÂMÂYANA.

"He who sings and hears this poem continually has attained to the highest state of enjoyment, and will finally be equal to the gods."

THE Râmâyana, the Hindu Iliad, is variously ascribed to the fifth, third, and first centuries B. C., its many interpolations making it almost impossible to determine its age by internal evidence. Its authorship is unknown, but according to legend it was sung by Kuça and Lava, the sons of Rama, to whom it was taught by Valmiki. Of the three versions now extant, one is attributed to Valmiki, another to Tuli Das, and a third to Vyasa.

Its historical basis, almost lost in the innumerable episodes and grotesque imaginings of the Hindu, is probably the conquest of southern India and Ceylon by the Aryans.

The Râmâyana is written in the Sanskrit language, is divided into seven books, or sections, and contains fifty thousand lines, the English translation of which, by Griffith, occupies five volumes.

The hero, Rama, is still an object of worship in India, the route of his wanderings being, each year, trodden by devout pilgrims. The poem is not a mere literary monument,—it is a part of the actual religion of the Hindu, and is held in such reverence that the mere reading or hearing of it, or certain passages of it, is believed to free from sin and grant his every desire to the reader or hearer.

BIBLIOGRAPHY AND CRITICISM, THE RÂMÂYANA.    G. W. Cox's Mythology and Folklore, 1881, p. 313 ; John Dowson's Classical Dictionary of Hindu Mythology, Religion, Geography, History, and Literature, 1879 ; Sir William Jones on the Literature of the Hindus (in his Works, vol. iv.) ; Maj.-Gen. Vans Kennedy's Researches into Hindu Mythology, 1831 ; James Mill's History of British India, 1840, vol. ii., pp. 47–123 ; F. Max Müller's Ancient Sanskrit Literature, 1859 ; E. A. Reed's Hindu Literature, 1891, pp. 153–271 ; Albrecht Weber's History of Indian Literature, 1878, pp. 191–195 ; J. T. Wheeler's History of India, 4 vols., 1876, vol. ii. ; Sir Monier Williams's Indian Wisdom, 1863, Indian Epic Poetry, 1863 ; Article on Sanskrit Literature in Encyclopædia Britannica ; R. M. Cust's The Râmâyana : a Sanskrit Epic (in his Linguistic and Oriental Essays, 1880, p. 56) ; T. Goldstuecker's Râmâyana (in his Literary Remains, 1879, vol. i., p. 155) ; C. J. Stone's Cradleland of Arts and Creeds, 1880, pp. 11–21 ; Albrecht Weber's On the Râmâyana, 1870 ; Westminster Review, 1849, vol. l., p. 34 ; J. C. Oman's Great Indian Epics, 1874, pp. 13–81.

STANDARD ENGLISH TRANSLATIONS, THE RÂMÂYANA. — The Râmâyana, Tr. by R. T. H. Griffith, 5 vols., 1870–1874 (Follows Bombay ed., Translated into metre of " Lady of the Lake ") ; Extracts from the Râmâyana, Tr. by Sir William Jones (in his Works, vol. 13) ; Iliad of the East, F. Richardson, 1873 (Popular translations of a set of legends from the Râmâyana) ; The Râmâyana translated into English Prose, edited and published by Naumatha Nath Dutt, 7 vols., Calcutta, 1890–1894.

## THE STORY OF THE RÂMÂYANA.

BRAHMA, creator of the universe, though all powerful, could not revoke a promise once made. For this reason, Ravana, the demon god of Ceylon, stood on his head in the midst of five fires for ten thousand years, and at the end of that time boldly demanded of Brahma as a reward that he should not be slain by gods, demons, or genii. He also requested the gift of nine other heads and eighteen additional arms and hands.

These having been granted, he began by the aid of his evil spirits, the Rakshasas, to lay waste the earth and to do violence to the good, especially to the priests.

At the time when Ravana's outrages were spreading terror throughout the land, and Brahma, looking down from his throne, shuddered to see the monster he had gifted with such fell power, there reigned in Ayodhya, now the city of Oude, a good and wise raja, Dasaratha, who had reigned over the splendid city for nine thousand years without once growing weary. He had but one grief, — that he was childless, — and at the opening of the story he was preparing to make the great sacrifice, Asva-medha, to propitiate the gods, that they might give him a son.

The gods, well pleased, bore his request to Brahma in person, and incidentally preferred a request that he provide some means of destroying the monster Ravana that was working such woe among their priests, and disturbing their sacrifices.

Brahma granted the first request, and, cudgeling his brains for a device to destroy Ravana, bethought himself that while he had promised that neither gods, genii, nor demons should slay him, he had said nothing of man. He accordingly led the appealing gods to Vishnu, who proclaimed that the monster should be slain by men and monkeys, and that he would himself be re-incarnated as the eldest son of Dasaratha and in this form compass the death of Ravana.

In course of time, as a reward for his performance of the great sacrifice, four sons were born to Dasaratha, Rama by Kausalya, his oldest wife, Bharata, whose mother was Kaikeyi, and twin sons, Lakshmana and Satrughna, whose mother was Sumitra.

Rama, the incarnation of Vishnu, destined to destroy Ravana, grew daily in grace, beauty, and strength. When he was but sixteen years old, having been sent for by a sage to destroy the demons who were disturbing the forest hermits in their religious rites, he departed unattended, save by his brother Lakshmana and a guide, into the pathless forests, where he successfully overcame the terrible Rakshasa, Tarika, and conveyed her body to the grateful sage.

While he was journeying through the forests, destroying countless Rakshasas, he chanced to pass near the kingdom of Mithila and heard that its king, Janaka, had offered his peerless daughter, Sita, in marriage to the man who could bend the mighty bow of Siva the destroyer, which, since its owner's death, had been kept at Janaka's court.

Rama at once determined to accomplish the feat, which had been essayed in vain by so many suitors. When he presented himself at court Janaka was at once won by his youth and beauty ; and when the mighty bow, resting upon an eight-wheeled car, was drawn in by five thousand men, and Rama without apparent effort bent it until it broke, he gladly gave him his beautiful daughter, and after the splendid wedding ceremonies were over, loaded the happy pair with presents to carry back to Ayodhya.

When Dasaratha, who had attended the marriage of his son at Mithila, returned home, he began to feel weary of reigning, and bethought himself of the ancient Hindu custom of making the eldest son and heir apparent a Yuva-Raja, — that is appointing him assistant king. Rama deserved this honor, and would, moreover, be of great assistance to him.

His happy people received the announcement of his intention with delight ; the priests approved of it as well, and the

whole city was in the midst of the most splendid preparations
for the ceremony, when it occurred to Dasaratha that all he
lacked was the congratulations of his youngest and favorite
wife, Kaikeyi, on this great event. The well-watered streets
and the garlanded houses had already aroused the suspicions
of Kaikeyi, — suspicions speedily confirmed by the report of
her maid. Angered and jealous because the son of Kausalya
and not her darling Bharata, at that time absent from the
city, was to be made Yuva-Raja, she fled to the "Chamber
of Sorrows," and was there found by the old Raja.

Though Kaikeyi was his youngest and most beautiful wife,
her tears, threats, and entreaties would have been of no avail
had she not recalled that, months before, the old Raja, in
gratitude for her devoted nursing during his illness, had
granted her two promises. She now demanded the fulfilment
of these before she would consent to smile upon him, and
the consent won, she required him, first, to appoint Bharata
Yuva-Raja ; and, second, to exile Rama for fourteen years to
the terrible forest of Dandaka.

The promise of a Hindu, once given, cannot be revoked.
In spite of the grief of the old Raja, of Kausalya, his old
wife, and of all the people, who were at the point of revolt at
the sudden disgrace of their favorite prince, the terrible news
was announced to Rama, and he declared himself ready to
go, to save his father from dishonor.

He purposed to go alone, but Sita would not suffer herself to be thus deserted. Life without him, she pleaded, was
worse than death ; and so eloquent was her grief at the thought
of parting that she was at last permitted to don the rough garment of bark provided by the malicious Kaikeyi.

The people of Ayodhya, determined to share the fate of
their favorites, accompanied them from the city, their tears
laying the dust raised by Rama's chariot wheels. But when
sleep overcame them, Rama, Sita, and Lakshmana escaped
from them, dismissed their charioteer, and, crossing the
Ganges, made their way to the mountain of Citra-kuta, where
they took up their abode.

No more beautiful place could be imagined. Flowers of

every kind, delicious fruits, and on every side the most pleasing prospects, together with perfect love, made their hermitage a paradise on earth.   Here the exiles led an idyllic existence until sought out by Bharata, who, learning from his mother on his return home the ruin she had wrought in the Raj, had indignantly spurned her, and hastened to Dandaka. The old Raja had died from grief soon after the departure of the exiles, and Bharata now demanded that Rama should return to Ayodhya and become Raja, as was his right, as eldest son.

When Rama refused to do this until the end of his fourteen years of exile, Bharata vowed that for fourteen years he would wear the garb of a devotee and live outside the city, committing the management of the Raj to a pair of golden sandals which he took from Rama's feet.   All the affairs of state would be transacted under the authority of the sandals, and Bharata, while ruling the Raj, would pay homage to them.

Soon after the departure of Bharata the exiles were warned to depart from their home on Citra-kuta and seek a safer hermitage, for terrible rakshasas filled this part of the forest. They accordingly sought the abode of Atri the hermit, whose wife Anasuya was so pleased with Sita's piety and devotion to her husband that she bestowed upon her the crown of immortal youth and beauty.   They soon found a new abode in the forest of Pancarati, on the banks of the river Godavari, where Lakshmana erected a spacious bamboo house.

Their happiness in this elysian spot was destined to be short-lived.   Near them dwelt a horrible rakshasa, Surpanakha by name, who fell in love with Rama.   When she found that he did not admire the beautiful form she assumed to win him, and that both he and Lakshmana laughed at her advances, she attempted to destroy Sita, only to receive in the attempt a disfiguring wound from the watchful Lakshmana.   Desiring revenge for her disfigured countenance and her scorned love, she hastened to the court of her brother Ravana, in Ceylon, and in order to induce him to avenge her wrongs, dwelt upon the charms of the beautiful wife of Rama.

Some days after, Sita espied a golden fawn, flecked with

silver, among the trees near their home. Its shining body, its jewel-like horns, so captivated her fancy that she implored Rama, if possible, to take it alive for her; if not, at least to bring her its skin for a couch. As Rama departed, he warned Lakshmana not to leave Sita for one moment; he would surely return, since no weapon could harm him. In the depths of the forest the fawn fell by his arrow, crying as it fell, "O Sita! O Lakshmana!" in Rama's very tones.

When Sita heard the cry she reproached Lakshmana for not going to his brother's aid, until he left her to escape her bitter words. He had no sooner disappeared in the direction of the cry than a hermit appeared and asked her to minister unto his wants.

Sita carried him food, bathed his feet, and conversed with him until, able no longer to conceal his admiration for her, he revealed himself in his true form as the demon god of Ceylon.

When she indignantly repulsed him he seized her, and mounting his chariot drove rapidly towards Ceylon.

When Rama and Lakshmana returned home, soon after, they found the house empty. As they searched through the forest for traces of her they found a giant vulture dying from wounds received while endeavoring to rescue the shrieking Sita. Going farther, they encountered the monkey king Sugriva and his chiefs, among whom Sita had dropped from the chariot her scarf and ornaments.

Sugriva had been deposed from his kingdom by his brother Bali, who had also taken his wife from him. Rama agreed to conquer Bali if Sugriva would assist in the search for Sita; and, the agreement made, they at once marched upon Kishkindha, together slew Bali, and gained possession of the wealthy city and the queen Tara. They were now ready to search for the lost Sita.

In his quest through every land, Hanuman, the monkey general, learned from the king of the vultures that she had been carried to Ceylon. He immediately set out for the coast with his army, only to find a bridgeless ocean stretching between them and the island. Commanding his soldiers to remain where they were, Hanuman expanded his body to enormous proportions, leaped the vast expanse of water, and alighted upon a mountain, from which he could look down upon Lanka, the capital city of Ceylon. Perceiving the city to be closely guarded, he assumed the form of a cat, and thus, unsuspected, crept through the barriers and examined the city. He found the demon god in his apartments, surrounded by beautiful women, but Sita was not among them. Continuing his search, he at last discovered her, her beauty dimmed by grief, seated under a tree in a beautiful asoka grove, guarded by hideous rakshasas with the faces of buffaloes, dogs, and swine.

Assuming the form of a tiny monkey, Hanuman crept down the tree, and giving her the ring of Rama, took one from her. He offered to carry her away with him, but Sita declared that Rama must himself come to her rescue. While they were talking together, the demon god appeared, and, after fruitless wooing, announced that if Sita did not yield herself to him in two months he would have her guards "mince her limbs with steel" for his morning repast.

In his rage, Hanuman destroyed a mango grove and was captured by the demon's guards, who were ordered to set his tail on fire. As soon as this was done, Hanuman made himself so small that he slipped from his bonds, and, jumping upon the roofs, spread a conflagration through the city of Lanka.

He leaped back to the mainland, conveyed the news of Sita's captivity to Rama and Sugriva, and was soon engaged in active preparations for the campaign.

As long as the ocean was unbridged it was impossible for any one save Hanuman to cross it. In his anger at being so thwarted, Rama turned his weapons against it, until from the terrified waves rose the god of the ocean, who promised him that if Nala built a bridge, the waves should support the materials as firmly as though it were built on land.

Terror reigned in Lanka at the news of the approach of Rama. Vibishana, Ravana's brother, deserted to Rama, because of the demon's rage when he advised him to make peace with Rama. Fiercely fought battles ensued, in which even the gods took part, Vishnu and Indra taking sides with Rama, and the evil spirits fighting with Ravana.

After the war had been carried on for some time, with varying results, it was decided to determine it by single combat between Ravana and Rama. Then even the gods were terrified at the fierceness of the conflict. At each shot Rama's mighty bow cut off a head of the demon, which at once grew back, and the hero was in despair until he remembered the all-powerful arrow given him by Brahma.

As the demon fell by this weapon, flowers rained from heaven upon the happy victor, and his ears were ravished with celestial music.

Touched by the grief of Ravana's widows, Rama ordered his foe a splendid funeral, and then sought the conquered city.

Sita was led forth, beaming with happiness at finding herself re-united to her husband; but her happiness was destined to be of short duration. Rama received her with coldness and with downcast eyes, saying that she could no longer be his wife, after having dwelt in the zenana of the demon. Sita assured him of her innocence; but on his continuing to revile her, she ordered her funeral pyre to be built, since she would rather die by fire than live despised by Rama. The sympathy of all the bystanders was with Sita, but Rama saw her enter the flames without a tremor. Soon Agni, the god of fire, appeared, bearing the uninjured Sita in his arms. Her innocence thus publicly proved by the trial by fire, she was welcomed by Rama, whose treatment she tenderly forgave.

The conquest made, the demon destroyed, and Sita restored, Rama returned in triumph to Ayodhya, and assumed the government. The city was prosperous, the people were happy, and for a time all went well. It was not long, however, before whispers concerning Sita's long abode in Ceylon spread abroad, and some one whispered to Rama that a famine in the country was due to the guilt of Sita, who had suffered the caresses of the demon while in captivity in Ceylon. Forgetful of the trial by fire, forgetful of Sita's devotion to him through weal and woe, the ungrateful Rama immediately ordered her to the forest in which they had spent together the happy years of their exile.

Without a murmur the unhappy Sita, alone and unbefriended, dragged herself to the forest, and, torn with grief of body and spirit, found the hermitage of Valmiki, where she gave birth to twin sons, Lava and Kuça. Here she reared them, with the assistance of the hermit, who was their teacher, and under whose care they grew to manhood, handsome and strong.

It chanced about the time the youths were twenty years old, that Rama, who had grown peevish and disagreeable with age, began to think the gods were angered with him because he had killed Ravana, who was the son of a Brahman. Determined to propitiate them by means of the great sacrifice, he caused a horse to be turned loose in the forest. When his men went to retake it, at the end of the year, it was caught by two strong and beautiful youths who resisted all efforts to capture them. In his rage Rama went to the forest in person, only to learn that the youths were his twin sons, Lava and Kuça. Struck with remorse, Rama recalled the sufferings of his wife Sita, and on learning that she was at the hermitage of Valmiki, ordered her to come to him, that he might take her to him again, having first caused her to endure the trial by fire to prove her innocence to all his court.

Sita had had time to recover from the love of her youth, and the prospect of life with Rama, without the *couleur de rose* of youthful love, was not altogether pleasant. At first, she even refused to see him; but finally, moved by the appeals of Valmiki and his wife, she clad herself in her richest robes, and, young and beautiful as when first won by Rama, she stood before him. Not deigning to look in his face, she appealed to the earth. If she had never loved any man but Rama, if her truth and purity were known to the earth, let it open its bosom and take her to it. While the armies stood trembling with horror, the earth opened, a gorgeous throne appeared, and the goddess of earth, seated upon it, took Sita beside her and conveyed her to the realms of eternal happiness, leaving the too late repentant Rama to wear out his remaining years in shame and penitence.

## SELECTIONS FROM THE RÂMÂYANA.

### THE DESCENT OF THE GANGES.

SAGARA, an early king of Ayodhya, had sixty thousand sons, whom he sent out one day to recover a horse that had been designed for the great sacrifice, but had been stolen by a rakshasa. Having searched the earth unsuccessfully, they proceeded to dig into the lower regions.

Cloven with shovel and with hoe, pierced by axes and by spades,
Shrieked the earth in frantic woe ; rose from out the yawning shades
Yells of anguish, hideous roars from the expiring brood of hell,—
Serpents, giants, and asoors, in the deep abyss that dwell.
Sixty thousand leagues in length, all unweary, full of wrath,
Through the centre, in their strength, clove they down their hellward path.
And downward dug they many a rood, and downward till they saw aghast,
Where the earth-bearing elephant stood, ev'n like a mountain tall and vast.
'T is he whose head aloft sustains the broad earth's forest-clothèd round,
With all its vast and spreading plains, and many a stately city crowned.
If underneath the o'erbearing load bows down his weary head, 't is then
The mighty earthquakes are abroad, and shaking down the abodes of men.
Around earth's pillar moved they slowly, and thus in humble accents blest
Him the lofty and the holy, that bears the region of the East.
And southward dug they many a rood, until before their shuddering sight
The next earth-bearing elephant stood, huge Mahapadmas' mountain height.
Upon his head earth's southern bound, all full of wonder, saw they rest.
Slow and awe-struck paced they round, and him, earth's southern pillar, blest.
Westward then their work they urge, king Sagara's six myriad race,
Unto the vast earth's western verge, and there in his appointed place
The next earth-bearing elephant stood, huge Saumanasa's mountain crest ;
Around they paced in humble mood, and in like courteous phrase addrest,
And still their weary toil endure, and onward dig until they see
Last earth-bearing Himapandure, glorying in his majesty.

*At last they reach the place where Vishnu appears with the horse. A flame issues from the mouth of the indignant deity and destroys the six myriad sons of Sagara. The adventure devolves on their brother Ansuman, who achieves it with perfect success. He is permitted to lead away the horse,*

*but the ashes of his brothers cannot be purified by earthly water; the god-*
*dess Ganga must first be brought to earth, and having undergone lustration*
*from that holy flood, the race of Sagara are to ascend to heaven. Brahma*
*at last gives his permission to Ganga to descend. King Bhagiratha takes*
*his stand on the top of Gokarna, the sacred peak of Himavan (the Himalaya),*
*and here —*

Stands with arms outstretch'd on high, amid five blazing fires, the one
Towards each quarter of the sky, the fifth the full meridian sun.
Mid fiercest frosts on snow he slept, the dry and withered leaves his food,
Mid rains his roofless vigil kept, the soul and sense alike subdued.
High on the top of Himavan the mighty Mashawara stood;
And "Descend," he gave the word to the heaven-meandering water —
Full of wrath the mandate heard Himavan's majestic daughter.
To a giant's stature soaring and intolerable speed,
From heaven's height down rushed she, pouring upon Siva's sacred head,
Him the goddess thought in scorn with her resistless might to sweep
By her fierce waves overborne, down to hell's remotest deep.

    Down on Sankara's holy head, down the holy fell, and there,
Amid the entangling meshes spread, of his loose and flowing hair,
Vast and boundless as the woods upon the Himalaya's brow,
Nor ever may the struggling floods rush headlong to the earth below.
Opening, egress was not there, amid those winding, long meanders.
Within that labyrinthine hair, for many an age, the goddess wanders.

    *By the penances of the king, Siva is propitiated, and the stream, by seven*
*channels, finds its way to the plains of India.*

    Up the Raja at the sign upon his glittering chariot leaps,
Instant Ganga the divine follows his majestic steps.
From the high heaven burst she forth first on Siva's lofty crown,
Headlong then, and prone to earth thundering rushed the cataract down,
Swarms of bright-hued fish came dashing; turtles, dolphins in their mirth,
Fallen or falling, glancing, flashing, to the many-gleaming earth.
And all the host of heaven came down, spirits and genii, in amaze,
And each forsook his heavenly throne, upon that glorious scene to gaze.
On cars, like high-towered cities, seen, with elephants and coursers rode,
Or on soft swinging palanquin, lay wondering each observant god.
As met in bright divan each god, and flashed their jewell'd vestures' rays,
The coruscating æther glow'd, as with a hundred suns ablaze.
And with the fish and dolphins gleaming, and scaly crocodiles and snakes,
Glanc'd the air, as when fast streaming the blue lightning shoots and breaks:
And in ten thousand sparkles bright went flashing up the cloudy spray,
The snowy flocking swans less white, within its glittering mists at play.
And headlong now poured down the flood, and now in silver circlets wound,
Then lake-like spread all bright and broad, then gently, gently flowed around,
Then 'neath the caverned earth descending, then spouted up the boiling tide,
Then stream with stream harmonious blending, swell bubbling up and smooth
    subside.
By that heaven-welling water's breast, the genii and the sages stood,
Its sanctifying dews they blest, and plung'd within the lustral flood.

Whoe'er beneath the curse of heaven from that immaculate world had fled,
To th' impure earth in exile driven, to that all-holy baptism sped ;
And purified from every sin, to the bright spirit's bliss restor'd,
Th' ethereal sphere they entered in, and through th' empyreal mansions
    soar'd.
The world in solemn jubilee beheld those heavenly waves draw near,
From sin and dark pollution free, bathed in the blameless waters clear.
Swift king Bhagiratha drave upon his lofty glittering car,
And swift with her obeisant wave bright Ganga followed him afar.

*Milman's Translation.*


## The Death of Yajnadatta.

THE Raja Dasaratha was compelled to banish his favorite
son Rama, immediately after his marriage to Sita, because his
banishment was demanded by the Raja's wife Kaikeyi, to
whom he had once promised to grant any request she might
make. His grief at the loss of his son is described in this
selection.

Scarce Rama to the wilderness had with his younger brother gone,
Abandoned to his deep distress, king Dasaratha sate alone.
Upon his sons to exile driven when thought that king, as Indra bright,
Darkness came o'er him, as in heaven when pales th' eclipsèd sun his
    light.
Six days he sate, and mourned and pined for Rama all that weary time.
At midnight on his wandering mind rose up his old forgotten crime.
His queen, Kausalya, the divine, addressed he, as she rested near :
    " Kausalya, if thou wakest, incline to thy lord's speech thy ready ear.
Whatever deed, or good or ill, by man, O blessed queen, is wrought,
Its proper fruit he gathers still, by time to slow perfection brought.
He who the opposing counsel's weight compares not in his judgment cool,
Or misery or bliss his fate, among the sage is deemed a fool.
As one that quits the Amra bower, the bright Palasa's pride to gain
Mocked by the promise of its flower, seeks its unripening fruit in vain,
So I the lovely Amra left for the Palasa's barren bloom,
Through mine own fatal error 'reft of banished Rama, mourn in gloom.
Kausalya ! in my early youth by my keen arrow, at his mark
Aimed with too sure and deadly truth, was wrought a deed most fell and
    dark.
At length, the evil that I did, hath fallen upon my fated head,
As when on subtle poison hid an unsuspecting child hath fed ;
Even as that child unwittingly hath made the poisonous fare his food,
Even so, in ignorance by me was wrought that deed of guilt and blood.
Unwed wert thou in virgin bloom, and I in youth's delicious prime,
The season of the rains had come, — that soft and love enkindling time.
Earth's moisture all absorbed, the sun through all the world its warmth had
    spread,

Turned from the north, its course begun, where haunt the spirits of the dead :
Gathering o'er all the horizon's bound on high the welcome clouds appeared,
Exulting, all the birds flew round, — cranes, cuckoos, peacocks, flew and veered.
And all down each wide-watered shore the troubled, yet still limpid floods,
Over their banks began to pour, as o'er them hung the bursting clouds.
And, saturate with cloud-born dew, the glittering verdant-mantled earth,
The cuckoos and the peacocks flew, disputing as in drunken mirth. —
   " In such a time, so soft, so bland, oh beautiful! I chanced to go,
With quiver and with bow in hand, where clear Sarayu's waters flow,
If haply to the river's brink at night the buffalo might stray,
Or elephant, the stream to drink, — intent my savage game to slay.
Then of a water cruse, as slow it filled, the gurgling sound I heard,
Nought saw I, but the sullen low of elephant that sound appeared.
The swift well-feathered arrow I upon the bowstring fitting straight,
Towards the sound the shaft let fly, ah, cruelly deceived by fate!
The winged arrow scarce had flown, and scarce had reached its destined aim,
' Ah me, I'm slain,' a feeble moan in trembling human accents came.
' Ah, whence hath come this fatal shaft against a poor recluse like me,
Who shot that bolt with deadly craft, — alas ! what cruel man is he ?
At the lone midnight had I come to draw the river's limpid flood,
And here am struck to death, by whom ? ah whose this wrongful deed of blood ?
Alas ! and in my parents' heart, the old, the blind, and hardly fed,
In the wild wood, hath pierced the dart, that here hath struck their offspring dead.
Ah, deed most profitless as worst, a deed of wanton useless guilt :
As though a pupil's hand accurs'd his holy master's blood had spilt.
But not mine own untimely fate, — it is not that which I deplore.
My blind, my aged parents' state — 'tis their distress afflicts me more.
That sightless pair, for many a day, from me their scanty food have earned ;
What lot is theirs when I'm away, to the five elements returned?
Alike, all wretched they, as I — ah, whose this triple deed of blood?
For who the herbs will now supply, — the roots, the fruit, their blameless food ? '
My troubled soul, that plaintive moan no sooner heard, so faint and low,
Trembled to look on what I'd done, fell from my shuddering hand my bow.
Swift I rushed up, I saw him there, heart-pierced, and fallen the stream beside,
The hermit boy with knotted hair, — his clothing was the black deer's hide.
On me most piteous turned his look, his wounded breast could scarce respire,
And these the words, O queen, he spoke, as to consume me in his ire :
' What wrong, O Kshatriya, have I done, to be thy deathful arrow's aim,
The forest's solitary son, to draw the limpid stream I came.
Both wretched and both blind they lie, in the wildwood all destitute,
My parents, listening anxiously to hear my home-returning foot.

By this, thy fatal shaft, this one, three miserable victims fall,
The sire, the mother, and the son — ah why? and unoffending all.
How vain my father's life austere, the Veda's studied page how vain,
He knew not with prophetic fear his son would fall untimely slain.
But had he known, to one as he, so weak, so blind, 't were bootless all,
No tree can save another tree by the sharp hatchet marked to fall.
But to my father's dwelling haste, O Raghu's son, lest in his ire
Thy head with burning curse he blast, as the dry forest tree the fire.
Thee to my father's lone retreat will quickly lead yon onward path,
Oh, haste his pardon to entreat, or ere he curse thee in his wrath.
Yet first that gently I may die, draw forth the barbèd steel from hence,
Allay thy fears, no Brahmin I, not thine of Brahmin blood the offence.
My sire, a Brahmin hermit he, my mother was of Sudra race.'
So spake the wounded boy, on me while turned his unreproaching face.
As from his palpitating breast I gently drew the mortal dart,
He saw me trembling stand, and blest that boy's pure spirit seemed to
    part.
As died that holy hermit's son, from me my glory seemed to go,      *952*
With troubled mind I stood, cast down t' inevitable endless woe.
That shaft that seemed his life to burn like serpent venom, thus drawn
    out,
I, taking up his fallen urn, t' his father's dwelling took my route.
There miserable, blind, and old, of their sole helpmate thus forlorn,
His parents did these eyes behold, like two sad birds with pinions shorn.
Of him in fond discourse they sate, lone, thinking only of their son,
For his return so long, so late, impatient, oh by me undone.
My footsteps' sound he seemed to know, and thus the aged hermit said,
' O Yajnadatta, why so slow? — haste, let the cooling draught be shed.
Long on the river's cooling brink hast thou been sporting in thy joy.
Thy mother's fainting spirits sink in fear for thee; but thou, my boy,
If aught to grieve thy gentle heart thy mother or thy sire do wrong,
Bear with us, nor, when next we part, on the slow way thus linger long,
The feet of those that cannot move, of those that cannot see the eye,
Our spirits live but in thy love, — oh wherefore, dearest, no reply?'
  " My throat thick swollen with bursting tears, my power of speech that
      seemed to choke,
With hands above my head, my fears breaking my quivering voice, I spoke :
' The Kshatriya Dasaratha I, O hermit sage, 't is not thy son !
Most holy ones, unknowingly a deed of awful guilt I 've done.
With bow in hand I took my way along Sarayu's pleasant brink,
The savage buffalo to slay, or elephant come down to drink.
  "' A sound came murmuring to my ear, — 't was of the urn that slowly
      filled,
I deemed some savage wild-beast near, — my erring shaft thy son had killed.
A feeble groan I heard, his breast was pierced by that dire arrow keen :
All trembling to the spot I pressed, lo there thy hermit boy was seen.
Flew to the sound my arrow, meant the wandering elephant to slay,
Toward the river brink it went, — and there thy son expiring lay.
The fatal shaft when forth I drew, to heaven his parting spirit soared,
Dying he only thought of you, long, long, your lonely lot deplored.

Thus ignorantly did I slay your child beloved, O hermit sage!
Turn thou on me, whose fated day is come, thy all-consuming rage!'
He heard my dreadful tale at length, he stood all lifeless, motionless;
Then deep he groaned, and gathering strength, me the meek suppliant did
    address.
' Kshatriya, 't is well that thou hast turned, thy deed of murder to rehearse,
Else over all thy land had burned the fire of my wide-wasting curse.
If with premeditated crime the unoffending blood thou 'dst spilt,
The Thunderer on his throne sublime had shaken at such tremendous guilt.
Against the anchorite's sacred head, hadst, knowing, aimed thy shaft
    accursed,
In th' holy Vedas deeply read, thy skull in seven wide rents had burst.
But since, unwitting, thou hast wrought that deed of death, thou livest still,
O son of Taghu, from thy thought dismiss all dread of instant ill.
Oh lead me to that doleful spot where my poor boy expiring lay,
Beneath the shaft thy fell hand shot, of my blind age the staff, the stay.
On the cold earth 't were yet a joy to touch my perished child again,
(So long if I may live) my boy in one last fond embrace to strain
His body all bedewed with gore, his locks in loose disorder thrown,
Let me, let her but touch once more, to the dread realm of Yama gone.'
Then to that fatal place I brought alone that miserable pair;
His sightless hands and hers I taught to touch their boy that slumbered there.
Nor sooner did they feel him lie, on the moist herbage coldly thrown,
But with a shrill and feeble cry upon the body cast them down.
The mother as she lay and groaned, addressed her boy with quivering
    tongue,
And like a heifer sadly moaned, just plundered of her new-dropped young :
  " ' Was not thy mother once, my son, than life itself more dear to thee?
Why the long way thou hast begun, without one gentle word to me?
One last embrace, and then, beloved, upon thy lonely journey go!
Alas! with anger art thou moved, that not a word thou wilt bestow?'
  " The miserable father now with gentle touch each cold limb pressed,
And to the dead his words of woe, as to his living son addressed :
' I too, my son, am I not here? — thy sire with thy sad mother stands;
Awake, arise, my child, draw near, and clasp each neck with loving hands.
Who now, 'neath the dark wood by night, a pious reader shall be heard?
Whose honeyed voice my ear delight with th' holy Veda's living word?
The evening prayer, th' ablution done, the fire adored with worship meet,
Who now shall soothe like thee, my son, with fondling hand, my aged
    feet?
And who the herb, the wholesome root, or wild fruit from the wood shall
    bring?
To us the blind, the destitute, with helpless hunger perishing?
Thy blind old mother, heaven-resigned, within our hermit-dwelling lone,
How shall I tend, myself as blind, now all my strength of life is gone?
Oh, stay, my child, oh, part not yet, to Yama's dwelling go not now,
To-morrow forth we all will set, — thy mother and myself and thou :
For both, in grief for thee, and both so helpless, ere another day,
From this dark world, but little loath, shall we depart, death's easy prey!
And I myself, by Yama's seat, companion of thy darksome way,

The guerdon to thy virtues meet from that great Judge of men will pray.
Because, my boy, in innocence, by wicked deed thou hast been slain,
Rise, where the heroes dwell, who thence ne'er stoop to this dark world
    again.
Those that to earth return no more, the sense-subdued, the hermits wise,
Priests their sage masters that adore, to their eternal seats arise.
Those that have studied to the last the Veda's, the Vedanga's page,
Where saintly kings of earth have passed, Nahusa and Yayati sage;
The sires of holy families, the true to wedlock's sacred vow;
And those that cattle, gold, or rice, or lands, with liberal hands bestow;
That ope th' asylum to th' oppressed, that ever love, and speak the truth;
Up to the dwellings of the blest, th' eternal, soar thou, best-loved youth.
For none of such a holy race within the lowest seat may dwell;
But that will be his fatal place by whom my only offspring fell.'
   "So groaning deep, that wretched pair, the hermit and his wife, essayed
The meet ablution to prepare, their hands their last faint effort made.
Divine, with glorious body bright, in splendid car of heaven elate,
Before them stood their son in light, and thus consoled their helpless state:
'Meed of my duteous filial care, I've reached the wished for realms of joy;
And ye, in those glad realms, prepare to meet full soon your dear-loved
    boy.
My parents, weep no more for me, yon warrior monarch slew me not,
My death was thus ordained to be, predestined was the shaft he shot.'
Thus as he spoke, the anchorite's son soared up the glowing heaven afar,
In air his heavenly body shone, while stood he in his gorgeous car.
But they, of that lost boy so dear the last ablution meetly made,
Thus spoke to me that holy seer, with folded hands above his head.
'Albeit by thy unknowing dart my blameless boy untimely fell,
A curse I lay upon thy heart, whose fearful pain I know too well.
As sorrowing for my son I bow, and yield up my unwilling breath,
So, sorrowing for thy son shalt thou at life's last close repose in death.'
That curse dread sounding in mine ear, to mine own city forth I set,
Nor long survived that hermit seer, to mourn his child in lone regret.
This day that Brahmin curse fulfilled hath fallen on my devoted head,
In anguish for my parted child have all my sinking spirits fled.
No more my darkened eyes can see, my clouded memory is o'ercast,
Dark Yama's heralds summon me to his deep, dreary realm to haste.
Mine eye no more my Rama sees, and grief-o'erborne, my spirits sink,
As the swoln stream sweeps down the trees that grow upon the crumbling
    brink.
Oh, felt I Rama's touch, or spake one word his home-returning voice,
Again to life I should awake, as quaffing nectar draughts, rejoice,
But what so sad could e'er have been, celestial partner of my heart,
As Rama's beauteous face unseen, from life untimely to depart?
His exile in the forest o'er, him home returned to Oude's high town,
Oh happy those, that see once more, like Indra from the sky come down.
No mortal men, but gods I deem, — moonlike, before whose wondering sight
My Rama's glorious face shall beam, from the dark forest bursting bright.
Happy that gaze on Rama's face with beauteous teeth and smile of love,
Like the blue lotus in its grace, and like the starry king above.

Like to the full autumnal moon, and like the lotus in its bloom,
That youth who sees returning soon, — how blest shall be that mortal's doom."
Dwelling in that sweet memory, on his last bed the monarch lay,
And slowly, softly seemed to die, as fades the moon at dawn away.

"Ah, Rama! ah, my son!" thus said, or scarcely said, the king of men,
His gentle hapless spirit fled in sorrow for his Rama then,
The shepherd of his people old at midnight on his bed of death,
The tale of his son's exile told, and breathed away his dying breath.

*Milman's Translation.*

# THE MAHÂ-BHÂRATA.

"It is a deep and noble forest, abounding in delicious fruits and fragrant flowers, shaded and watered by perennial springs."

THOUGH parts of the Mahâ-Bhârata, or story of the great war, are of great antiquity, the entire poem was undoubtedly collected and re-written in the first or second century A. D. Tradition ascribes the Mahâ-Bhârata to the Brahman Krishna Dwaipayana Vyasa.

The Mahâ-Bhârata, unlike the Râmâyana, is not the story of some great event, but consists of countless episodes, legends, and philosophical treatises, strung upon the thread of a single story. These episodes are called Upakhyanani, and the five most beautiful are called, in India, the five precious stones.

Its historical basis is the strife between the Aryan invaders of India and the original inhabitants, illustrated in the strife between the sons of the Raja Pandu and the blind Raja, Dhrita-rashtra, which forms the main story of the poem.

Though marred by the exaggerations peculiar to the Hindu, the poem is a great treasure house of Indian history, and from it the Indian poets, historical writers, and philosophers have drawn much of their material.

The Mahâ-Bhârata is written in the Sanskrit language ; it is the longest poem ever written, its eighteen cantos containing two hundred thousand lines.

It is held in even higher regard than the Râmâyana, and the reading of it is supposed to confer upon the happy reader every good and perfect gift.

BIBLIOGRAPHY AND CRITICISM, THE MAHÂ-BHÂRATA. G. W. Cox's Mythology and Folklore, 1881, p. 313; John

Dowson's Classical Dictionary of Hindu Mythology, Religion, Geography, History, and Literature, 1879; F. Max Müller's Ancient Sanskrit Literature, 1859 (Introduction); E. A. Reed's Hindu Literature, 1891, pp. 272–352; Albrecht Weber's History of Indian Literature, 1878, pp. 184–191; J. T. Wheeler's History of India, 4 vols., 1876, vol. ii.; J. C. Oman's Great Indian Epics, 1874, pp. 87–231; T. Goldstuecker's Hindu Epic Poetry; the Mahâ-Bhârata (in his Literary Remains, 1879, vol. ii., pp. 86–145); M. Macmillan's Globe-trotter in India, 1815, p. 193; J. Peile's Notes on the Tales of Nala, 1882; C. J. Stone's Cradle-land of Arts and Creeds, 1880, pp. 36–49; H. H. Wilson's Introduction to the Mahâ-Bhârata and a Translation of three Extracts (in his Works, vol. iii., p. 277); Westminster Review, 1868, vol. xxxiii., p. 380.

STANDARD ENGLISH TRANSLATIONS, THE MAHÂ-BHÂRATA. The Mahâ-Bhârata, Selections from the, Tr. by Sir Edwin Arnold, in his Indian Poetry, 1886; in his Indian Idylls, 1883; Nala and Damayanti and other Poems, Tr. from the Mahâ-Bhârata by H. H. Milman, 1834 (his translation of the Story of Nala is edited with notes by Monier Williams, 1879); Metrical translations from Sanskrit writers by John Muir, 1879, pp. 13–37; Last Days of Krishna, Tr. from the Mahâ-Bhârata, by David Price (Oriental Translation Fund: Miscellaneous Translations); The Mahâ-Bhârata, an English Prose Translation with notes, by Protap Chandra Roy, Published in one hundred parts, 1883–1890; Asiatic Researches, Tr. by H. H. Wilson, from the Mahâ-Bhârata, vol. xv., p. 101; Translations of episodes from the Mahâ-Bhârata, in Scribner's Monthly, 1874, vol. vii., p. 385; International Review, vol. x., pp. 36, 297; Oriental Magazine, Dec., 1824, March, Sept., 1825, Sept., 1826.

# THE STORY OF THE MAHÂ-BHÂRATA.

LONG ago there dwelt in India two great Rajas who were brothers, the Raja Pandu and the blind Raja, Dhrita-rashtra. The former had five noble sons called the Pandavas, the eldest of whom was Yudhi-sthira, the second Bhima, the third Arjuna, and the youngest, twin sons, Nakalu and Sahadeva. All were gifted in every way, but Arjuna was especially noble in form and feature.

The blind Raja had a family of one hundred sons, called the Kauravas from their ancestor, Kura. The oldest of these was Duryodhana, and the bravest, Dhusasana.

Before the birth of Pandu's sons, he had left his kingdom in charge of Dhrita-rashtra, that he might spend his time in hunting in the forests on the slopes of the Himalayas. After his death Dhrita-rashtra continued to rule the kingdom; but on account of their claim to the throne, he invited the Pandavas and their mother to his court, where they were trained, together with his sons, in every knightly exercise.

There was probably jealousy between the cousins from the beginning, and when their teacher, Drona, openly expressed his pride in the wonderful archery of Arjuna, the hatred of the Kauravas was made manifest. No disturbance occurred, however, until the day when Drona made a public tournament to display the prowess of his pupils.

The contests were in archery and the use of the noose and of clubs. Bhima, who had been endowed by the serpent king with the strength of ten thousand elephants, especially excelled in the use of the club, Nakalu was most skillful in taming and driving the horse, and the others in the use of the sword and spear. When Arjuna made use of the bow and the noose the plaudits with which the spectators greeted his skill so enraged the Kauravas that they turned the contest of clubs, which was to have been a friendly one, into a degrading and blood-shedding battle. The spectators left

the splendid lists in sorrow, and the blind Raja determined
to separate the unfriendly cousins before further harm could
come from their rivalry.

Before this could be done, another event increased their
hostility. Drona had agreed to impart to the Kauravas and
the Pandavas his skill in warfare, on condition that they
would conquer for him his old enemy, the Raja of Panchala.
On account of their quarrel the cousins would not fight together, and the Kauravas, marching against the Raja, were
defeated. On their return, the Pandavas went to Panchala,
and took the Raja prisoner.

After Yudhi-sthira had been appointed Yuva-Raja, a step
Dhrita-rashtra was compelled by the people of Hastinapur to
take, the Kauravas declared that they could no longer remain
in the same city with their cousins.

A plot was laid to destroy the Pandavas, the Raja's con-
science having been quieted by the assurances of his Brahman counsellor that it was entirely proper to slay one's foe,
be he father, brother, or friend, openly or by secret means.
The Raja accordingly pretended to send his nephews on a
pleasure-trip to a distant province, where he had prepared for
their reception a "house of lac," rendered more combustible
by soaking in clarified butter, in which he had arranged to
have them burned as if by accident, as soon as possible after
their arrival.

All Hastinapur mourned at the departure of the Pandavas,
and the princes themselves were sad, for they had been
warned by a friend that Dhrita-rashtra had plotted for their
destruction. They took up their abode in the house of lac,
to which they prudently constructed a subterranean outlet, and one evening, when a woman with five sons attended
a feast of their mother's, uninvited, and fell into a drunken
sleep, they made fast the doors, set fire to the house, and
escaped to the forest. The bodies of the five men and
their mother were found next day, and the assurance was
borne to Hastinapur that the Pandavas and their mother
Kunti had perished by fire.

The five princes, with their mother, disguised as Brahmans,

spent several years wandering through the forests, having many strange adventures and slaying many demons. While visiting Ekachakra, which city they freed from a frightful rakshasa, they were informed by the sage Vyasa that Draupadi, the lovely daughter of the Raja Draupada of Panchala, was going to hold a Svayamvara in order to select a husband. The suitors of a princess frequently attended a meeting of this sort and took part in various athletic contests, at the end of which the princess signified who was most pleasing to her, usually the victor in the games, by hanging around his neck a garland of flowers.

Vyasa's description of the lovely princess, whose black eyes were large as lotus leaves, whose skin was dusky, and her locks dark and curling, so excited the curiosity of the Pandavas that they determined to attend the Svayamvara. They found the city full of princes and kings who had come to take part in the contest for the most beautiful woman in the world. The great amphitheatre in which the games were to take place was surrounded by gold and jewelled palaces for the accommodation of the princes, and with platforms for the convenience of the spectators.

After music, dancing, and various entertainments, which occupied sixteen days, the contest of skill began. On the top of a tall pole, erected in the plain, was placed a golden fish, below which revolved a large wheel. He who sent his arrow through the spokes of the wheel and pierced the eye of the golden fish was to be the accepted suitor of Draupadi.

When the princes saw the difficulty of the contest, many of them refused to enter it; as many tried it only to fail, among them, the Kaurava Duryodhana. At last Arjuna, still in his disguise, stepped forward, drew his bow, and sent his arrow through the wheel into the eye of the golden fish.

Immediately a great uproar arose among the spectators because a Brahman had entered a contest limited to members of the Kshatriya, or warrior class. In the struggle which ensued, however, Arjuna, assisted by his brothers, especially Bhima, succeeded in carrying off the princess, whose father did not demur.

When the princes returned to their hut they went into the inner room and informed their mother that they had brought home a prize. Supposing that it was some game, she told them it would be well to share it equally. The mother's word was law, but would the gods permit them to share Draupadi? Their troubled minds were set at rest by Vyasa, who assured them that Draupadi had five different times in former existences besought Siva for a good husband. He had refused her requests then, but would now allow her five husbands at once. The princes were well satisfied, and when the Raja Draupada learned that the Brahmans were great princes in disguise, he caused the five weddings to be celebrated in great state.

Not satisfied with this, the Raja at once endeavored to make peace between the Pandavas and their hostile cousins, and succeeded far enough to induce Dhrita-rashtra to cede to his nephews a tract of land in the farthest part of his kingdom, on the river Jumna, where they set about founding a most splendid city, Indra-prastha.

Here they lived happily with Draupadi, conquering so many kingdoms and accumulating so much wealth that they once more aroused the jealousy of their old enemies, the Kauravas. The latter, knowing that it would be impossible to gain the advantage of them by fair means, determined to conquer them by artifice, and accordingly erected a large and magnificent hall and invited their cousins thither, with a great show of friendliness, to a gambling match.

The Pandavas knew they would not be treated fairly, but as such an invitation could not be honorably declined by a Kshatriya, they went to Hastinapur. Yudhi-sthira's opponent was Shakuni, the queen's brother, an unprincipled man, by whom he was defeated in every game.

Yudhi-sthira staked successively his money, his jewels, and his slaves; and when these were exhausted, he continued to play, staking his kingdom, his brothers, and last of all his peerless wife, Draupadi.

At this point, when the excitement was intense, the brutal Dhusasana commanded Draupadi to be brought into the hall, and insulted her in every way, to the great rage of the help-less Pandavas, until Dhrita-rashtra, affrighted by the evil omens by which the gods signified their disapproval, rebuked Dhusasana for his conduct, and giving Draupadi her wish, released her husbands and herself and sent them back to their kingdom.

To prevent the Pandavas from gaining time to avenge their insult, the Kauravas induced their father to invite their cousins to court to play a final game, this time the conditions being that the losing party should go into exile for thirteen years, spending twelve years in the forest and the thirteenth in some city. If their disguise was penetrated by their enemies during the thirteenth year, the exile was to be ex-tended for another thirteen years.

Though they knew the outcome, the Pandavas accepted the second invitation, and in consequence again sought the forest, not departing without the most terrible threats against their cousins.

In the forest of Kamyaka, Yudhi-sthira studied the science of dice that he might not again be defeated so disastrously, and journeyed pleasantly from one point of interest to an-other with Draupadi and his brothers, with the exception of Arjuna, who had sought the Himalayas to gain favor with the god Siva, that he might procure from him a terrible weapon for the destruction of his cousins.

After he had obtained the weapon he was lifted into the heaven of the god Indra, where he spent five happy years. When he rejoined his wife and brothers, they were visited by the god Krishna and by the sage Markandeya, who told them the story of the creation and destruction of the uni-verse, of the flood, and of the doctrine of Karma, which in-structs one that man's sufferings here below are due to his actions in former and forgotten existences. He also related to them the beautiful story of how the Princess Sâvitrî had wedded the Prince Satyavan, knowing that the gods had de-creed that he should die within a year; how on the day set for his death she had accompanied him to the forest, had there followed Yama, the awful god of death, entreating him until, for very pity of her sorrow and admiration of her courage and devotion, he yielded to her her husband's soul.

Near the close of the twelfth year of their exile, the princes, fatigued from a hunt, sent Nakalu to get some water from a lake which one had discovered from a tree-top. As the prince approached the lake he was warned by a voice not to touch it, but thirst overcoming fear, he drank and fell dead. The same penalty was paid by Sahadeva, Arjuna, and Bhima, who in turn followed him. Yudhi-sthira, who went last, obeyed the voice, which, assuming a terrible form, asked the king questions on many subjects concerning the universe. These being answered satisfactorily, the being declared himself to be Dharma, the god of justice, Yudhi-sthira's father, and in token of his affection for his son, restored the princes to life, and granted them the boon of being unrecognizable during the remaining year of their exile.

The thirteenth year of their exile they spent in the city of Virata, where they entered the service of the Raja, — Yudhi-sthira as teacher of dice-playing, Bhima as superintendent of the cooks, Arjuna as a teacher of music and dancing to the ladies, Nakalu as master of horse, and Sahadeva as superintendent of the cattle. Draupadi, who entered the service of the queen, was so attractive, even in disguise, that Bhima was forced to kill the queen's brother, Kechaka, for insulting her. This would have caused the Pandavas' exile from Virata had not their services been needed in a battle between Virata and the king of the Trigartas.

The Kauravas assisted the Trigartas in this battle, and the recognition, among the victors, of their cousins, whose thirteenth year of exile was now ended, added to the bitterness of their defeat.

Their exile over, the Pandavas were free to make preparations for the great war which they had determined to wage against the Kauravas. Both parties, anxious to enlist the services of Krishna, sent envoys to him at the same time. When Krishna gave them the choice of himself or his armies, Arjuna was shrewd enough to choose the god, leaving his hundreds of millions of soldiers to swell the forces of the Kauravas.

When their preparations were completed, and the time had come to wreak vengeance on their cousins, the Pandavas were loath to begin the conflict. They seemed to understand that, war once declared, there could be no compromise, but that it must be a war for extinction. But the Kauravas received their proposals of peace with taunts, and heaped insults upon their emissary.

When the Pandavas found that there was no hope of peace, they endeavored to win to their side Karna, who was really a son of Kunti, and hence their half-brother, though this fact had not been made known to him until he had long been allied with the Kauravas. In anticipation of this war, the gods, by a bit of trickery, had robbed Karna of his god-given armor and weapons. However, neither celestial artifice, the arguments of Krishna, nor the entreaties of Kunti were able to move Karna from what he considered the path of duty, though he promised that while he would fight with all his strength, he would not slay Yudhi-sthira, Bhima, and the twins.

The forces of the two armies were drawn up on the plain of Kuruk-shetra. The army of the Kauravas was under the command of the terrible Bhishma, the uncle of Pandu and Dhrita-rashtra, who had governed the country during the minority of Pandu.

Each side was provided with billions and billions of infantry, cavalry, and elephants; the warriors were supplied with weapons of the most dangerous sort. The army of the Kauravas was surrounded by a deep trench fortified by towers, and further protected by fireballs and jars full of scorpions to be thrown at the assailants.

As night fell, before the battle, the moon's face was stained with blood, earthquakes shook the land, and the images of the gods fell from their places.

The next morning, when Arjuna, from his chariot, beheld the immense army, he was appalled at the thought of the bloodshed to follow, and hesitated to advance. Krishna in-

sisted that it was unnecessary for him to lament, setting forth
his reasons in what is known as the Bhagavat-gita, the divine
song, in which he said it was no sin to slay a foe, since death
is but a transmigration from one form to another.  The soul
can never cease to be ; who then can destroy it?  Therefore, when Arjuna slew his cousins he would merely remove
their offensive bodies ; their souls, unable to be destroyed,
would seek other habitations.  To further impress Arjuna
Krishna boasted of himself as embodying everything, and as
having passed through many forms.  Faith in Krishna was
indispensable, for the god placed faith above either works or
contemplation.  He next exhibited himself in his divine
form to Arjuna, and the warrior was horror-stricken at the
terrible divinity with countless arms, hands, and heads, touching the skies.  Having been thus instructed by Krishna,
Arjuna went forth, and the eighteen days' battle began.

The slaughter was wholesale ; no quarter was asked or
given, since each side was determined to exterminate the
other.  Flights of arrows were stopped in mid-air by flights
of arrows from the other side.  Great maces were cut in
pieces by well-directed darts.  Bhima, wielding his great
club with his prodigious strength, wiped out thousands of the
enemy at one stroke, and Arjuna did the same with his swift
arrows.  Nor were the Kauravas to be despised.  Hundreds
of thousands of the Pandavas' followers fell, and the heroic
brothers were themselves struck by many arrows.

Early in the battle the old Bhishma was pierced by so
many arrows that, falling from his chariot, he rested upon
their points as on a couch, and lay there living by his own
desire, until long after the battle.

After eighteen days of slaughter, during which the field
reeked with blood and night was made horrible by the cries
of the jackals and other beasts of prey that devoured the
bodies of the dead, the Kauravas were all slain, and the five
Pandavas, reconciled to the blind Raja, accompanied him
back to Hastinapur, where Yudhi-sthira was crowned Raja,
although the Raj was still nominally under the rule of his
old uncle.

Yudhi-sthira celebrated his accession to the throne by the performance of the great sacrifice, which was celebrated with the utmost splendor.    After several years the unhappy Dhrita-rashtra retired with his wife to a jungle on the banks of the Ganges, leaving Yudhi-sthira in possession of the kingdom.    There the Pandavas visited him, and talked over the friends who had fallen in the great war.    One evening the sage Vyasa instructed them to bathe in the Ganges and then stand on the banks of the river.    He then went into the water and prayed, and coming out stood by Yudhi-sthira and called the names of all those persons who had been slain at Kuruk-shetra.    Immediately the water began to foam and boil, and to the great surprise and terror of all, the warriors lost in the great battle appeared in their chariots, at perfect peace with one another, and cleansed of all earthly stain. Then the living were happy with the dead ; long separated families were once more united, and the hearts that had been desolate for fifteen long years were again filled with joy. The night sped quickly by in tender conversation, and when morning came, all the dead mounted into their chariots and disappeared.    Those who had come to meet them prepared to leave the river, but with the permission of Vyasa, the widows drowned themselves that they might rejoin their husbands.

Not long after his return to Hastinapur, Yudhi-sthira heard that the old Raja and his wife had lost their lives in a jungle-fire ; and soon after this, tidings came to him of the destruction of the city of the Yadavas, the capital of Krishna, in punishment for the dissipation of its inhabitants.

Yudhi-sthira's reign of thirty-six years had been a succession of gloomy events, and he began to grow weary of earth and to long for the blessing promised above.    He therefore determined to make the long and weary pilgrimage to Heaven without waiting for death.    According to the Mahâ-Bhârata, the earth was divided into seven concentric rings, each of which was surrounded by an ocean or belt separating it from the next annular continent.    The first ocean was of salt water ; the second, of the juice of the sugar-cane ; the third, of wine ; the fourth, of clarified butter ; the fifth, of curdled milk ; the sixth, of sweet milk ; the seventh, of fresh water. In the centre of this vast annular system Mount Meru rose to the height of sixty-four thousand miles.

Upon this mountain was supposed to rest the heaven of the Hindus, and thither Yudhi-sthira proposed to make his pilgrimage. His brothers and their wife Draupadi insisted on going with him, for all were equally weary of the world. Their people would fain have accompanied them, but the princes sent them back and went unaccompanied save by their faithful dog. They kept on, fired by their high resolves, until they reached the long and dreary waste of sand that stretched before Mount Meru. There Draupadi fell and yielded up her life, and Yudhi-sthira, never turning to look back, told the questioning Bhima that she died because she loved her husbands better than all else, better than heaven. Next Sahadeva fell, then Nakalu, and afterwards Arjuna and Bhima. Yudhi-sthira, still striding on, informed Bhima that pride had slain the first, self-love the second, the sin of Arjuna was a lie, and Bhima had loved too well the good things of earth.

Followed by the dog, Yudhi-sthira pushed across the barren sand until he reached the mount and stood in the presence of the god. Well pleased with his perseverance, the god promised him the reward of entering into heaven in his own form, but he refused to go unless the dog could accompany him. After vainly attempting to dissuade him, the god allowed the dog to assume its proper form, and lo ! it was Dharma, the god of justice, and the two entered heaven together.

But where were Draupadi and the gallant princes, her husbands ? Yudhi-sthira could see them nowhere, and he questioned only to learn that they were in hell. His determination was quickly taken. There could be no heaven for him unless his brothers and their wife could share it with him. He demanded to be shown the path to hell, to enter which he walked over razors, and trod under foot mangled human forms. But joy of joys ! The lotus-eyed Draupadi called to him, and his brothers cried that his presence in hell brought a soothing breeze that gave relief to all the tortured souls.

Yudhi-sthira's self-sacrifice sufficiently tested, the gods proclaimed that it was all but an illusion shown to make him enjoy the more, by contrast, the blisses of heaven. The king Yudhi-sthira then bathed in the great river flowing through three worlds, and, washed from all sins and soils, went up, hand in hand with the gods, to his brothers, the Pandavas, and

> " Lotus-eyed and loveliest Draupadi,
>   Waiting to greet him, gladdening and glad."

## SELECTIONS FROM THE MAHÂ–BHÂRATA.

### SÂVITRÎ, OR LOVE AND DEATH.

THE beautiful princess Sâvitrî of her own choice wedded the prince Satyavan, son of a blind and exiled king, although she knew that he was doomed by the gods to die within a year. When the year was almost gone, she sat for several days beneath a great tree, abstaining from food and drink, and imploring the gods to save him from death. On the fateful day she accompanied him to the forest to gather the sacred wood for the evening sacrifice. As he struck the tree with the axe he reeled in pain, and exclaiming, " I cannot work ! " fell fainting.

> Thereon that noble lady, hastening near,
> Stayed him that would have fallen, with quick arms ;
> And, sitting on the earth, laid her lord's head
> Tenderly in her lap. So bent she, mute,
> Fanning his face, and thinking 't was the day —
> The hour — which Narad named — the sure fixed date
> Of dreadful end — when, lo ! before her rose
> A shade majestic. Red his garments were,
> His body vast and dark ; like fiery suns
> The eyes which burned beneath his forehead-cloth ;
> Armed was he with a noose, awful of mien.
> This Form tremendous stood by Satyavan,
> Fixing its gaze upon him. At the sight
> The fearful Princess started to her feet.
> Heedfully laying on the grass his head,

Up started she, with beating heart, and joined
Her palms for supplication, and spake thus
In accents tremulous : " Thou seem'st some God;
Thy mien is more than mortal ; make me know
What god thou art, and what thy purpose here."

And Yama said (the dreadful god of death):
" Thou art a faithful wife, O Sâvitrî,
True to thy vows, pious, and dutiful;
Therefore I answer thee.   Yama I am !
This Prince thy lord lieth at point to die ;
Him will I straightway bind and bear from life ;
This is my office, and for this I come."

Then Sâvitrî spake sadly : " It is taught
Thy messengers are sent to fetch the dying ;
Why is it, Mightiest, thou art come thyself ? "

In pity of her love, the Pityless
Answered — the King of all the Dead replied :
" This was a Prince unparalleled, thy lord;
Virtuous as fair, a sea of goodly gifts,
Not to be summoned by a meaner voice
Than Yama's own : therefore is Yama come."

With that the gloomy God fitted his noose
And forced forth from the Prince the soul of him —
Subtile, a thumb in length — which being reft,
Breath stayed, blood stopped, the body's grace was gone,
And all life's warmth to stony coldness turned.
Then, binding it, the Silent Presence bore
Satyavan's soul away toward the South.

But Sâvitrî the Princess followed him ;
Being so bold in wifely purity,
So holy by her love ; and so upheld,
She followed him.

Presently Yama turned.
"Go back," quoth he.   " Pay for him funeral dues.
Enough, O Sâvitrî, is wrought for love ;
Go back !   Too far already hast thou come."

Then Sâvitrî made answer : " I must go
Where my lord goes, or where my lord is borne ;
Naught other is my duty.   Nay, I think,
By reason of my vows, my services,
Done to the Gurus, and my faultless love,
Grant but thy grace, I shall unhindered go.
The sages teach that to walk seven steps
One with another, maketh good men friends ;
Beseech thee, let me say a verse to thee : —

> " *Be master of thyself, if thou wilt be*
> *Servant of Duty.  Such as thou shalt see*
> *Not self-subduing, do no deeds of good*
> *In youth or age, in household or in wood.*
> *But wise men know that virtue is best bliss,*
> *And all by some one way may reach to this.*
> *It needs not men should pass through orders four*
> *To come to knowledge: doing right is more*
> *Than any learning; therefore sages say*
> *Best and most excellent is Virtue's way.*"

Spake Yama then: " Return! yet I am moved
By those soft words; justly their accents fell,
And sweet and reasonable was their sense.
See now, thou faultless one.  Except this life
I bear away, ask any boon from me;
It shall not be denied."

Sâvitrî said:
" Let, then, the King, my husband's father, have
His eyesight back, and be his strength restored,
And let him live anew, strong as the sun."

" I give this gift," Yama replied.  " Thy wish,
Blameless, shall be fulfilled.  But now go back;
Already art thou wearied, and our road
Is hard and long.  Turn back, lest thou, too, die."

The Princess answered: " Weary am I not,
So I walk near my lord.  Where he is borne,
Thither wend I.  Most mighty of the Gods,
I follow wheresoe'er thou takest him.
A verse is writ on this, if thou wouldst hear:—

> " *There is naught better than to be*
> *With noble souls in company:*
> *There is naught better than to wend*
> *With good friends faithful to the end.*
> *This is the love whose fruit is sweet,*
> *Therefore to bide within is meet.*"

Spake Yama, smiling: " Beautiful! thy words
Delight me; they are excellent, and teach
Wisdom unto the wise, singing soft truth.
Look, now! Except the life of Satyavan,
Ask yet another — any — boon from me."

Sâvitrî said: " Let, then, the pious King,
My husband's father, who hath lost his throne,
Have back the Raj; and let him rule his realm
In happy righteousness.  This boon I ask."

"He shall have back the throne," Yama replied,
"And he shall reign in righteousness : these things
Will surely fall.   But thou, gaining thy wish,
Return anon ; so shalt thou 'scape sore ill."


"Ah, awful God! who hold'st the world in leash,"
The Princess said, " restraining evil men,
And leading good men — even unconscious — there,
Where they attain, hear yet those famous words : —


> *" The constant virtues of the good are tenderness and love*
> *To all that lives — in earth, air, sea — great, small — be-*
> *    low, above ;*
> *Compassionate of heart, they keep a gentle thought for each,*
> *Kind in their actions, mild in will, and pitiful of speech ;*
> *Who pitieth not, he hath not faith ; full many an one so lives,*
> *But when an enemy seeks help, a good man gladly gives."*


"As water to the thirsty," Yama said,
" Princess, thy words melodious are to me.
Except the life of Satyavan, thy lord,
Ask one boon yet again, for I will grant."


Answer made Sâvitrî : " The King, my sire,
Hath no male child.   Let him see many sons
Begotten of his body, who may keep
The royal line long regnant.   This I ask."


"So shall it be," the Lord of Death replied ;
" A hundred fair preservers of his race
Thy sire shall boast.   But this wish being won,
Return, dear Princess ; thou hast come too far."


" It is not far for me," quoth Sâvitrî,
" Since I am near my husband ; nay, my heart
Is set to go as far as to the end ;
But hear these other verses, if thou wilt : —


> *" By that sunlit name thou bearest,*
> *Thou, Vaivaswata ! art dearest ;*
> *Those that as their Lord proclaim thee,*
> *King of Righteousness do name thee :*
> *Better than themselves the wise*
> *Trust the righteous.   Each relies*
> *Most upon the good, and makes*
> *Friendship with them.   Friendship takes*
> *Fear from hearts ; yet friends betray,*
> *In good men we may trust alway."*

"Sweet lady," Yama said, "never were words
Spoke better ; never truer heard by ear ;
Lo! I am pleased with thee.   Except this soul,
Ask one gift yet again, and get thee home."

"I ask thee then," quickly the Princess cried,
"Sons, many sons, born of my body ; boys ;
Satyavan's children ; lovely, valiant, strong ;
Continuers of their line.   Grant this, kind God."

"I grant it," Yama answered ; "thou shalt bear
These sons thy heart desireth, valiant, strong.
Therefore go back, that years be given thee.
Too long a path thou treadest, dark and rough."

But sweeter than before, the Princess sang : —

> *" In paths of peace and virtue*
> *Always the good remain ;*
> *And sorrow shall not stay with them,*
> *Nor long access of pain ;*
> *At meeting or at parting*
> *Joys to their bosom strike ;*
> *For good to good is friendly,*
> *And virtue loves her like.*
> *The great sun goes his journey*
> *By their strong truth impelled ;*
> *By their pure lives and penances*
> *Is earth itself upheld ;*
> *Of all which live and shall live*
> *Upon its hills and fields,*
> *Pure hearts are the protectors,*
> *For virtue saves and shields.*
>
> *" Never are noble spirits*
> *Poor while their like survive ;*
> *True love has gems to render,*
> *And virtue wealth to give.*
> *Never is lost or wasted*
> *The goodness of the good ;*
> *Never against a mercy,*
> *Against a right, it stood ;*
> *And seeing this, that virtue*
> *Is always friend to all,*
> *The virtuous and true-hearted,*
> *Men their protectors call."*

"Line for line, Princess, as thou sangest so,"
Quoth Yama, "all that lovely praise of good,
Grateful to hallowed minds, lofty in sound,

And couched in dulcet numbers — word by word —
Dearer thou grew'st to me.  O thou great heart,
Perfect and firm ! ask any boon from me, —
Ask an incomparable boon !"

                              She cried
Swiftly, no longer stayed : "Not Heaven I crave,
Nor heavenly joys, nor bliss incomparable,
Hard to be granted, even by thee ; but him,
My sweet lord's life, without which I am dead ;
Give me that gift of gifts !  I will not take
Aught less without him, — not one boon — no praise,
No splendors, no rewards, — not even those sons
Whom thou didst promise.  Ah, thou wilt not now
Bear hence the father of them and my hope !
Make thy free word good ; give me Satyavan
Alive once more."

                              And thereupon the God —
The Lord of Justice, high Vaivaswata —
Loosened the noose and freed the Prince's soul,
And gave it to the lady, saying this,
With eyes grown tender : "See, thou sweetest queen
Of women, brightest jewel of thy kind !
Here is thy husband.   He shall live and reign
Side by side with thee, saved by thee, — in peace
And fame and wealth, and health, many long years,
For pious sacrifices world-renowned.
Boys shalt thou bear to him, as I did grant, —
Kshatriya kings, fathers of kings to be,
Sustainers of thy line.   Also thy sire
Shall see his name upheld by sons of sons,
Like the immortals, valiant, Mâlavas."

                              ARNOLD : *Indian Idylls.*


## FROM "THE GREAT JOURNEY."

THE shadow of the Great War hung over King Yudhi-sthira,
whose reign was one long succession of gloomy events, culmi-
nating in the death of the blind Raja and his wife in a jungle fire,
and the destruction of the capital city of Krishna because of the
dissipation of its inhabitants.

On tidings of the wreck of Vrishni's race,
King Yudhi-sthira of the Pandavas
Was minded to be done with earthly things,
And to Arjuna spake : "O noble prince,

Time endeth all; we linger, noose on neck,
Till the last day tightens the line, and kills.
Let us go forth to die, being yet alive."
And Kunti's son, the great Arjuna, said:
"Let us go forth! Time slayeth all.
We will find Death, who seeketh other men."
And Bhimasena, hearing, answered: "Yea,
We will find Death!" and Sahadev cried: "Yea!"
And his twin brother Nakalu; whereat
The princes set their faces for the Mount.

. . . . . . .

So ordering ere he went, the righteous King
Made offering of white water, heedfully,
To Vasudev, to Rama, and the rest, —
All funeral rites performing; next he spread
A funeral feast. . . .

And all the people cried, " Stay with us, Lord!"
But Yudhi-sthira knew his time was come,
Knew that life passes and that virtue lasts,
And put aside their love. . . .

So, with farewells
Tenderly took of lieges and of lords,
Girt he for travel with his princely kin,
Great Yudhi-sthira, Dharma's royal son.
Crest-gem and belt and ornaments he stripped
From off his body, and for broidered robe
A rough dress donned, woven of jungle bark;
And what he did — O Lord of men! — so did
Arjuna, Bhima, and the twin-born pair,
Nakalu with Sahadev, and she, — in grace
The peerless, — Draupadi. Lastly those six, —
Thou son of Bharata! — in solemn form
Made the high sacrifice of Naishtiki,
Quenching their flames in water at the close;
And so set forth, midst wailing of all folk
And tears of women, weeping most to see
The Princess Draupadi — that lovely prize
Of the great gaming, Draupadi the Bright —
Journeying afoot; but she and all the five
Rejoiced because their way lay heavenward.

Seven were they, setting forth, — Princess and King,
The King's four brothers and a faithful dog.
Those left Hastinapur; but many a man,
And all the palace household, followed them
The first sad stage : and ofttimes prayed to part,

Put parting off for love and pity, still
Sighing, " A little farther ! " till day waned ;
Then one by one they turned.

    .     .     .     .     .     .

                             Thus wended they,
Pandu's five sons and loveliest Draupadi,
Taking no meat and journeying due east,
On righteousness their high hearts fed, to heaven
Their souls assigned ; and steadfast trod their feet —
By faith upborne — past nullah ran, and wood,
River and jheel and plain.   King Yudhi-sthir
Walked foremost, Bhima followed, after him
Arjuna, and the twin-born brethren next,
Nakalu with Sahadev ; in whose still steps —
O Best of Bharat's offspring ! — Draupadi,
That gem of women paced, with soft dark face, —
Clear-edged like lotus petals ; last the dog
Following the Pandavas.

    .     .     .     .     .     .

                     While yet those heroes walked,
Now to the northward bending, where long coasts
Shut in the sea of salt, now to the north,
Accomplishing all quarters, journeyed they ;
The earth their altar of high sacrifice,
Which these most patient feet did pace around
Till Meru rose.

               At last it rose !   These Six,
Their senses subjugate, their spirits pure,
Wending along, came into sight — far off
In the eastern sky — of awful Himavat ;
And midway in the peaks of Himavat,
Meru, the mountain of all mountains. rose,
Whose head is heaven ; and under Himavat
Glared a wide waste of sand, dreadful as death.

Then, as they hastened o'er the deathly waste,
Aiming for Meru, having thoughts at soul
Infinite, eager, — lo ! Draupadi reeled,
With faltering heart and feet ; and Bhima turned,
Gazing upon her ; and that hero spake
To Yudhi-sthira : " Master, Brother, King !
Why doth she fail ?   For never all her life
Wrought our sweet lady one thing wrong, I think.
Thou knowest ; make us know, why hath she failed ? "

Then Yudhi-sthira answered : " Yea, one thing.
She loved our brothers better than all else, —
Better than Heaven : that was her tender sin,
Fault of a faultless soul : she pays for that."

So spake the monarch, turning not his eyes,
Though Draupadi lay dead, — striding straight on
For Meru, heart-full of the things of Heaven,
Perfect and firm.   But yet a little space
And Sahadev fell down ; which Bhima seeing,
Cried once again : " O King, great Madri's son
Stumbles and sinks.   Why hath he sunk ? — so true,
So brave and steadfast, and so free from pride !"

" He was not free," with countenance still fixed,
Quoth Yudhi-sthira ; " he was true and fast
And wise ; yet wisdom made him proud ; he hid
One little hurt of soul, but now it kills."

So saying, he strode on, Kunti's strong son,
And Bhima ; and Arjuna followed him,
And Nakalu and the hound ; leaving behind
Sahadev in the sands.   But Nakalu,
Weakened and grieved to see Sahadev fall —
His dear-loved brother — lagged and stayed ; and then
Prone on his face he fell, that noble face
Which had no match for beauty in the land, —
Glorious and godlike Nakalu !   Then sighed
Bhima anew : " Brother and Lord ! the man
Who never erred from virtue, never broke
Our fellowship, and never in the world
Was matched for goodly perfectness of form
Or gracious feature, — Nakalu has fallen !"

But Yudhi-sthira, holding fixed his eyes, —
That changeless, faithful, all-wise king, — replied :
" Yea, but he erred !   The god-like form he wore
Beguiled him to believe none like to him,
And he alone desirable, and things
Unlovely, to be slighted.   Self-love slays
Our noble brother.   Bhima, follow !   Each
Pays what his debt was."

Which Arjuna heard,
Weeping to see them fall ; and that stout son
Of Pandu, that destroyer of his foes,
That Prince, who drove through crimson waves of war,
In old days, with his milk-white chariot-steeds,
Him, the arch hero, sank !   Beholding this, —
The yielding of that soul unconquerable,

4

Fearless, divine, from Sakra's self derived,
Arjuna's, — Bhima cried aloud : "O King!
This man was surely perfect.  Never once,
Not even in slumber, when the lips are loosed,
Spake he one word that was not true as truth.
Ah, heart of gold! why art thou broke?  O King!
Whence falleth he?"

                 And Yudhi-sthira said,
Not pausing : "Once he lied, a lordly lie!
He bragged — our brother — that a single day
Should see him utterly consume, alone,
All those his enemies, — which could not be.
Yet from a great heart sprang the unmeasured speech.
Howbeit a finished hero should not shame
Himself in such a wise, nor his enemy,
If he will faultless fight and blameless die :
This was Arjuna's sin.  Follow thou me!"

So the King still went on.  But Bhima next
Fainted, and stayed upon the way, and sank ;
But, sinking, cried behind the steadfast Prince :
"Ah, Brother, see!  I die!  Look upon me,
Thy well beloved!  Wherefore falter I,
Who strove to stand?"

                 And Yudhi-sthira said :
"More than was well the goodly things of earth
Pleased thee, my pleasant brother!  Light the offence
And large thy spirit ; but the o'erfed soul
Plumed itself over others.  Pritha's son,
For this thou fallest, who so near didst gain."

Thenceforth alone the long-armed monarch strode,
Not looking back, — nay, not for Bhima's sake, —
But walking with his face set for the Mount ;
And the hound followed him, — only the hound.

After the deathly sands, the Mount! and lo!
Sakra shone forth, — the God, — filling the earth
And Heavens with the thunders of his chariot wheels.
"Ascend," he said, "with me, Pritha's great son!"
But Yudhi-sthira answered, sore at heart
For those his kinsfolk, fallen on the way :
"O Thousand-eyed, O Lord of all the gods,
Give that my brothers come with me, who fell!
Not without them is Swarga sweet to me.
She too, the dear and kind and queenly, — she
Whose perfect virtue Paradise must crown, —
Grant her to come with us!  Dost thou grant this?"

The God replied: " In Heaven thou shalt see
Thy kinsmen and the Queen — these will attain —
And Krishna.  Grieve no longer for thy dead,
Thou chief of men!  their mortal coverings stripped,
These have their places; but to thee, the gods
Allow an unknown grace: thou shalt go up,
Living and in thy form, to the immortal homes."

But the King answered: " O thou wisest One,
Who know'st what was, and is, and is to be,
Still one more grace!  This hound hath ate with me,
Followed me, loved me; must I leave him now?"

" Monarch," spake Indra, " thou art now as we, —.
Deathless, divine; thou art become a god;
Glory and power and gifts celestial,
And all the joys of heaven are thine for aye:
What hath a beast with these?  Leave here thy hound."

Yet Yudhi-sthira answered: " O Most High,
O Thousand-Eyed and Wisest!  can it be
That one exalted should seem pitiless?
Nay, let me lose such glory: for its sake
I cannot leave one living thing I loved."

Then sternly Indra spake: " He is unclean,
And into Swarga such shall enter not.
The Krodhavasha's wrath destroys the fruits
Of sacrifice, if dog defile the fire.
Bethink thee, Dharmaraj; quit now this beast!
That which is seemly is not hard of heart."

Still he replied: " 'T is written that to spurn
A suppliant equals in offence to slay
A twice-born; wherefore, not for Swarga's bliss
Quit I, Mahendra, this poor clinging dog, —
So without any hope or friend save me,
So wistful, fawning for my faithfulness;
So agonized to die, unless I help
Who among men was called steadfast and just."

Quoth Indra: " Nay, the altar flame is foul
Where a dog passeth; angry angels sweep
The ascending smoke aside, and all the fruits
Of offering, and the merit of the prayer
Of him whom a hound toucheth.  Leave it here!
He that will enter Heaven must enter pure.
Why didst thou quit thy brethren on the way,
And Krishna, and the dear-loved Draupadi,
Attaining firm and glorious to this Mount
Through perfect deeds, to linger for a brute?"

Hath Yudhi-sthira vanquished self, to melt
With one pure passion at the door of bliss?
Stay'st thou for this, who did not stay for them, —
Draupadi, Bhima?"

     But the King yet spake:
"'T is known that none can hurt or help the dead.
They, the delightful ones, who sank and died,
Following my footsteps, could not live again
Though I had turned — therefore I did not turn;
But could help profit, I had stayed to help.
There be four sins, O Sakra, grievous sins:
The first is making suppliants despair,
The second is to slay a nursing wife,
The third is spoiling Brahmans' goods by force,
The fourth is injuring an ancient friend.
These four I deem not direr than the crime,
If one, in coming forth from woe to weal,
Abandon any meanest comrade then."

 Straight as he spake, brightly great Indra smiled;
Vanished the hound, and in its stead stood there
The Lord of Death and Justice, Dharma's self!
Sweet were the words which fell from those dread lips,
Precious the lovely praise: "O thou true King,
Thou that dost bring to harvest the good seed
Of Pandu's righteousness; thou that hast ruth
As he before, on all which lives! — O Son!

  .  .  .  .  .  .  .

Hear thou my word! Because thou didst not mount
This car divine, lest the poor hound be shent
Who looked to thee, lo! there is none in heaven
Shall sit above thee, King! Bharata's son!
Enter thou now to the eternal joys,
Living and in thy form. Justice and Love
Welcome thee, Monarch! thou shalt throne with us!"

        ARNOLD: *Indian Idylls*

# THE ILIAD.

THE Iliad, or story of the fall of Ilium (Troy), is supposed to have been written by Homer, about the tenth century B. C. The legendary history of Homer represents him as a schoolmaster and poet of Smyrna, who while visiting in Ithaca became blind, and afterwards spent his life travelling from place to place reciting his poems, until he died in Ios. Seven cities, Smyrna, Chios, Colophon, Ithaca, Pylos, Argos, and Athens, claimed to be his birthplace.

In 1795, Wolf, a German scholar, published his " Prolegomena," which set forth his theory that Homer was a fictitious character, and that the Iliad was made up of originally unconnected poems, collected and combined by Pisistratus.

Though for a time the Wolfian theory had many advocates, it is now generally conceded that although the stories of the fall of Troy were current long before Homer, they were collected and recast into one poem by some great poet. That the Iliad is the work of one man is clearly shown by its unity, its sustained simplicity of style, and the centralization of interest in the character of Achilles.

The destruction of Troy, for a time regarded as a poetic fiction, is now believed by many scholars to be an actual historical event which took place about the time of the Æolian migration.

The whole story of the fall of Troy is not related in the Iliad, the poem opening nine years after the beginning of the war, and closing with the death of Hector.

The Iliad is divided into twenty-four books, and contains nineteen thousand four hundred and sixty-five lines.

As a work of art the Iliad has never been excelled; moreover, it possesses what all works of art do not, — " the touches of things human " that make it ours, although the centuries lie between us and its unknown author, who told his stirring story in such swift-moving verses, with such touches of pathos and humor, and with such evident joy of living. Another evidence of the perfection of Homer's art is that while his heroes are perfect types of Greeks and Trojans, they are also typical men, and for that reason, still keep their hold upon us. It is this human interest, simplicity of style, and grandeur of treatment that have rendered Homer immortal and his work imperishable.

BIBLIOGRAPHY AND CRITICISM, THE ILIAD. M. Arnold's Essay on Homer, 1876, pp. 284–425 ; H. Bonitz's Origin of the Homeric Poems, tr. 1880 ; R. C. Jebb's Introduction to Homer, 1887 ; F. B. Jevons's History of Greek Literature, 1886, pp. 7–17 ; A. Lang's Homer and the Epic, 1893 ; W. Leaf's Companion to the Iliad for English Readers, 1892 ; J. A. Symonds's Studies in Greek Poets, ed. 3, 1893.

STANDARD ENGLISH TRANSLATIONS, THE ILIAD. The Iliad, Tr. into English blank verse by W. C. Bryant, 2 vols., 1871 (Primitive in spirit, like Homer. Union of literalness with simplicity) ; The Iliad, Tr. according to the Greek with introduction and notes by George Chapman [1615], Ed. 2, 2 vols., 1874 (Written in verse. Pope says a daring and fiery spirit animates this translation, something like that in which one might imagine Homer would have written before he came to years of discretion) ; The Iliad, Tr. by William Cowper (Very literal and inattentive to melody, but has more of simple majesty and manner of Homer than Pope) ; The Iliad, rendered into English blank verse by the Earl of Derby, 2 vols., 1864 ; The Iliad, Tr. by Alexander Pope, with notes by the Rev. T. W. A. Buckley, n. d. (Written in couplets. Highly ornamented paraphrase).

## THE STORY OF THE ILIAD.

FOR nine years a fleet of one thousand one hundred and eighty-six ships and an army of more than one hundred thousand Greeks, under the command of Agamemnon, lay before King Priam's city of Troy to avenge the wrongs of Menelaus, King of Sparta, and to reclaim Helen, his wife, who had been carried away by Priam's son Paris, at the instigation of Venus.

Though they had not succeeded in taking Troy, the Greeks had conquered many of the surrounding cities. From one of these, Agamemnon had taken as his share of the booty Chryseis, the beautiful daughter of the priest Chryses; and when her father had come to ransom her, he had been insulted and driven away by the king. Chryses had prayed to Apollo for revenge, and the god had sent upon the Greeks a pestilence which was slaying so many thousands that a meeting was called to consult upon what to do to check the plague and conciliate the god.

Calchas the seer had declared that the plague was sent because of the detention of Chryseis, and Agamemnon, though indignant with the priest, announced that he would send her back to save his army from destruction. " Note, however," said he, " that I have now given up my booty. See that I am recompensed for what I lose."

Then rose the leader of the Myrmidons, swift-footed Achilles, in his wrath, and denounced Agamemnon for his greediness.

" Thou hast ever had thy share and more of all the booty, and thou knowest well that there is now no common store from which to give thee spoil. But wait until Troy town is sacked, and we will gladly give thee three and fourfold thy recompense."

The angry Agamemnon declared that if he were not given the worth of what he had lost he would seize the maidens of Ajax and Ulysses, or Achilles' maid, Briseis.

Achilles was beside himself with rage. He had not come to Troy to contribute to Agamemnon's glory. He and his followers had long borne the brunt of battle only to see the largest share of booty given to Agamemnon, who lay idle in his ships. Sooner than endure longer such indignity he would return home to Phthia.

"Go!" replied Agamemnon. "I detest thee and thy ways. Go back over the sea and rule over thy Myrmidons. But since Phœbus has taken away my maid, I will carry off thy prize, thy rosy-cheeked Briseis, that thou may'st learn that I am indeed king."

Warned by Pallas Athene, Achilles took his hand from his sword hilt, and contented himself with telling Agamemnon that he would see the day when he would fret to think he had driven Achilles from the Grecian ranks.

Though the persuasive orator, Nestor, endeavored to make peace between the chiefs, Agamemnon could not be softened. As soon as the black ship bearing Chryseis set sail, he sent his unwilling men to where Achilles sat by his tent, beside the barren deep, to take the fair Briseis, whom Achilles ordered to be led forth to them. Then the long days dragged by in the tent where the chief sat eating his heart out in idleness, while his men engaged in athletic sports, and the rest of the Greeks fought before Troy.

Both armies, worn out with indecisive battles, gladly hailed Hector's proposal that a combat between Paris and Mene-laus should decide the war.

As the armies stood in silence, watching the preparations for the combat, Helen, summoned by Iris, left her room in Priam's palace, where she was weaving among her maidens, and, robed and veiled in white, and shedding tears at the recollection of her former home and husband, went down to the Scæan gates, where sat Priam and the men too old for war. When they saw bright-haired Helen they whispered among themselves that it was little wonder that men warred for her sake, so fair was she, so like unto the deathless goddesses.

In response to Priam's tender greeting she seated herself

beside him and pointed out the Greek heroes, — Agamemnon, ruler over wide lands, crafty Ulysses, and the mighty Ajax; but she strained her eyes in vain for a sight of her dearly loved brothers, Castor and Pollux, not knowing that they already lay dead in pleasant Lacedæmon.

In the single combat between Paris and Menelaus, the spear of the Greek was fixed in Paris's buckler, and his sword was shivered on his helmet without injury to the Trojan. But, determined to overcome his hateful foe, Menelaus seized Paris by the helm and dragged him towards the Grecian ranks. Great glory would have been his had not the watchful Venus loosed the helm and snatched away the god-like Paris in a cloud. While the Greeks demanded Helen and her wealth as the price of Menelaus's victory, Pandarus, prompted by Pallas, broke the truce by a shot aimed at Menelaus, and the battle soon raged with greater fury than before.

Diomed, having received new strength and courage from Pallas, rushed madly over the field, falling upon the affrighted Trojans like a lion in the sheepfold; then, made more presumptuous by his success, and forgetful of the few years promised the man who dares to meet the gods in battle, the arrogant warrior struck at Venus and wounded her in the wrist, so that, shrieking with pain, she yielded Æneas to Apollo, and fled to Olympus.

Perceiving that the Trojans were unable to withstand the fury of Diomed, assisted as he was by Pallas and Juno, Hector hastened homeward to order a sacrifice to Pallas that she might look with more favor upon their cause.

Having instructed his mother to lay her richest robe on Pallas's shrine, Hector sought his wife, the white-armed Andromache, and their babe, Astyanax. Andromache entreated Hector to go forth no more to battle, to lose his life and leave their babe fatherless; but Hector, upon whom the cares of war sat heavily, bade her a tender farewell, and kissing the babe, returned with Paris to the field.

Incited by Pallas and Apollo, Helenus suggested to his brother Hector that he should challenge the bravest of the

Greeks to single combat. The lot fell to Ajax the Greater, and the two mighty heroes contested with spears and stones until twilight fell, and they were parted by a herald.

That night the Greeks feasted, and when, the next morning, a Trojan messenger offered them the treasures of Helen if they would withdraw from Troy, and proposed a truce, they indignantly rejected the offer, declaring that they would not even accept Helen herself, but agreed upon a truce in which to bury the dead.

When the battle was renewed, Jupiter forbade the gods to take part. Opposed by no celestial foes, the Trojans were this day successful, and having pursued the Greeks to the ships, sat all night, full of hope, around their thousand watch fires, waiting for the morn.

In the Grecian camp, however, a different scene was being enacted. Disheartened by their defeat, Agamemnon proposed that the armies give up the siege and return to Greece.

Angry at his weakness, Diomed thus reproached him : —

"The gods have granted thee high rank and rule, but thou hast no fortitude. Return if thou desirest. Still enough long-haired Achaians will remain to take the city. If they desire to go as well, at least Sthenelus and I will remain until Troy is ours. We have the gods with us."

At the suggestion of Nestor a banquet was spread, and after the hunger of all was appeased, the peril of the Greeks was discussed in the Council of the Elders. Here Nestor showed Agamemnon that the trouble began at the hour when he drove Achilles from their ranks by appropriating Briseis.

Ill fortune had humbled the haughty Agamemnon, and he confessed that he had done wrong. "For this wrong, however," said he, " I am ready to make ample amends. Priceless gifts I will send to Achilles : seven tripods, six talents of pure gold, twenty shining caldrons, twelve steeds, seven damsels, among them Briseis ; not only this, when Priam's citadel falls, he shall be the first to load his galley down with gold and silver and with Trojan maidens. Better yet, I will unite him to me by the ties of marriage. I will give him my daughter for a wife, and with her for a dower will go seven cities near the sea, rich in flocks and herds. Then let him yield, and join us in taking Troy."

Joyfully the messengers — Ajax, Ulysses, and the aged Phœnix, carefully instructed by Nestor — set forth on their embassy. As they neared the tents of the Myrmidons their ears were struck by the notes of a silver harp touched by Achilles to solace him in his loneliness. His friend Patroclus sat beside him in silence. Achilles and Patroclus greeted the messengers warmly, mingled the pure wine, and spread a feast for them. This over, Ulysses, at a nod from Ajax, drank to Achilles' health, and then told him of the sore need of the Greeks, pressed by the Trojans. If he did not come to their aid, he whose very name frightened the enemy, the time would surely come when he would greatly lament his idleness.

Achilles' passion, the greater for its fifteen days' repression, burst forth in his reply : " I will say what I have in my heart," he cried, " since concealment is hateful to me. What thanks does the victor in countless battles gain ? He and the idler are equally honored, and die the same death. Many nights' slumber have I lost on the battle field ; many cities have I conquered, abroad and here upon the Trojan coast, and of the spoil, the greater part has gone to Agamemnon, who sat idle in his fleet ; yet from me, who suffered much in fighting, he took my prize, my dearly loved Briseis ; now let him keep her. Let him learn for himself how to conquer Hector, — this Hector, who, when I went out against him, was afraid to leave the shelter of the Scæan gates. To-morrow, if you but watch, you will see my galleys sailing upon the Hellespont on our return to Phthia. Evil was the hour in which I left its fertile coasts for this barren shore, where my mother Thetis foretold I should win deathless renown but bitter death.

" Tell Agamemnon that I will never wed a child of his. On my return to Phthia my father will select a bride for me with whom, on his broad fields, I can live the life I have dreamed of."

The entreaties of the aged Phœnix, who had helped to rear Achilles, and his arguments against his mercilessness, were of no avail; neither were the words of Ajax. However, he at last sent the message that he would remain by the sea watching the course of the war, and that he would encounter Hector whenever he approached to set fire to the galleys of the Myrmidons.

That night sleep did not visit the eyes of Agamemnon. Long he reflected on the reply of Achilles, and wondered at the watch fires on the plain before Troy. The other chiefs were likewise full of anxiety, and when Nestor offered a reward to any one who would go as a spy to the Trojan camp, Diomed quickly volunteered. Selecting the wary Ulysses as his companion, he stole forth to where the Trojans sat around their camp fires. The pair intercepted and slew Dolon the spy, and finding Rhesus and his Thracian band wrapped in slumber, slew the king with twelve of his chiefs, and carried away his chariot and horses.

Encouraged by this bold deed, the Greeks went forth to battle the next morning. Fortune still favored the Trojans, however, and many Greeks fell by the hand of Hector, until he was checked by Ulysses and Diomed. In the fight, Agamemnon was wounded, and Diomed, Ulysses, and Machaon. And when Achilles from his tent saw the physician borne back from battle wounded, in the chariot of Nestor, he sent Patroclus to inquire of his injury. Nestor sent word that Ulysses, Agamemnon, Diomed, Machaon, and Eurypylus were wounded; perhaps these tidings would induce Achilles to forget his grievances, and once more go forth to battle. If not, he urged Patroclus to beseech Achilles to permit him, Patroclus, to go forth with the Myrmidons, clad in Achilles' armor, and strike terror to the hearts of the Trojans.

The Trojans, encouraged by their success, pushed forward to the trench which the Greeks had dug around the wall thrown up before the ships, and, leaving their chariots on the brink, went on foot to the gates. After a long struggle, — because the Trojans could not break down the wall and the

Greeks could not drive back the Trojans, — Hector seized a mighty stone, so large that two men could scarcely lift it, and bearing it in one hand, battered the bolted gates until they gave way with a crash; and the Trojans sprang within, pursuing the affrighted Greeks to the ships.

From the heights of Olympus the gods kept a strict watch on the battle; and as soon as Neptune discovered that Jove, secure in the belief that no deity would interfere with the successful Trojans, had turned away his eyes, he went to the aid of the Greeks. Juno, also, furious at the sight of the Greeks who had fallen before the mighty Hector, determined to turn the attention of Jove until Neptune had had an opportunity to assist the Greeks. Jove sat upon the peaks of Mount Ida, and thither went Juno, after rendering herself irresistible by borrowing the cestus of Venus. Jove, delighted with the appearance of his wife, and still further won by her tender words and caresses, thought no longer of the armies fighting at the Grecian wall.

Great was his anger when, after a time, he again looked towards Troy and saw that Neptune had employed his time in aiding the Greeks, and that Hector had been wounded by Ajax. By his orders Neptune was quickly recalled, Hector was healed by Apollo, and the Trojans, strengthened again by Jupiter, drove back the Greeks to the ships, and attempted to set fire to the fleet.

Seeing the Greeks in such desperate straits, Achilles at last gave his consent that Patroclus should put on his armor, take his Myrmidons, and drive the Trojans from the ships, stipulating, however, that he should return when this was done, and not follow the Trojans in their flight to Troy.

The appearance of the supposed Achilles struck fear to the hearts of the Trojans, and Patroclus succeeded in driving them from the fleet and in slaying Sarpedon. Intoxicated by his success, he forgot Achilles' warning, and pursued the fleeing Trojans to the walls of Troy. The strength of the Trojans was not sufficient to cope with that of Patroclus; and Troy would have been taken had not Apollo stood upon a tower to thrust him down each time he attempted to scale

the walls.   At last Hector and Patroclus encountered each
other, and fought furiously.   Seeing the peril of Hector,
Apollo smote Patroclus's helmet off, broke his spear, and
loosed his buckler.   Still undaunted, the hero fought until he
fell, and died with the boasting words of Hector in his ears.

Speedily the swift-footed Antilochus conveyed to Achilles
the tidings of his friend's death.   Enveloped in "a black
cloud of sorrow," Achilles rolled in the dust and lamented
for his friend until warned by Iris that the enemy were about
to secure Patroclus's body.   Then, without armor, — for
Hector had secured that of Patroclus and put it on, — he
hastened to the trench, apart from the other Greeks, and
shouted thrice, until the men of Troy, panic-stricken, fell
back in disorder, and the body of his friend was carried away
by the triumphant Greeks.

Through the long night the Achaians wept over Patroclus;
but deeper than their grief was the sorrow of Achilles, for he
had promised Menœtius to bring back his son in honor,
laden with spoils, and now the barren coast of Troy would
hold the ashes of both.   Then Achilles made a solemn vow
not to celebrate the funeral rites of Patroclus until he brought
to him the head and arms of Hector, and had captured on
the field twelve Trojan youths to slaughter on his funeral
pile.   The hated Hector slain and Patroclus's funeral rites
celebrated, he cared not for the future.   The fate his mother
had foretold did not daunt him.   Since, by his own folly,
his dearest friend had been taken from him, the sooner their
ashes rested together the better.   If he was not to see the
rich fields of Phthia, his was to be, at least, a deathless
renown.

To take the place of the arms which Hector had taken
from Patroclus, Vulcan, at Thetis's request, had fashioned for
Achilles the most beautiful armor ever worn by man.   Brass,
tin, silver, and gold composed the bright corselet, the solid
helm, and the wondrous shield, adorned with such pictures
as no mortal artist ever wrought.

After having feasted his eyes on this beautiful armor, whose
clanking struck terror even to the hearts of the Myrmidons,

Achilles sought out the Greeks and Agamemnon, and in the assembly acknowledged his fault. " Let these things belong to the dead past," said he. " My wrath is done. Let us now stir the long-haired Greeks to war."

" Fate, not I, was the cause of our trouble," replied Agamemnon. " The goddess of discord created the dissension, that Até who troubled even the gods on Olympus until expelled by Jupiter. But I will make amends with liberal gifts."

Peace having been made between the chiefs, Achilles returned to his tent without partaking of the banquet spread by Agamemnon, as he had vowed not to break his fast until he had avenged his friend. Agamemnon's gifts were carried to the tents of Achilles by the Myrmidons, and with them went Briseis, who, when she saw the body of Patroclus, threw herself upon it and wept long for the one whose kindness to her — whose lot had been sorrow upon sorrow — she could never forget. All the women mourned, seemingly for Patroclus, really for their own griefs. Achilles likewise wept, until, strengthened by Pallas, he hastened to put his armor on and urge the Greeks to battle.

As he mounted his chariot he spoke thus to his fleet steeds, Xanthus and Balius : " Bring me back when the battle is over, I charge you, my noble steeds. Leave me not on the field, as you left Patroclus."

Then Xanthus, with the long-flowing mane, endowed with power of speech by Juno, thus spake : " This day, at least, we will bring thee home, Achilles ; but the hour of thy death is nigh, and, since the fates have decreed it, we could not save thee, were we swift as the winged winds. Nor was it through fault of ours that Patroclus fell."

Angry at the reminder of his doom, Achilles drove hurriedly to the field, determined to fight until he had made the Trojans sick of war.

Knowing that the war was drawing rapidly to a close, Jupiter gave permission to the gods to take part in it, and a terrible combat ensued. Juno, Pallas, Neptune, Hermes, and Vulcan went to the fleet of the Greeks, while Mars, Apollo, Diana, Latona, Venus, and Xanthus arrayed themselves with the Trojans. When the gods joined in the combat and Neptune shook the earth and Jupiter thundered from above, there was such tumult in the air that even the dark god of the underworld was terrified. In the battle of the gods, Apollo encountered Neptune, Pallas fought against Mars, Diana and Juno opposed each other, Hermes was pitted against Latona, and Xanthus or Scamander, the river god, strove against Vulcan. It was not long before Jupiter's fear was realized, and the mortals needed the aid of the gods. Æneas, encouraged by Apollo to confront Achilles, was rescued only by the intervention of Neptune, who, remembering that it was the will of fate that Æneas should be spared to perpetuate the Dardan race, snatched him away in a cloud, although he was himself aiding the Greeks.

Mad with rage and spattered with blood, Achilles pursued the flying Trojans about the plain, sparing none except the twelve youths who were to be butchered on the funeral pile of Patroclus. He stood in the river, filling it with slaughtered bodies until, indignant at the insults offered him, the river god Scamander caused his waters to rush after Achilles so that he fled for his life. Far across the plain it chased him, and was only stopped by the fires of Vulcan, summoned by Juno.

By an artifice of Apollo, Achilles was decoyed away from the gates of Troy long enough to allow the Trojans to enter. Hector, however, stayed without, unmoved by the prayers of Priam and Hecuba. Too late he saw his error in not heeding the advice of Polydamas to keep within the walls after the re-appearance of Achilles; he feared the reproaches of the Trojan warriors and dames, and determined to meet his fate, whatever it might be. Even death at the hands of Achilles would be preferable to the insults and reproaches that might await him within the walls.

When he saw Achilles approach in his god-given armor, fear seized the noble Hector, and he fled from his enemy. Thrice around the walls he fled, Achilles pursuing, and the gods looked down from heaven in sorrow, for, according to the decrees of fate, Hector must fall this day by the hand of

Achilles. To hasten the combat, Pallas assumed the form of Hector's brother Deiphobus, and stood by his side, encouraging him to turn and meet his foe.

Hector soon perceived the deception, but boldly faced Achilles, who sprang at him, brandishing his awful spear. Quickly stooping, Hector avoided the weapon and hurled his spear at Achilles. It was an unequal conflict. The armor of Achilles was weapon proof, and Pallas stood at his elbow to return to him his weapons. Achilles knew well the weak spots in his old armor worn by Hector, and selecting a seam unguarded by the shield, he gave Hector a mortal wound, and insulted him as he lay dying at his feet.

Tears and wailing filled the city as the Trojans watched the combat; and despair fell upon them when they saw the body of Hector fastened to the chariot of Achilles and dragged thrice around the Trojan walls. From her chamber where she sat weaving, unaware of the mortal combat waged before the walls, Andromache came forth to see great Hector fallen and his corpse insulted by his enemy.

While Priam sat in his palace with dust strewn on his head, and the wailings of the women filled the streets of Troy, the Greeks were hastening to their camps to celebrate the funeral rites of Patroclus, whose body had been saved from corruption by Thetis. A massive funeral pile was constructed of wood brought from the forests on Mount Ida. The chiefs in their chariots and thousands of men on foot followed the body of Patroclus. The comrades of the dead warrior cut off their long hair and strewed it on the dead, and Achilles sheared his yellow hair and placed the locks in Patroclus's hands. He had suffered the flowing curls to grow long because of a vow made by his father to the river Sperchius that he would sacrifice these locks to him on his son's return home, a useless vow, since now he was to lose his life by this dark blue sea.

Next the sacrifice was offered, many fatlings of the flock, and countless oxen, noble steeds, dogs, jars of honey, and lastly the bodies of the twelve Trojan youths were heaped upon the fire.

After the flames had consumed the pile, Achilles and his friends quenched the ashes with red wine, and gathered the bones of Patroclus in a golden vase which Achilles commanded his friends not to bury until he, too, fell before Troy, that their ashes might be mingled and buried under one mound by the remaining Greeks.

After the funeral rites were celebrated, the funeral games were held, in which the warriors vied with each other in chariot racing, boxing, wrestling, foot racing, throwing the spear, and archery.

So ended the funeral of Patroclus, and the gods, looking down from heaven, sorrowed for Hector, whose corpse Achilles was treating with such indignity, intending that the dogs should destroy it. The gods had kept the body unstained, and now they determined to soften Achilles' heart, that he might restore it to Priam.

Iris descended from heaven, and standing at the side of Priam as he sat with dust-strewn head, in his palace halls, gave him Jove's command that he should take gifts and visit Achilles, to ransom Hector's body. Heeding not the prayers of Hecuba, Priam gathered together whatever was most choice, talents of pure gold, beautiful goblets, handsome robes and tunics, and seating himself in his polished car, drawn by strong-hoofed mules, set forth unaccompanied save by an aged herald. Above him soared Jove's eagle, in token of the god's protection.

Priam had not gone far when he met Mercury in the guise of a Greek youth, who guided him unseen through the slumbering Greek lines to the tent of Achilles.

The hero was just finishing his repast when the old king entered, fell on his knees, kissed the cruel hands that had slain so many of his sons, and prayed him to give up the body of his loved Hector in return for the ransom he had brought with him. Achilles, recognizing the fact that Priam had made his way there uninjured only by the assistance and protection of some god, and touched by the thought of his own aged father, whom he should never again gladden by his return to Phthia, granted the request, and bade Priam seat himself at the table and banquet with him. He also granted a twelve days' truce for the celebration of the funeral rites of Hector, and then invited Priam to pass the night in his tent. Warned by Mercury, Priam rose early in the morning, and, unseen by the Greeks, conveyed Hector's body back to Troy.

When the polished car of Priam entered the city of Troy, great were the lamentations and wailings over the body of Hector. Hecuba and Andromache vied with each other in the bitterness of their grief, and Helen lamented because the only friend she had in Troy had departed, and no one who remained would be kind to her.

During the twelve days granted as a truce, wood was brought from Ida, and the funeral rites of Hector were celebrated as befitted the son of a great king.

## SELECTIONS FROM THE ILIAD.

### HELEN AT THE SCÆAN GATES.

PARIS, moved by the reproaches of Hector, proposed that the nine years' indecisive war be settled by single combat between himself and Menelaus, the victor to take Helen and the treasure. Greeks and Trojans agreed to this proposition, and the tidings of the approaching combat were borne to Helen by Iris.

> In the heart of Helen woke
> Dear recollections of her former spouse
> And of her home and kindred. Instantly
> She left her chamber, robed and veiled in white,
> And shedding tender tears ; yet not alone,
> For with her went two maidens, — Æthra, child
> Of Pitheus, and the large-eyed Clymene.
> Straight to the Scæan gates they walked, by which
> Panthoüs, Priam, and Thymœtes sat,
> Lampus and Clytius, Hicetaon sprung
> From Mars, Antenor and Ucalegon,
> Two sages, — elders of the people all.
> Beside the gates they sat, unapt, through age,
> For tasks of war, but men of fluent speech,
> Like the cicadas that within the wood
> Sit on the trees and utter delicate sounds.

Such were the nobles of the Trojan race
Who sat upon the tower. But when they marked
The approach of Helen, to each other thus
With winged words, but in low tones, they said : —
    " Small blame is theirs, if both the Trojan knights
And brazen-mailed Achaians have endured
So long so many evils for the sake
Of that one woman. She is wholly like
In feature to the deathless goddesses.
So be it : let her, peerless as she is,
Return on board the fleet, nor stay to bring
Disaster upon us and all our race."
    So spake the elders. Priam meantime called
To Helen : " Come, dear daughter, sit by me.
Thou canst behold thy former husband hence,
Thy kindred and thy friends. I blame thee not ;
The blame is with the immortals who have sent
These pestilent Greeks against me. Sit and name
For me this mighty man, the Grecian chief,
Gallant and tall. True, there are taller men ;
But of such noble form and dignity
I never saw : in truth, a kingly man."
    And Helen, fairest among women, thus
Answered : " Dear second father, whom at once
I fear and honor, would that cruel death
Had overtaken me before I left,
To wander with thy son, my marriage bed,
And my dear daughter, and the company
Of friends I loved. But that was not to be ;
And now I pine and weep. Yet will I tell
What thou dost ask. The hero whom thou seest
Is the wide-ruling Agamemnon, son
Of Atreus, and is both a gracious king
And a most dreaded warrior. He was once
Brother-in-law to me, if I may speak —
Lost as I am to shame — of such a tie."
    She said, the aged man admired, and then
He spake again : " O son of Atreus, born
Under a happy fate, and fortunate
Among the sons of men ! A mighty host
Of Grecian youths obey thy rule. I went
To Phrygia once, — that land of vines, — and there
Saw many Phrygians, heroes on fleet steeds,
The troops of Otreus, and of Mygdon, shaped
Like one of the immortals. They encamped
By the Sangarius. I was an ally ;
My troops were ranked with theirs upon the day
When came the unsexed Amazons to war.
Yet even there I saw not such a host
As this of black-eyed Greeks who muster here."

Then Priam saw Ulysses, and inquired: —
" Dear daughter, tell me also who is that,
Less tall than Agamemnon, yet more broad
In chest and shoulders.  On the teeming earth
His armor lies, but he, from place to place,
Walks round among the ranks of soldiery,
As when the thick-fleeced father of the flocks
Moves through the multitude of his white sheep."

And Jove-descended Helen answered thus : —
" That is Ulysses, man of many arts,
Son of Laertes, reared in Ithaca,
That rugged isle, and skilled in every form
Of shrewd device and action wisely planned."

Then spake the sage Antenor: " Thou hast said
The truth, O lady.  This Ulysses once
Came on an embassy, concerning thee,
To Troy with Menelaus, great in war;
And I received them as my guests, and they
Were lodged within my palace, and I learned
The temper and the qualities of both.
When both were standing 'mid the men of Troy,
I marked that Menelaus's broad chest
Made him the more conspicuous, but when both
Were seated, greater was the dignity
Seen in Ulysses.  When they both addressed
The council, Menelaus briefly spake
In pleasing tones, though with few words, — as one
Not given to loose and wandering speech, — although
The younger.  When the wise Ulysses rose,
He stood with eyes cast down, and fixed on earth,
And neither swayed his sceptre to the right
Nor to the left, but held it motionless,
Like one unused to public speech.  He seemed
An idiot out of humor.  But when forth
He sent from his full lungs his mighty voice,
And words came like a fall of winter snow,
No mortal then would dare to strive with him
For mastery in speech.  We less admired
The aspect of Ulysses than his words."

Beholding Ajax then, the aged king
Asked yet again : " Who is that other chief
Of the Achaians, tall, and large of limb, —
Taller and broader-chested than the rest?"

Helen, the beautiful and richly-robed,
Answered: "Thou seest the mighty Ajax there,
The bulwark of the Greeks.  On the other side,
Among his Cretans, stands Idomeneus,
Of godlike aspect, near to whom are grouped
The leaders of the Cretans.  Oftentimes
The warlike Menelaus welcomed him

Within our palace, when he came from Crete.
I could point out and name the other chiefs
Of the dark-eyed Achaians. Two alone,
Princes among their people, are not seen, —
Castor the fearless horseman, and the skilled
In boxing, Pollux, — twins; one mother bore
Both them and me. Came they not with the rest
From pleasant Lacedæmon to the war?
Or, having crossed the deep in their good ships,
Shun they to fight among the valiant ones
Of Greece, because of my reproach and shame?"
   She spake; but they already lay in earth
In Lacedæmon, their dear native land.

*Bryant's Translation, Book III.*

## THE PARTING OF HECTOR AND ANDROMACHE.

THE single combat between Paris and Menelaus broke up in
a general battle unfavorable to the Trojans, and Hector returned
to Troy to order the Trojan matrons to sacrifice to Pallas. He
then sought his dwelling to greet his wife and child, but learned
from one of the maids that Andromache, on hearing that the
Greeks were victorious, had hastened to the city walls with the
child and its nurse.

Hector left in haste
The mansion, and retraced his way between
The rows of stately dwellings, traversing
The mighty city. When at length he reached
The Scæan gates, that issue on the field,
His spouse, the nobly-dowered Andromache,
Came forth to meet him, — daughter of the prince
Eëtion, who among the woody slopes
Of Placos, in the Hypoplacian town
Of Thebê, ruled Cilicia and her sons,
And gave his child to Hector great in arms.
She came attended by a maid, who bore
A tender child — a babe too young to speak —
Upon her bosom, — Hector's only son,
Beautiful as a star, whom Hector called
Scamandrius, but all else Astyanax, —
The city's lord, — since Hector stood the sole
Defence of Troy. The father on his child
Looked with a silent smile. Andromache
Pressed to his side meanwhile, and, all in tears,
Clung to his hand, and, thus beginning, said:—

"Too brave! thy valor yet will cause thy death.
Thou hast no pity on thy tender child
Nor me, unhappy one, who soon must be
Thy widow.   All the Greeks will rush on thee
To take thy life.   A happier lot were mine,
If I must lose thee, to go down to earth,
For I shall have no hope when thou art gone, —
Nothing but sorrow.   Father have I none,
And no dear mother.   Great Achilles slew
My father when he sacked the populous town
Of the Cilicians, — Thebè with high gates.
'T was there he smote Eëtion, yet forbore
To make his arms a spoil ; he dared not that,
But burned the dead with his bright armor on,
And raised a mound above him.   Mountain-nymphs,
Daughters of ægis-bearing Jupiter,
Came to the spot and planted it with elms.
Seven brothers had I in my father's house,
And all went down to Hades in one day.
Achilles the swift-footed slew them all
Among their slow-paced bullocks and white sheep.
My mother, princess on the woody slopes
Of Placos, with his spoils he bore away,
And only for large ransom gave her back.
But her Diana, archer-queen, struck down
Within her father's palace.   Hector, thou
Art father and dear mother now to me,
And brother and my youthful spouse besides.
In pity keep within the fortress here,
Nor make thy child an orphan nor thy wife
A widow.   Post thine army near the place
Of the wild fig-tree, where the city-walls
Are low and may be scaled.   Thrice in war
The boldest of the foe have tried the spot, —
The Ajaces and the famed Idomeneus,
The two chiefs born to Atreus, and the brave
Tydides, whether counselled by some seer
Or prompted to the attempt by their own minds."

   Then answered Hector, great in war : "All this
I bear in mind, dear wife ; but I should stand
Ashamed before the men and long-robed dames
Of Troy, were I to keep aloof and shun
The conflict, coward-like.   Not thus my heart
Prompts me, for greatly have I learned to dare
And strike among the foremost sons of Troy,
Upholding my great father's fame and mine ;
Yet well in my undoubting mind I know
The day shall come in which our sacred Troy,
And Priam, and the people over whom
Spear-bearing Priam rules, shall perish all.

But not the sorrows of the Trojan race,
Nor those of Hecuba herself, nor those
Of royal Priam, nor the woes that wait
My brothers many and brave, — who all at last,
Slain by the pitiless foe, shall lie in dust, —
Grieve me so much as thine, when some mailed Greek
Shall lead thee weeping hence, and take from thee
Thy day of freedom.   Thou in Argos then
Shalt at another's bidding ply the loom,
And from the fountain of Messeis draw
Water, or from the Hypereian spring,
Constrained unwilling by thy cruel lot.
And then shall some one say who sees thee weep,
'This was the wife of Hector, most renowned
Of the horse-taming Trojans, when they fought
Around their city.'   So shall some one say,
And thou shalt grieve the more, lamenting him
Who haply might have kept afar the day
Of thy captivity.   O let the earth
Be heaped above my head in death before
I hear thy cries as thou art borne away!"
　　So speaking, mighty Hector stretched his arms
To take the boy; the boy shrank crying back
To his fair nurse's bosom, scared to see
His father helmeted in glittering brass,
And eying with affright the horsehair plume
That grimly nodded from the lofty crest.
At this both parents in their fondness laughed;
And hastily the mighty Hector took
The helmet from his brow and laid it down
Gleaming upon the ground, and, having kissed
His darling son and tossed him up in play,
Prayed thus to Jove and all the gods of heaven: —
　　"O Jupiter and all ye deities,
Vouchsafe that yet this my son may yet become
Among the Trojans eminent like me,
And nobly rule in Ilium.   May they say,
'This man is greater than his father was!'
When they behold him from the battle-field
Bring back the bloody spoil of the slain foe, —
That so his mother may be glad at heart."
　　So speaking, to the arms of his dear spouse
He gave the boy; she on her fragrant breast
Received him, weeping as she smiled.   The chief
Beheld, and, moved with tender pity, smoothed
Her forehead gently with his hand, and said: —
　　"Sorrow not thus, beloved one, for me.
No living man can send me to the shades
Before my time; no man of woman born,
Coward or brave, can shun his destiny.

But go thou home, and tend thy labors there, —
The web, the distaff, — and command thy maids
To speed the work. The cares of war pertain
To all men born in Troy, and most to me."
   Thus speaking, mighty Hector took again
His helmet, shadowed with the horsehair plume,
While homeward his beloved consort went,
Oft looking back, and shedding many tears.
Soon was she in the spacious palace-halls
Of the man-queller Hector. There she found
A troop of maidens, — with them all she shared
Her grief ; and all in his own house bewailed
The living Hector, whom they thought no more
To see returning from the battle-field,
Safe from the rage and weapons of the Greeks.

*Bryant's Translation, Book VI.*

# THE ODYSSEY.

"The surge and thunder of the Odyssey."

THE Odyssey relates the adventures of Ulysses on his
return to Ithaca after the Trojan war.

It consists of twenty-four books, the first four of which are
sometimes known as the Telemachia, because Telemachus is
the principal figure.

The difference in style of the Iliad and Odyssey has caused
some critics to assert that the latter is not the work of Homer ;
this is accounted for, however, by the difference of subject,
and it is probable that the Odyssey, though of a later date, is
the work of the same hand, "the work of Homer's old age,
— an epic bathed in a mellow light of sunset."

If the Odyssey alone had come down to us, its authorship
would have passed unquestioned, for the poem is so compact, its plot so carefully planned and so skilfully carried
out, that there can be no doubt that it is the work of one
hand.

The Odyssey is as great a work of art as the Iliad, and is
even more popular ; for the Odyssey is a domestic romance,
and as such appeals to a larger audience than a tale of
war alone, — the romance of the wandering Ulysses and
the faithful Penelope. Interwoven with it are the ever-pop-
ular fairy tales of Ulysses's wanderings and descriptions of
home life. It is marked by the same pagan enjoyment of
life, the same freshness and charm that lend enchantment
to the Iliad.

BIBLIOGRAPHY AND CRITICISM, THE ODYSSEY. F. B.
Jevons's History of Greek Literature, 1886, pp. 17–25 ; A.
Lang's Homer and the Epic, 1893, chaps. 8–13 ; J. A.

Symonds's Studies of the Greek Poets, ed. 3, 1893 ; J. E. Harrison's Myths of the Odyssey in Art and Literature, 1882 ; W. J. Stillman's On the Track of Ulysses, 1888 ; F. W. Newman's The Authorship of the Odyssey (in his Miscellanies, vol. v.) ; J. Spence's Essay on Pope's Translation of the Odyssey, 1837.

STANDARD ENGLISH TRANSLATIONS, THE ODYSSEY. The Odyssey, Tr. into English blank verse by W. C. Bryant, 2 vols., 1871 ; The Odyssey, Tr. according to the Greek, with introduction and notes by George Chapman, ed. 2, 2 vols., 1874 ; The Odyssey, Tr. by William Cowper ; The Odyssey, Tr. by G. H. Palmer, 1894 (prose) ; The Odyssey, Tr. by Alexander Pope, with notes by Rev. T. W. A. Buckley, n. d. ; The Odyssey, Tr. by S. H. Butcher and A. Lang, 1879 (prose).

## THE STORY OF THE ODYSSEY.

AFTER the fall of Troy, Agamemnon returned to Argos, where he was treacherously slain by Ægisthus, the corrupter of his wife; Menelaus reached Sparta in safety, laden with spoil and reunited to the beautiful Helen; Nestor resumed the rule of Pylos, but Ulysses remained absent from Ithaca, where his wife Penelope still grieved for him, though steadfast in her belief that he would return. One hundred and fourteen suitors, princes from Dulichium, Samos, Zacynthus, and Ithaca, determined to wed Penelope that they might obtain the rich possessions of Ulysses, spent their time in revelling in his halls and wasting his wealth, thinking in this way to force Penelope to wed some one of them.

Penelope, as rich in resources as was her crafty husband, announced to them that she would wed when she had woven a funeral garment for Laertes, the father of Ulysses. During the day she wove industriously, but at night she unravelled what she had done that day, so that to the expectant suitors the task seemed interminable. After four years her artifice was revealed to the suitors by one of her maids, and she was forced to find other excuses to postpone her marriage. In the mean time, her son Telemachus, now grown to manhood, disregarded by the suitors on account of his youth, and treated as a child by his mother, was forced to sit helpless in his halls, hearing the insults of the suitors and seeing his rich possessions wasted.

Having induced Jove to end the sufferings of Ulysses, Pallas caused Hermes to be dispatched to Calypso's isle to release the hero, while she herself descended to Ithaca in the guise of Mentes. There she was received courteously by the youth, who sat unhappy among the revellers. At a table apart from the others, Telemachus told the inquiring stranger who they were who thus wasted his patrimony.

"Something must needs be done speedily," said Mentes, "and I shall tell thee how to thrust them from thy palace gates. Take a ship and go to Pylos to inquire of the aged and wise Nestor what he knows of thy father's fate. Thence go to Menelaus, in Sparta; he was the last of all the mailed Greeks to return home. If thou hear encouraging tidings, wait patiently for a year. At the end of that time, if thy father come not, celebrate his funeral rites, let thy mother wed again, and take immediate steps for the destruction of the suitor band. Thou art no longer a child; the time has come for thee to assert thyself and be a man."

Telemachus, long weary of inactivity, was pleased with this advice, and at once announced to the incredulous suitors his intention of going to learn the fate of his father. A boat was procured and provided with a crew by the aid of Pallas, and provisioned from the secret store-room guarded by the old and faithful servant Eurycleia. From among the treasures of Ulysses — garments, heaps of gold and brass, and old and delicate wines — Telemachus took sweet wine and meal to be conveyed to the ship at night, and instructing Eurycleia not to tell his mother of his absence until twelve days had passed, he departed as soon as sleep had overcome the suitors. Pallas, in the guise of Mentor, accompanied him.

His courage failed him, however, as they approached the shore of Pylos, where Nestor and his people were engaged in making a great sacrifice to Neptune. "How shall I approach the chief?" he asked. "Ill am I trained in courtly speech."

But, encouraged by Pallas, he greeted the aged Nestor, and after he and his companion had assisted in the sacrifice and partaken of the banquet that followed, he revealed his name and asked for tidings of his father, boldly and confidently, as befitted the son of Ulysses. The old king could tell him nothing, however. After Troy had fallen, a dissension had rent the camp, and part of the Greeks had remained with Agamemnon, part had sailed with Menelaus. Sailing with Menelaus, Nestor had parted with Diomed at Argos, and had sailed on to Pylos. Since his return he had heard of the death of Agamemnon, and of the more recent return of Menelaus, but had heard no tidings of Ulysses, who had remained with Agamemnon.

To Menelaus he advised Telemachus to go, warning him, however, not to remain long away from Ithaca, leaving his home in the possession of rude and lawless men.

In a car provided by Nestor and driven by his son, Pisistratus, Telemachus reached Sparta after a day and a night's rapid travel, and found Menelaus celebrating the nuptial feast of his daughter Hermione, betrothed at Troy to the son of Achilles, and his son Megapenthes, wedded to the daughter of Alector. The two young men were warmly welcomed, and were invited to partake of the banquet without being asked their names. After the feast they wondered at the splendor of the halls of gold, amber, and ivory, the polished baths, and the fleecy garments in which they had been arrayed ; but Menelaus assured them that all his wealth was small compensation to him for the loss of the warriors who had fallen before Troy, and above all, of the great Ulysses, whose fate he knew not. Though Telemachus's tears fell at his father's name, Menelaus did not guess to whom he spoke, until Helen, entering from her perfumed chamber, saw the likeness between the stranger and the babe whom Ulysses had left when he went to Troy, and greeted their guest as Telemachus.

Then they sat in the splendid hall and talked of Troy, — Menelaus broken by his many toils, Helen beautiful as when she was rapt away by Paris, weaving with her golden distaff wound with violet wool, and the two young men, who said little, but listened to the wondrous tale of the wanderings of Menelaus. And they spoke of Ulysses : of the times when he had proved his prudence as well as his craft ; of his entering Troy as a beggar and revealing the Achaian plots to Helen ; of how he had prevented their breaking out of the wooden horse too soon. Then the king told of his interview with the Ancient of the Deep, in which he had learned the fate of his comrades ; of Agamemnon's death, and of the detention of Ulysses on Calypso's isle, where he languished, weeping bitterly, because he had no means of escape.

This information gained, Telemachus was anxious to return home; but his host detained him until he and Helen had descended to their fragrant treasure-chamber and brought forth rich gifts, — a double cup of silver and gold wrought by Vulcan, a shining silver beaker, and an embroidered robe for his future bride.

Mercury, dispatched by Jove, descended to the distant isle of Calypso, and warned the bright-haired nymph, whom he found weaving in her charmed grotto, that she must let her mortal lover go or brave the wrath of the gods. The nymph, though loath to part with her lover, sought out the melancholy Ulysses, where he sat weeping beside the deep, and giving him tools, led him to the forest and showed him where to fell trees with which to construct a raft. His labor finished, she provided the hero with perfumed garments, a full store of provisions, and saw him set forth joyfully upon the unknown deep.

For seventeen days his journey was a prosperous one; but on the eighteenth day, just as the land of the Phæacians came in sight, Neptune returned from Ethiopia, and angry at what the gods had contrived to do in his absence, determined to make the hero suffer as much as possible before he attained the promised end of his troubles.

Soon a great storm arose and washed Ulysses from the raft. Clinging to its edge, buffeted here and there by the angry waves, he would have suffered death had not a kind sea nymph urged him to lay aside his heavy garments, leave the raft, and binding a veil that she gave him about his chest, swim to the land of the Phæacians. The coast was steep and rocky, but he found at last a little river, and swimming up it, landed, and fell asleep among some warm heaps of dried leaves.

The Phæacians were a people closely allied to the gods, to whom they were very dear. They had at one time been neighbors of the Cyclops, from whose rudeness they had suffered so much that they were compelled to seek a distant home. They were a civilized people, who had achieved great results as sailors, having remarkably swift and well-equipped ships.

To the Princess Nausicaa, beautiful as a goddess, Pallas appeared in a dream the night that Ulysses lay sleeping on the isle, warning her that since her wedding day was near at hand, when all would need fresh garments, it was fitting that she should ask her father's permission to take the garments of the household to the river side to wash them.

Nausicaa's father willingly granted his permission, and ordered the strong car in which to carry away the soiled garments. A hamper of food and a skin of wine were added by her mother, as the princess climbed into the chariot and drove towards the river, followed by her maids.

When the garments had been washed in the lavers hollowed out by the river side, and the lunch had been eaten, the maids joined in a game of ball. Joyous they laughed and frolicked, like Dian's nymphs, until they roused the sleeper under the olive-trees on the hillside.

All save Nausicaa fled affrighted as he came forth to speak to them, covered with sea foam, his nakedness hidden only by a leafy branch woven round his waist; but she, strengthened by the goddess, heard his story, and provided him with clothing and materials for the bath. When he appeared, cleansed from the sea foam, and made more handsome by the art of Pallas, Nausicaa's pity was changed to admiration, and she wished that she might have a husband like him.

Food and wine were set before the hero, and while he refreshed himself the dried clothes were folded and placed in the cart. As the princess prepared to go she advised the stranger to follow the party until they reached a grove outside the city, and to remain there until she had time to reach her father's palace, lest some gossip should connect Nausicaa's name with that of a stranger. She told him how to find her father's palace, and instructed him to win the favor of her mother, that he might be received with honor and assisted on his homeward way.

Ulysses obeyed, and when he reached the city gates was met by Pallas, in the guise of a virgin with an urn. She answered his questions, directed him to the palace, and told him to throw himself first at the feet of Queen Arete, who was looked on by the people as if she were a goddess. Wrapped in a cloud by Pallas, the unseen Ulysses admired the spacious halls of Alcinoüs. Walls of brass supported blue steel cornices, golden doors guarded by gold and silver mastiffs opened into the vast hall, along which were ranged thrones covered with delicately woven mantles, for which the Phæacian women were famous.

Around the palace lay a spacious garden filled with pear, pomegranate, fig, and apple trees, that knew no change of season, but blossomed and bore fruit throughout the year. Perennially blooming plants scattered perfume through the garden kept fresh by water from two sparkling fountains.

As Ulysses knelt at the feet of Arete, the cloud enveloping him fell away, and all were astonished at the sight of the stranger imploring protection. Arete received Ulysses with favor, and Alcinoüs was so pleased with him that he offered him his daughter in marriage, if he was unmarried, a palace and riches if he would remain on the island, and a safe passage home if he desired to leave them. The king then invited the chiefs of the isle to a great banquet in honor of his guest. At this banquet Demodocus, the blind minstrel, sang so touchingly of the heroes of the Trojan war that Ulysses was moved to tears, a fact observed by the king alone. After the feast the guests displayed their strength in athletic games; and Ulysses, provoked by the taunts of the ill-bred Euryalus, cast a broader, heavier quoit than had yet been used far beyond the mark. The Phæacians were amazed, and the king confessed that his people were weak in athletic sports but excelled in the dance, — a statement to which Ulysses readily agreed when he saw the beautiful and graceful dance of the princes Laodamas and Halius to the music of Demodocus's silver harp.

When the games were over, all the chiefs presented Ulysses with garments and with talents of gold, for the reception of which Arete gave a beautiful chest. As he corded up the chest, and stepped forth to the banquet, refreshed from the bath, Nausicaa, standing beside a pillar, bade him farewell.

" Remember, in thy native land, O stranger, that thou owest thy life to me."

When they sat again in the banqueting hall, Ulysses besought Demodocus to sing again of the fall of Troy; but when the minstrel sang of the strategy of the wooden horse which wrought the downfall of Troy, the hero was again melted to tears, — and this time his host, unable to repress his curiosity, asked him to reveal his name and history.

" Thou hast spoken, O king, and I proceed to tell the story of my calamitous voyage from Troy; for I am Ulysses, widely known among men for my cunning devices. Our first stop was among the Ciconians, whose city we laid waste. Here, in spite of my warning, my men tarried to drink red wine until the Ciconians had had time to recruit their forces, and, attacking us, slew six men from each galley. When we who survived reached the land of the lotus-eaters, some of my men ate of the sweet plant, after which a man thinks never more of wife, or friends, or home; and it was with the utmost difficulty that we succeeded in dragging them to the ships.

" At the Cyclopean land I myself, with a few of my men, disembarked, and went up to seek the inhabitants and conciliate them with gifts of food and wine. The Cyclops were huge one-eyed giants who did not cultivate the land, had no government, and cared nought for the gods. The first cave to which we came was empty, and we went in to await the arrival of the owner, appeasing our appetites, meanwhile, with some of his cheeses. Presently he arrived, and after he had closed up the entrance of the cave with a huge stone, and had milked his goats, he questioned us as to who we were. Our story told, he seized two of my companions, dashed their heads against the rocks, and devoured them. The next morning, after devouring two others, he drove out his flocks, leaving us shut up in the huge cave. All that day I revolved plans for his destruction and our escape; and at last, drawing lots with my companions to determine who should assist me, I determined, with their aid, to bore out his great eye with a huge olive-wood stick that I found in the cave. We spent the day sharpening it and hardening it in the fire, and at night hid it under a heap of litter. Two more of my men made his evening meal, after which I plied him with the wine I had brought, until, softened by the liquor, he inquired my name, assuring me that as return for my gift, he would devour me last. My name, I told him, was Noman.

" As soon as he had fallen into a drunken slumber I put the stake to heat, and, strengthening the courage of my men, I drew it forth and plunged it into his eye. Steadily we spun it round until the monster, screaming with pain, drew it forth, crying to the other Cyclops to come to his aid. When they, from without, questioned who hurt him, he replied, ' Noman destroyeth me by guile.' ' If it is " Noman," ' said they, departing, ' it must be Jove. Then pray to Neptune.'

" During the night I tied together the rams, three and three with osier twigs, and instructed my comrades, as he drove them out, to cling under the middle one. I hid myself under the fleecy belly of a huge ram, the finest of the flock. He touched their backs as he drove them out, but he did not penetrate my cunning, and we all escaped. After we had driven the flock on board, however, and had pushed out our galley, I could not forbear a taunting shout, at which he hurled a huge fragment of rock after us, just missing our galley.

" With Æolus, King of the Winds, we remained a month, reciting the events connected with the fall of Troy. So pleased was the king with my story, that on our departure he presented me with a bag tied up with a silver cord, which contained the adverse winds. One day, as I slumbered, my unhappy sailors, suspecting some treasure concealed therein, opened it, and we were immediately blown back to Æolus's isle, from which he, enraged at our folly, indignantly drove us.

" At the land of the Læstrygonians all our galleys were lost and our men devoured by the cannibal inhabitants, with the exception of my own ship, which by good fortune I had moored without the harbor. Overcome with grief, we rowed wearily along until we arrived at the land of Circe. With caution born of experience, we drew lots to see who should venture into the unknown isle. The lot fell to Eurylochus, who, with twenty-two brave men, went forward to the fair palace of Circe, around which fawned tamed mountain lions and wolves. Within sat the bright-haired goddess, singing while she threw her shuttle through the beautiful web she was weaving.

"All the men entered the palace at her invitation but Eurylochus, who, suspecting some guile, remained without. He saw his comrades led within, seated upon thrones and banqueted; but no sooner was the feast over, than she touched them with her wand, and transformed them into swine that she drove scornfully to their cells.

"Eurylochus hastened back to our ships with the sorrowful tidings. As soon as grief had permitted him to tell the story, I flung my sword over my shoulders and hastened away to the palace. As I entered the valley, not far from the palace, I was met by a youth, none save the Argus-queller himself, who revealed to me Circe's guile, and presented me with a plant, the moly, which would enable me to withstand her charms.

"The goddess received me kindly, seated me upon a throne, and invited me to feast with her. After the feast she struck me with her wand, as she had done my comrades, ordering me to go to my sty; but when I remained unchanged, she perceived that her guest was Ulysses, whose coming had long been foretold to her.

"Softened by her entreaties, I sheathed my sword, after having made her promise to release my friends and do us no further harm. Then the others were called from the ships, and we banqueted together.

"Time passed so happily on Circe's isle that we lingered a whole year, until, roused by the words of my friends, I announced my intended departure, and was told by Circe that I must first go to the land of the dead to get instructions as to my future course from Tiresias. Provided with the proper sacrifices by Circe, we set sail for the land of the Cimmerians, on the confines of Oceanus. The sacrifices having been duly performed, the spirits appeared, — Elpenor, my yet unburied comrade, whose body lay on Circe's isle, my own dead mother, and the Theban seer, Tiresias, with his golden wand. 'Neptune is wroth with thee,' he said, 'but thou mayst yet return if thou and thy comrades leave undisturbed the cattle of the Sun. If thou do not, destruction awaits thee. If thou escape and return home it will be after long journeyings and much suffering, and there thou wilt slay the insolent suitor crew that destroy thy substance and wrong thy household.' After Tiresias had spoken I lingered to speak with other spirits, — my mother, Ajax, Antiope, Agamemnon, Achilles, Patroclus, and Antilochus. Having conversed with all these, we set sail for Circe's isle, and thence started again on our homeward voyage.

"Circe had instructed me to stop the ears of my men with wax as we approached the isle of the Sirens, and to have myself tied to the boat that I might not leap into the ocean to go to the beautiful maidens who sang so entrancingly. We therefore escaped without adding our bones to those on the isle of the Sirens, and came next to Scylla and Charybdis. Charybdis is a frightful whirlpool. The sailor who steers too far away in his anxiety to escape it, is seized by the six arms of the monster Scylla and lifted to her cavern to be devoured. We avoided Charybdis; but as we looked down into the abyss, pale with fear, six of my comrades were seized by Scylla and snatched up to her cave.

"As we neared the Island of the Sun I told my comrades again of the warning of Tiresias, and begged them to sail past without stopping. I was met, however, by the bitterest reproaches, and at last consented to a landing if they would bind themselves by a solemn oath not to touch the cattle of the Sun. They promised, but when adverse winds prolonged our stay and food became scarce, fools, madmen, they slew the herds, and in spite of the terrible omens, the meat lowing on the spits, the skins crawling, they feasted for six days. When, on the seventh, the tempest ceased and we sailed away, we went to our destruction. I alone was saved, cling-

ing to the floating timbers for nine long days, until on
the tenth I reached Calypso's isle, Ogygia, where, out of
love for me, the mighty goddess cherished me for seven
years."

The Phæacians were entranced by this recital, and in addition to their former gifts, heaped other treasures upon the
" master of stratagems" that he might return home a wealthy
man. The swift ship was filled with his treasures, and after
the proper sacrifices and long farewells, the chieftain embarked. It was morn when the ship arrived in Ithaca, and
Ulysses, worn out from his long labors, was still asleep.
Stopping at the little port of Phorcys, where the steep shores
stretch inward and a spreading olive-tree o'ershadows the
grotto of the nymphs, the sailors lifted out Ulysses, laid him
on the ground, and piling up his gifts under the olive-tree,
set sail for Phæacia.  But the angry Neptune smote the
ship as it neared the town and changed it to a rock, thus fulfilling an ancient prophecy that Neptune would some day
wreak his displeasure on the Phæacians for giving to every
man who came to them safe escort home.

When Ulysses awoke he did not recognize the harbor, and
thinking that he had been treated with deceit, he wept bitterly.  Thus Pallas, in the guise of a young shepherd, found
him, and showed him that it was indeed his own dear land.
She helped him to conceal his treasures in the grotto, and
told him that Telemachus was even now away on a voyage
of inquiry concerning him, and his wife was weeping over
his absence and the insolence of the suitors.  But he must
act with caution.  To give him an opportunity to lay his
plans for the destruction of these men without being recognized, she changed him to a beggar, wrinkled and old, and
clad in ragged, soiled garments.  Then directing him to the
home of his old herdsman, she hastened to warn Telemachus
to avoid the ship the suitors had stationed to destroy him on
his way home.

The old Eumæus was sitting in his lodge without whose
hedge lay the many sties of swine that were his care.  He
greeted the beggar kindly, and spread food before him,

lamenting all the while the absence of his noble master and the wickedness of the suitors. Ulysses told him that he was a wanderer who had heard of his master, and could speak surely of his return. Though Eumæus regarded this as an idle speech spoken to gain food and clothing, he continued in his kindness to his guest.

To this lodge came Telemachus after the landing of his ship, that he might first hear from Eumæus the news from the palace, — Telemachus, who had grown into sudden manliness from his experience among other men. He also was kind to the beggar, and heard his story. While he remained with the beggar, Eumæus having gone to acquaint Penelope of her son's return, Pallas appearing, touched the beggar with her golden wand, and Ulysses, with the presence of a god, stood before his awed and wondering son.

Long and passionate was their weeping as the father told the son of his sufferings, and the son told of the arrogance of the one hundred and fourteen suitors.

" There are we two with Pallas and her father Jove against them," replied his father. "Thinkest thou we need to fear with two such allies?"

On the day after Telemachus's return, Ulysses, accompanied by Eumæus, visited the palace. No one recognized him except his old dog, Argus, long neglected and devoured by vermin, who, at the sound of his master's voice, drew near, wagged his tail, and fell dead.

According to their carefully laid plans, Telemachus feigned not to know his father, but sent to the beggar some food. Ulysses asked the same of the suitors, but was repulsed with taunts and insults, Antinoüs, the most insolent, striking him with a footstool.

To Penelope, weaving in her chamber, was carried the story of the beggar at whom the abhorred Antinoüs had thrown a stool, and she sent for him to ask if he had tidings of Ulysses. He refused to go to her, however, until the suitors had withdrawn for the night ; and as he sat among the revellers, he caught the first glimpse of his wife, as she came down among her maids, to reproach her son for exposing himself to danger among the suitors, and for allowing the beggar to be injured.

When darkness fell and the hall was deserted, Telemachus, with the assistance of his father, removed all the weapons from the walls. After Telemachus had retired to his chamber, Penelope came down, and sitting upon her ivory throne conversed with the beggar, questioning him about his story until he was driven to invent tales that seemed like truth, and asking about her husband while the tears ran down her fair cheeks. By a great effort Ulysses kept his tears from falling as he beheld his wife weeping over him; he assured her that her husband would soon return, but he would accept no clothing as a reward for his tidings. The aged Eurycleia, who was called forth to wash his feet, came near betraying her master when she recognized a scar made by a wild boar's tusk, but he threatened her into silence. Soon after, Penelope and her maids withdrew, and left Ulysses to meditate vengeance through the night.

The next morning, when the suitors again sat in the banquet-hall, Penelope descended to them and declared that she had determined to give her hand to the one of the suitors who could draw the great bow of Ulysses and send the arrow through twelve rings set on stakes planted in the ground. Up to the polished treasure-chamber she went, and took down the great bow given to Ulysses by Iphitus. As she took it from its case her tears fell, but she dried them and carried it and the steel rings into the hall. Gladly Ulysses hailed this hour, for he knew the time had come when he should destroy the suitor band. That morn many omens had warned him, and he had revealed himself to his faithful men, Eumæus, and Philœtius the master-herdsman, that they might assist him. Telemachus, though astonished at his mother's decision, first took the bow; if he succeeded in bending it, his mother would not have to leave her home. He would have bent the bow at the fourth attempt had not his father's glance warned him to yield it to the suitors.

Although the bow was rubbed and softened with oil, all failed in their attempts to draw it; and when the beggar asked to be allowed to try, their wrath burst forth. What shame would be theirs if the beggar succeeded in doing that in which they had failed! But Telemachus, who asserted his rights more day by day, insisted that the beggar should try to bend the bow, if he so desired. Sending his mother and her maids to their bower, he watched his father as he easily bent the mighty bow, snapped the cord with a sound at which the suitors grew pale, and sent the arrow through the rings. Then casting aside his rags, the supposed beggar sprang upon the threshold, and knowing that by his orders, Eumæus, Philœtius, and Eurycleia had secured the portals so that escape was impossible, he sent his next shaft through the throat of Antinoüs. "Dogs! ye thought I never would return! Ye dreaded not the gods while ye devoured my substance and pursued my wife! Now vengeance is mine! Destruction awaits you all!"

Too late Eurymachus sprang up and besought the monarch to grant them their lives if they made good their waste and returned to their homes. Ulysses had brooded too long over his injuries; his wife and son had suffered too many years from their persecutions for him to think of mercy. Eurymachus fell by the next brass-tipped shaft, and for every arrow in the quiver a suitor lay dead until the quiver was empty. Then Telemachus, Philœtius, and Eumæus, provided with weapons and armor, stood forth with Ulysses, and withstood the suitors until all were slain, save Medon the herald and Phemius the minstrel, for both of whom Telemachus pleaded, since they had been coerced by the others. Giving the destruction of the false serving-maids to his three assistants, Ulysses ordered the hall to be cleansed, and after greeting his faithful servants and weeping with them, sent Eurycleia up to the bower to tell Penelope that her master had at last arrived.

Penelope was too fearful of deceit to believe instantly that the beggar sitting beside the lofty column was her husband, though as she looked at him wonderingly, she sometimes fancied that she saw Ulysses, and again could not believe that it was he. So long was she silent that Telemachus reproached her for her hardness of heart; but Ulysses, better guessing the difficulty, ordered that all should take the bath and array themselves in fresh garments while the harper played gay melodies, that those passing should not guess the slaughter that had occurred, but should fancy that a wedding was being celebrated. When Ulysses again appeared, refreshed and handsomely attired, Penelope, still uncertain, determined to test his knowledge of her chamber. "Bear out the bed made by his own hands," she commanded Eurycleia, "that he may rest for the night."

"Who has dared move my bed?" cried Ulysses; "the couch framed upon the stump of an olive-tree, round which I built a stone chamber! I myself cunningly fitted it together, and adorned it with gold, silver, and ivory."

Then Penelope, who knew that no one save herself, Ulysses, and one handmaiden had ever seen the interior of that chamber, fell on his neck and welcomed the wanderer home. "Pray, be not angry with me, my husband. Many times my heart has trembled lest some fraud be practised on me, and I should receive a stranger to my heart."

Welcome as land to the shipwrecked mariner was Ulysses to Penelope. Both wept as he held her in his arms, and the rosy-fingered morn would have found them thus, weeping, with her fair, white arms encircling his neck, had not Pallas prolonged the night that he might relate to her the story of his wanderings. Then, happy in their reunion, the years of sorrow all forgotten, sleep overcame them. At dawn, bidding a brief farewell to his wife, Ulysses went forth to visit his father, and settle as best he might the strife which he knew would result from the slaughter of the suitors.

After Ulysses' mother had died of grief at the prolonged absence of her son, Laertes passed his days wretchedly in a little habitation remote from the palace. There Ulysses found him and made himself known; and there he, Laertes, Telemachus, the aged Dolius, and his six sons faced the people who had been roused to battle by the speech of Eupeithes, whose son Antinoüs had been the first of the suitors to fall by the hand of Ulysses. Not heeding the warning of the herald Medon that the suitors had been slain justly, they attacked Ulysses and his handful of followers.

Eupeithes fell first by the spear of Laertes, and a great slaughter would have ensued, had not the combatants been silenced by the voice of Pallas, who commanded all strife to cease. Frightened by this divine command, the enemy fled; and Pallas, descending in the form of Mentor, plighted a covenant between them that Ulysses might live peacefully among them the remainder of his life.

# SELECTIONS FROM THE ODYSSEY.

## The Palace of Alcinoüs.

Ulysses, having been directed by Nausicaa, reached the gate of the city, and was there met by Pallas in the guise of a maiden with an urn, who instructed him how to approach the king and queen. He passed through the town, wrapped in a cloud by Pallas, and paused on the threshold of Alcinoüs's palace.

> For on every side beneath
> The lofty roof of that magnanimous king
> A glory shone as of the sun or moon.
> There from the threshold, on each side, were walls
> Of brass that led towards the inner rooms,
> With blue steel cornices. The doors within
> The massive building were of gold, and posts
> Of silver on the brazen threshold stood,
> And silver was the lintel, and above
> Its architrave was gold; and on each side
> Stood gold and silver mastiffs, the rare work
> Of Vulcan's practised skill, placed there to guard
> The house of great Alcinoüs, and endowed
> With deathless life, that knows no touch of age.
> Along the walls within, on either side,
> And from the threshold to the inner rooms,
> Were firmly planted thrones on which were laid
> Delicate mantles, woven by the hands
> Of women. The Phæacian princes here
> Were seated; here they ate and drank, and held
> Perpetual banquet. Slender forms of boys
> In gold upon the shapely altars stood,
> With blazing torches in their hands to light

At eve the palace guests ; while fifty maids
Waited within the halls, where some in querns
Ground small the yellow grain ; some wove the web
Or twirled the spindle, sitting, with a quick
Light motion, like the aspen's glancing leaves.
The well-wrought tissues glistened as with oil.
As far as the Phæacian race excel
In guiding their swift galleys o'er the deep,
So far the women in their woven work
Surpass all others. Pallas gives them skill
In handiwork and beautiful design.
Without the palace-court and near the gate,
A spacious garden of four acres lay.
A hedge enclosed it round, and lofty trees
Flourished in generous growth within, — the pear
And the pomegranate, and the apple-tree
With its fair fruitage, and the luscious fig
And olive always green. The fruit they bear
Falls not, nor ever fails in winter time
Nor summer, but is yielded all the year.
The ever-blowing west-wind causes some
To swell and some to ripen ; pear succeeds
To pear ; to apple, apple, grape to grape,
Fig ripens after fig. A fruitful field
Of vines was planted near ; in part it lay
Open and basking in the sun, which dried
The soil, and here men gathered in the grapes,
And there they trod the wine-press. Farther on
Were grapes unripened yet, which just had cast
The flower, and others still which just began
To redden. At the garden's furthest bound
Were beds of many plants that all the year
Bore flowers. There gushed two fountains : one of them
Ran wandering through the field ; the other flowed
Beneath the threshold to the palace-court,
And all the people filled their vessels there.
Such were the blessings which the gracious gods
Bestowed on King Alcinoüs and his house.

*Bryant's Translation, Book VII.*

## THE BENDING OF THE BOW.

PENELOPE, weary of the importunities of the suitors, determined to end the contest by giving them the bow of Ulysses
and allowing the one who could successfully send the arrow
through the steel rings to become her husband. Having an-

nounced her intention, she ascended the stairs to the treasure
chamber, where the bow was kept.

> Now when the glorious lady reached the room,
> And stood upon the threshold, wrought of oak
> And polished by the workman's cunning hand,
> Who stretched the line upon it, and set up
> Its posts, and hung its shining doors, she loosed
> With a quick touch the thong that held the ring,
> Put in the key, and with a careful aim
> Struck back the sounding bolts. As when a bull
> Roars in the field, such sound the beautiful doors,
> Struck with the key, gave forth, and instantly
> They opened to her. Up the lofty floor
> She stepped, where stood the coffer that contained
> The perfumed garments. Reaching forth her hand,
> The queen took down the bow, that hung within
> Its shining case, and sat her down, and laid
> The case upon her knees, and, drawing forth
> The monarch's bow, she wept aloud. As soon
> As that new gush of tears had ceased to fall,
> Back to the hall she went, and that proud throng
> Of suitors, bearing in her hand the bow
> Unstrung, and quiver, where the arrows lay
> Many and deadly. Her attendant maids
> Brought also down a coffer, where were laid
> Much brass and steel, provided by the king
> For games like these. The glorious lady then,
> In presence of the suitors, stood beside
> The columns that upheld the stately roof.
> She held a lustrous veil before her cheeks,
> And while on either side of her a maid
> Stood modestly, bespake the suitors thus : —
> "Hear, noble suitors ! ye who throng these halls,
> And eat and drink from day to day, while long
> My husband has been gone ; your sole excuse
> For all this lawlessness the claim ye make
> That I become a bride. Come then, for now
> A contest is proposed. I bring to you
> The mighty bow that great Ulysses bore.
> Whoe'er among you he may be whose hand
> Shall bend this bow, and send through these twelve rings
> An arrow, him I follow hence, and leave
> This beautiful abode of my young years,
> With all its plenty, — though its memory,
> I think, will haunt me even in my dreams."
> She spake, and bade the master of the swine,
> The good Eumæus, place the bow and rings
> Of hoary steel before the suitor train.
> In tears he bore the bow and laid it down.

The herdsman also wept to see again
His master's bow.

.    .    .    .    .    .    .    .

   He (Telemachus) spake and, rising, from his shoulders
     took
The purple cloak, and laid the trenchant sword
Aside; and first he placed the rings of steel
In order, opening for them in the ground
A long trench by a line, and stamping close
The earth around them.   All admired the skill
With which he ranged them, never having seen
The game before.   And then he took his place
Upon the threshold, and essayed the bow;
And thrice he made the attempt, and thrice gave o'er,
Yet hoping still to draw the cord, and send
An arrow through the rings.   He would have drawn
The bow at the fourth trial, but a nod
Given by his father caused him to forbear,
Though eager for the attempt.

.    .    .    .    .    .    .    .

      . . . And then Eupeithes' son,
Antinoüs, to the crowd of suitors said : —
   " Rise one by one, my friends, from right to left.
Begin where he begins who pours the wine."
So spake Antinoüs, and the rest approved.
Then rose Leiodes, son of Œnops, first.
He was their seer, and always had his seat
Beside the ample bowl.   From deeds of wrong
He shrank with hatred, and was sore incensed
Against the suitors all.   He took the bow
And shaft, and, going to the threshold, stood
And tried the bow, yet bent it not; it galled
His hands, for they were soft, and all unused
To such a task.
        . . . The swineherd went
Forward along the hall, and, drawing near
The wise Ulysses, gave into his hands
The bow.

.    .    .    .    .    .    .

      . . . but when the wary chief
Had poised and shrewdly scanned the mighty bow,
Then, as a singer, skilled to play the harp,
Stretches with ease on its new fastenings
A string, the twisted entrails of a sheep,
Made fast at either end, so easily
Ulysses bent that mighty bow.   He took
And drew the cord with his right hand; it twanged
With a clear sound as when a swallow screams.

The suitors were dismayed, and all grew pale.
Jove in loud thunder gave a sign from heaven.
The much-enduring chief, Ulysses, heard
With joy the friendly omen, which the son
Of crafty Saturn sent him.   He took up
A winged arrow, that before him lay
Upon a table drawn; the others still
Were in the quiver's womb; the Greeks were yet
To feel them.   This he set with care against
The middle of the bow, and toward him drew
The cord and arrow-notch, just where he sat,
And aiming opposite, let fly the shaft.
He missed no ring of all; from first to last
The brass-tipped arrow threaded every one.
Then to Telemachus Ulysses said : —

   " Telemachus, the stranger sitting here
Hath not disgraced thee.   I have neither missed
The rings, nor found it hard to bend the bow ;
Nor has my manly strength decayed, as these
Who seek to bring me to contempt pretend ;
And now the hour is come when we prepare
A supper for the Achaians, while the day
Yet lasts, and after supper the delights
Of song and harp, which nobly grace a feast."

   He spake, and nodded to Telemachus,
His well-beloved son, who girded on
His trenchant sword, and took in hand his spear,
And, armed with glittering brass for battle, came
And took his station by his father's seat.


   Then did Ulysses cast his rags aside,
And, leaping to the threshold, took his stand
On its broad space, with bow and quiver filled
With arrows.   At his feet the hero poured
The winged shafts, and to the suitors called : —

   " That difficult strife is ended.   Now I take
Another mark, which no man yet has hit.
Now I shall see if I attain my aim,
And, by the aid of Phœbus, win renown."

   He spake ; and, turning, at Antinoüs aimed
The bitter shaft, — Antinoüs, who just then
Had grasped a beautiful two-eared cup of gold,
About to drink the wine.   He little thought
Of wounds and death ; for who, when banqueting
Among his fellows, could suspect that one
Alone against so many men would dare,
However bold, to plan his death, and bring
On him the doom of fate?   Ulysses struck
The suitor with the arrow at the throat.
The point came through the tender neck behind,

Sideways he sank to earth; his hand let fall
The cup; the dark blood in a thick warm stream
Gushed from the nostrils of the smitten man.
He spurned the table with his feet, and spilled
The viands; bread and roasted meats were flung
To lie polluted on the floor. Then rose
The suitors in a tumult, when they saw
The fallen man; from all their seats they rose
Throughout the hall, and to the massive walls
Looked eagerly; there hung no buckler there,
No sturdy lance for them to wield. They called
Then to Ulysses with indignant words : —

"Stranger! in evil hour hast thou presumed
To aim at men; and thou shalt henceforth bear
Part in no other contest. Even now
Is thy destruction close to thee. Thy hand
Hath slain the noblest youth in Ithaca.
The vultures shall devour thy flesh for this."

So each one said; they deemed he had not slain
The suitor wittingly; nor did they see,
Blind that they were, the doom which in that hour
Was closing round them all. Then with a frown
The wise Ulysses looked on them, and said : —

"Dogs! ye had thought I never would come back
From Ilium's coast, and therefore ye devoured
My substance here, and offered violence
To my maid-servants, and pursued my wife
As lovers, while I lived. Ye dreaded not
The gods who dwell in the great heaven, nor feared
Vengeance hereafter from the hands of men;
And now destruction overhangs you all."

He spake, and all were pale with fear, and each
Looked round for some escape from death.

*Bryant's Translation, Books XXI., XXII.*

# THE KALEVALA.

"Songs preserved from distant ages."

THE national epic of Finland, the Kalevala, or Place of Heroes, stands midway between the purely epical structure, as exemplified in Homer, and the epic songs of certain nations.

It is a purely pagan epic, and from its complete silence as to Finland's neighbors, the Russians, Germans, and Swedes, it is supposed to date back at least three thousand years.

The first attempt to collect Finnish folk-song was made in the seventeenth century by Palmsköld and Peter Bäng. In 1733, Maxenius published a volume on Finnish national poetry, and in 1745 Juslenius began a collection of national poems. Although scholars saw that these collected poems were evidently fragments of a Finnish epic, it remained for two physicians, Zacharias Topelius and Elias Lönnrot, to collect the entire poem. Topelius, though confined to his bed by illness for eleven years, took down the songs from travelling merchants brought to his bedside. His collections were published in 1822 and 1831. Lönnrot travelled over Finland, collecting the songs, which he published, arranged in epical form, in 1835. A revised edition was published in 1849.

The Kalevala consists of fifty parts, or runes, containing twenty-two thousand seven hundred and ninety-three lines. Its historical foundation is the contests between the Finns and the Lapps.

Its metre is the "eight syllabled trochaic with the part-line echo," alliteration also being used, a metre familiar to us through Longfellow's "Hiawatha."

The labors of a Wolf are not necessary to show that the Kalevala is composed of various runes or lays, arranged by a compiler. Topelius and Lönnrot were conscientious collectors and compilers, but they were no Homers, who could fuse these disconnected runes into one great poem. The Kalevala recites many events in the lives of different heroes who are not types of men, like Rama, or Achilles, or Ulysses, but the rude gods of an almost savage people, or rather, men in the process of apotheosis, all alike, save in the varying degrees of magic power possessed by each.

The Finnish lays are interesting to us because they are the popular songs of a people handed down with few changes from one generation to another; because they would have formed the material for a national epic if a great poet had arisen; because of their pictures of ancient customs, and particularly the description of the condition of women, and because of their frequently beautiful descriptions of nature. But because they are simply runes "loosely stitched together" we can regard them only with interest and curiosity, not with admiration.

BIBLIOGRAPHY AND CRITICISM, THE KALEVALA. Andrew Lang's Homer and the Epic, pp. 412–419; Andrew Lang's Kalevala, or the Finnish National Epic (in his Custom and Myth), 1885, pp. 156–179; C. J. Billson's Folk-songs, comprised in the Finnish Kalevala, Folk-Lore, 1895, vi. pp. 317–352; F. C. Cook's Kalevala, Contemporary, 1885, xlvii., pp. 683–702; Preface of J. M. Crawford's Translation of the Kalevala, 1891.

STANDARD ENGLISH TRANSLATIONS, THE KALEVALA. The Kalevala, Tr. by J. M. Crawford, 2 vols., 1891; The Kalevala, Tr. by W. F. Kirby, through the German translation of Schiefner; Selections from the Kalevala, Tr. from a German version by J. A. Porter, with an introduction and analysis of the Poem, 1868.

## THE STORY OF THE KALEVALA.

WAINAMOINEN was born upon the ocean after his mother, Ilmatar, daughter of the illimitable Ether, had floated upon its surface for more than seven hundred years. During this time Ilmatar had created the islands, the rocks, and the continents. After eight years of swimming through the ocean, studying his surroundings, Wainamoinen left the waters and swam to a barren promontory, where he could rest himself on dry land and study the sun, the moon, and the starry skies. At last he called to him Pellerwoinen, that the slender youth might scatter seeds broadcast upon the island, sowing in their proper places the birch, the alder, the linden, the willow, the mountain ash, and the juniper. It was not long until the eyes of the sower were gladdened by the sight of trees rising above the hitherto barren soil.

But as Wainamoinen cast his eyes over the place he perceived that the oak, the tree of heaven, was wanting. The acorn planted in the sterile soil developed not until Tursas, the giant, arose from the ocean, burned some meadow grasses, and raking together the ashes, planted therein the acorn, from which soon sprang up a mighty oak-tree whose branches hid the sun rays and the starlight.

The oak-tree must be felled if the land was to prosper, but who could fell it? "Help me, Kapé, daughter of the Ether, help me, my ancient mother, to uproot this terrible tree that shuts out the sunshine," cried Wainamoinen.

Straightway arose from the ocean a little being clad in copper, — cap, boots, gloves, and belt. He was no longer than a man's forefinger, and the blade of the hatchet at his belt was but a finger's breadth. "Art thou divine, or human?" queried Wainamoinen. "Tell me who thou art. Thou surely hast the bearing of a hero, though so small. But thou must be of the race of the pygmies, and therefore useless."

"I came here to fell the oak," replied the pygmy. "I am a god and a hero from the tribes that rule the ocean."

"Never canst thou lop the branches of this mighty tree," replied Wainamoinen.

As he spoke, the pygmy became a giant; with one step he left the ocean, and stood piercing the clouds with his head. He whetted his hatchet on the great rocks, and with three steps reached the tree; with four blows felled it. The trunk fell eastward, its tops westward, the leaves to the south, the hundred branches to the north. Full of magic power were the parts of this tree, and happy was he who possessed himself of some part of it.

Then vegetation flourished, the birds sang happily in the trees, and all was well except that barley was wanting. On the ocean strand Wainamoinen discovered the barley seed; and, advised by the birds how to plant it, was soon gratified by the sight of the growing barley. His next act was to clear the forest; but he left the slender birch for the birds to nest in, thus winning the gratitude of the silver-voiced singers.

In the land of Kalevala, Wainamoinen passed many happy years, and the fame of his wonderful songs of wit and wisdom spread even to the land of the Lapps, in the dismal north, where lived Youkahainen, a young minstrel. Against the advice of his parents, the youth, filled with jealousy, visited Kalevala, to hold a singing contest with Wainamoinen.

He proudly displayed his wisdom to the old minstrel, who laughed at it as "women's tales and children's wisdom," and when Youkahainen declared in song that he was present at the creation, Wainamoinen called him the prince of liars, and himself began to sing. As he sang, the copper-bearing mountains, the massive rocks and ledges, trembled, the hills re-echoed, and the very ocean heaved with rapture. The boaster stood speechless, seeing his sledge transformed into reed grass and willows, his beautiful steed changed to a statue, his dog to a block of stone, and he himself fast sinking in a quicksand. Then comprehending his folly, he begged his tormentor to free him. Each precious gift he offered for a ransom was refused, until he named his beautiful sister Aino. Wainamoinen, happy in the promise of Aino for a wife, freed the luckless youth from his enchantment, and sent him home.

Aino's mother was rejoiced to hear that her daughter had been promised to the renowned Wainamoinen; but when the beautiful girl learned that she was tied by her brother's folly to an old man, she wandered weeping through the fields. In vain her mother and father sought to console her; she wept for her vanished childhood, for all her happiness and hope and pleasure forever gone. To console her daughter, the mother told her of a store of beautiful ornaments that she herself had worn in girlhood; they had been given her by the daughters of the Moon and Sun, — gold, ribbons, and jewels. Beautifully arrayed in these long-concealed ornaments, Aino wandered through the fields for many days, bewailing her sad fate. On the fourth day, she laid her garments on the sea shore, and swam out to the standing rock, a little distance from the shore. No sooner had she clambered on the rainbow-colored rock than it turned and fell to the bottom of the sea, carrying with it the weeping maiden, chanting a farewell to her family. The fleet and haughty hare bore the news of her death to the household, where her unfortunate mother sat weeping, urging other mothers never to force their daughters to wed against their choice. The tears that rolled down her cheeks formed three streamlets, that, growing larger, became torrents with foaming cataracts. From the cataracts towered three pillared rocks upon which rose three hillocks, and upon each hillock sprang a birch-tree. On the summit of each tree sat a golden bird singing; and the first sang, for three moons, his song of "Love! O Love!" the second called for six moons, "Suitor! Suitor!" but the third bird sang forever his sad song of "Consolation! Consolation!"

Wainamoinen was deeply grieved when he heard of the fate of the lovely Aino, and he at once went to angle in the deep where dwelt the mermaids, the daughters of Wellamo.

After he had fished many days in vain, he caught a wondrous salmon, larger and more beautiful than he had ever before caught. But as he took out his silver knife to cut it, the fish sprang from his hand into the deep, telling him that it was Aino who had thus come to him, and whom he had now lost forever by his stupidity. Then indeed the song of the golden bird seemed sad to Wainamoinen, and he was disconsolate until his mother spoke to him from her grave: "My son, go north and seek thy wife. Take not a silly Lapp, but choose one of the daughters of Suomi."

Quickly Wainamoinen prepared for his journey, and mounted his magic steed, that galloped over the plains of Kalevala and crossed the waste of blue sea-water as though it were land.

But the envious Youkahainen was informed of the journey, and had prepared a cruel cross-bow and three poisoned arrows. In spite of the protests of his mother, he waited for the hero and shot at him three times. The third arrow struck Wainamoinen's horse, which sank to the bottom of the ocean, leaving the hapless rider struggling in the water. "Seven summers must he tread the waves," chuckled Youkahainen; "eight years ride the billows."

For six days Wainamoinen floated on the waters; then he was rescued by a huge eagle that carried him on its back to Pohyola, the dismal Sariola, and left him on a barren promontory, where he bemoaned his unhappy fate. Here he was found by Louhi, the toothless dame of Pohyola, who took him home and fed him. Then she promised to provide him with a sledge that he might journey safely home if he would forge for her the Sampo, a magical jewel that gave success to its possessor. If he could make her this, she would also give him her daughter in marriage. "I cannot forge the Sampo, but if thou wilt help me to my distant country I will send thee my brother Ilmarinen, the blacksmith, who can forge for thee the magic Sampo, and win thy beautiful daughter."

Louhi provided a sledge and horse, and as Wainamoinen seated himself she warned him, as he journeyed, not to look upward before nightfall, or some great misfortune would befall him.

The maiden of the Rainbow, beautiful daughter of Pohyola, was sitting on the rainbow weaving, and Wainamoinen, hearing the whizzing of the loom, forgot the warning, and, looking up, was filled with love for the maiden.

" Come to me," he cried.

"The birds have told me," she replied, " that a maiden's life, as compared to a married woman's, is as summer to coldest winter. Wives are as dogs enchained in kennels."

When Wainamoinen further besought her, she told him that she would consider him a hero when he had split a golden hair with edgeless knives and snared a bird's egg with an invisible snare. When he had done these things without difficulty, she demanded that he should peel the sandstone, and cut her a whipstick from the ice without making a splinter. This done, she commanded that he should build her a boat from the fragments of her distaff, and set it floating without the use of his knee, arm, hand, or foot to propel it.

While Wainamoinen was engaged in this task Hisi, the god of evil, caused him to cut his knee with the axe. None of his charms availed to stanch the blood, so he dragged himself to his sledge and sought the nearest village. In the third cottage he found a graybeard, who caused two maids to dip up some of the flowing blood, and then commanded Wainamoinen to sing the origin of iron. The daughters of Ukko the Creator had sprinkled the mountains with black, white, and red milk, — from this was formed iron. Fire caught the iron and carried it to its furnace, and later Ilmarinen worked the unwilling metal into various articles. As he sought something to harden it, Hisi's bird, the hornet, dropped poison into the water ; and the iron dipped into it, formed the hard steel, which, angry because it could not be broken, cut its brother, and vowed that it would ever cause man's blood to flow in torrents.

The old man then addressed the crimson stream flowing from the wound, and prayed to mighty Ukko to stop it.

When it ceased to flow at his prayer, he sent forth his son to gather various charmed plants, steep them, and make a magic balsam. After many attempts the son was successful ; and the balsam, applied to Wainamoinen's wound, healed it immediately.

Wainamoinen returned home and sought Ilmarinen, who refused to go north to forge the Sampo. Inducing his brother to climb a lofty fir-tree to bring down the Moon and the Bear he had conjured there, the wizard caused a great storm-wind to arise and blow Ilmarinen to the woodlands of Pohyola.

There the blacksmith at once set up a forge, and after four days' work saw the Sampo rising from the furnace, its many colored lid rocking and grinding, every day, many measures of meal.

Joyfully Louhi received the magic Sampo and locked it in a secret chamber under the copper-bearing mountains. But when Ilmarinen asked for the hand of the Rainbow Maid, he was refused. "Never shall I, in my lifetime, say farewell to maiden freedom." So the blacksmith was compelled to return alone to Wainola.

While Ilmarinen was forging the Sampo and Wainamoinen was building the magic boat, Lemminkainen, or Ahti, the reckless wizard, king of the islands, was longing for a bride from Ehstland. In spite of his mother's entreaties, Lemminkainen went to Ehstland, and when he found it was impossible to gain the favor of Kylliki, the Sahri maid of beauty, he carried her off by force in his sledge. She became reconciled to him when he promised that he would never go to battle, and she in turn vowed that she would not visit the village dances. They lived happily together until Lemminkainen tarried late at the fishing one evening, and Kylliki went to the village dance. When Lemminkainen returned, his sister told him of Kylliki's broken vow ; and in spite of the prayers of his mother and wife, the hero declared that he would break his promise and go to war. To the North-land he would go, and win another wife. "When my brush bleeds, then you may know that misfortune has overtaken me," he said angrily, flinging his hairbrush at the wall.

Through many dangers he passed unscathed by the aid of his magic, until he stood in the halls of Louhi and asked for her daughter, the Rainbow Maiden.

"First bring me the wild moose from the Hisi-fields and forests," said Louhi.

From Kauppi, able smith, Lemminkainen procured the wondrous snow-shoes; but Hisi, who heard the boasts of the hero, fashioned a wild moose that ran so rapidly that Lemminkainen could not overtake it, but broke his snow-shoes in the race. He besought Ukko and the mistress of the forest and her king, and at last, with their aid, the moose was captured and led home to Louhi.

"Now bridle the flaming horse of Hisi," said she.

The mighty stallion stood on the Hisi mountain, breathing fire and smoke. When the hero saw him he prayed to Ukko, "Let the hail and icy rain fall upon him." His prayer was granted; and, going forward, Lemminkainen prayed the steed to put its head into the golden head-stall, promising to treat it with all gentleness. Then he led it to the courts of Sariola.

"Now kill for me the swan that swims in Tuoni, the black death-river. One shot only canst thou have. If thou succeed, then mayst thou claim thy bride."

When Lemminkainen entered Pohyola he had slain all his opponents but one blind shepherd, whom he spared because he despised his helplessness. This object of his scorn was waiting for him, and when Lemminkainen approached the river he fell by a shot from the enemy, regretting, as he died, that he had not asked his mother's advice before attempting to reach Tuoni.

Nasshut, the shepherd, threw the hero's body into the river, where it was seized and cut in pieces by the son of Tuoni.

At home the mother and wife awaited anxiously tidings of their hero. When they saw blood trickling from the brush, the mother could wait no longer, but at once set out for the dreary Northland. After repeated threats, she wrested from Louhi the fact that her son had gone to Tuoni; from the Sun she learned his fate.

Quickly seeking Ilmarinen, the mother bade him forge for her a mighty rake. With this she raked the deep death-river, collected the pieces of the hero, bound them together with the aid of the goddess Suonetar, and making a balsam, the materials for which were brought her by the bee, she healed her hero son, comforted him, and led him back to Kalevala.

In the mean time, Wainamoinen, who was building his boat for the Rainbow Maid, found that he had forgotten three magic words with which to fasten in the ledges and complete the boat's forecastle.

After examining in vain the mouths of the wild animals, he sought the dead hero Wipunen, forced open his jaws, and accidentally fell into his mouth. Wipunen quickly swallowed him; but Wainamoinen, setting up a forge in his body, caused him such discomfort that the giant was glad to give his information, and get rid of his unwelcome visitor. Having thus learned the secrets of the ages, and among them the three magic words, Wainamoinen hastened home and finished his boat.

The boat builded, he at once set out for the Northland to woo the Rainbow Maid. The boat was bedecked with silver and gold, and the linen sails were blue, white, and scarlet. The sails were merely for ornament, however, for the boat moved over the ocean without the aid of oars or sails. Wainamoinen's departure from Kalevala was observed by Anniki, the sister of Ilmarinen, who at once told her brother. With her assistance, Ilmarinen cleansed the black from his ruddy countenance, and jumping into his sledge, was soon on the way to Sariola. The approach of the heroes was perceived by Louhi. " Daughter," said she, " the old man brings thee a boat full of treasures; take him. Do not wed the empty-handed youth."

"Thy advice is good, but I will not take it. The young man shall be my husband."

When Wainamoinen was refused in spite of his gifts, Louhi addressed herself to Ilmarinen, and set him, in turn, three tasks : to plough the serpent field of Hisi, to muzzle Tuoni's bear, and to catch the pike of Mana, in the river of Tuoni.

With the help of his sweetheart, Ilmarinen accomplished these tasks, and the wedding day was set. Old Wainamoinen, heavy hearted, journeyed homeward, and sent the edict to his people that in the future old men should not go wooing, or strive with younger men.

Great preparations were made for the wedding feast; the mighty ox of Karjala was slain, and for the first time, beer was brewed in Pohyola. Invitations were sent to all the people of Pohyola and the tribes of Kalevala, to all save Lemminkainen.

When Ilmarinen returned for his bride, he was received with honor, and the wedding feast was merry. But when the time came to take the bride away, the Rainbow Maid was unwilling, she who before had been so ready to go with him. Many times had she been told of the miseries of the wife: her husband's slave, her whole life one of service, one long endeavor to please her husband's mother and father. After her lament, Osmatar, the Bride-adviser, instructed her how to please her husband's family, and admonished Ilmarinen to guard well his Bride of Beauty. Then the two set forth together, the Rainbow Maid shedding many tears at parting with her loved ones.

The bride and groom were received with joy by Ilmarinen's family, and old Wainamoinen himself sang at the wedding feast.

But Lemminkainen was angry because he had received no invitation to the wedding, and in spite of his mother's advice, set out to make war against the Lapps. He successfully overcame all the terrors that beset him, and reached Sariola, but was so coldly received there that, enraged at such treatment, he slew his host, the landlord of Pohyola, and fled homeward to escape the hosts whom Louhi called to defend her.

His mother sent him to the isle of refuge to escape the northern hosts. In the centre of the tenth ocean it rose, the refuge of his father; there he must abide three years, and must take a vow not to fight again for sixty summers.

The three years passed speedily on the happy isle, where

dwelt many maidens who admired the reckless hero, and he
departed just in time to escape the swords of the jealous
heroes of the isle. His ancient home was in ashes when he
returned, his mother missing; but while he mourned for
her, he chanced upon her, hiding from the Lapps in the
forest. Again he determined to seek out his enemies and
be revenged on them. Taking with him his friend Tiera he
sought the north, but was met by the Frost-Fiend and compelled to return.

To the house of Ilmarinen the blacksmith, was sold by
Untamoinen a slave, Kullervo. He was a giant who had
done naught but evil, until in despair his master sold him
to the blacksmith. Kullervo, or Kullerwoinen, was made a
shepherd and sent forth with the flocks. But rage at the
blacksmith's wife, who baked a stone in his bread on which
he broke the magic knife of his people, caused him to transform the flocks into wolves, who tore the Rainbow Wife to
pieces when she went to milk them.

Then Kullerwoinen fled from the blacksmith, and set out
to find his tribe-people, but on the way unknowingly corrupted his sister, and in despair at his evil deeds, destroyed
himself.

Ilmarinen was full of grief at the loss of his wife. Unhappy and restless, he forged for himself a bride of gold; but
the image failed to satisfy him, and Wainamoinen, reproving
him, forbade his people in the future to worship any graven
image. Then the blacksmith again sought the north to win
the sister of his former bride, but was met with bitter reproaches for the sorrow he had brought upon the family.
Nevertheless, he seized the maiden to carry her away, but she
was so angry and so unhappy that he changed her to a sea-
gull and came home wifeless and sad.

Wainamoinen and Ilmarinen soon conceived the idea of
going to the Northland to win back the Sampo. On the
way they allied to themselves the wizard Lemminkainen.
As they approached the whirlpool near Pohyola, their vessel
stuck on the shoulders of a great pike. When neither Lemminkainen nor Ilmarinen could slay it, Wainamoinen impaled

it on his fire-sword, and the three banqueted on the great fish. From its bones, Wainamoinen framed the first harp. No one could win music from it but its creator ; but when he touched its strings and sang, the very trees danced about him, wild animals lay in peace at his feet, and the hearts of men were ravished. As his listeners wept at the strains, Wainamoinen's tears rolled down into the ocean. Thence the duck brought them, changed to pearls, receiving for a reward its beautiful coat. Such was the origin of sea-pearls.

When Wainamoinen had put the inhabitants of Pohyola to sleep with his magic music, the heroes found the Sampo with little difficulty, and bore it away from the copper mountain. But as they hastened home, the discordant voice of Lemminkainen, who sang for joy of their capture, caused the crane to screech, and the bird's cry roused the people of Pohyola. Louhi speedily discovered her loss, and started in pursuit of the heroes. In various ways she attacked them, — with war ships that were stopped by a reef conjured up by Wainamoinen, by a terrible storm, and by a giant eagle that perched on their boat. In their struggle with her the Sampo was broken and its fragments scattered on the ocean. Louhi left them, uttering dire threats ; and Wainamoinen, gathering up what fragments of the Sampo he could find, buried them where they would bring prosperity to his people.

Now Wainamoinen longed to sing to his harp to rejoice the hearts of his people, but the magic instrument had been lost in the storm conjured by Louhi. After raking the sea for it in vain, he constructed a new harp from the birch-tree, and delighted the people with his songs.

In revenge for the theft of the Sampo, Louhi sent nine diseases upon Wainamoinen's people, — colic, pleurisy, fever, ulcer, plague, consumption, gout, sterility, and cancer, the offspring of the fell Lowyatar ; but by the use of vapor baths and balsams Wainamoinen healed his people. Then Louhi sent Otso the Bear, the honey-eater, but he was slain by the hero, who made a banquet of his flesh for the people. Enraged at her failures, she stole the sun, moon, and fire, and left Kalevala in darkness. Ukko, taking pity on his people, struck lightning from his fire-sword and gave the fire-child to a virgin to be cared for. In an unguarded moment it sprang earthward, fell into the sea, and was swallowed by a fish, that, in the agonies of torment, was swallowed by another. Wainamoinen went fishing with Ilmarinen, and at last caught the gray pike,— found in it the trout, found in the trout the whiting, and in the whiting the fireball. When he attempted to seize the fireball he burned his fingers, and dropped it. Ilmarinen did likewise. Then the ball rolled rapidly away until Wainamoinen caught it in an elm-tree, and took it home to gladden his people. Still they were cheerless without the sun and moon, and Wainamoinen was obliged to go to Louhi and compel her to give up the sun and moon. When he returned there was joy in Kalevala.

In the Northland dwelt a happy maiden, Mariatta, who, eating of the magic berry, as she wandered one day in the fields, bore by it a child which she called Flower. Her parents cast her off, and as no one would take her in, she was compelled to go to the flaming steed of Hisi, in whose manger the child was born. Once when she slumbered the child vanished, and she sought for it in vain, until told by the sun that it was in Wainola, sleeping among the reeds and rushes.

The child grew in grace and beauty, but no priest would baptize him, all saying that he was a wizard. Wainamoinen, too, counselled that he be destroyed; but when the two weeks old babe lifted its head and reproached him, saying that he had committed many follies but had been spared by his people, Wainamoinen baptized him, and gave him the right to grow a hero and become a mighty ruler over Karyala.

As Wainamoinen grew feeble with the passing years, he built himself a boat of copper, and singing a plaintive song in which he said the people of Suomi would look forward to his return as a time of peace and plenty, he set forth, sailing through the dusk of evening to the fiery sunset, and anchored in the purple horizon, leaving behind him for an heritage his harp, his wondrous songs, and his wisdom-sayings.

## SELECTIONS FROM THE KALEVALA.

### ILMARINEN'S WEDDING FEAST.

ILMARINEN, the blacksmith, visited the Northland, won the
Rainbow Maid, and successfully performed the tasks set by her
mother Louhi. Great preparations were made in Pohyola for
the wedding, and the coming of the bridegroom was anxiously
expected.

Louhi, hostess of the Northland,
Ancient dame of Sariola,
While at work within her dwelling,
Heard the whips crack on the fenlands,
Heard the rattle of the sledges ;
To the northward turned her glances,
Turned her vision to the sunlight,
And her thoughts ran on as follow :
" Who are these in bright apparel,
On the banks of Pohya-waters,
Are they friends or hostile armies ? "
Then the hostess of the Northland
Looked again and well considered,
Drew much nearer to examine,
Found they were not hostile armies,
Found that they were friends and suitors ;
In the midst was Ilmarinen,
Son-in-law to ancient Louhi.
When the hostess of Pohyola
Saw the son-in-law approaching,
She addressed the words that follow :
" I had thought the winds were raging,
That the piles of wood were falling,
Thought the pebbles in commotion,
Or perchance the ocean roaring ;
Then I hastened nearer, nearer,
Drew still nearer and examined,
Found the winds were not in battle,
Found the piles of wood unshaken,
Found the ocean was not roaring,
Nor the pebbles in commotion ;
Found my son-in-law was coming
With his heroes and attendants,
Heroes counted by the hundreds.
" Should you ask of me the question,
How I recognized the bridegroom
Mid the host of men and heroes,

I should answer, I should tell you:
' As the hazel-bush in copses,
As the oak-tree in the forest,
As the moon among the planets ;
Drives the groom a coal-black courser,
Running like a famished black-dog,
Flying like the hungry raven,
Graceful as the lark at morning,
Golden cuckoos, six in number,
Twitter on the birchen cross-bow ;
There are seven blue-birds singing
On the racer's hame and collar.' "

Noises hear they in the court-yard,
On the highway hear the sledges.
To the court comes Ilmarinen,
With his body-guard of heroes ;
In the midst the chosen suitor,
Not too far in front of others,
Not too far behind his fellows.
Spake the hostess of Pohyola :

" Hie ye hither, men and heroes,
Haste, ye watchers, to the stables,
There unhitch the suitor's stallion,
Lower well the racer's breast-plate,
There undo the straps and buckles,
Loosen well the shafts and traces,
And conduct the suitor hither,
Give my son-in-law good welcome ! "

Ilmarinen turned his racer
Into Louhi's yard and stables,
And descended from his snow-sledge
Spake the hostess of Pohyola :

"Come, thou servant of my bidding,
Best of all my trusted servants,
Take at once the bridegroom's courser
From the shafts adorned with silver,
From the curving arch of willow,
Lift the harness trimmed in copper,
Tie the white-face to the manger,
Treat the suitor's steed with kindness,
Lead him carefully to shelter
By his soft and shining bridle,
By his halter tipped with silver ;
Let him roll among the sand-hills,
On the bottoms soft and even,
On the borders of the snow-banks,
In the fields of milky color.
Lead the hero's steed to water,
Lead him to the Pohya-fountains,
Where the living streams are flowing,

Sweet as milk of human kindness,
From the roots of silvery birches,
Underneath the shade of aspens.

"Feed the courser of the suitor,
With the sweetest corn and barley,
With the summer-wheat and clover,
In the caldron steeped in sweetness;
Feed him at the golden manger,
In the boxes lined with copper,
At my manger richly furnished,
In the warmest of the hurdles;
Tie him with a silk-like halter,
To the golden rings and staples,
To the hooks of purest silver,
Set in beams of birch and oak-wood;
Feed him on the hay the sweetest,
Feed him on the grains nutritious,
Give the best my barns can furnish.

"Curry well the suitor's courser
With the curry-comb of fish-bone,
Brush his hair with silken brushes,
Put his mane and tail in order,
Cover well with silken blankets,
Blankets wrought in gold and silver,
Buckles forged from shining copper.

"Come, ye small lads of the village,
Lead the suitor to my chambers,
With your auburn locks uncovered,
From your hands remove your mittens,
See if ye can lead the hero
Through the door without his stooping,
Lifting not the upper cross-bar,
Sinking not the oaken threshold,
Moving not the oaken casings,
Great the hero who must enter.

"Ilmarinen is too stately,
Cannot enter through the portals,
Not the son-in-law and bridegroom,
Till the portals have been lengthened;
Taller by a head the suitor
Than the doorways of the mansion."
Quick the servants of Pohyola
Tore away the upper cross-bar,
That his cap might not be lifted;
Made the oaken threshold lower
That the hero might not stumble;
Made the birch-wood portals wider,
Opened full the door of welcome,
Easy entrance for the suitor.

Speaks the hostess of the Northland

As the bridegroom freely passes
Through the doorway of her dwelling:
  " Thanks are due to thee, O Ukko,
That my son-in-law has entered !
Let me now my halls examine;
Make the bridal chambers ready,
Finest linen on my tables,
Softest furs upon my benches,
Birchen flooring scrubbed to whiteness,
All my rooms in perfect order."
  Then the hostess of Pohyola
Visited her spacious dwelling,
Did not recognize her chambers;
Every room had been remodelled,
Changed by force of mighty magic;
All the halls were newly burnished,
Hedgehog bones were used for ceilings,
Bones of reindeer for foundations,
Bones of wolverine for door-sills,
For the cross-bars bones of roebuck,
Apple-wood were all the rafters,
Alder-wood, the window casings,
Scales of trout adorned the windows,
And the fires were set in flowers.
All the seats were made of silver,
All the floors of copper-tiling,
Gold-adorned were all the tables,
On the floor were silken mattings,
Every fire-place set in copper,
Every hearth-stone cut from marble,
On each shelf were colored sea-shells,
Kalew's tree was their protection.
  To the court-room came the hero,
Chosen suitor from Wainola,
These the words of Ilmarinen :
  " Send, O Ukko, health and pleasure
To this ancient home and dwelling,
To this mansion richly fashioned ! "
Spake the hostess of Pohyola :
  " Let thy coming be auspicious
To these halls of thee unworthy,
To the home of thy affianced,
To this dwelling lowly fashioned,
Mid the lindens and the aspens.
  " Come, ye maidens that should serve me,
Come, ye fellows from the village,
Bring me fire upon the birch-bark,
Light the fagots of the fir-tree,
That I may behold the bridegroom,
Chosen suitor of my daughter,

Fairy Maiden of the Rainbow,
See the color of his eyeballs,
Whether they are blue or sable,
See if they are warm and faithful."

    Quick the young lads from the village
Brought the fire upon the birch-bark,
Brought it on the tips of pine-wood;
And the fire and smoke commingled
Roll and roar about the hero,
Blackening the suitor's visage,
And the hostess speaks as follows:

    " Bring the fire upon a taper,
On the waxen tapers bring it! "

    Then the maidens did as bidden,
Quickly brought the lighted tapers,
Made the suitor's eyeballs glisten,
Made his cheeks look fresh and ruddy;
Eyes were neither blue nor sable,
Sparkled like the foam of waters,
Like the reed-grass on the margin,
Colored as the ocean-jewels,
Iridescent as the rainbow.

    "Come, ye fellows from the hamlets,
Lead my son-in-law and hero
To the highest seat at table,
To the seat of greatest honor,
With his back upon the blue-wall,
Looking on my bounteous tables,
Facing all the guests of Northland."

    Then the hostess of Pohyola
Served her guests in great abundance,
Richest drinks and rarest viands,
First of all she served the bridegroom;
On his platters honeyed biscuit,
And the sweetest river-salmon,
Seasoned butter, roasted bacon,
All the dainties of Pohyola.
Then the servants served the others,
Filled the plates of all invited
With the varied food of Northland.
Spake the hostess of Pohyola:

    "Come, ye maidens from the village,
Hither bring the beer in pitchers,
In the urns with double handles,
To the many guests in-gathered.
Ere all others, serve the bridegroom."

    Thereupon the merry maidens
Brought the beer in silver pitchers
From the copper-banded vessels,
For the wedding guests assembled;

And the beer, fermenting, sparkled
On the beard of Ilmarinen,
On the beards of many heroes.
    When the guests had all partaken
Of the wondrous beer of barley,
Spake the drink in merry accents
Through the tongues of the magicians,
Through the tongue of many a hero,
Through the tongue of Wainamoinen,
Famed to be the sweetest singer
Of the Northland bards and minstrels.

          .        .        .

    "Grant, O Ukko, my Creator,
God of love, and truth, and justice,
Grant thy blessing on our feasting,
Bless this company assembled,
For the good of Sariola,
For the happiness of Northland !
May this bread and beer bring joyance,
May they come in rich abundance,
May they carry full contentment
To the people of Pohyola,
To the cabin and the mansion ;
May the hours we spend in singing,
In the morning, in the evening,
Fill our hearts with joy and gladness !
Hear us in our supplications,
Grant to us thy needed blessings,
Send enjoyment, health, and comfort,
To the people here assembled,
To the host and to the hostess,
To the bride and to the bridegroom,
To the sons upon the waters,
To the daughters at their weavings,
To the hunters on the mountains,
To the shepherds in the fenlands,
That our lives may end in honor,
That we may recall with pleasure
Ilmarinen's magic marriage
To the Maiden of the Rainbow,
Snow-white virgin of the Northland."
                    *Crawford's Translation, Rune XXI.*

### THE BIRTH OF THE HARP.

WAINAMOINEN, Ilmarinen, and the wizard Lemminkainen
started to the Northland to win back the Sampo forged for
Louhi by Ilmarinen.  On the way their boat stuck on the

shoulders of a great pike, which was killed by Wainamoinen.
The three then landed, ordered the pike to be cooked by the
maidens, and feasted until nothing remained of the fish but a
heap of bones.

> Wainamoinen, ancient minstrel,
> Looked upon the pile of fragments,
> On the fish-bones looked and pondered,
> Spake these words in meditation :
>     " Wondrous things might be constructed
> From the relics of this monster,
> Were they in the blacksmith's furnace,
> In the hands of the magician,
> In the hands of Ilmarinen."
>     Spake the blacksmith of Wainola :
>     " Nothing fine can be constructed
> From the bones and teeth of fishes
> By the skilful forger-artist,
> By the hands of the magician."
> These the words of Wainamoinen :
>     " Something wondrous might be builded
> From these jaws, and teeth, and fish-bones ;
> Might a magic harp be fashioned,
> Could an artist be discovered
> That could shape them to my wishes."
>     But he found no fish-bone artist
> That could shape the harp of joyance
> From the relics of their feasting,
> From the jaw-bones of the monster,
> To the will of the magician.
> Thereupon wise Wainamoinen
> Set himself at work designing ;
> Quick became a fish-bone artist,
> Made a harp of wondrous beauty,
> Lasting joy and pride of Suomi.
> Whence the harp's enchanting arches ?
> From the jaw-bones of the monster.
> Whence the necessary harp-pins ?
> From the pike-teeth, firmly fastened.
> Whence the sweetly singing harp-strings ?
> From the tail of Lempo's stallion.
> Thus was born the harp of magic
> From the mighty pike of Northland,
> From the relics from the feasting
> Of the heroes of Wainola.
> All the young men came to view it,
> All the aged with their children,
> Mothers with their beauteous daughters,
> Maidens with their golden tresses ;

All the people on the islands
Came to view the harp of joyance,
Pride and beauty of the Northland.
   Wainamoinen, ancient minstrel,
Let the aged try the harp-strings,
Gave it to the young magicians,
To the dames and to their daughters,
To the maidens, silver-tinselled,
To the singers of Wainola.
When the young men touched the harp-strings,
Then arose the notes of discord;
When the aged played upon it,
Dissonance their only music.
Spake the wizard, Lemminkainen:
  "O ye witless, worthless children,
O ye senseless, useless maidens,
O ye wisdom-lacking heroes,
Cannot play this harp of magic,
Cannot touch the notes of concord!
Give to me this thing of beauty,
Hither bring the harp of fish-bones,
Let me try my skillful fingers."
Lemminkainen touched the harp-strings,
Carefully the strings adjusted,
Turned the harp in all directions,
Fingered all the strings in sequence,
Played the instrument of wonder,
But it did not speak in concord,
Did not sing the notes of joyance.
Spake the ancient Wainamoinen:
  "There is none among these maidens,
None among these youthful heroes,
None among the old magicians,
That can play the harp of magic,
Touch the notes of joy and pleasure.
Let us take the harp to Pohya,
There to find a skillful player
That can touch the strings in concord."
   Then they sailed to Sariola,
To Pohyola took the wonder,
There to find the harp a master.
All the heroes of Pohyola,
All the boys and all the maidens,
Ancient dames and bearded minstrels,
Vainly touched the harp of beauty.
   Louhi, hostess of the Northland,
Took the harp-strings in her fingers;
All the youth of Sariola,
Youth of every tribe and station,
Vainly touched the harp of fish-bone;

Could not find the notes of joyance,
Dissonance their only pleasure;
Shrieked the harp-strings like the whirlwinds,
All the tones were harsh and frightful.

.    .    .    .    .    .    .

Wainamoinen, ancient minstrel,
The eternal wisdom-singer,
Laves his hands to snowy whiteness,
Sits upon the rock of joyance,
On the stone of song he settles,
On the mount of song he settles,
On the mount of silver clearness,
On the summit, golden colored,
Takes the harp by him created,
In his hands the harp of fish-bone,
With his knee the arch supporting,
Takes the harp-strings in his fingers,
Speaks these words to those assembled:
    "Hither come, ye Northland people,
Come and listen to my playing,
To the harp's entrancing measures,
To my songs of joy and gladness."
    Then the singer of Wainola
Took the harp of his creation,
Quick adjusting, sweetly tuning,
Deftly plied his skillful fingers
To the strings that he had fashioned.
Now was gladness rolled on gladness,
And the harmony of pleasure
Echoed from the hills and mountains;
Added singing to his playing,
Out of joy did joy come welling,
Now resounded marvellous music,
All of Northland stopped and listened.
Every creature in the forest,
All the beasts that haunt the woodlands
On their nimble feet came bounding,
Came to listen to his playing,
Came to hear his songs of joyance.
Leaped the squirrels from the branches,
Merrily from birch to aspen;
Climbed the ermines on the fences,
O'er the plains the elk deer bounded,
And the lynxes purred with pleasure;
Wolves awoke in far-off swamp-lands,
Bounded o'er the marsh and heather,
And the bear his den deserted,
Left his lair within the pine-wood,
Settled by a fence to listen,
Leaned against the listening gate-posts,

But the gate-posts yield beneath him ;
Now he climbs the fir-tree branches
That he may enjoy and wonder,
Climbs and listens to the music
Of the harp of Wainamoinen.

Tapiola's wisest senior,
Metsola's most noble landlord,
And of Tapio, the people,
Young and aged, men and maidens,
Flew like red-deer up the mountains
There to listen to the playing,
To the harp of Wainamoinen.
Tapiola's wisest mistress,
Hostess of the glen and forest,
Robed herself in blue and scarlet,
Bound her limbs with silken ribbons,
Sat upon the woodland summit,
On the branches of a birch-tree,
There to listen to the playing,
To the high-born hero's harping,
To the songs of Wainamoinen.

All the birds that fly in mid-air
Fell like snow-flakes from the heavens,
Flew to hear the minstrel's playing,
Hear the harp of Wainamoinen.
Eagles in their lofty eyrie
Heard the songs of the enchanter ;
Swift they left their unfledged young ones,
Flew and perched around the minstrel.
From the heights the hawks descended,
From the clouds down swooped the falcon,
Ducks arose from inland waters,
Swans came gliding from the marshes ;
Tiny finches, green and golden,
Flew in flocks that darkened sunlight,
Came in myriads to listen,
Perched upon the head and shoulders
Of the charming Wainamoinen,
Sweetly singing to the playing
Of the ancient bard and minstrel.
And the daughters of the welkin,
Nature's well-beloved daughters,
Listened all in rapt attention ;
Some were seated on the rainbow,
Some upon the crimson cloudlets,
Some upon the dome of heaven.

In their hands the Moon's fair daughters
Held their weaving-combs of silver ;
In their hands the Sun's sweet maidens
Grasped the handles of their distaffs,

Weaving with their golden shuttles,
Spinning from their silver spindles,
On the red rims of the cloudlets,
On the bow of many colors.
As they hear the minstrel playing,
Hear the harp of Wainamoinen,
Quick they drop their combs of silver,
Drop the spindles from their fingers,
And the golden threads are broken,
Broken are the threads of silver.

All the fish in Suomi-waters
Heard the songs of the magician,
Came on flying fins to listen
To the harp of Wainamoinen.
Came the trout with graceful motions,
Water-dogs with awkward movements,
From the water-cliffs the salmon,
From the sea-caves came the whiting,
From the deeper caves the bill-fish;
Came the pike from beds of sea-fern,
Little fish with eyes of scarlet,
Leaning on the reeds and rushes,
With their heads above the surface;
Came to hear the harp of joyance,
Hear the songs of the enchanter.

Ahto, king of all the waters,
Ancient king with beard of sea-grass,
Raised his head above the billows,
In a boat of water-lilies,
Glided to the coast in silence,
Listened to the wondrous singing,
To the harp of Wainamoinen.
These the words the sea-king uttered:
" Never have I heard such playing,
Never heard such strains of music,
Never since the sea was fashioned,
As the songs of this enchanter,
This sweet singer, Wainamoinen."

Satko's daughters from the blue-deep,
Sisters of the wave-washed ledges,
On the colored strands were sitting,
Smoothing out their sea-green tresses
With the combs of molten silver,
With their silver-handled brushes,
Brushes forged with golden bristles.
When they hear the magic playing,
Hear the harp of Wainamoinen,
Fall their brushes on the billows,
Fall their combs with silver handles
To the bottom of the waters,

Unadorned their heads remaining,
And uncombed their sea-green tresses.
　　Came the hostess of the waters,
Ancient hostess robed in flowers,
Rising from her deep sea-castle,
Swimming to the shore in wonder,
Listened to the minstrel's playing,
To the harp of Wainamoinen.
As the magic tones re-echoed,
As the singer's song outcircled,
Sank the hostess into slumber,
On the rocks of many colors,
On her watery couch of joyance,
Deep the sleep that settled o'er her.
　　Wainamoinen, ancient minstrel,
Played one day and then a second,
Played the third from morn to even.
There was neither man nor hero,
Neither ancient dame nor maiden,
Not in Metsola a daughter,
Whom he did not touch to weeping ;
Wept the young and wept the aged,
Wept the mothers, wept the daughters,
At the music of his playing,
At the songs of the magician.

　　　　　　*Crawford's Translation, Runes XL.-XLI.*

# THE ÆNEID.

THE Æneid was written by Publius Vergilius Maro, commonly known as Vergil, who was born at Andes, near Mantua, Oct. 15, 70 B. C., and died at Brundusium, Sept. 22, 19 B. C.

He was educated at Cremona, Milan, Naples, and Rome. When the lands near Cremona and Mantua were assigned by Octavianus to his soldiers after the battle of Philippi, Vergil lost his estates; but they were afterwards restored to him through Asinius Pollio.

He became a favorite of Augustus, and spent part of his time in Rome, near his patron, Mæcenas, the emperor's minister.

Vergil's first work was the Bucolics, in imitation of Theocritus. His second work, the Georgics, treats of husbandry. The Æneid relates the adventures of Æneas, the legendary ancestor of the Romans.

The Æneid is in twelve books, of which the first six describe the wanderings of Æneas, and the last six his wars in Italy. Its metre is the dactyllic hexameter.

Vergil worked for eleven years on the poem, and considered it incomplete at his death.

The Æneid tells the story of the flight of Æneas from burning Troy to Italy, and makes him an ancestor of the Romans. With the story of his wanderings are interwoven praises of the Cæsars and the glory of Rome.

It is claimed that because Vergil was essentially a poet of rural life, he was especially fitted to be the national poet, since the Roman life was founded on the agricultural country life. He also chose a theme which particularly appealed to the patriotism of the Romans. For this reason, the poem was immediately received into popular favor, and was made a text-book of the Roman youths.

It is often said of Vergil by way of reproach, that his work was an imitation of Homer, and the first six books of the Æneid are compared to the Odyssey, the last six to the Iliad. But while Vergil may be accused of imitation of subject matter, his style is his own, and is entirely different from that of Homer. There is a tender grace in the Roman writer which the Greek does not possess. Vergil also lacks that purely pagan enjoyment of life; in its place there is a tender melancholy that suggests the passing of the golden age. This difference of treatment, this added grace and charm, which are always mentioned as peculiarly Vergil's own, united with his poetical feeling, and skill in versification, are sufficient to absolve him from the reproach of a mere imitator.

The Æneid was greatly admired and imitated during the Middle Ages, and still retains its high place in literature.

BIBLIOGRAPHY AND CRITICISM, THE ÆNEID. R. W. Brown's History of Roman Classical Literature, n. d., pp. 257–265; John Alfred Church's Story of the Æneid, 1886; Domenico Comparetti's Virgil in the Middle Ages, Tr. by Benecke, 1895; C. T. Cruttwell's Virgil (see his History of Roman Literature, n. d. pp. 252–375); John Davis's Observations on the poems of Homer and Virgil, out of the French, 1672; James Henry's Æneidea: or Critical, Exegetical, and Æsthetical Remarks on the Æneis, 1873; James Henry's Notes of Twelve Years' Voyage of Discovery in the first six Books of the Æneid, 1853; J. W. Mackail's Virgil (see his Latin Literature, 1895, pp. 91–106); H. Nettleship's The Æneid (see his Vergil, 1880, pp. 45–74); H. T. Peck and R. Arrowsmith's Roman Life in Latin Prose and Verse, 1894, pp. 68–70; Leonhard Schmitz's History of Latin Literature, 1877, pp. 106–108; W. Y. Sellar's Roman Poets of the Augustan Age, Vergil, Ed. 2, 1883; W. S. Teuffel's Æneis (see his History of Roman Literature, 1891, pp. 434–439); J. S. Tunison's Master Virgil, the author of the Æneid, as he seemed in the Middle Ages, 1888 ; Robert Y. Tyrrell's Virgil (see his Latin Poetry, 1895, pp. 126–161) ; A Forgotten Virtue, Macmillan, 1895, xii. 51–56, an article on the Æneid, "the epic of piety ;" Scene of the last six books of the Æneid, Blackwood, 1832, xxxii. 76–87 ; A. A. Knight's The Year in the Æneid, Education, 1886, vi. 612–616 ; William C. Cawton's The Underworld in Homer, Virgil, and Dante, Atlantic, 1884, liv. 99–110.

STANDARD ENGLISH TRANSLATIONS, THE ÆNEID. The Æneid, Tr. by J. Conington, 1887 ; The Æneid, Tr. by C. P. Cranch, 1872 ; The Æneid, Tr. by John Dryden (1697), 1884 ; The Æneid, Tr. by William Morris, 1882 ; The Æneid, Tr. by W. S. Thornhill, 1886 ; The Æneid, Tr. by J. A. Wilstach, 1884 ; The Æneid, Tr. by J. W. Mackail, 1890.

## THE STORY OF THE ÆNEID.

FOR many years the heroic Æneas, who escaped from falling Troy to seek the shores of Italy, there to found the lofty walls of Rome, was tossed upon the sea by the wrath of cruel Juno.

The fates foretold that these future Romans would overthrow a city dearer to her than Samos, — Carthage, founded by the Tyrians, opposite Italy, and far from the Tiberine mouths. For this rich city Juno desired boundless rule, — hence her hatred of the Trojans. Moreover, she had not forgotten the judgment of Paris, her slighted charms, and the supplanting of Hebe by Ganymede.

After having tossed the unhappy hero and his men over many seas, Juno, observing their approach to Italy, hastened to Æolia, where King Æolus ruled over the struggling winds and tempests, chained in vast caves.

Bribed by Juno, Æolus sent forth a tempest that scattered the ships of Æneas, and would have destroyed them had it not been for the interposition of Neptune.

Suspecting his sister's treachery, Neptune angrily dismissed the winds, and hastened to the relief of the Trojans. Cymothoë and Triton pushed the ships from the rocks, he himself assisting with his trident. Then, driving over the rough waves in his chariot, he soothed the frenzy of the sea.

The wearied Æneans speedily sought a harbor on the Libyan shore, a long and deep recess bordered by a dense grove. In the cliffs was a cave, with sweet waters and seats carved from the living rock, — the abode of the nymphs. Gathering here the seven ships that survived the fury of the storm, Æneas landed, and feasted with his comrades.

The next morning Æneas, accompanied by his friend Achates, sallied forth from the camp at dawn, to learn, if possible, something of the land on which they had been thrown. They had gone but a little way in the depths of the forest when they met Æneas's mother, Venus, in the guise of a Spartan maid, her bow hung from her shoulders, her hair flowing to the wind.

"Hast thou seen my sister?" she inquired, "hunting the boar, wrapped in a spotted lynx hide, her quiver at her back?"

"Nay, we have seen no one," replied Æneas. "But what shall I call thee, maiden? A goddess, a nymph? Be kind, I pray thee, and tell us among what people we have fallen, that before thy altars we may sacrifice many a victim."

"I am unworthy of such honors," Venus answered. "This land is Libya, but the town is Tyrian, founded by Dido, who fled hither from her brother Pygmalion, who had secretly murdered her husband, Sichæus, for his gold. To Dido, sleeping, appeared the wraith of Sichæus, pallid, his breast pierced with the impious wound, and revealed to her her brother's crime, showed where a hoard of gold was concealed, and advised her to leave the country.

"Gathering together a company of those who wished to flee from the tyrant, Dido seized the ships, loaded them with the gold, and fled to Libya, where she is now erecting the walls and towers of New Carthage. I would advise thee to hasten forward and seek our queen. If augury fail me not, I read from yonder flight of swans the return of thy missing ships and comrades."

As she turned to go, her neck shone with a rosy refulgence, ambrosial fragrance breathed from her, her robe flowed down about her feet and revealed the goddess. As she vanished, her son stretched longing hands after her. "Ah, mother, why dost thou thus trifle with me? Why may not I clasp thy loved hands and exchange true words with thee?"

Wrapped in a cloud by Venus, Æneas and Achates mounted a hill that overlooked the city, and looked down wondering on the broad roofs and the paved streets of Carthage. The busy Tyrians worked like the bees in early summer: some moving the immense masses of stone, some founding the citadel, others laying off the sites for the law courts and sacred Senate House. " O happy ye whose walls now rise ! " exclaimed Æneas, as he and Achates mingled with the crowd, still cloud-wrapped, and entered the vast temple built to Juno. Here Æneas's fear fell from him ; for as he waited for the queen's coming, he saw pictured on the walls the fall of his own dear city, and wept as he gazed upon the white tents of Rhesus, and Hector's disfigured body.

As he wept, the beautiful Dido entered, joyously intent on her great work, and, seating herself on her throne, proceeded to give laws to the Tyrians, and assign their work to them.

Suddenly, to the amazement of Æneas and Achates, in burst their lost comrades, Antheus, Sergestus, Gyas, Cloanthus, and other Trojans, demanding of Dido a reason for their rough reception. To whom the queen replied : —

" Let fear desert your hearts ; I, too, have suffered, and know how to aid the unfortunate. And whither hath not the fame of Troy penetrated? I will aid you in leaving this coast, or give you a home with me, treating you as I treat my Tyrians. Would only that Æneas's self stood with you ! "

Then burst Æneas forth from his cloud-wrapping, made more beautiful by Venus, the purple bloom of youth on his face, joy in his eyes. " Here am I, Trojan Æneas, to render thanks to thee, divine Dido."

Dido, charmed with the hero, prepared a banquet for him in her splendid hall, curtained with rich drapery, and adorned with costly plate, whereon were pictured the proud deeds of her ancestors. Hither came the Trojans with gifts for Dido, — a rich robe stiff with gold embroidery, a veil embroidered with the yellow acanthus, ornaments of Helen, the sceptre of Ilione, a pearl and gold necklace, and a double crown of gems and gold.

Beside Achates tripped Cupid, for Venus, suspecting the craft of the Tyrians, had hidden Ascanius on Mount Ida, and sent her own son in his guise, to complete Æneas's conquest of Dido.

After the feast was over, the great beakers were brought in

and crowned with garlands. Dido called for the beaker used by Belus and all his descendants, and pouring a libation, drank to the happiness of the Trojan wanderers, and passed the cup around the board. Iopas, the long-haired minstrel, sang, and the night passed by in various discourse. Dido, forgetting Sichæus, hung on the words of Æneas, questioning him of Priam and Hector, and at last demanding the story of his wanderings.

"Thou orderest me, O queen, to renew my grief, the destruction of Troy by the Greeks, which deeds I have seen, and a part of which I have been.

" Despairing of conquering Troy, the Greeks attempted to take it by stratagem. By the art of Pallas, they framed a heaven-high horse, within which were concealed picked men for our destruction. Leaving this behind them, they sailed, ostensibly for home, in reality for Tenedos.

" When we supposed them gone we joyfully went forth to examine the deserted camp and the giant horse. As we wondered at it, and Laocoön, priest of Neptune, urged us to destroy it, a crowd of shepherds approached with a youth whom they had found hiding in the sedges. His name was Sinon. He was a Greek, but he was hated by Ulysses, and had fled to save his life. The Greeks had sailed home, he assured us, leaving the horse as a votive offering to Pallas. They had hoped that its great bulk would prevent the Trojans from taking it inside their walls, for once within the city, Troy could never be taken.

" We Trojans were credulous, and Sinon's tale was plausible. To increase our belief in it, while Laocoön was sacrificing a bull to Neptune, we saw coming over the sea from Tenedos two huge serpents, their crimson crests towering high, their breasts erect among the waves, their long folds sweeping over the foaming sea. As we fled affrighted, they seized the two sons of Laocoön, twining their coils around the wretched boys ; and when their father hastened to their aid, caught him in their huge coils, staining his fillets with black blood. ' Laocoön suffered for his crime,' we said, when, the priest slain, the serpents crept to Pallas's altar, and curled themselves around the feet of the goddess. Then joyfully we made a breach in the walls, put rollers under the horse, and, with music and dancing, dragged it within the walls.

"That night as we lay sleeping after revelry and feasting, Sinon crept down, opened the horse, and freed the men, who were soon joined by the other Greeks, returned from Tenedos.

"In a dream Hector's shade appeared to me, and, weeping, bade me fly. 'Troy falls. Do thou go forth and save her household deities!' As I woke, sounds of battle penetrated to my palace halls, removed somewhat from the city, and embowered in trees; and I rushed forth, forgetful of Hector's warning. I saw the streets swimming in Trojan blood, Trojan women and children led captive, Cassandra dragged from her shrine. Enraged, I gathered a band and slew many Greeks. But when I saw the impious Pyrrhus enter the palace and slay Priam at the altar, I recognized the uselessness of my struggle, and turned to my home.

"Taking my old father Anchises on my back, and leading Iulus by the hand, I set forth, followed by my wife Creusa. But when I looked behind me at the city gates, my wife was gone. Mad with despair, I rushed back to the citadel, crying, 'Creusa! Creusa!' Our homestead was in flames, the streets filled with Greeks; but as I roamed through the town, I met her pallid shape. 'O husband, rage not against heaven's decrees! Happy days will come for thee on the banks of the Tiber. Farewell, and love with me our boy!'

"Without the gates I was joined by other fugitives; and after the departure of the Greeks we built ships from the timbers of Mount Ida, and loading these with our household gods and a few spoils from the city, we departed to seek new homes.

"In Thrace, our first stopping-place, I learned that Polydore, Priam's son, who had been entrusted to the care of the Thracian king, had been slain by him for his gold, when the fortunes of Troy fell. We hastened to leave this accursed land, and sought Delos, only to be instructed by

Apollo that we must seek the home from which our fore-fathers had come. Anchises, who remembered the legends of our race, thought this must be Crete; so to Crete we sailed, and there laid the foundations of a city, only to be driven thence by a plague and a threatened famine.

" In a dream my household gods instructed me that Dardanus, the founder of our race, had come from Hesperia, and thither we must bend our course. Tempests drove us about the sea for three suns, until, on the fourth, we landed at the isle of the Harpies, — loathsome monsters, half woman, half bird, who foul everything they touch. When we had slain the cattle and prepared to banquet, they drove us from the tables; and when attacked by us, uttered dire threats of future famine.

" At Epirus we heard that Andromache had wed Prince Helenus, who had succeeded to the rule of Pyrrhus, two Trojans thus being united. As I landed here, anxious to prove the truth of the rumor, I met Andromache herself in a grove near the town, sacrificing at an empty tomb dedicated to Hector. Pyrrhus had made her his slave after the fall of Troy, but after he wedded Hermione, he had given her to Helenus, himself a slave. When Pyrrhus died, part of his realm fell to Helenus, and here the two had set up a little Troy.

" Helenus received us kindly, instructed us as to our route, and gave us rich gifts; and Andromache, remembering her dead Astyanax, wept over Iulus as she parted with him.

" As we passed Sicily we took up a Greek, Achemenides, a companion of Ulysses, who had been left behind, and had since been hiding in deadly terror from the Cyclops. We ourselves caught sight of the monster Polyphemus, feeling his way to the shore to bathe his wounded eye.

" Instructed by Helenus, we avoided Scylla and Charybdis, and reached Sicily, where my father died. We were just leaving the island when the storm arose that brought us hither. The rest thou knowest."

The guests departed from the banquet hall; but the unhappy Dido, consumed with love, imparted her secret to her sister Anna.

"Why shouldst thou weep, sister dear? Why regret that thou hast at last forgotten Sichæus? Contend not against love, but strive to unite Trojan and Tyrian. Winter comes on, and thou canst detain him while the sea rages and the winds are fierce and the rains icy."

Her ambitious plans for her city forgotten, Dido wandered through the streets, mad with love and unable to conceal her passion. She led Æneas among the walls and towers, made feasts for him, and begged again and again to hear the story of his wandering. At other times she fondled Ascanius, leaving her youths undrilled, and the city works abandoned.

Perceiving that Æneas, well content, seemed to forget that his goal was Hesperia, Mercury was dispatched by Jupiter to warn him to depart from Carthage.

"Why stoppest thou here?" questioned the herald of the gods. "If thou carest not for thyself, think of Ascanius, thine heir. His must be the Italian realms, the Roman world."

The horror-stricken Æneas stood senseless with fear. He longed to escape, but how leave the unhappy Dido? Quickly calling his comrades, he commanded them to fit out the fleet in silence, hoping to find a time when he could break the news to Dido gently.

But who can deceive a lover? Rumor bore the report to Dido, who, mad with grief, reproached Æneas. "Perfidious one! didst thou think to escape from me? Does not our love restrain thee, and the thought that I shall surely die when thou art gone? I have sacrificed all to thee; now leave me not lonely in my empty palace."

Æneas remained untouched. He would ever retain the kindest memories of his stay in Carthage. He had never held out the hope of wedlock to her. A higher power called him, and, bidden by Jove, he must depart, for Ascanius's sake, to Italy.

The fainting Dido was carried to her palace, whence she could watch the hurried preparations for the departure. As she watched, life became intolerable to her. Pretending to her sister that she was preparing to perform a magic spell to release her from the bonds of love, she reared a mighty pyre in her court, wreathed it with funereal garlands, and placed thereon Æneas's couch, garments, and sword. With her hair dishevelled, she then invoked Hecate, and sprinkling Avernian water and poisons on it, and casting thereon various love-charms, she called the gods to witness that she was determined to die. As the ships left the harbor, she tore her hair, one moment accusing herself because she had not torn Æneas to pieces when in her power, at another vowing to follow him. Then, anxious to forget her grief, she mounted the pyre, and threw herself on the sword of her faithless lover.

Far out at sea, the Æneans, looking back, dimly guessed the meaning of the flames that brightened the stormy skies.

Contrary winds compelled Æneas to seek harbor in Sicily. Its king, Acestes, was his friend, and there he had buried his father Anchises. A year had elapsed since his death, and in honor of the anniversary, Æneas instituted funeral games, in which there were trials of skill in rowing, foot-racing, archery, and boxing.

While the spectators were applauding the feats of skill, the Trojan women, at the instigation of Juno, set fire to the ships, that they might compel Æneas to remain in Sicily. By Jupiter's aid, some of the vessels were saved, and Æneas, acting on the advice of Nautes, allowed the women and those Trojans who so desired, to remain in Sicily, and himself marked out for them the foundations of their city.

While here Æneas was urged by Anchises in a dream to visit the Cumæan Sibyl, that, with her assistance, he might visit Elysium and talk with him.

In the lofty temple, the Sibyl, inspired by the god, encouraged the hero. "Success will at last be thine, and Juno will be won over to thee. But great labors must thou undergo."

To visit the underworld was no easy task, she assured him. "The gates of Dis stand open night and day; small trouble it is to descend thereto, but to retrace one's steps, and regain the upper air, there lies the toil." Æneas must first possess a golden branch to present to Proserpina, and celebrate the funeral rites of his friend, Misenus, who yet lay unburied.

While Æneas worked in the forest, felling trees for Misenus's bier, the doves of Venus descended and aided him to find the tree, from which he plucked the gleaming branch.

Across the Styx, past the dread Cerberus, Æneas and the Sibyl went, through the abode of babes and those who died for deeds they did not do, and into the mourning fields, where the disappointed in love were hedged in with myrtle sprays. Here Æneas descried Dido dimly through the clouds, and wept to see her fresh wound. Many were his protestations of his faithfulness, and strong his declaration that he left her only at the command of the gods. But without raising her eyes, Dido turned coldly away to where her former husband returned her love for love. Past the chamber of torture, beyond Phlegethon, guarded by Tisiphone and Tartarus, in whose depths the wicked were punished, they went, and entered the beautiful fields of Elysium, where Æneas found his father.

To his son, Anchises explained that the souls that visited the underworld were punished according to their deserts, and then sent into Elysium. Cleansed there of all impurities, and with the memories of the past washed from them by Lethe, they again visited the world in another form. Pointing out a crowd that passed them, he indicated to Æneas the illustrious men who would make his race famous in Italy. First his son Silvius, born of Lavinia, his Italian wife to be ; Numitor, Romulus, the founder of Rome, Cæsar, and greatest of all, Augustus Cæsar, who would usher in the golden age.

Comforted by the prophecies of Anchises, Æneas sought the upper world, and collecting his companions, set sail for the mouth of the Tiber.

Latinus the king welcomed Æneas, and received his proposals for his daughter Lavinia's hand with favor, remembering an ancient prophecy that Lavinia was to wed a foreign prince. But queen Amata, aroused by Juno, insisted that Lavinia should be espoused to Turnus, chief of the Rutulians. Stung by the fury Alecto, she stirred up the people until they demanded that Latinus declare war against Æneas ; and when he hesitated, Juno herself threw open the gates of the temple of Janus.

Leaving part of his forces in Latium with Ascanius, Æneas, instructed in a dream by father Tiber, sailed up the river to Pallanteum, the future site of Rome, to gain the alliance of Evander, an Arcadian king unfriendly to Turnus.

Evander, who was celebrating a solemn feast to Hercules, together with his only son Pallas, and his senate, welcomed the warriors to his modest home, promised his alliance, and sent forth with Æneas his son Pallas and four hundred knights. He also advised him to go to Argylla, whose people were stirred up against Turnus because he protected their tyrant king Mezentius.

While Æneas was thus seeking allies, his troops in Latium had been attacked and besieged by Turnus, and were greatly in need of the hero's aid. While the hosts of Turnus were sleeping after their drunken revelry, Nisus proposed to his beloved Euryalus that they steal through the Latin line with messages to Æneas. Their proposal was applauded by the elders, and Iulus, weeping, promised to cherish them forever for their courage.

As the youths passed among the sleeping Latins, the desire for slaughter overcame them, and they slew Rhamnes, as he lay upon his gorgeous rugs, Lamus, and many others, Euryalus taking Rhamnes's golden-studded belt and Messapus's helmet as booty. Unfortunately they had delayed too long in slaughter ; as they neared the camp of Turnus, Volscens, returning with reinforcements, caught sight of the shining helmet of Euryalus. The youth, flying, became separated from Nisus, and was captured by the enemy. Nisus, who returned to rescue his friend, sent weapon after weapon from his retreat, and when he saw Euryalus about to suffer death from Volscens, rushed forth to save him, only to fall dead upon the body of his slaughtered friend.

Angry at the slaughter committed by Nisus and Euryalus, Turnus, on his return, attempted to scale the intrenchments. The fight raged fiercely around the walls and towers; but just as the victory seemed to be with Turnus, Æneas returned with his Tuscan allies, effected a landing, and began to put the enemy to flight, slaying the tyrant Mezentius and his son.

Turnus, hearing of the danger of his friend Lausus, at the hands of Pallas, who had already wrought great slaughter, sought him out, amazing the young warrior by his great size. Pallas faced him bravely; but while his spear only grazed the shoulder of Turnus, the spear of the Rutulian crushed the folds of iron, bronze, and hides, the corselet's rings of steel, and buried itself in Pallas's breast.

Turnus took the sword-belt from Pallas's body; but because of the merit of the young warrior, yielded his body to the Arcadians to be carried to King Evander.

Enraged at the death of his friend, Æneas fought more fiercely. Especially anxious was he to meet Turnus; but Juno, determined, if possible, to save her favorite, decoyed Turnus off the battle-field by assuming the guise of Æneas.

After a truce, during which the armies buried their dead, and the body of Pallas was sent home to his father, the armies again came together, the Latins being reinforced by the Amazons, under the leadership of Camilla. Camilla had been reared by her father, the exile Metabus, and, early trained to warlike pursuits, had consecrated herself to Diana. Beautiful as a goddess was she, and so light of foot that she could fly over the tops of the tallest wheat without harming the ears.

Within the walls of Latium there was quarrelling between the parties, Drances, leader of the peace party, accusing Turnus of bringing on and continuing the hostilities. The approach of Æneas brought these disputes to an abrupt conclusion, and Camilla, with Turnus, hastened to battle. Many victims fell by Camilla's hand that day, as she rode about the field, her breast bare, her hand clasping her double battle-axe, before Aruns struck her down and fled, frightened at his victory.

In Latium the unhappiness increased, and Turnus, enraged at the reproaches heaped upon him, declared that he would decide the war by single combat with Æneas. Latinus made no secret of his regret at having been compelled to break his compact with Æneas ; but Amata, still furious, raged against Æneas, and declared that she would die if he were made her son-in-law.

The preparations were made for the single combat, the sacrifices at the altars, the crowds assembled to witness the combat ; but just as the kings were solemnizing the agreement, Turnus's sister, Juturna, a river goddess, beloved of Jupiter, renewed the hostilities that Turnus might be saved. A weapon hurled from the Latin ranks caused the indignant Trojans to rise in arms, forgetful of the treaty, and the fight raged more fiercely than before.

Juturna, fearful from Juno's words of the fate of Turnus, assumed the guise of Metiscus, his charioteer, and drove her brother over the field far from the angry Æneas, who, weary of waiting for Turnus, turned towards Latium. The frightened people rushed hither and thither, and the queen, seeing the approaching foe, the roofs in flames, and no troops of Turnus in sight, supposed the Rutulian dead, and hanged herself.

In the mean time, Turnus, remote from the fight, reproached his sister. " Think'st thou not I recognized thee? Thy deceit is in vain. Is to die so wretched a thing? Let us go to the battle. At least, I will die not unworthy of my ancestry."

As he spoke, Saces, wounded and bleeding, rushed to him, imploring : " Turnus, have pity on us ; come to our rescue ! The Latins call thee, the queen is dead, the phalanxes crowd thick around the gates, while thou drivest idly here."

Turnus, amazed, confused, and shamed, saw flames consuming the towers of Latium.

" Now, sister, the fates control. Desist ! It is too late,

I will be shamed no more!" Leaping from his chariot, he rushed forward, demanding that war cease in order that he and Æneas might decide the battle in single combat.

When Turnus's sword broke on the helmet of Æneas, — the sword of his charioteer, that he had seized by mistake instead of his own Styx-hardened blade, — he turned and fled, Æneas pursuing.

Above, in Olympus, Jupiter and Juno quarrelled, as they watched the heroes circling over the yellow sand.

"Give over thy enmity," said the omnipotent father. "Thou hast caused the treaty to be violated; even now thou hast made Juturna return the lost sword to Turnus — in vain. Grieve no more, and goad no longer these suffering men of Troy."

Then Juno yielded, stipulating only that the Trojans lay aside their ancient name, that Latium remain Latium, and the future growth Roman.

Juturna, warned by Jove's messenger, a bird of evil omen, tore her locks and beat her breast, regretting the gift of immortality conferred on her by Jove. Then wrapping her gray veil about her, she fled to her watery throne that she might not see the death of her brother. The frightened Turnus, still fleeing from Æneas, abandoned his sword and took up instead a mighty rock, a landmark such as scarce six men could uplift.

Hurling this at Æneas, he stood, his blood running chill, his eyes cast towards the Rutuli, the town, and the spear of Æneas, that, shrieking through the air, doom laden, wrecked his heavy shield and pierced his thigh.

"Mercy!" he prayed. "Fate hath given thee the advantage. Think, thou duteous son, of my old father, Daunus."

As Æneas stood, softened, and ready to grant the request, the sword-belt of Pallas caught his eye.

"Shalt thou escape, decked out with Pallas's spoils? No, not I slay thee, but Pallas! His hand immolates thee!" As he spoke he plunged his sword in Turnus's breast.

Chilly death came, and the warrior's spirit fled, groaning to the shades.

## SELECTION FROM THE ÆNEID.

### NISUS AND EURYALUS.

WHILE Æneas, finding the Latins hostile to him, sailed up the Tiber in search of allies, the troops he left behind under Ascanius were attacked by Turnus, and their slight fortifications besieged. They were sorely pressed, and longed to be able to inform Æneas of their need.

Nisus was guardian of the gate,
No bolder heart in war's debate,
The son of Hyrtacus, whom Ide
Sent, with his quiver at his side,
From hunting beasts in mountain brake
To follow in Æneas' wake:
With him Euryalus, fair boy;
None fairer donned the arms of Troy;
His tender cheek as yet unshorn
And blossoming with youth new-born.
Love made them one in every thought:
In battle side by side they fought;
And now in duty at the gate
The twain in common station wait.
"Can it be Heaven," said Nisus then,
"That lends such warmth to hearts of men,
Or passion surging past control
That plays the god to each one's soul?
Long time, impatient of repose,
My swelling heart within me glows,
And yearns its energy to fling
On war, or some yet grander thing.
See there the foe, with vain hope flushed!
Their lights are scant, their stations hushed:
Unnerved by slumber and by wine
Their bravest chiefs are stretched supine.
Now to my doubting thought give heed
And listen where its motions lead.
Our Trojan comrades, one and all,
Cry loud, Æneas to recall,
And where, they say, the men to go
And let him of our peril know?
Now if the meed I ask they swear
To give you — nay, I claim no share,
  Content with bare renown —

Meseems, beside yon grassy heap
The way I well might find and keep,
  To Pallanteum's town."
The youth returns, while thirst of praise
Infects him with a strange amaze:
"Can Nisus aim at heights so great,
Nor take his friend to share his fate?
Shall I look on, and let you go
Alone to venture 'mid the foe?
Not thus my sire Opheltes, versed
In war's rude toil, my childhood nursed,
When Argive terror filled the air
And Troy was battling with despair:
Nor such the lot my youth has tried,
In hardship ever at your side,
Since, great Æneas' liegeman sworn,
I followed Fortune to her bourne:
Here, here within this bosom burns
A soul that mere existence spurns,
And holds the fame you seek to reap,
Though bought with life, were bought full cheap."

"Not mine the thought," brave Nisus said,
"To wound you with so base a dread:
So may great Jove, or whosoe'er
Marks with just eyes how mortals fare,
Protect me going, and restore
In triumph to your arms once more.
But if — for many a chance, you wis,
Besets an enterprise like this —
If accident or power divine
The scheme to adverse end incline,
Your life at least I would prolong:
Death does your years a deeper wrong.
Leave me a friend to tomb my clay,
Rescued or ransomed, which you may;
Or, e'en that boon should chance refuse,
To pay the absent funeral dues.
Nor let me cause so dire a smart
To that devoted mother's heart,
Who, sole of all the matron train,
Attends her darling o'er the main,
Nor cares like others to sit down
An inmate of Acestes' town."
He answers brief: "Your pleas are naught:
Firm stands the purpose of my thought:
  Come, stir we: why so slow?"
Then calls the guards to take their place,
Moves on by Nisus, pace with pace,
  And to the prince they go.

All other creatures wheresoe'er
Were stretched in sleep, forgetting care:
Troy's chosen chiefs in high debate
Were pondering o'er the reeling state,
What means to try, or whom to speed
To show Æneas of their need.
There stand they, midway in the field,
Still hold the spear, still grasp the shield:
When Nisus and his comrade brave
With eager tones admittance crave;
The matter high; though time be lost,
The occasion well were worth the cost.
Iulus hails the impatient pair,
Bids Nisus what they wish declare.
Then spoke the youth: " Chiefs! lend your ears,
Nor judge our proffer by our years.
The Rutules, sunk in wine and sleep,
Have ceased their former watch to keep:
A stealthy passage have we spied
Where on the sea the gate opes wide:
The line of fires is scant and broke,
And thick and murky rolls the smoke.
Give leave to seek, in these dark hours,
Æneas at Evander's towers,
Soon will you see us here again
Decked with the spoils of slaughtered men.
Nor strange the road: ourselves have seen
The city, hid by valleys green,
Just dimly dawning, and explored
In hunting all the river-board."
Out spoke Aletes, old and gray:
" Ye gods, who still are Ilium's stay,
No, no, ye mean not to destroy
Down to the ground the race of Troy,
When such the spirit of her youth,
And such the might of patriot truth."
Then, as the tears roll down his face,
He clasps them both in strict embrace:
" Brave warriors! what rewards so great,
For worth like yours to compensate?
From Heaven and from your own true heart
Expect the largest, fairest part:
The rest, and at no distant day,
The good Æneas shall repay,
Nor he, the royal youth, forget
Through all his life the mighty debt."
" Nay, hear me too," Ascanius cried,
" Whose life is with my father's tied:
O Nisus! by the home-god powers
We jointly reverence, yours and ours,

The god of ancient Capys' line,
And Vesta's venerable shrine,
By these dread sanctions I appeal
To you, the masters of my weal;
Oh, bring me back my sire again!
Restore him, and I feel no pain.
Two massy goblets will I give;
Rich sculptures on the silver live;
   The plunder of my sire,
What time he took Arisba's hold;
Two chargers, talents twain of gold,
A bowl beside of antique mould
   By Dido brought from Tyre.
Then, too, if ours the lot to reign
O'er Italy by conquest ta'en,
   And each man's spoil assign, —
Saw ye how Turnus rode yestreen,
His horse and arms of golden sheen?
That horse, that shield and glowing crest
I separate, Nisus, from the rest
   And count already thine.
Twelve female slaves, at your desire,
Twelve captives with their arms entire,
My sire shall give you, and the plain
That forms Latinus' own domain.
But you, dear youth, of worth divine,
Whose blooming years are nearer mine,
Here to my heart I take, and choose
My comrade for whate'er ensues.
No glory will I e'er pursue,
Unmotived by the thought of you:
Let peace or war my state befall,
Thought, word, and deed, you share them all."
The youth replied: "No after day
This hour's fair promise shall betray,
Be fate but kind.   Yet let me claim
One favor, more than all you name:
A mother in the camp is mine,
   Derived from Priam's ancient line:
No home in Sicily or Troy
Has kept her from her darling boy.
She knows not, she, the paths I tread;
I leave her now, no farewell said;
By night and this your hand I swear,
A parent's tears I could not bear.
Vouchsafe your pity, and engage
To solace her unchilded age:
And I shall meet whate'er betide
By such assurance fortified."
With sympathy and tender grief
All melt in tears, Iulus chief,

As filial love in other shown
Recalled the semblance of his own:
And, " Tell your doubting heart," he cries,
" All blessings wait your high emprise:
I take your mother for my own,
Creusa, save in name alone,
Nor lightly deem the affection due
To her who bore a child like you.
Come what come may, I plight my troth
By this my head, my father's oath,
The bounty to yourself decreed
Should favoring gods your journey speed,
The same shall in your line endure,
To parent and to kin made sure."
He spoke, and weeping still, untied
A gilded falchion from his side,
Lycaon's work, the man of Crete,
With sheath of ivory complete:
Brave Mnestheus gives for Nisus' wear
A lion's hide with shaggy hair;
Aletes, old in danger grown,
His helmet takes, and gives his own.
Then to the gates, as forth they fare,
The band of chiefs with many a prayer
    The gallant twain attends:
Iulus, manlier than his years,
Oft whispering, for his father's ears
    Full many a message sends:
But be it message, be it prayer,
Alike 't is lost, dispersed in air.


The trenches past, through night's deep gloom
    The hostile camp they near:
Yet many a foe shall meet his doom
    Or ere that hour appear.
There see they bodies stretched supine,
O'ercome with slumber and with wine;
The cars, unhorsed, are drawn up high;
'Twixt wheels and harness warriors lie,
With arms and goblets on the grass
In undistinguishable mass.
" Now," Nisus cried, " for hearts and hands:
This, this the hour our force demands.
Here pass we: yours the rear to mind,
Lest hostile arm be raised behind;
Myself will go before and slay,
While carnage opes a broad highway."
So whispers he with bated breath,
And straight begins the work of death
    On Rhamnes, haughty lord;

On rugs he lay, in gorgeous heap,
From all his bosom breathing sleep,
A royal seer by Turnus loved:
But all too weak his seer-craft proved
   To stay the rushing sword.
Three servants next the weapon found
Stretched 'mid their armor on the ground:
Then Remus' charioteer he spies
Beneath the coursers as he lies,
   And lops his downdropt head;
The ill-starred master next he leaves,
A headless trunk, that gasps and heaves:
Forth spouts the blood from every vein,
And deluges with crimson rain,
   Green earth and broidered bed.
Then Lamyrus and Lamus died,
Serranus, too, in youth's fair pride:
That night had seen him long at play:
Now by the dream-god tamed he lay:
Ah, had his play but matched the night,
Nor ended till the dawn of light!
So famished lion uncontrolled
Makes havoc through the teeming fold,
   As frantic hunger craves;
Mangling and harrying far and near
The meek, mild victims, mute with fear,
   With gory jaws he raves.
Nor less Euryalus performs:
The thirst of blood his bosom warms;
'Mid nameless multitudes he storms,
Herbesus, Fadus, Abaris kills
Slumbering and witless of their ills,
While Rhœtus wakes and sees the whole,
But hides behind a massy bowl.
There, as to rise the trembler strove,
Deep in his breast the sword he drove,
   And bathed in death withdrew.
The lips disgorge the life's red flood,
A mingled stream of wine and blood:
   He plies his blade anew.
Now turns he to Messapus' band,
   For there the fires he sees
Burnt out, while coursers hard at hand
   Are browsing at their ease,
When Nisus marks the excess of zeal,
The maddening fever of the steel,
And checks him thus with brief appeal:
"Forbear we now; 't will soon be day:
Our wrath is slaked, and hewn our way."
Full many a spoil they leave behind

Of solid silver thrice refined,
Armor and bowls of costliest mould
And rugs in rich confusion rolled.
A belt Euryalus puts on
With golden knobs, from Rhamnes won ;
Of old by Cædicus 't was sent,
An absent friendship to cement,
To Remulus, fair Tibur's lord,
  Who, dying, to his grandson left
The shining prize : the Rutule sword
  In after days the trophy reft.
Athwart his manly chest in vain
He binds these trappings of the slain;
Then 'neath his chin in triumph laced
Messapus' helm, with plumage graced,
The camp at length they leave behind,
And round the lake securely wind.

Meanwhile a troop is on its way,
  From Latium's city sped,
An offshoot from the host that lay
Along the host in close array,
Three hundred horsemen, sent to bring
A message back to Turnus, king,
  With Volscens at their head.
Now to the camp they draw them nigh,
  Beneath the rampart's height,
When from afar the twain they spy,
  Still steering from the right ;
The helmet through the glimmering shade
At once the unwary boy betrayed,
  Seen in the moon's full light.
Not lost the sight on jealous eyes :
" Ho ! stand ! who are ye ? " Volscens cries,
  " Whence come, or whither tend ? "
No movement deign they of reply,
But swifter to the forest fly,
  And make the night their friend.
With fatal speed the mounted foes
Each avenue as with network close,
  And every outlet bar.
It was a forest bristling grim
With shade of ilex, dense and dim :
Thick brushwood all the ground o'ergrew :
The tangled ways a path ran through,
  Faint glimmering like a star.
The darkling boughs, the cumbering prey
Euryalus's flight delay :
His courage fails, his footsteps stray :
  But Nisus onward flees ;

No thought he takes, till now at last
The enemy is all o'erpast,
E'en at the grove, since Alban called,
Where then Latinus' herds were stalled:
Sudden he pauses, looks behind
In eager hope his friend to find:
    In vain: no friend he sees.
" Euryalus, my chiefest care,
Where left I you, unhappy? where?
What clue may guide my erring tread
This leafy labyrinth back to thread?"
Then, noting each remembered track,
He thrids the wood, dim-seen and black.
Listening, he hears the horse-hoofs' beat,
The clatter of pursuing feet.
A little moment — shouts arise,
And lo! Euryalus he spies,
Whom now the foemen's gathered throng
Is hurrying helplessly along.
While vain resistance he essays,
Trapped by false night and treacherous ways.
What should he do? what force employ
To rescue the beloved boy?
Plunge through the spears that line the wood,
And death and glory win with blood?
Not unresolved, he poises soon
A javelin, looking to the Moon:
" Grant, goddess, grant thy present aid,
Queen of the stars, Latonian maid,
    The greenwood's guardian power;
If, grateful for success of mine,
With gifts my sire has graced thy shrine,
If e'er myself have brought thee spoil,
The tribute of my hunter's toil,
To ornament thy roof divine,
    Or glitter on thy tower,
These masses give me to confound.
And guide through air my random wound."
He spoke, and hurled with all his might;
The swift spear hurtles through the night:
Stout Sulmo's back the stroke receives:
The wood, though snapped, the midriff cleaves.
He falls, disgorging life's warm tide,
And long-drawn sobs distend his side.
All gaze around: another spear
The avenger levels from his ear,
    And launches on the sky.
Tagus lies pierced through temples twain,
The dart deep buried in his brain.
Fierce Volscens storms, yet finds no foe,

Nor sees the hand that dealt the blow,
    Nor knows on whom to fly.
" Your heart's warm blood for both shall pay,"
He cries, and on his beauteous prey
    With naked sword he sprang.
Scared, maddened, Nisus shrieks aloud :
No more he hides in night's dark shroud,
    Nor bears the o'erwhelming pang :
" Me, guilty me, make me your aim,
O Rutules ! mine is all the blame ;
He did no wrong, nor e'er could do ;
That sky, those stars attest 't is true ;
Love for his friend too freely shown,
This was his crime, and this alone."
In vain he spoke : the sword, fierce driven,
That alabaster breast had riven.
Down falls Euryalus, and lies
In death's enthralling agonies :
Blood trickles o'er his limbs of snow ;
" His head sinks gradually low " :
Thus, severed by the ruthless plough,
    Dim fades a purple flower :
Their weary necks so poppies bow,
    O'erladen by the shower.
But Nisus on the midmost flies,
With Volscens, Volscens in his eyes :
In clouds the warriors round him rise,
    Thick hailing blow on blow :
Yet on he bears, no stint, no stay ;
Like thunderbolt his falchion's sway :
Till as for aid the Rutule shrieks
Plunged in his throat the weapon reeks :
The dying hand has reft away
    The life-blood of its foe.
Then, pierced to death, asleep he fell
On the dead breast he loved so well.

Blest pair ! if aught my verse avail,
No day shall make your memory fail
    From off the heart of time,
While Capitol abides in place,
The mansion of the Æneian race,
And throned upon that moveless base
    Rome's father sits sublime.
            *Conington's Translation, Book IX.*

# BEOWULF.

BEOWULF, the only Anglo-Saxon epic preserved entire, was composed in southwest Sweden probably before the eighth century, and taken to England, where it was worked over and Christianized by the Northumbrian poets.

It is variously attributed to the fifth, seventh, and eighth centuries; but the seventh is most probably correct, since the Higelac of the poem has been identified with Chocilaicus of the " Gesta Regum Francorum," a Danish king who invaded Gaul in the days of Theuderic, son of Clovis, and died near the close of the sixth century.

The only manuscript of the poem in existence is thought to be of the tenth century. It is preserved in the British Museum. Since 1837 much interest has been manifested in the poem, and many editions of it have been given to the public.

Beowulf contains three thousand one hundred and eighty-four lines. It is written in alliterative verse. The lines are written in pairs, and each perfect line contains three alliterating words, — two in the first part, and one in the second.

The unknown writer of Beowulf cannot be praised for his skill in composition; the verse is rude, as was the language in which it was written. But it is of the greatest interest to us because of the pictures it gives of the everyday lives of the people whose heroic deeds it relates, — the drinking in the mead-halls, the relation of the king to his warriors, the description of the armor, the ships, and the halls. The heroes are true Anglo-Saxon types, — bold, fearless, ready to go to the assistance of any one in trouble, no matter how great the risk to themselves; and as ready to drink mead and boast of their valor after the peril is over. In spite of

the attempt to Christianize the poem, it is purely pagan; the
most careless reader can discover the priestly interpolations.
And it has the greater value to us because it refused to be
moulded by priestly hands, but remained the rude but heroic
monument of our Saxon ancestors.

BIBLIOGRAPHY AND CRITICISM, BEOWULF.   B. Ten Brink's
Early English Literature, Tr. by Kennedy; S. A. Brooke's
History of Early English Literature, 1892, p. 12; W. F.
Collier's History of English Literature, p. 19; G. W. Cox
and E. H. Jones's Popular Romances of the Middle Ages,
1871, pp. 382–398; in 1880 ed. pp. 189–201; Isaac Disraeli's Amenities of Literature, i. 65–73; J. Earle's Anglo-
Saxon Literature; T. W. Hunt's Ethical Teaching in
Beowulf (in his Ethical Teachings in Old English Literature,
1892, pp. 66–77); H. Morley's English Writers, 1887, pp.
276–354; H. A. Taine's History of English Literature, 1886,
i. 62; S. Turner's Anglo-Saxons, iii. 326; in ed. 3, i. 456;
J. Harrison's Old Teutonic Life in Beowulf (in the Over-
land Monthly, July, 1894); F. A. March's The World of
Beowulf (in Proceedings of American Philological Associa-
tion, 1882).

STANDARD ENGLISH TRANSLATIONS, BEOWULF.   Beowulf,
edition with English translation, notes and glossary by Thomas
Arnold, 1876; The Deeds of Beowulf, 1892; Beowulf, Tr.
by J. M. Garnett, 1882 (translated line for line); Beowulf,
Tr. by J. L. Hall, 1892, metrical translation; Beowulf, Tr. by
J. M. Kemble, with copious glossary, preface, and philological notes, 2 vols., 1833–37; Beowulf translated into modern
rhymes, by H. W. Lumsden, 1881; Beowulf, Tr. by Benja-
min Thorpe, Literal translation, notes and glossary, 1875.

## THE STORY OF BEOWULF.

A MIGHTY man was Scyld, ruler of the Gar-Danes. From far across the whale-path men paid him tribute and bore witness to his power. Beowulf was his son, a youth endowed with glory, whose fame spread far and wide through all the Danish land.

When the time came for Scyld to die he ordered his thanes to prepare the ring-stemmed ship, laden with treasures, battle-weed, and swords, and place him in the death-chamber. Laden with his people's gifts, and sailing under a golden banner, he passed from sight, none knew whither.

After him ruled Beowulf, and after him Healfdene, — brave warriors and kind monarchs. When, after Healfdene's death, his son Hrothgar succeeded him, his fame in war inclined all his kinsmen towards him, and he, too, became a mighty monarch.

To the mind of Hrothgar it came to build a lordly mead-hall where he and his men could find pleasure in feasting, drinking mead, and hearing the songs of the minstrels. Heorot it was called, and when its high spires rose glistening in the air, all hailed it with delight.

But, alas ! The joy in hall, the melody of the harp, and the shouts of the warriors penetrated to the dismal fen where lay concealed the monster Grendel, descendant of sin-cursed Cain. At night came Grendel to the hall, found sleeping the troop of warriors, and bore away in his foul hands thirty of the honored thanes. Great was the sorrow in Heorot when in the morning twilight the deed of Grendel became known.

For twelve long winters did this sorrow continue ; for so long a time was Hrothgar plunged in grief ; for so many years did this beautiful mead-hall, destined for joyful things, stand idle.

While thus the grief-stricken lord of the Scyldings brooded over his wrongs, and the people besought their idols vainly for aid, the tidings of Grendel's ravages were conveyed to the court of the Gothic king, Higelac, and thus reached the ears of a highborn thane, Beowulf. A strong man was he, his grasp equal to that of thirty men.

Straightway commanded he a goodly ship to be made ready, chose fifteen of his bravest Goths, and swiftly they sailed over the swan-path to the great headlands and bright sea-cliffs of the Scyldings.

High on the promontory stood the guard of Hrothgar. "What men be ye who hither come?" cried he. "Not foes, surely. Ye know no pass word, yet surely ye come on no evil errand. Ne'er saw I a greater lord than he who leads the band. Who are ye?"

"Higelac's man am I," answered the leader. "Ecgtheow, my sire; my name, Beowulf. Lead me, I pray thee, to thy lord, for I have come over seas to free him forever from his secret foe, and to lift the cloud that hangs over the stately mead-hall."

Over the stone-paved streets the warder led the warriors, their armor clanking, their boar-tipped helmets sparkling, to the goodly hall, Heorot. There were they warmly welcomed, for Hrothgar had known Beowulf's sire; the fame of the young man's strength had also reached him, and he trusted that in his strong grasp Grendel should die.

All took their seats on the mead-benches, and a thane passed from warrior to warrior, bearing the chased wine-cup. Sweet was the minstrel's song, and the warriors were happy in Heorot.

But Hunferd sat at the banquet, and envious of Beowulf's fame, taunted him with his swimming match with Breca. "Seven days and nights thou didst swim with Breca; but he was stronger, and he won. Worse will befall thee, if thou dar'st this night await Grendel!"

"Easy it is to brag of Breca's deeds when drunk with beer, friend Hunferd!" replied Beowulf. "Seven days and nights I swam through the sea-water, slaying the monsters of the deep. Rough was the wave, terrible were the water beasts; but I reached the Finnish land. Wert thou as brave as thou claim'st to be, Grendel would ne'er have wrought such havoc in thy monarch's land."

Decked with gold, Queen Waltheow passed through the hall, greeted the warriors, and proffered the mead-cup to Beowulf, thanking God that she had found an earl who would deliver them from their enemy.

When dusky night fell over Heorot, the king uprose. "To no other man have I ever entrusted this hall of gold. Have now and keep it! Great reward shall be thine if thou come forth alive!"

The knights left in the lordly hall composed themselves for slumber, all save Beowulf, who, unarmed, awaited the coming of Grendel.

He came, with wrathful step and eyes aflame, bursting open the iron bolts of the great door, and laughing at the goodly array of men sleeping before him. On one he laid hands and drank his blood; then he clutched the watchful Beowulf.

Ne'er had he found a foe like this! Fearful, he turned to flee to his home in the fen, but the grip of Beowulf forbade flight. Strongly was Heorot builded, but many a gilded mead-bench was torn from the walls as the two combated within the hall. The sword blade was of no avail, and him must Beowulf bring to death by the strength of his grip alone. At last, with a scream that struck terror to every Dane's heart, the monster sprang from Beowulf and fled, leaving in the warrior's grasp his arm and shoulder. Great was Beowulf's joy, for he knew that the wound meant death.

When the king and queen came forth in the morning with their nobles and maids, and saw the grisly arm of Grendel fastened upon the roof of Heorot, they gave themselves up to rejoicing. Gifts were heaped upon Beowulf, — a golden crest, a banner bright, a great and goodly sword and helm and corselet, eight steeds with headstalls ornamented with gold plate, and a richly decorated saddle. Nor were his comrades forgotten, but to each were given rich gifts.

When the mead-hall had been cleansed and refitted, they gathered therein and listened to the song of the bard who

told how Healfdene's knight, Hnæf, smote Finn.  The song
over, the queen, crowned with gold, gave gifts to Beowulf,
the liberator from the horrors of Grendel, — two armlets, a
necklace, raiment, and rings.  When the drinking and feasting were over, the king and Beowulf withdrew, leaving many
earls to keep the hall.  Little guessed they that one of them
was that night doomed to die !

The haunt of Grendel was a mile-wide mere.  Around it
were wolf-haunted cliffs, windy promontories, mist-covered
mountains.  Close around the mere hung the woods, shroud-
ing the water, which, horrible sight, was each night covered
with fire.  It was a place accursed ; near it no man might
dwell ; the deer that plunged therein straightway died.

In a palace under the mere dwelt Grendel and his mother ;
she, a foul sprite, whom the peasants had sometimes seen
walking with her son over the meadows.  From her dwelling-
place she now came forth to avenge the death of her son,
and snatched away from the group of sleeping Ring-Danes
the good Æschere, dearest of all his thanes to Hrothgar.

Loud was Hrothgar's wailing when at morning Beowulf
came forth from his bower.

" Sorrow not, O wise man," spake Beowulf.  " I fear not.
I will seek out this monster and destroy her.  If I come not
back it will at least be better than to have lost my glory.
She can never hide from me.  I ween that I will this day
rid thee of thine enemy."

Accompanied by Hrothgar, some of the Ring-Danes and
his Goths, Beowulf sought the dismal mere, on whose brink
they found the head of Æschere.  Among the bloody waves
swam horrible shapes, Nicors and sea-drakes, that fled at a
blast of the war-horn.  Beowulf slew one of the monsters,
and while his companions were marvelling at the grisly form,
he prepared himself for the combat.  His breast was guarded
by a coat of mail woven most cunningly ; upon his head
shone the gold-adorned helmet, and in his hand was Hunferd's sword, Hrunting, made of iron steeped in twigs of
bitter poison, annealed in battle blood, and fearful to every
foe.

"Hearken unto me, O Hrothgar," cried the hero. "If I return not, treat well my comrades and send my gifts to Higelac, that he may see the deed I have accomplished, and the generous ring-lord I have gained among the Scyldings." And without waiting for a reply, he leaped into the waves and was lost to sight.

There was the monster waiting for him; and catching him in her grip, which bruised him not because of his strong mail-coat, she dragged him to her cave, in whose lighted hall he could see the horrible features of the woman of the mere. Strong was Hrunting, but of no avail was its mighty blade against her. Soon he threw it down, and gripped her, reckless of peril. Once he threw her on the ground, but the second time she threw him, and drew her glaive to pierce his breast. Strong was the linked mail, and Beowulf was safe. Then his quick eye lighted on a sword, — a magic, giant sword; few men could wield it. Quickly he grasped it, and smote the neck of the sea-woman. Broken were the bone-rings, and down she fell dead. Then Ecgtheow's son looked around the hall and saw the body of the dead Grendel. Thirsting to take his revenge, he smote him with his sword. Off flew the head; but when the red drops of blood touched the magic blade it melted, leaving but the massive golden hilt in the hands of the hero. Beowulf took no treasure from the cave, but rose through the waves, carrying only the head of the monster and the hilt of the sword.

When Hrothgar and his men saw the mere red and boiling with blood they deemed that Beowulf was dead, and departed to their citadel. Sorrowful sat the comrades of Beowulf, waiting and hoping against hope for his reappearance. Up sprang they when they saw him, joyfully greeted him, relieved him of his bloody armor, and conducted him to Hrothgar, bearing — a heavy task — the head of Grendel.

When Hrothgar saw the hideous head and the mighty sword-hilt, whose history he read from its Runic inscriptions, he hailed Beowulf with joy, and proclaimed him mightiest of men. "But ever temper thy might with wisdom," advised the king, "that thou suffer not the end of

Heremod, or be punished as I have been, in this my spacious mead-hall."

After a night's rest, Beowulf prepared to return to his
country.  Returning Hrunting to Hunferd, he praised the
sword, saying nothing of its failure in the fight.  Then to
Hrothgar: " Farewell.  If e'er thou art harried by foes, but
let me know, — a thousand fighting men I 'll bring.  Higelac,
well I know, will urge me on to honor thee.  If e'er thy son
seeks Gothic halls, I will intercede and win friends for him."

The old king, weeping, bade Beowulf farewell.  " Peace
be forever between the Goths and the Gar-Danes ; in common their treasures !  May gifts be interchanged between
them ! "

The bark was filled with the gifts heaped upon Beowulf
and his men ; and the warder, who had hailed them so
proudly at their coming, now bade them an affectionate
farewell.  Over the swan-path sailed they, and soon reached
the Gothic coast, and landed their treasures.

Then went Beowulf before Higelac and told him of his
adventures.  Higelac was a mighty king ; lofty his house
and hall, and fair and gentle was his wife, Hygd.  To him,
after he had related his adventures, Beowulf presented the
boar-head crest, the battle-mail and sword, four of the
steeds, and much treasure, and upon the wise and modest
Hygd bestowed he the wondrous necklace given him by
Waltheow.  So should a good thane ever do !

There had been a time when Beowulf was accounted a
sluggish knight, but now the land rang with his glory.

When Higelac died and Hardred was slain, Beowulf succeeded to the throne, and for fifty years ruled the people
gloriously.

At this time a great fire-drake cherished a vast hoard in a
cave on a high cliff, difficult of access, and known to few
men.  Thither one day fled a thrall from his master's wrath,
and saw the hoard buried by some weary warrior, and now
guarded by the dragon.  While the drake slept, the thrall
crept in and stole a cup as a peace-offering to his master.

When the drake awoke, he scented the foot-prints of the

foe, and discovered his loss. When even was come, he hastened to wreak his revenge on the people, spewing out flames of fire, and laying waste the land.

Far and near were the lands of the Goths devastated, and ere long, tidings were borne to Beowulf that his great hall, his gift seat, was destroyed by fire. Saddened, and fearing that he had in some way angered God, he turned his mind to vengeance, and girded on his armor. A stout shield of iron he took, knowing that the dragon's fiery breath would melt the wood, and with foreboding of his fate, bade farewell to his hearth-mates. "Many times have I battled, great deeds have I done with sword and with hand-grip; now must I go forth and battle with hand and sword against the hoard-keeper."

Commanding the men who had accompanied him to remain upon the hillside, leaving him to combat with the dragon alone, Beowulf went proudly forward, shouting his battle-cry. Out rushed the dragon, full of deadly hate. His fiery breath was stronger than the king had deemed it. Stroke upon stroke he gave his enemy, who continued to cast forth his death-fire, so that Beowulf stood girt with flames.

From afar, among the watching thanes, Wiglaf saw his monarch's peril. "Comrades," he cried, "do you remember our promises to our king? Was it for this he stirred us up to glorious deeds? Was it for this he heaped gifts upon us? Let us go to his rescue. It is not right that we should see our lord fall, and bear away our shields untouched!"

Rushing forward, he cried, "Beowulf, here am I! Now strike for thy life! Thou hast said that thou never wouldst let thy fame depart from thee!"

Again the dragon came forth; again it enveloped its foeman in flames. The linden shield of Wiglaf burned in his hands, and he sought shelter behind Beowulf's shield of iron. Again and again Wiglaf smote the monster, and when the flames burnt low, Beowulf seized his dirk and pierced the dragon so that he fell dead.

The dragon lay dead, but Beowulf felt the poison in his

wounds and knew that he had not long to live. He commanded Wiglaf to bring forth the treasure that he might gaze upon the hoard, — jewel work and twisted gold, — that he had wrested from the fire-drake.

The den was filled with rings of gold, cups, banners, jewels, dishes, and the arms of the old owner of the treasure. All these did Wiglaf bear forth to his lord, who surveyed them, and uttered thanks to his Maker, that he could win such a treasure. Then, turning to Wiglaf, he said, " Now I die. Build for me upon the lofty shore a bright mound that shall ever remind my people of me. Far in the distance their ships shall descry it, and they shall call it Beowulf's mound." Then, giving his arms to Wiglaf, he bade him enjoy them. " Thou art the last of our race. All save us, fate-driven, are gone to doom. Thither go I too."

Bitterly did Wiglaf denounce his comrades when he saw them steal from their hiding-places. " Well may it be said of you that he who gave you your arms threw them away. No thanks deserve ye for the slaughter of the dragon! I did my little, but it was not in my power to save my kinsman. Too few helpers stood about him! Now shall your kin be wanting in gifts. Void are ye of land-rights! Better is it for an earl to die than to live with a blasted name! "

Sorrowful were the people when they heard of the death of Beowulf. Full well they knew with what joy the tidings would be hailed by their enemies, who would hasten to harry the land, now that their great leader was gone. The Frisians, the Merovingians, the Franks, the Swedes, — all had their grievances, which they would hasten to wreak on the Goths when they learned that the dreaded king was gone. Dreary would be the land of the Goths; on its battle-fields the wolves would batten; the ravens would call to the eagles as they feasted on the slain.

Straight to the Eagle's Nest went the band, and found their dead monarch; there, too, lay the loathsome fire-drake, full fifty feet long, and between them the great hoard, rust-eaten from long dwelling in the earth. Ever had that hoard brought ill with it.

Down from the cliff they thrust the dragon into the deep, and carried their chief to Hronésness. There they built a lofty pile, decked it with his armor, and burned thereon the body of their glorious ruler. According to his wish, they reared on the cliff a broad, high barrow, surrounded it with a wall, and laid within it the treasure. There yet it lies, of little worth to men!

Then around the barrow rode twelve of the bravest, boldest nobles, mourning their king, singing his praises, chanting a dirge, telling of his glorious deeds, while over the broad land the Gothic folk lamented the death of their tender prince, their noble king, Beowulf.


## SELECTION FROM BEOWULF.

### GRENDEL'S MOTHER.

THERE was great rejoicing in Heorot when Beowulf slew Grendel, and at night the earls again slept in the hall as they had not dared to do since the coming of the fiend. But Grendel's mother came to avenge her son's death and slew Æschere, a favorite liegeman of Hrothgar's. In the morning, Beowulf, who had slept in another part of the palace, was sent for and greeted Hrothgar, unaware of his loss.

> Hrothgar rejoined, helm of the Scyldings:
> "Ask not of joyance! Grief is renewed to
> The folk of the Danemen. Dead is Æschere,
> Yrmenlaf's brother, older than he,
> My true-hearted counsellor, trusty adviser,
> Shoulder-companion, when fighting in battle
> Our heads we protected, when troopers were clashing,
> And heroes were dashing; such an earl should be ever,
> An erst-worthy atheling, as Æschere proved him.
> The flickering death-spirit became in Heorot
> His hand-to-hand murderer; I cannot tell whither
> The cruel one turned, in the carcass exulting,
> By cramming discovered. The quarrel she wreaked then,
> The last night igone Grendel thou killedst
> In grewsomest manner, with grim-holding clutches,
> Since too long he had lessened my liege-troop and wasted
> My folk-men so foully. He fell in the battle
> With forfeit of life, and another has followed,
> A mighty crime-worker, her kinsman avenging,

And henceforth hath 'stablished her hatred unyielding,
As it well may appear to many a liegeman,
Who mourneth in spirit the treasure-bestower,
Her heavy heart-sorrow; the hand is now lifeless
Which availed you in every wish that you cherished.
Land-people heard I, liegemen, this saying,
Dwellers in halls, they had seen very often
A pair of such mighty march-striding creatures,
Far-dwelling spirits, holding the moorlands:
One of them wore, as well they might notice,
The image of woman, the other one wretched
In guise of a man wandered in exile,
Except that he was huger than any of earthmen;
Earth-dwelling people entitled him Grendel
In days of yore; they knew not their father,
Whe'r ill-going spirits any were borne him
Ever before.   They guard the wolf-coverts,
Lands inaccessible, wind-beaten nesses,
Fearfullest fen-deeps, where a flood from the mountains
'Neath mists of the nesses netherward rattles,
The stream under earth: not far is it henceward
Measured by mile-lengths that the mere-water standeth,
Which forests hang over, with frost-whiting covered,
A firm-rooted forest, the floods overshadow.
There ever at night one an ill-meaning portent
A fire-flood may see; 'mong children of men
None liveth so wise that wot of the bottom;
Though harassed by hounds the heath-stepper seek for,
Fly to the forest, firm-antlered he-deer,
Spurred from afar, his spirit he yieldeth,
His life on the shore, ere in he will venture
To cover his head.   Uncanny the place is:
Thence upward ascendeth the surging of waters,
Wan to the welkin, when the wind is stirring
The weathers unpleasing, till the air groweth gloomy,
And the heavens lower.   Now is help to be gotten
From thee and thee only!   The abode thou know'st not,
The dangerous place where thou 'rt able to meet with
The sin-laden hero: seek if thou darest!
For the feud I will fully fee thee with money,
With old-time treasure, as erstwhile I did thee,
With well-twisted jewels, if away thou shalt get thee."

Beowulf answered, Ecgtheow's son:
"Grieve not, O wise one! for each it is better,
His friend to avenge than with vehemence wail him;
Each of us must the end-day abide of
His earthly existence; who is able accomplish
Glory ere death!   To battle-thane noble
Lifeless lying, 't is at last most fitting.

Arise, O king, quick let us hasten
To look at the footprint of the kinsman of Grendel!
I promise thee this now: to his place he 'll escape not,
To embrace of the earth, nor to mountainous forest,
Nor to depths of the ocean, wherever he wanders.
Practice thou now patient endurance
Of each of thy sorrows, as I hope for thee soothly!"
Then up sprang the old one, the All-Wielder thanked he,
Ruler Almighty, that the man had outspoken.
Then for Hrothgar a war-horse was decked with a bridle,
Curly-maned courser. The clever folk-leader
Stately proceeded: stepped then an earl-troop
Of linden-wood bearers. Her foot-prints were seen then
Widely in wood-paths, her way o'er the bottoms,
Where she far-away fared o'er fen-country murky,
Bore away breathless the best of retainers
Who pondered with Hrothgar the welfare of country.
The son of the athelings then went o'er the stony,
Declivitous cliffs, the close-covered passes,
Narrow passages, paths unfrequented,
Nesses abrupt, nicker-haunts many;
One of a few of wise-mooded heroes,
He onward advanced to view the surroundings,
Till he found unawares woods of the mountain
O'er hoar-stones hanging, holt-wood unjoyful;
The water stood under, welling and gory.
'T was irksome in spirit to all of the Danemen,
Friends of the Scyldings, to many a liegeman
Sad to be suffered, a sorrow unlittle
To each of the earlmen, when to Æschere's head they
Came on the cliff. The current was seething
With blood and with gore (the troopers gazed on it).
The horn anon sang the battle-song ready.
The troop were all seated; they saw 'long the water then
Many a serpent, mere-dragons wondrous
Trying the waters, nickers a-lying
On the cliffs of the nesses, which at noonday full often
Go on the sea-deeps their sorrowful journey,
Wild-beasts and worm-kind; away then they hastened
Hot-mooded, hateful, they heard the great clamor,
The war-trumpet winding. One did the Geat-prince
Sunder from earth-joys, with arrow from bowstring,
From his sea-struggle tore him, that the trusty war-missile
Pierced to his vitals; he proved in the currents
Less doughty at swimming whom death had off-carried.
Soon in the waters the wonderful swimmer
Was straitened most sorely and pulled to the cliff-edge:
The liegemen then looked on the loath-fashioned stranger.
Beowulf donned then his battle-equipments,
Cared little for life; inlaid and most ample,
The hand-woven corselet which could cover his body,

Must the wave-deeps explore, that war might be powerless
To harm the great hero, and the hating one's grasp might
Not peril his safety ; his head was protected
By the light-flashing helmet that should mix with the bottoms,
Trying the eddies, treasure-emblazoned,
Encircled with jewels, as in seasons long past
The weapon-smith worked it, wondrously made it,
With swine-bodies fashioned it, that thenceforward no longer
Brand might bite it, and battle-sword hurt it.
And that was not least of helpers in prowess
That Hrothgar's spokesman had lent him when straitened ;
And the hilted hand-sword was Hrunting entitled,
Old and most excellent 'mong all of the treasures ;
Its blade was of iron, blotted with poison,
Hardened with gore ; it failed not in battle
Any hero under heaven in hand who it brandished,
Who ventured to take the terrible journeys,
The battle-field sought ; not the earliest occasion
That deeds of daring 't was destined to 'complish.
Ecglaf's kinsman minded not soothly,
Exulting in strength, what erst he had spoken
Drunken with wine, when the weapon he lent to
A sword-hero bolder ; himself did not venture
'Neath the strife of the currents his life to endanger,
To fame-deeds perform ; there he forfeited glory,
Repute for his strength.    Not so with the other
When he, clad in his corselet, had equipped him for battle.

Beowulf spoke, Ecgtheow's son :
" Recall now, oh, famous kinsman of Healfdene,
Prince very prudent, now to part I am ready,
Gold-friend of earl-men, what erst we agreed on,
Should I lay down my life in lending thee assistance,
When my earth-joys were over, thou wouldst evermore serve me
In stead of a father ; my faithful thanemen,
My trusty retainers, protect thou and care for,
Fall I in battle : and, Hrothgar belovèd,
Send unto Higelac the high-valued jewels
Thou to me hast allotted.    The lord of the Geatmen
May perceive from the gold, the Hrethling may see it
When he looks on the jewels, that a gem-giver found I
Good over-measure, enjoyed him while able.
And the ancient heirloom Unferth permit thou,
The famed one to have, the heavy-sword splendid,
The hard-edged weapon ; with Hrunting to aid me,
I shall gain me glory, or grim death shall take me."
The atheling of Geatmen uttered these words and
Heroic did hasten, not any rejoinder
Was willing to wait for ; the wave-current swallowed
The doughty-in-battle.    Then a day's-length elapsed ere
He was able to see the sea at its bottom.

Early she found then who fifty of winters
The course of the currents kept in her fury,
Grisly and greedy, that the grim one's dominion
Some one of men from above was exploring.
Forth did she grab them, grappled the warrior
With horrible clutches; yet no sooner she injured
His body unscathèd: the burnie out-guarded,
That she proved but powerless to pierce through the armor,
The limb-mail locked, with loath-grabbing fingers.
The sea-wolf bare then, when bottomward came she,
The ring-prince homeward, that he after was powerless.
(He had daring to do it) to deal with his weapons,
But many a mere-beast tormented him swimming,
Flood-beasts no few with fierce-biting tusks did
Break through his burnie, the brave one pursued they.
The earl then discovered he was down in some cavern
Where no water whatever anywise harmed him,
And the clutch of the current could not come anear him,
Since the roofed-hall prevented; brightness a-gleaming
Fire-light he saw, flashing, resplendent.
The good one saw then the sea-bottom's monster,
The mighty mere-woman; he made a great onset
With weapon-of-battle, his hand not desisted
From striking, that war-blade struck on her head then
A battle-song greedy. The stranger perceived then
The sword would not bite, her life would not injure,
But the falchion failed the folk-prince when straitened:
Erst had it often onsets encountered,
Oft cloven the helmet, the fated one's armor:
'T was the first time that ever the excellent jewel
Had failed of its fame. Firm-mooded after,
Not heedless of valor, but mindful of glory,
Was Higelac's kinsman; the hero-chief angry
Cast then his carved-sword covered with jewels
That it lay on earth, hard and steel-pointed;
He hoped in his strength, his hand-grapple sturdy.
So any must act whenever he thinketh
To gain him in battle glory unending,
And is reckless of living. The lord of the War-Geats
(He shrank not from battle) seized by the shoulder
The mother of Grendel; then mighty in struggle
Swung he his enemy, since his anger was kindled,
That she fell to the floor. With furious grapple
She gave him requital early thereafter,
And stretched out to grab him; the strongest of warriors
Faint-mooded stumbled, till he fell in his traces,
Foot-going champion. Then she sat on the hall-guest
And wielded her war-knife wide-bladed, flashing.
For her son would take vengeance, her one only bairn.
His breast-armor woven bode on his shoulder;
It guarded his life, the entrance defended

'Gainst sword-point and edges.  Ecgtheow's son there
Had fatally journeyed, champion of Geatmen,
In the arms of the ocean, had the armor not given,
Close-woven corselet, comfort and succor,
And had God most holy not awarded the victory,
All-knowing Lord; easily did heaven's
Ruler most righteous arrange it with justice;
Uprose he erect ready for battle.

Then he saw 'mid the war-gems a weapon of victory,
An ancient giant-sword, of edges a-doughty,
Glory of warriors: of weapons 't was choicest,
Only 't was larger than any man else was
Able to bear in the battle-encounter,
The good and splendid work of the giants.
He grasped then the sword-hilt, knight of the Scyldings,
Bold and battle-grim, brandished his ring-sword,
Hopeless of living, hotly he smote her,
That the fiend-woman's neck firmly it grappled,
Broke through her bone-joints, the bill fully pierced her
Fate-cursèd body, she fell to the ground then :
The hand-sword was bloody, the hero exulted.
The brand was brilliant, brightly it glimmered,
Just as from heaven gemlike shineth
The torch of the firmament.  He glanced 'long the building,
And turned by the wall then, Higelac's vassal
Raging and wrathful raised his battle-sword
Strong by the handle.  The edge was not useless
To the hero-in-battle, but he speedily wished to
Give Grendel requital for the many assaults he
Had worked on the West-Danes not once, but often,
When he slew in slumber the subjects of Hrothgar,
Swallowed down fifteen sleeping retainers
Of the folk of the Danemen, and fully as many
Carried away, a horrible prey.
He gave him requital, grim-raging champion,
When he saw on his rest-place weary of conflict
Grendel lying, of life-joys bereavèd,
As the battle at Heorot erstwhile had scathed him ;
His body far bounded, a blow when he suffered,
Death having seized him, sword-smiting heavy,
And he cut off his head then.  Early this noticed
The clever carles who as comrades of Hrothgar
Gazed on the sea-deeps, that the surging wave-currents
Were mightily mingled, the mere-flood was gory :
Of the good one the gray-haired together held converse,
The hoary of head, that they hoped not to see again
The atheling ever, that exulting in victory
He 'd return there to visit the distinguished folk-ruler :
Then many concluded the mere-wolf had killed him.
The ninth hour came then.  From the ness-edge departed

The bold-mooded Scyldings; the gold-friend of heroes
Homeward betook him. The strangers sat down then
Soul-sick, sorrowful, the sea-waves regarding:
They wished and yet weened not their well-loved friend-lord
To see any more. The sword-blade began then,
The blood having touched it, contracting and shrivelling
With battle-icicles; 't was a wonderful marvel
That it melted entirely, likest to ice when
The Father unbindeth the bond of the frost and
Unwindeth the wave-bands, He who wieldeth dominion
Of time and of tides: a truth-firm Creator.
Nor took he of jewels more in the dwelling,
Lord of the Weders, though they lay all around him,
Than the head and the handle handsome with jewels;
The brand early melted, burnt was the weapon:
So hot was the blood, the strange-spirit poisonous
That in it did perish. He early swam off then
Who had bided in combat the carnage of haters,
Went up through the ocean; the eddies were cleansèd,
The spacious expanses, when the spirit from farland
His life put aside and this short-lived existence.
The seamen's defender came swimming to land then
Doughty of spirit, rejoiced in his sea-gift,
The bulky burden which he bore in his keeping.
The excellent vassals advanced then to meet him,
To God they were grateful, were glad in their chieftain,
That to see him safe and sound was granted them.
From the high-minded hero, then, helmet and burnie
Were speedily loosened: the ocean was putrid,
The water 'neath welkin weltered with gore.
Forth did they fare, then, their footsteps retracing,
Merry and mirthful, measured the earth-way,
To highway familiar: men very daring
Bare then the head from the sea-cliff, burdening
Each of the earlmen, excellent-valiant.
Four of them had to carry with labor
The head of Grendel to the high towering gold-hall
Upstuck on the spear, till fourteen most-valiant
And battle-brave Geatmen came there going
Straight to the palace: the prince of the people
Measured the mead-ways, their mood-brave companion,
The atheling of earlmen entered the building,
Deed-valiant man, adorned with distinction,
Doughty shield-warrior, to address King Hrothgar:
Then hung by the hair, the head of Grendel
Was borne to the building, where beer-thanes were drinking,
Loth before earlmen and eke 'fore the lady:
The warriors beheld then a wonderful sight.

*J. L. Hall's Translation, Parts XXI.-XXIV.*

# THE NIBELUNGEN LIED.

THE Nibelungen Lied, or Song of the Nibelungen, was written about the beginning of the thirteenth century, though the events it chronicles belong to the sixth or seventh century. The manuscript poem was discovered about the middle of the eighteenth century.

Lachmann asserts that the Nibelungen Lied consists of twenty songs of various dates and authorship; other scholars, while agreeing that it is the work of a single author, ascribe it variously to Conrad von Kurenburger, Wolfram von Eschenbach, Heinrich von Ofterdingen, and Walther von der Vogelweide.

Whoever was its author, he was only a compiler of legends that were the property of the people for centuries, and are found in many other of the popular German epics of the Middle Ages.

The poem consists of thirty-nine adventures, containing two thousand four hundred and fifty-nine stanzas of four lines each. The action covers thirty years. It is based on material obtained from four sources: (1) The Frankish saga-cycle, whose hero is Siegfried; (2) the saga-cycle of Burgundy, whose heroes are Günther, king of Worms, and his two brothers; (3) the Ostrogothic saga-cycle, whose hero is Dietrich of Bern; and (4) the saga-cycle of Etzel, king of the Huns, with his allies and vassals.

Dietrich of Bern is supposed to be Theodoric of Italy, in exile at the Hunnish court. Etzel is Attila the Hun, and Günther, Gunducarius, king of the Burgundians, who was destroyed by the Huns with his followers in the year 436.

The Nibelungen Lied very much resembles the Iliad, not only in the uncertainty of its origin and the impersonality of its author, but also in its objectivity, its realism, the primitive passions of its heroes, and the wondrous acts of valor performed by them. It contains many passages of wonderful beauty, and gives a striking picture of the social customs and the religious belief of the time.

BIBLIOGRAPHY AND CRITICISM, THE NIBELUNGEN LIED. Mary Elizabeth Burt's Story of the German Iliad, 1892 ; Thomas Carlyle's Nibelungen Lied (see his Miscellaneous Essays, 1869, vol. iii., pp. 111–162) ; Sir G. W. Cox and E. H. Jones's Nibelungen Lied (see their Tales of the Teutonic Lands, 1872, pp. 79–132) ; G. T. Dippold's Nibelungenlied (see his Great Epics of Mediæval Germany, 1882, pp. 1–117) ; William T. Dobson's Nibelungenlied Epitomized (see his Classic Poets, 1878) ; Auber Forestier's Echoes from Mistland, or the Nibelungen Lay Revealed, Tr. by A. A. Woodward, 1877 ; Joseph Gostwick's and Robert Harrison's Nibelungenlied (see their Outlines of German Literature, n. d., pp. 16–24) ; Hugh Reginald Haweis's Nibelungenlied (see his Musical Memories, 1887, pp. 225–250) ; Frederick Henry Hedge's Nibelungenlied (see his Hours with the German Classics, 1887, pp. 25–55) ; James K. Hosmer's Nibelungen Lied (see his Short History of German Literature, 1891, pp. 23–77) ; J. P. Jackson's Ring of the Nibelung, Cosmopolitan, 1888, vol. vi. pp. 415– 433 ; Henry W. Longfellow's Nibelungenlied (see his Poets and Poetry of Europe, new ed., enlarged, 1882, pp. 217–227) ; J. M. F. Ludlow's Lay and Lament of the Niblungs (see his Popular Epics of the Middle Ages, 1865, pp. 105–183) ; E. Magnusson and William Morris's Völsunga Saga, story of the Völsungs and Niblungs, 1870 ; William Morris's Story of Sigurd the Volsung and the Fall of the Niblungs, 1887 ; F. Max Müller's Das Nibelungenlied (see his German Classics, new ed., 1893, vol. i., pp. 112– 136) ; Ernst Raupach's Nibelungen Treasure, a tragedy from the German with remarks, 1847 ; A. M. Richey's Teutonic and the Celtic Epic, Fraser's Magazine, 1874, vol. lxxxix., pp. 336–354 ; Wilhelm Scherer's Nibelungenlied (see his History of German Literature, 1893, vol. i., pp. 101–115) ; Leda M. Schoonamaker's Nibelungen Lied, Harper's Magazine, 1877, vol. lv., pp. 38-51 ; Bayard Taylor's Nibelungen Lied (see his Studies in German Literature, 1893, pp. 101–134) ; Wilhelm Wagner's Nibelungenlied (see his Epics and Romances of the Middle Ages, 1883, pp. 229–306) ; Henry Weber's The Song of the Nibelungen (see Weber and Jamieson, Illustrations of Northern Antiquities, 1874, pp. 167–213).

STANDARD ENGLISH TRANSLATIONS, THE NIBELUNGEN. The Nibelungen Lied, Tr. by Alfred G. Foster Barham, 1887 ; The Lay of the Nibelungers, Tr. into English text after Lachman's text by Jonathan Birch, ed. 3, 1887 ; The Nibelungenlied, Tr. by Joseph Gostwick (see his Spirit of German Poetry, 1843) ; The Fall of the Nibelungers, Tr. by William Nanson Lettsom, ed. 2, 1874.

## THE STORY OF THE NIBELUNGEN LIED.

IN the beautiful city of Worms, in Burgundy, dwelt the maiden Kriemhild, surpassing all others in beauty. Her father, long since dead, was Dancrat ; her mother, Uta, and her three brothers, — Günther, Gernot, and Giselher, — puissant princes whose pride it was to guard their lovely sister. Among the noble lords their liegemen were Hagan of Trony, Dankwart, his brother, Ortwine of Metz, Eckewart, Gary, Folker, Rumolt the steward, Sindolt the butler, and Humolt the chamberlain.

The peace of the beautiful Kriemhild was one night disturbed by a dream, in which she saw a young falcon that she had long reared with tender care torn to pieces by two fierce eagles. When she confided this dream to her mother, the wise Uta declared that it meant that she would one day wed a fair prince threatened with a dreadful doom.

" Then I will never wed ! " cried Kriemhild. " Better to forego the bliss thou tellest me attends only the wedded state than to taste the anguish foretold by my dream." Alas ! little could she guess of what the future held in store for her.

In the wide country of the Netherlands, in the city of Xanten, dwelt the great prince Siegmund and his wife Sieglind. Their kingdom was wide, their wealth great, but nothing gave them so much happiness as the renown of their glorious son Siegfried. Such mighty deeds of valor had he performed that his fame was already world-wide, though he was but a youth. To Xanten the fame of the peerless princess Kriemhild had penetrated, and the young prince declared to his parents his intention of seeking her out in Burgundy, and wooing her for his wife. All entreaties were in vain ; with but twelve companions, each fitted out with the most gorgeous vestments, by the care of the queen mother, the haughty prince advanced into Burgundy.

King Günther, surprised at the sight of the splendidly attired strangers, called one after another of his knights to inform him who they were. None knew, until Hagan was at last called because he was familiar with the warriors of every land. He did not know them. "But," said he, "though I have never set eyes on him, I'll wager that is the noble Siegfried, the mighty warrior who slew the Nibelungers. Once, so I have heard the story, when he was riding alone, he saw the two kings Nibelung and Shilbung dividing the treasure of the Niblungs. They had just brought it out from the cavern where it was guarded by the dwarf Albric, and they called Siegfried to come and divide it for them. The task was so great that he did not finish it, and when the angry kings set upon him he slew them both, their giant champions and chiefs, and then overcame the dwarf Albric, and possessed himself of his wondrous cloud-cloak. So he is now lord of the Nibelungers and owner of the mighty treasure. Not only this, my king; he once slew a poison-spitting dragon and bathed in its blood, so that his skin is invulnerable. Treat the young prince with respect. It would be ill-advised to arouse his hatred."

While the king and his counsellors were admiring his haughty bearing, Siegfried and his followers advanced to the hall and were fittingly welcomed. Siegfried haughtily declared that he had come to learn if Günther's renown for knighthood was correct, and wished to fight with him, with their respective kingdoms as stakes. Günther had no desire to fight with such a doughty warrior, and he hastened to soothe Siegfried's wrath with gentle words, inviting him to remain as his guest.

So happy was Siegfried in the tourneys and games enjoyed by Günther's court, that he remained in Worms for a year, and in all that time never set eyes on Kriemhild. How enraptured would he have been had he known that the gentle maiden watched for him daily at her lattice, and came to long for a glimpse of the handsome stranger!

At the end of the year tidings were brought to Worms that the Saxons, led by King Lüdeger, and Lüdegast, king of Denmark, were marching against Burgundy. The Burgundians were terrified at the news; but Siegfried, delighted at the thought of war, begged Günther to give him but a thousand Burgundians, in addition to the twelve comrades he had brought with him, and he would pledge himself to defeat, unaided, the presumptuous enemy. Many were the camps of the foe; full forty thousand were there mustered out to fight, but Siegfried quickly scattered them, slew many thousands, and took the two kings prisoners.

How joyful the melancholy Kriemhild became when the messenger bore to her the glad tidings! Ruddy gold and costly garments he gained for his good news.

On Siegfried's return he first met and loved Kriemhild. More blooming than May, sweeter than summer's pride, she stood by the gallant warrior, who dared not yet to woo her. The twelve days of revel in celebration of the victory were one long dream of bliss to the happy lovers.

While Siegfried was still lingering at Günther's court, tidings were brought thither of the beauty, prowess, and great strength of Brunhild, Queen of Issland, and Günther determined to go thither and woo her. Siegfried implored him not to go.

"Thou knowest not what thou must undertake," he said. "Thou must take part in her contests, throw the javelin, throw the stone and jump after it, and if thou fail in even one of these three games thou must lose thy life and that of thy companions."

When Siegfried found that he could not move Günther, he promised to go with him and assist him, on condition that on their return Günther would give him the beautiful Kriemhild for his wife.

Attired in the most splendid raiment, prepared by the willing fingers of Kriemhild and her maids, Günther, with only three companions, Siegfried, Hagan, and Dankwart, set forth to Issland. Siegfried requested his companions to inform Brunhild that he was Günther's man; and when she welcomed him first, he himself told her to speak first to his master.

The little party was greatly impressed with the splendor of Brunhild's three turreted palaces, and with the beauty and prodigious strength of the queen. When they saw her huge golden shield, steel-studded, beneath whose weight four chamberlains staggered, and the immense javelin of the war-like maid, the warriors trembled for their lives, all save Siegfried, who, wrapped in his cloud-cloak, invisible to all, stood behind the bewildered Günther.

"Give me thy buckler," he whispered. "Now make but the motions, and I will hurl both spear and stone. But keep this a secret if thou wouldst save both our lives."

To the surprise of every one Günther won the games, and Brunhild, surprised and mortified, ordered her followers to bow to her better, and returned to the castle to make ready for the journey to Worms.

Siegfried carried the tidings to Worms, and the bridal party was met and welcomed at the banks of the Rhine by the Queen Uta, Kriemhild, and a large following. During the wedding feast, Siegfried reminded Günther of his promise, and the king, calling Kriemhild to him, affianced the two in the presence of the company.

When the suspicious Brunhild saw Siegfried sitting at the table of the king, she was angered, for she had been told that he was a vassal. Although she could get no satisfaction from Günther, she suspected some secret. When she and Günther retired for the night she conquered him, tied him hand and foot with her magic girdle, and hung him on the wall until morning. Günther, overcome with wrath and vexation, told his humiliation to Siegfried the next morning at the minster. "Be comforted," said Siegfried. "To-night I will steal into thy chamber wrapped in my mist-cloak, and when the lights are extinguished I will wrestle with her until I deprive her of the magic ring and girdle."

After some hesitation, Günther assented, and Brunhild, supposing she was conquered by Günther, yielded herself willingly to her husband and lost all her former strength. Siegfried carried away her girdle and ring and gave them to his wife, little suspecting what harm they would do him in the years to come.

The wedding festivities over, Siegfried took his bride home to the Netherlands, where their arrival was celebrated with the greatest festivities. Siegmund placed the crown on his son's head, and Siegfried and Kriemhild ruled happily over the kingdom for ten years, during which time a son was born to them, christened Günther for his uncle.

During these years Brunhild had been fretting that the supposed vassal, Siegfried, had never come to pay homage to his king. At last, affecting a great longing to see Kriemhild once more, she induced Günther to invite his sister and her husband to visit them. This he did gladly, and on their arrival many days were spent in feasting, merrymaking, and the tourney.

But one day, when the two queens were watching the tilting in the castle court, Kriemhild, excited by the victories of her husband, declared that Siegfried, because of his might, ought to be ruler of Burgundy. This angered Brunhild, who reproached the wife of a vassal for such presumption.

"My husband a vassal!" exclaimed the indignant Kriemhild. "He, ruler of the Netherlands, who holds a higher place than my brother Günther! I cannot endure thy insolence longer."

"I will see," said Brunhild, "this very day whether thou receivest the public respect and honor paid to me."

"I am ready for the test," responded Kriemhild, "and I will show thee to-day, before our following, that I dare to enter the church before Günther's queen."

When the two queens met on the minster steps, and Brunhild declared that no vassaless should enter before her, Kriemhild reproached her for being the leman of Siegfried, and displayed in proof the ring and girdle he had taken from Brunhild. Rage and fury rendered Brunhild speechless. The kings were summoned, and both denied the truth of Kriemhild's words. But the two queens were now bitter enemies, and the followers of Brunhild, among them the gloomy Hagan of Trony, were deeply angered at Siegfried and his queen. Hagan laid a plot to destroy Siegfried, and Günther, though at first unwilling, was at last induced to enter it.

Pretended messengers came to announce to Günther that the Saxons again threatened war against him. Siegfried proposed to take part in the war, and preparations were at once begun. Hagan, with pretended tenderness, told Kriemhild of the coming danger, and asked her if her lord had a weak place, that he might know and guard it for him. Kriemhild confided to him her husband's secret. When Siegfried was bathing in the dragon's blood, a leaf fell between his shoulders, and that spot was vulnerable. There she would embroider a cross on his vesture that Hagan might protect him in the shock of battle.

The war was now abandoned and a great hunt undertaken. Gernot and Giselher, though they did not see fit to warn Siegfried, refused to take part in the plot and go to the hunt. Many a lion, elk, and boar fell by Siegfried's hand that day before the hunters were called together to the royal breakfast; when they at last sat down in the flowery meadow the wine was wanting, and the warriors were compelled to quench their thirst at a brooklet near by.

" A race ! " cried the hero ; and he, Hagan, and Günther ran for the brook, Siegfried gaining it first. After the king had quenched his thirst, Siegfried threw down his arms and stooped to drink. Then Hagan, picking up his ashen spear, threw it at the embroidered cross, and Siegfried fell in the agonies of death, reproaching his traitorous friends whom he had served so faithfully.

To add cruelty to cruelty, the vindictive Hagan placed the body of Siegfried outside Kriemhild's chamber door, where she would stumble over it as she went out to early mass next morning. Down she fell fainting when she recognized her husband, and reviving, shrieked in her anguish, "Brunhild planned it ; Hagan struck the blow ! "

Her grief was terrible to see. One moment the unhappy queen was accusing herself for revealing her husband's secret ; again she was vowing revenge against Hagan, and at another time she reviled the traitorous Günther.

When her father-in-law Siegmund returned home, she would not go with him, but remained near the body of her husband, under the protection of her brothers Gernot and Giselher and in the company of her mother.

Kriemhild, living in joyless state in her lonely palace, was at last induced to speak to Günther and pardon him. The pardon granted, Günther and Hagan at once plotted to have the Nibelungen hoard, Siegfried's morning-gift to Kriemhild, brought to Worms. Never before was such a treasure seen. Twelve huge wagons, journeying thrice a day, required four nights and days to carry it from the mountain to the bay. It consisted of nothing but precious stones and gold, and with it was the magic wishing-rod. It filled Kriemhild's towers and chambers to overflowing, and won many friends for the queen, who distributed it liberally.

When the envious Hagan could not induce Günther to take the treasure from Kriemhild, he selected a time when the king and his brothers were away from home, and seizing the treasure, cast it into the Rhine, hoping to get it again. In this he failed, so the great treasure was forever lost.

Thus ends the first part of the Lay of the Nibelungen. The second part is sometimes called the Need or Fall of the Nibelungen.

While Kriemhild was bewailing her loss and revolving plans for revenge, Etzel, King of the Huns, who had heard of the charms of Siegfried's widow, sent the noble Margrave Rüdeger into Burgundy with proposals for her hand.

Gunther and his brothers begged Kriemhild to accept the offer ; their counsellors advised it ; only the sage Hagan protested. He knew too well how Kriemhild longed for revenge. " When once she gets among the Huns, she will make us rue the day," said he.

But the others laughed at Hagan's scruples. The land of the Huns was far away, and they need never set foot in it. Moreover, it was their duty to make Kriemhild happy.

Moved by the eloquence of Rüdeger, Kriemhild consented to wed Etzel, and set out in great state to meet the king.

She was splendidly entertained along the way, tarried a

short time at the home of the Margrave Rüdeger, and at
Tulna met the great monarch Etzel, riding to meet her,
among his hosts of Russians, Polacks, Greeks, and Wal-
lachians.

The splendid wedding-feast was held at Vienna. Kriemhild was received with the greatest honor, and so lavish was
she of the gold and jewels she had brought with her, and
so gracious to the attendant Huns, that every one loved her,
and willingly worked her will.

For seven long years she and Attila lived happy together,
and to them was given a son whom they christened Ortlieb.
Then Kriemhild, still remembering her loss and the cruelties
of her Burgundian relatives and friends, bethought herself of
her revenge.

Feigning a great desire to see her brothers, she entreated
Etzel to invite them to visit her; and the king, not suspecting
her fell purpose, and glad of an opportunity to welcome her
friends, at once despatched messengers with the invitation.

This time other counsellors besides Hagan mistrusted the
queen, and advised King Günther and his brothers to decline
the invitation. But the princes grew angry at their advice;
and Hagan, who could not endure to be laughed at, set forth
with them, accompanied with a great train of warriors.

The Rhine was too swollen to ford, and Hagan was sent
up the stream to find a ferryman. As he looked for the
boatman, he spied some mermaids bathing, and seizing their
garments, would not restore them until they told him what
would befall the Burgundians in Hungary.

"Safe will you ride to Etzel's court, and safe return,"
said one, as he returned the garments. But as he turned to
go, another called: "My aunt has lied to thee that she
might get back her raiment. Turn now, or you will never
live to see Burgundy. None save the chaplain will return
in safety."

Hagan went on gloomily and found the ferryman, who,
proud and sullen, refused to take the party across. Hagan
slew him, and, returning with the boat, threw the unfortunate
chaplain into the river, thinking by drowning him to prove

the mermaid's prophecy untrue. But the chaplain escaped to the other side, and walked back to Burgundy. Then Hagan told the party of the prophecy and they resolved to go on together, though they realized that they were going to their doom.

Because of the slaughter of the ferryman, they were attacked by Gelfrat, the ruler of the land; but he was overcome and slain by Dankwart.

The Margrave Rüdeger received the travellers hospitably, and betrothed his fair daughter to Giselher. He then accompanied the Burgundians to Etzel's court.

The Burgundians suspected Kriemhild from the first. Giselher was the only one of her brothers whom she kissed, and she and Hagan quarrelled over the treasure at their first meeting.

They were warned by Eckewart, who had accompanied Kriemhild from Burgundy, and by Dietrich of Bern, an exile at the court of Etzel, who told them that every morning since her stay in Hunland she had moaned and wailed for Siegfried. By Hagan's advice they all kept on their armor, telling Etzel that it was the custom in their country to wear it for the first three days.

Kriemhild's design was to destroy Hagan and spare her brothers. But Hagan, on his guard, drove her warriors away from his room at night, and saved himself at church from the jostling Hunnish lords, never, in the mean time, sparing his insults to Kriemhild.

The Huns, who were devoted to their queen, were not slow in showing their anger at Hagan's treatment of her, and the ill feeling between the warriors increased as the days passed by.

As the Burgundians sat at the banquet with Etzel and his wife, in burst Dankwart, exclaiming that he had been attacked by Bloedel, who had slain all his followers.

" Be stirring, brother Hagan ! " he cried. " Help me to avenge my wrongs ! "

At this moment the little prince Ortlieb had been brought into the hall and passed around among the guests.

" Let us drink to friendship with moody Kriemhild in king's wine ! " cried Hagan, and with one blow of the sword sent the child's head in his mother's lap. Then arose a fearful clamor. Spear rang against shield, and the cries of the fierce Huns mingled with the defiant shouts of the Burgundians.

Dietrich of Bern, leaping upon a bench, asked King Günther, that, as a friend to both parties, he might be permitted to withdraw from the hall with his friends. When the Burgundians assented, he led forth the king and queen. The same privilege was accorded to Rüdeger.

Then, while the terrible Folker guarded the door with his fiddle bow, one side of which was a trenchant sword, the battle began. The Burgundians taunted the Huns with their weakness and cowardice until they ventured into the hall and were cut down by Hagan and his desperate men. When evening fell the thousand and four who had entered the hall all lay dead by the hands of the Burgundians.

When Kriemhild's offer to give her brothers their lives if they would surrender Hagan was refused, she ordered fire to be set to the four corners of the hall, thinking thus to drive them forth. But the burning rafters fell into the rivers of blood and were quenched, and the Burgundians derived new courage and strength from huge draughts of blood from their fallen foes.

Then Kriemhild and Etzel, seeing how their Hunnish men had fallen, and perceiving that the Burgundians were in no wise injured by the fire, reproached the Margrave Rüdeger that he did not enter the fight. In vain he told them of his friendship with the princes ; of the betrothal of his daughter and Giselher. Kriemhild persisted in reminding him of the promise he had made to serve her to her dying day. At last he reluctantly summoned his men, and bidding farewell to his cruel king and queen, he entered the hall. Gladly was he welcomed by the Burgundians, who could not believe that he came to do battle with them. He explained how he was forced to fight them, and amid the tears of both sides, he exchanged shields with

Hagan, whose buckler was broken. Then was the grim
Hagan moved to tears, and he vowed not to touch Rüdeger
in the fight. Fearful was the clatter of shield and blade as
Rüdeger fought with Gernot, and fell at last by the blade he
had himself given the prince.

Great was the wailing of the Huns when they saw the
lifeless body of Rüdeger, and deeply did Etzel regret the
loss of the valiant and true margrave.

Dietrich of Bern, who sat afar off, sent some of his best
warriors under his man Hildebrand, to inquire of the
truth of the report of Rüdeger's death. These fiery men dis-
obeyed the orders of their master, and fought with the Burgundians until none remained save Günther and Hagan on
one side, and Hildebrand on the other.

When Dietrich heard of the slaughter of his followers, he
was overcome with sorrow, and himself sought the hall. He
promised Günther and Hagan that if they would surrender,
he would himself lead them back in safety to Burgundy ;
but to this they would not consent. By this time they were
so worn out, however, from the long battle, that Dietrich
easily overpowered them and led them captive before Kriemhild, who promised to show them fair treatment.

But Kriemhild's mind had become so warped by her desire for revenge, that she could not think of mercy. She
cast her prisoners into separate dungeons, and visiting Hagan
first, demanded her treasure. " But give it to me again,
and thou shalt return living into Burgundy."

" Pray not to me, haughty queen," replied Hagan. " I
swore that while my lords were living I would ne'er tell
where it lies. Thy prayer is thrown away."

Straightway the savage Kriemhild ordered the head of
Günther to be struck off, and bearing it by the hair, she
displayed it to Hagan, asking him now to tell her the
secret.

" Now that all my lords are dead," said he, " no one shall
know, thou least of all, she-fiend ! "

Kriemhild, beside herself with grief and rage, snatched
from him the sword Balmung that he had taken from Sieg-

fried, and ever since carried, and raising it high with both hands, struck off the head of her hated enemy.

At this the grief of Etzel broke forth, and the aged Hildebrand, enraged to see a woman do such deeds, sprang upon Kriemhild and smote her to death with his sword.

Bitterly wept King Etzel and Dietrich as they gazed on the corpses scattered round, and the disfigured body of the fair queen. Nothing remained for the Hunnish people but grief and woe.

Here on earth pain ever follows in the steps of pleasure.

## SELECTIONS FROM THE NIBELUNGEN LIED.

### How Brunhild was received at Worms.

Brunhild, queen of Issland, was won by Günther of Worms with the aid of Siegfried, whom Günther sent forward to Worms to announce the coming of the royal pair. Queen Uta and Princess Kriemhild, with many followers from the Burgundian court, went forward to the Rhine to meet and welcome the royal bridal party.

> Beyond the Rhine King Günther, with many a well-arm'd rank
> And all his guests about him, rode towards the river's bank;
> You might see by the bridle led forward many a maid.
> Those, who were to receive them, were ready all array'd.

> Soon as the men of Issland came to the shallops down,
> And eke the Nibelungers, lieges of Siegfried's crown,
> To th' other shore they hasten'd (busy was every hand)
> Where them the friends of Günther awaited on the strand.

> Now hear, by wealthy Uta what a device was wrought.
> Down with her from the castle a virgin train she brought,
> That rode where she was riding in that procession bright;
> So many a maid acquainted became with many a knight.

> Kriemhild by the bridle the Margrave Gary led,
> But only from the castle; then forward Siegfried sped,
> And did that gentle service; fair was the blushing maid;
> Full well for that thereafter the warrior she repaid.

Ortwine, the fearless champion, rode by Dame Uta's rein;
Knights and maids together follow'd, a social train.
At such a stately meeting, all must confess, I ween,
So many lovely ladies were ne'er together seen.

Full many a famous champion careering you might spy
(Ill there was sloth and idlesse) beneath fair Kriemhild's eye
E'en to the place of landing; by knights of fair renown
There many a high-born lady from steed was lifted down.

The king was now come over, and many a worthy guest.
Ah, before the ladies what spears were laid in rest!
How many went in shivers at every hurtling close!
Buckler clashed with buckler; ah, what a din arose!

Now might you see the ladies fast by the haven stand.
With his guests King Günther debark'd upon the strand,
In his hand soft leading the martial maiden fair.
Then each on each flash'd radiance, rich robes and jewels rare.

With that the smiling Kriemhild forth stepp'd a little space,
And Brunhild and her meiny greeted with gentle grace,
Each with snowy fingers back her headband drew,
And either kiss'd the other lovingly and true.

Then spoke in courteous manner Kriemhild the fair and free,
"In this our land, dear Brunhild, ever welcome be
To me and to my mother and all by us allow'd
For faithful friends and liegemen." Then each to th' other bow'd.

Next to greet Dame Brunhild approach'd Dame Uta too;
Oft she and oft her daughter their arms about her threw,
And on her sweet mouth lavish'd many a loving kiss.
Never was known a welcome so kind and frank as this.

Soon as Brunhild's women were all come to the strand,
Many a courtly warrior took by her lily hand
A lady fair, and gently her mincing steps upstay'd,
Now before Dame Brunhild stood many a noble maid.

'T was long before the greeting had gone through all the list.
On either part in plenty rosy mouths were kiss'd.
Still the two fair princesses were standing side by side,
A pair with love and rapture by longing warriors ey'd.

What erst had been but rumour, was now made clear to sight,
That nought had yet been witness'd so beautiful and bright
As those two lovely damsels; 't was plain to every eye;
None the slightest blemish in either form could spy.

Whoever look'd on women with but the sight for guide,
Such for her faultless beauty praised Günther's stately bride;
But those whose thoughts went deeper, and div'd into the mind,
Maintain'd that gentle Kriemhild left Brunhild far behind.

Now met the dames and damsels in friendly converse free;
Fair robes and fairer beauties were there in store to see;
Many a silk pavilion and many a gorgeous tent
The plain before the city fill'd in its whole extent.

King Günther's kinsmen ceas'd not to press to that fair show.
And now was begg'd each princess from the sun to go
Close by, with their attendants, where shade was overhead.
By bold Burgundian warriors thither were they led.

Then clomb to horse the heroes, and scour'd the sounding field;
Many a joust was practis'd with order'd spear and shield;
Right well were prov'd the champions, and o'er the trampled plain,
As though the land were burning, the dust curl'd up amain.

So all before the ladies display'd their skill and force,
Nor doubt I that Sir Siegfried rode many a knightly course
Before the rich pavilions, and ever as he sped,
His thousand Nibelungers, a stately squadron, led.

Then came the knight of Trony by the good king's command;
In friendly wise he parted the jousters on the strand,
For fear the dust, now thick'ning, the ladies might molest.
Him with ready reverence obey'd each gentle guest.

Then spake the noble Gernot, " Let each now rest his steed
Till the air be cooler, 't will then be ours to lead
These lovely ladies homeward e'en to the palace wide.
So keep yourselves all ready till it please the king to ride."

Thus ended was the tourney, and now the warriors went
To join the dames and damsels beneath each lofty tent,
And there in gentle converse their grace and favor sought;
So flew the hours in pastime till of riding home they thought.

Now as drew on the twilight, when cooler grew the air
And the sun was setting, they would not linger there,
But up rose lords and ladies to seek the castle high;
Many a fair dame was cherish'd by many a love-lit eye.

So on the fair they waited as from good knights is due.
Then hardy squires, hot spurring before the nobles' view,
After the country's custom rode for the prize of weed
As far as to the palace, where sprung the king from steed.

There too the proud queens parted, each taking thence her way.
Dame Uta and her daughter with their handmaids gay
Into a spacious chamber both together went.
There might you see on all sides the sound of merriment.

In hall the seats were order'd; the king would instant hie
With all his guests to table; beside him you might spy
His lovely bride, Queen Brunhild; her royal crown she wore
There in King Günther's country; so rich was none before.

Seats were there plac'd unnumber'd with tables broad and good,
As is to us reported, full heap'd with costly food.
How little there was wanted that passes for the best!
There with the king was seated full many a noble guest.

The chamberlains of Günther in ewers of ruddy gold
Brought to the guests the water; should you be ever told
That at a prince's table service was better done,
'T were labor lost to say so, 't would be believ'd by none.

Then, ere the lord of Rhineland touch'd the water bright,
Up to him, as befitted, went Siegfried the good knight,
And brought to his remembrance the promise made him there,
Ere yet afar in Issland he look'd on Brunhild fair.

Said he, "You must remember what swore to me your hand,
That soon as Lady Brunhild were come into this land,
To me you'd give your sister, your oaths now where are they?
On me throughout your journey much toil and travail lay."

"Well did you to remind me," the noble king replied,
"By what my hand has promis'd, I ever will abide,
And in this thing to serve you will do my best, my all."
Then sent he to beg Kriemhild to come into the hall.

Straight to the hall came Kriemhild begirt with many a maid,
When from the lofty staircase young Giselher thus said,
"Send back your maidens, Kriemhild, this bus'ness is your own;
On this the king, our brother, would speak with you alone."

Then forward led was Kriemhild, as Günther gave command,
Where stood the king, and round him from many a prince's land
Were noble knights unnumber'd; at once all silence kept;
At that same instant Brunhild had just to table stepp'd.

Thence came it she knew nothing of what was to be done.
Then to his gather'd kinsmen spoke Dancrat's royal son,
"Help me to move my sister Siegfried for lord to take."
"Such match," they all made answer, "with honour she may make.'

Then spoke the king to Kriemhild, "Sister, I ask of thee
From an oath to set me by thy kindness free.
Thee to a knight I promis'd ; if thou become his bride,
Thou 'lt do the will of Günther, and show thy love beside."

Then spake the noble maiden, "Dearest brother mine,
It needed not to ask me ; whate'er command be thine,
I'll willingly perform it ; so now, for thy sake,
Whom thou for husband giv'st me, fain I, my lord, will take."

With love and eke with pleasure redden'd Siegfried's hue ;
At once to Lady Kriemhild he pledg'd his service true.
They bade them stand together in the courtly circle bright,
And ask'd her if for husband she took that lofty knight.

In modest maiden fashion she blush'd a little space,
But such was Siegfried's fortune and his earnest grace,
That not altogether could she deny her hand.
Then her for wife acknowledg'd the noble king of Netherland.

He thus to her affianc'd, and to him the maid,
Straight round the long-sought damsel in blushing grace array'd
His arms with soft emotion th' enamour'd warrior threw,
And kiss'd the high-born princess before that glitt'ring crew.

*Lettsom's Translation, Tenth Adventure.*


## How Margrave Rüdeger was Slain.

THE Margrave Rüdeger did not take part in the battle fought
in Etzel's hall between the Burgundians visiting the Hunnish
court and the Huns, because of his friendship for the Burgundians, and the betrothal of his daughter to Prince Giselher. Because of this, he was taunted by a Hun, who said to the queen
that although Rüdeger had accepted many favors from Etzel he
did not fight for him. When the Hun fell dead under Rüdeger's blow, Etzel reproached him for slaying one of his followers
when he had need of so many.

Then came the fair Queen Kriemhild ; she too had seen full well
What from the hero's anger the luckless Hun befell ;
And she too mourn'd it deeply ; with tears her eyes were wet.
Thus spake she to Rüdeger, " How have we ever yet

" Deserv'd that you, good Rüdeger, should make our anguish more?
Now sure to me and Etzel you 've promised o'er and o'er,
That you both life and honour would risk to do us right.
That you 're the flower of knighthood is own'd by every knight.

"Now think upon the homage that once to me you swore,
When to the Rhine, good warrior, King Etzel's suit you bore,
That you would serve me ever to either's dying day.
Ne'er can I need so deeply, that you that vow should pay."

"'T is true, right noble lady; in this we 're not at strife;
I pledg'd, to do you service, my honour and my life,
But my soul to hazard never did I vow.
I brought the princes hither, and must not harm them now."

.    .    .    .    .    .    .

With that, to beg and pray him the king began as well;
King and queen together both at his feet they fell.
Then might you the good margrave have seen full ill bestead,
And thus in bitterest anguish the faithful hero said : —

"Woe 's me the heaven-abandon'd, that I have liv'd to this!
Farewell to all my honours! woe for my first amiss!
My truth — my God-giv'n innocence — must they be both forgot?
Woe 's me, O God in heaven! that death relieves me not!"

Then thus bespake him Kriemhild, 'Right noble Rüdeger,
Take pity on our anguish; thou see'st us kneeling here,
The king and me before thee; both clasp thy honour'd knees.
Sure never host yet feasted such fatal guests as these."

With that the noble margrave thus to the queen 'gan say,
"Sure must the life of Rüdeger for all the kindness pay,
That you to me, my lady, and my lord the king have done.
For this I 'm doom'd to perish, and that ere set of sun.

"Full well I know, this morning my castles and my land
Both will to you fall vacant by stroke of foeman's hand,
And so my wife and daughter I to your grace commend,
And all at Bechelaren, each trusty homeless friend."

.    .    .    .    .    .    .

So to war the margrave under helmet strode ;
Sharpest swords his meiny brandished as they rode;
Each in hand, bright-flashing, held his shield before.
That saw the dauntless minstrel, and seeing sorrow'd sore.

Then too was by young Giselher his lady's father seen
With helm laced as for battle. "What," thought he, "can he mean?
But nought can mean the margrave but what is just and right."
At the thought full joyous wax'd the youthful knight.

"I know not what you trust in ; " thus the stern minstrel spake;
"Where saw you warriors ever for reconcilement's sake
With helmets laced advancing, and naked swords in hand?
On us will earn Sir Rüdeger his castles and his land."

Scarcely the valiant minstrel his words had utter'd all,
When the noble Rüdeger was close before the hall.
His shield, well proved in battle, before his feet he laid,
But neither proffered service, nor friendly greeting made.

To those within he shouted, " Look not for succor hence;
Ye valiant Nibelungers, now stand on your defence.
I 'd fain have been your comrade ; your foe I now must be.
We once were friends together ; now from that bond I 'm free."

" Now God forbid," said Günther, " that such a knight as you
To the faith wherein we trusted, should ever prove untrue,
And turn upon his comrades in such an hour as this.
Ne'er can I think that Rüdeger can do so much amiss."

" I can't go back," said Rüdeger, " the deadly die is cast;
I must with you do battle ; to that my word is pass'd.
So each of you defend him as he loves his life.
I must perform my promise ; so wills King Etzel's wife."

.    .    .    .    .    .    .

" Tarry yet a little, right noble Rüdeger !
I and my lords a moment would yet with you confer ;
Thereto hard need compels us, and danger gathering nigh ;
What boot were it to Etzel though here forlorn we die ?

" I 'm now," pursued Sir Hagan, " beset with grievous care ;
The shield that Lady Gotelind gave me late to bear,
Is hewn, and all-to broken by many a Hunnish brand.
I brought it fair and friendly hither to Etzel's land.

" Ah ! that to me this favour heaven would be pleas'd to yield,
That I might to defend me bear so well-prov'd a shield
As that, right noble Rüdeger, before thee now display'd !
No more should I in battle need then the hauberk's aid."

" Fain with the same I 'd serve thee to th' height of thy desire,
But that I fear such proffer might waken Kriemhild's ire.
Still, take it to thee, Hagan, and wield it well in hand.
Ah ! might'st thou bring it with thee to thy Burgundian land !"

While thus with words so courteous so fair a gift he sped,
The eyes of many a champion with scalding tears were red.
'T was the last gift, that buckler, e'er given to comrade dear
By the lord of Bechelaren, the blameless Rüdeger.

However stern was Hagan, and of unyielding mood,
Still at the gift he melted, which one so great and good
Gave in his last few moments, e'en on the eve of fight,
And with the stubborn warrior mourn'd many a noble knight.

"Now God in heaven, good Rüdeger, thy recompenser be!
Your like on earth, I 'm certain, we never more shall see,
Who gifts so good and gorgeous to homeless wanderers give.
May God protect your virtue, that it may ever live!

"Alas! this bloody bus'ness!" Sir Hagan then went on,
"We have had to bear much sorrow, and more shall have anon.
Must friend with friend do battle, nor heaven the conflict part?"
The noble margrave answer'd, "That wounds my inmost heart."

"Now for thy gift I 'll quit thee, right noble Rüdeger!
What e'er may chance between thee and my bold comrades here,
My hand shall touch thee never amidst the heady fight,
Not e'en if thou shouldst slaughter every Burgundian knight."

For that to him bow'd courteous the blameless Rüdeger.
Then all around were weeping for grief and doleful drear,
Since none th' approaching mischief had hope to turn aside.
The father of all virtue in that good margrave died.

.      .      .      .      .      .

What a fearful clatter of clashing blades there rang!
From shields beneath the buffets how the plates they sprang,
And precious stones unnumber'd rain'd down into the gore!
They fought so fell and furious as man will never more.

The lord of Bechelaren went slashing here and there,
As one who well in battle knew how himself to bear.
Well prov'd the noble Rüdeger in that day's bloody fight,
That never handled weapon a more redoubted knight.

.      .      .      .      .      .

Loud o'er the din of battle stout Gernot shouted then,
"How now, right noble Rüdeger? not one of all my men
Thou 'lt leave me here unwounded; in sooth it grieves me sore
To see my friends thus slaughter'd; bear it can I no more.

"Now must thy gift too surely the giver harm to-day,
Since of my friends so many thy strength has swept away.
So turn about and face me, thou bold and high-born man!
Thy goodly gift to merit, I 'll do the best I can."

Ere through the press the margrave could come Sir Gernot nigh,
Full many a glittering mail-coat was stain'd a bloody die.
Then those fame-greedy champions each fierce on th' other leapt,
And deadly wounds at distance with wary ward they kept.

So sharp were both their broadswords, resistless was their dint,
Sudden the good Sir Rüdeger through th' helmet hard as flint
So struck the noble Gernot, that forth the blood it broke;
With death the stern Burgundian repaid the deadly stroke.

He heaved the gift of Rüdeger with both his hands on high,
And to the death though wounded, a stroke at him let fly
Right through both shield and morion ; deep was the gash and wide.
At once the lord of Gotelind beneath the swordcut died.

In sooth a gift so goodly was worse requited ne'er.
Down dead dropp'd both together, Gernot and Rüdeger.
Each slain by th' other's manhood, then prov'd, alas! too well.
Thereat first Sir Hagan furious wax'd and fell.

Then cried the knight of Trony, "Sure we with ills are cross'd ;
Their country and their people in both these chiefs have lost
More than they 'll e'er recover ; — woe worth this fatal day !
We have here the margrave's meiny, and they for all shall pay ! "

All struck at one another, none would a foeman spare.
Full many a one, unwounded, down was smitten there,
Who else might have 'scap'd harmless, but now, though whole and sound,
In the thick press was trampled, or in the blood was drown'd.

"Alas ! my luckless brother who here in death lies low !
How every hour I 'm living brings some fresh tale of woe !
And ever must I sorrow for the good margrave too.
On both sides dire destruction and mortal ills we rue."

Soon as the youthful Giselher beheld his brother dead,
Who yet within were lingering by sudden doom were sped.
Death, his pale meiny choosing, dealt each his dreary dole.
Of those of Bechelaren 'scaped not one living soul.

King Günther and young Giselher, and fearless Hagan too,
Dankwart as well as Folker, the noble knights and true,
Went where they found together out-stretched the valiant twain.
There wept th' assembled warriors in anguish o'er the slain.

"Death fearfully despoils us," said youthful Giselher,
"But now give over wailing, and haste to th' open air
To cool our heated hauberks, faint as we are with strife.
God, methinks, no longer, will here vouchsafe us life."

This sitting, that reclining, was seen full many a knight ;
They took repose in quiet ; around (a fearful sight ! )
Lay Rüdeger's dead comrades; all was hush'd and still;
From that long dreary silence King Etzel augur'd ill.

"Alas for this half friendship !" thus Kriemhild frowning spake,
"If it were true and steadfast, Sir Rüdeger would take
Vengeance wide and sweeping on yonder murderous band ;
Now back he'll bring them safely to their Burgundian land.

"What boot our gifts, King Etzel? was it, my lord, for this
We gave him all he asked us? The chief has done amiss.
He, who should have reveng'd us, will now a treaty make."
Thereto in answer Folker, the gallant minstrel, spake,

"Not so the truth is, lady! the more the pity too!
If one the lie might venture to give a dame like you,
Most foully against the margrave you 've lied, right noble queen!
Sore trick'd in that same treaty he and his men have been.

"With such good will the margrave his king's commands obey'd,
That he and all his meiny dead on this floor are laid.
Now look about you, Kriemhild! for servants seek anew;
Well were you served by Rüdeger; he to the death was true.

"The fact if still you 're doubting, before your eyes we 'll bring."
'T was done e'en of set purpose her heart the more to wring.
They brought the mangled margrave, where Etzel saw him well.
Th' assembled knights of Hungary such utter anguish ne'er befell.

When thus held high before them they saw the margrave dead,
Sure by the choicest writer could ne'er be penn'd nor said
The woeful burst of wailing from woman and eke from man,
That from the heart's deep sorrow to strike all ears began.

Above his weeping people King Etzel sorrow'd sore;
His deep-voic'd wail resounded loud as the lion's roar
In the night-shaded desert; the like did Kriemhild too;
They mourn'd in heart for Rüdeger, the valiant and the true.

*Lettsom's Translation, Thirty-seventh Adventure.*

# THE SONG OF ROLAND.

THE Song of Roland is one of the many mediæval romances that celebrate the deeds of Charlemagne.

The oldest text now in existence was written about 1096, but the poem was current in other forms long before this.

The author was a Norman, for the poem is written in the Norman dialect; but it is uncertain whether the Turoldus or Théroulde named in the last line of the poem, "Thus endeth here the geste Turoldus sang," was the author, a copyist, or a *jongleur*.

It is said that Taillefer, the minstrel of Normandy, sang the Song of Roland at the battle of Hastings. "Taillefer, who right well sang, mounted on his rapid steed, went before them singing of Charlemagne, and of Roland, and Olivier, and of the vassals who died in Roncesvalles."

The only text of the poem now in existence is one of the thirteenth century, preserved in the Bodleian library at Oxford.

On the fifteenth of August, 778, in the valley of Ronces-valles, in the Pyrenees, Charlemagne's rear guard, left under the command of Roland, Prefect of the Marches of Brittany, was attacked and slaughtered by a large army of Gascons.

This incident forms the historical basis of the poem; but the imagination of the poet has made of Charlemagne, then a young man, the old emperor, with "beard all blossom white," and transformed his Gascon foes to Saracens.

The Song of Roland is written in the heroic pentameter; it is divided into "laisses," or stanzas, of irregular length, and contains about three thousand seven hundred and eight

13

lines. It is written in the assonant, or vowel rhyme, that was universal among European nations in the early stage of their civilization.

Each stanza ends with the word "aoi," for which no satisfactory translation has yet been offered, although "away" and "it is done" have been suggested.

The author of the Song of Roland undertook, like Homer, to sing of one great event about which all the interest of the poem centres; but unlike Homer, his poem is out of all proportion, the long-drawn out revenge being in the nature of an anti-climax. The Song of Roland is a fair exponent of the people among whom it originated. It contains no ornament; it is a straightforward relation of facts; it lacks passion, and while it describes fearful slaughter, it never appeals to the emotions. Though the French army shed many tears, and fell swooning to the ground at the sight of the fearful slaughter at Roncesvalles, we are rather moved to smile at the violence of their emotion than to weep over the dead, so little power has the poet to touch the springs of feeling. However, there are passages in which the poem rises to sublimity, and which have been pronounced Homeric by its admirers.

BIBLIOGRAPHY AND CRITICISM, THE SONG OF ROLAND. J. Banquier's Bibliographie de la Chanson de Roland, 1877; T. Bulfinch's Legends of Charlemagne, 1863; Sir G. W. Cox and E. H. Jones's Popular Romances of the Middle Ages, 1871, pp. 320–347; Léon Gautier's Les épopées françaises, vol. i., 1878; J. Malcolm Ludlow's Story of Roland (see his Popular Epics of the Middle Ages, 1865, vol. i., pp. 362–427); Gaston Paris's La poésie épique (see his Histoire poétique de Charlemagne, 1865, pp. 1–33); Gaston Paris's Les Chansons de Gestes françaises (see his Histoire poétique de Charlemagne, 1865, pp. 69–72); George Saintsbury's The Chansons de Gestes (see his Short History of French Literature, 1892, pp. 10–25); Henri Van Laun's The Carlovingian Cycle (see his History of French Literature, 1876, vol. i., pp. 141–148); Ancient Literature of

France, Quarterly Review, 1866, cxx. 283–323 ; The Chanson de Roland, Westminster Review, 1873, c. 32–44 ; M. Hayden's The Chansons de Geste, Dublin Review, 1894, cxiv. 346–357 ; Charles Francis Keary's The Chansons de Geste ; the Song of Roland, Fraser's Magazine, 1881, civ. 777–789 ; J. M. L.'s The Song of Roland, Macmillan's Magazine, 1862, vi. 486–501 ; Agnes Lambert's The oldest epic of Christendom, Nineteenth Century, 1882, xi. 77–101 ; Andrew Lang's The Song of Roland and the Iliad, National Review, 1892, xx. 195–205 ; Legend of Roland, Encyclopædia Britannica, vol. xx. ; Gustave Masson's The Chanson de Roland, Leisure Hour, 1877, xxvi. 618–620 ; The Song of Roland, Catholic World, 1873 and 1874, xviii. 378–388, 488–500 ; The Song of Roland, Harper's Monthly, 1882, lxiv. 505–515 ; The Month, 1880, xl. 515–527 ; Temple Bar, 1886, lxxviii. 534–540.

Standard English Translations, the Song of Roland. The Song of Roland, as chanted before the Battle of Hastings by the Minstrel Taillefer, Tr. from the French translation of Vitet by Mrs. Anne Caldwell Marsh, 1854 ; The Song of Roland, Tr. into English verse by John O'Hagan, ed. 2, 1883 ; La Chanson de Roland, Tr. from the seventh ed. of Léon Gautier, by Leonce Rabillon, 1885.

## THE STORY OF THE SONG OF ROLAND.

FOR full seven years had Charlemagne tarried in Spain, and all the land lay conquered save the city of Saragossa. There, in an orchard, upon a terrace paved with blue marble, sat its king, Marsile, taking counsel with his lords.

"No army have I," said the king; "no people to array against the hosts of the great emperor. Advise me, my lords, what I shall do to save ourselves from disgrace and shame."

The wily Blancandrin, wisest and greatest among the pagans, advanced before him. " Where might cannot prevail, often craft gains the day. My lord, send gifts to mighty Carle. Drive forth a long train of camels ; heap many mules with gold ; send chariots filled with precious gifts. Advise him that on the day of Saint Michael's feast you will seek him at Aix, and there become a Christian, and his vassal. Yea, even send hostages ; my own son shall go, even though he lose his head. Then will Carle depart for France. The day set by you will come, but he will hear naught from us. The hostages' heads will fall. What of it ? Better this than for us to lose forever Spain the fair."

The king, pleased with the craft of Blancandrin, dismissed his council, and ordered ten of his fiercest barons to seek Charlemagne at Cordova, bearing the olive-branch, and make the offer suggested by Blancandrin.

Cordova, filled with rich spoils, had been taken, and its surviving inhabitants given the choice of the sword or Christian baptism. Therefore the happy emperor sat at his ease in a wide-spreading orchard. Around him stood Roland, Olivier, Samsun the duke, Anseis, Gefrei d'Anjou, and Gerier. At least fifteen thousand French knights were diverting themselves with different games in the beautiful orchard, where, under a pine-tree, the great King of France sat upon a golden chair. His white hair and flowing white beard added majesty to his already majestic figure, so that the olive-bearing messengers needed not to have great Carle pointed out to them.

The emperor heard the message of Marsile in silence, and dismissing the pagans for the night to a pavilion, called together in council his wisest barons, Duke Ogier, Archbishop Turpin, Gerier, Roland, Olivier, a thousand Franks, among them Ganelon, the step-father of Roland, and laid before them the message of Marsile.

"Rich gifts he offers me, but he demands that I return to France; thither will he follow me, and at Aix will become a Christian and a vassal. A fair promise, but what is in his heart I cannot tell."

After a moment's silence Roland stood forth.

"Sire, have no faith in the words of Marsile. When have we found aught but treachery in the Saracen? For seven years I have been winning victories for you here in Spain. Once before you yielded to such a message as this, from this same Marsile, and lost, in consequence, the heads of your Counts Bazan and Bazile. War on as you have begun. Besiege his city! subdue Saragossa!"

Then strode forth the angry Ganelon. "My king, this young hot-head is a fool; hearken not unto him. Accept the offer of Marsile, and lose no more lives by the foolhardiness of one who cares more for his own glory than for human life."

The voice of the others, among them Duke Naimes, Charlemagne's wisest counsellor and truest vassal, was with Ganelon. The emperor stroked his white beard. "My lords, whom shall we send to meet Marsile at Saragossa?"

"I will go," said Duke Naimes.

"Nay, I cannot spare you from my councils," replied the king.

"I am here!" cried Roland.

"Not you! You are too hot-headed to venture into the court of the enemy!" cried his friend Olivier. "Let me go instead, sire!"

"Nay!" cried the king. "Silence! Not one of the twelve peers sets his foot in the kingdom of the Moors."

"Then let my step-father go," suggested Roland. "No wiser man than he can be found."

"Come forward," said the king, as the Franks murmured assent, "and receive the staff and glove. The Franks have chosen you."

Ganelon rose, wrathful, casting off his fur robe. His eyes were gray, his face fierce, his form noble.

"This is Roland's work. I shall hate him forever, and Olivier, and the twelve peers, because they love him. Ne'er shall I return ; full well I know it. If e'er I do, it will be to wreak vengeance on my enemy."

"Go !" said the king. "You have said enough !"

As Ganelon went forward, full of rage, to receive the king's glove, it fell ere he touched it. "A bad omen !" exclaimed the French.

"Sirs, ye shall hear of this !" said Ganelon.

On his way to Saragossa with the legates of Marsile, Ganelon laid the impious plot that was to result in the destruction of Roland and the peers. It saved his life at Saragossa, where Marsile threatened to kill him on reading Charlemagne's message. He explained carefully to the Saracens how the rear guard, left at Roncesvalles under the command of Roland and the twelve peers, could be destroyed by the pagan forces before the knowledge of the battle could reach Charlemagne, and that, with these props of his kingdom gone, the king's power would be so diminished that Marsile could easily hold out against him. Then the traitor hastened back to Cordova, laden with rich gifts.

When Ganelon rode back, the emperor was preparing to return to sweet France. "Barons," said Carle, "whom shall I leave in charge of these deep defiles and narrow passes?"

"My step-son Roland is well able to take the command," said Ganelon ; "he your nephew, whom you prize most of all your knights."

Rage filled the hearts of both Roland and Carle ; but the word was spoken, and Roland must remain. With him remained the twelve peers, his friends, Olivier, his devoted comrade, the gallant Archbishop Turpin, and twenty thousand valiant knights.

While Charlemagne's army toiled over the terrible gorges and high mountains into Gascony, the emperor, ever grieving over the untimely death his nephew might meet in the defiles of Spain, down came the pagans, who had been gathering on the high mountains and in the murky valleys, — emirs, sons of noble counts were they, brave as the followers of Charlemagne.

When Olivier descried the pagan horde he at once exclaimed, —

"This is the work of Ganelon!"

"Hush!" replied Roland. "He is my step-father. Say no more."

Then Olivier, when from the hill he saw the one hundred thousand Saracens, their helmets bedecked with gold, their shields shining in the sun, besought his friend to sound his horn, the olifant, and summon the king to their aid.

"Never will I so disgrace myself!" exclaimed Roland. "Never shall sweet France be so dishonored. One hundred thousand blows shall I give with my sword, my Durendal, and the Moors will fall and die!"

When Olivier found his pleading vain, he mounted his steed and rode with Roland to the front of the lines.

Long was the fight and terrible. If gallantry and strength sat with the twelve peers and their followers, they were with their opponents as well. No sooner had Roland, or Olivier, or Turpin, or Engelier cleft the body of a Moorish knight down to the saddle, than down fell a Christian, his helmet broken, his hauberk torn by the lance of his dreaded foe. The nephew of Marsile fell by the hand of Roland, who taunted him as he lay in death; Olivier struck down Marsile's brother. "A noble stroke!" cried Roland.

"A baron's stroke!" exclaimed the archbishop, as Samsun pierced the Almazour with his lance and he fell dead. Olivier spurred over the field, crushing the pagans and beating them down with his broken lance.

"Comrade, where is thy sword, thy Halteclere?" called Roland to his friend.

"Here, but I lack time to draw it," replied the doughty Olivier.

More than a thousand blows struck Turpin; the pagans fell by hundreds and by thousands, and over the field lay scattered those who would nevermore see sweet France.

Meanwhile, in France, hail fell and rain; the sky was vivid with lightning bolts. The earth shook, and the land lay in darkness at noonday. None understood the portent. Alas! it was Nature's grief at the death of Count Roland.

When Roland perceived that in spite of their mighty efforts the passes were still filled with heathen knights, and the French ranks were fast thinning, he said to Olivier, "What think you if we call the king?"

"Never!" exclaimed Olivier. "Better death now than shame!"

"If I blow, Carle will hear it now and return. I shall blow my olifant," cried Roland.

"When I begged you to blow it," said Olivier, "you refused, when you could have saved the lives of all of us. You will show no valor if you blow it now."

"Great is the strife," said Roland. "I will blow that Carle may come."

"Then," said Olivier, "if I return to France, I pledge you my word my sister Aude shall never be your wife. Your rashness has been the cause of our destruction. Now you shall die here, and here ends our friendship."

Across the field the archbishop spurred to reconcile the friends. "Carle will come too late to save our lives," said he, "but he will reach the field in time to preserve our mangled bodies and wreak vengeance on our foes."

Roland put his horn to his lips and blew with such force that his temples burst and the crimson blood poured forth from his mouth. Three times he sounded his horn, and each time the sound brought anguish to the heart of Carle, who heard it, riding thirty leagues away. "Our men make battle!" cried he; but this Ganelon hastened to deny, insisting that Roland was but hunting and blowing the horn, taking sport among the peers. But Duke Naimes exclaimed,

"Your nephew is in sore distress. He who would deceive you is a traitor. Haste! Shout your war-cry, and let us return to the battle-field. You yourself hear plainly his call for help!"

Commanding Ganelon to be seized and given to the scullions of his house to be kept for punishment until his return, Carle ordered his men to arm and return to Roncesvalles, that they might, if possible, save the lives of the noble peers. All the army wept aloud as they thought of the doom of Roland. High were the mountains, deep the valleys, swift the rushing streams. The French rode on, answering the sound of the olifant; the emperor rode, filled with grief and rage; the barons spurred their horses, but in vain.

After Roland had sounded the horn he again grasped Durendal, and, mounted on his horse Veillantif, scoured the battle-field, cutting down the heathen. But still their troops pressed him, and when he saw the Ethiopian band led by the uncle of Marsile, he knew his doom had come. Olivier, riding forth to meet the accursed band, received his death-wound from the Kalif, but lived to cut his enemy down, and call Roland to him. Alas! sight had forsaken his eyes, and as he sat on his steed he lifted his bright sword Halteclere, and struck Roland a fearful blow that clove his crest but did not touch his head. "Was the blow meant for me, my comrade?" asked Roland softly. "Nay, I can see no more. God pity me! Pardon me, my friend!" and as the two embraced each other, Olivier fell dead.

Then, in the agony of his grief, Roland fainted, sitting firm in his saddle, and again recovering consciousness, became aware of the terrible losses of the French. Only himself, the archbishop, and the gallant Gaultier de l'Hum were left to defend the honor of the French. After Gaultier fell, Roland, unassisted save by Turpin, who fought transfixed by four spear shafts, put the enemy to flight. Feeling his death wounds, Roland besought Turpin to let him bring together the bodies of his fallen comrades that they might receive the blessing of the archbishop. Weak and trembling from loss of blood, Roland passed to and fro over the

corpse-bestrewn field, and gathered together his comrades:
here, Gerin and Gerier, Berengier and Otun; there, Anseis,
Samsun, and Gerard de Roussillon, and last of all, his beloved Olivier, and placing them before the knees of Turpin,
he saw them receive his blessing.

In his great grief at the sight of the dead Olivier, Roland
again fainted, and Turpin hastened to a little brook near by
for water to revive him. But the strain was too great for his
already weakened body, and, when Roland revived, it was
to find the archbishop dead.

Then Roland, realizing that his hour, too, had come,
sought out a place in which to die. Upon a hill between
two lofty trees, where was a marble terrace, he placed himself
with his head towards the enemy's country; and there a
Saracen, who had feigned death to escape it, tried to wrest
from him his beloved Durendal.

Roland crushed the pagan's head with his olifant, but now
he was troubled, for he feared that his sword would fall into
other than Christian hands. Ill could he bear to be parted
from his beloved sword. Its golden hilt contained rare
relics, — a tooth of Saint Peter, blood, hair, and bones of
other saints, and by the strength of these holy relics it had
conquered vast realms. Ten and more mighty blows he
struck with Durendal upon the hard rock of the terrace, in
the endeavor to break it; but it neither broke nor blunted.
Then, counting over his great victories, he placed it and the
olifant beneath him, and committed his soul to the Father,
who sent down his angels to bear it to Paradise.

When the French army, led by Charlemagne, found the
passes heaped high with the bodies of the dead and no living soul to tell the story of the slaughter, they wept, and
many fell swooning to the earth. But the enraged Charlemagne, unwilling then to give time for mourning, spurred
on his soldiers, overtook the fleeing enemy, and drove them
into the Ebro, so that those who survived the sword, perished by the wave. Then, returning to the field of Roncesvalles, he wept over his beloved Roland and the peers.

Great was his grief; handfuls of hair he tore from his

head, and many times wished that his soul were in Paradise, and his body beside that of Roland. He commanded that the hearts of Roland, Olivier, and Turpin be taken from their bodies, wrapped, and inurned, and the bodies borne home in chariots. The bodies of the others were gathered together in one tomb, and assoiled and blessed by the priests who accompanied the army.

As Charlemagne prepared to start for France, he saw a new army approaching. The aged Emir Baligant, from Babylon, who had long ago been summoned by Marsile, had just arrived in Saragossa, and hastened forth to meet Charlemagne. The emir's army was countless, and Charlemagne's was weakened by its great loss. But the thought of the slaughtered peers spurred on the French, and with great Carle for their leader, they quickly put the pagans to flight.

The Franks pursued the enemy to Saragossa, where the wounded Marsile expired on hearing of his defeat. The city was taken, its inhabitants either slain, or converted and baptized, and Queen Bramimunde taken to France to be won to the true faith by gentler means.

When Charlemagne entered his stately palace at Aix, he was met by the fair lady Aude.

" Where is Roland, my betrothed? "

Carle wept, tearing his white beard.

" Thou askest of one who is no more. But in his place I will give thee my son. I can do no better."

" Nay, God forbid that I should live if Roland is dead ; " and so saying, Aude, the beautiful, fell dead at the feet of the emperor.

From all his lands Carle summoned men to Aix for the trial of Ganelon.

" Judge him according to the law, my barons," said the king. " He lost me twenty thousand of my Franks. My nephew Roland, Olivier, my twelve peers, he sold."

" My king," pleaded Ganelon, " call it not treason. I was ever loyal to you. I thought not of gain, but of revenge against my rebellious and haughty step-son."

The sentiment of many was with Ganelon, and Pinabel

offered to fight for him against Thierri, the champion of the king. Thirty knights of his kin gave themselves as legal sureties of his pledge, and the combat began. Pinabel was conquered and slain, and Ganelon was condemned to be torn to pieces by wild horses. His thirty sureties were also compelled to suffer death.

Ganelon was punished; Bramimunde was made a Christian, and the emperor thought at last to have peace. But as night fell and he sought rest in his lofty room, Gabriel appeared to him.

"Summon thy hosts and march into Bire to succor King Vivien. The Christians look to thee for help."

The king wept and tore his beard. "So troubled is my life!" said he.

## SELECTIONS FROM THE SONG OF ROLAND.

### The Horn.

The Rear Guard of the French army, left behind at Roncesvalles, under Roland, was attacked by a great host of Moors. In the beginning of the battle Olivier besought Roland to recall the emperor by blowing the olifant, whose sound could be heard for many leagues, but Roland refused. But when he saw the overwhelming forces of the Moors, and the field strewn with the corpses of the French, he resolved to blow the horn.

> Seeing so many warriors fall'n around,
> Rollánd unto his comrade Olivier
> Spoke thus: "Companion fair and dear, for God
> Whose blessing rests on you, those vassals true
> And brave lie corses on the battle-field:
> Look! We must mourn for France so sweet and fair,
> From henceforth widowed of such valiant knights.
> Carle, 'would you were amongst us, King and friend!
> What can we do, say, brother Olivier,
> To bring him news of this sore strait of ours!"
> Olivier answers: "I know not; but this
> I know; for us is better death than shame."
>                                        Aoi.

Rollánd says : " I will blow mine olifant,
And Carle will hear it from the pass.   I pledge
My word the French at once retrace their steps."
Said Olivier : " This a great shame would be,
One which to all your kindred would bequeathe
A lifetime's stain.   When this I asked of you,
You answered nay, and would do naught.   Well, now
With my consent you shall not ; — if you blow
Your horn, of valor true you show no proof.
Already, both your arms are drenched with blood."
Responds the count : " These arms have nobly struck."

Aoi.

" The strife is rude," Rollánd says ;  " I will blow
My horn, that Carle may hear." — Said Olivier :
" This would not courage be.   What I desired,
Companion, you disdained.   Were the king here,
Safe would we be, but yon brave men are not
To blame." — " By this my beard," said Olivier,
I swear, if ever I see again sweet Aude,
My sister, in her arms you ne'er shall lie."

Aoi.

Rollánd asked Olivier — " Why show to me
Your anger, friend ? " — " Companion, yours the fault ;
True courage means not folly.   Better far
Is prudence than your valiant rage.   Our French
Their lives have lost, your rashness is the cause.
And now our arms can never more give Carle
Their service good.   Had you believed your friend,
Amongst us would he be, and ours the field,
The King Marsile, a captive or a corse.
Rollánd, your valor brought ill fortune, nor
Shall Carle the great e'er more our help receive,
A man unequalled till God's judgment-day.
Here shall you die, and dying, humble France, . . .
This day our loyal friendship ends — ere falls
The Vesper-eve, dolorously we part ! "

Aoi.

The archbishop heard their strife.   In haste he drives
Into his horse his spurs of purest gold,
And quick beside them rides.   Then chiding them,
Says : " Sire Rollánd, and you, Sire Olivier,
In God's name be no feud between you two ;
No more your horn shall save us ; nathless 't were
Far better Carle should come and soon avenge
Our deaths.   So joyous then these Spanish foes
Would not return.   But as our Franks alight,
Find us, or slain or mangled on the field,
They will our bodies on their chargers' backs

Lift in their shrouds with grief and pity, all
In tears, and bury us in holy ground:
And neither wolves, nor swine, nor curs shall feed
On us — "   Replied Rollánd: " Well have you said."

Rollánd raised to his lips the olifant,
Drew a deep breath, and blew with all his force.
High are the mountains, and from peak to peak
The sound re-echoes ; thirty leagues away
'T was heard by Carle and all his brave compeers.
Cried the king : " Our men make battle !"  Ganelon
Retorts in haste : " If thus another dared
To speak, we should denounce it as a lie."

                                        Aoi.

The Count Rollánd in his great anguish blows
His olifant so mightily, with such
Despairing agony, his mouth pours forth
The crimson blood, and his swol'n temples burst.
Yea, but so far the ringing blast resounds ;
Carle hears it, marching through the pass, Naimes harks,
The French all listen with attentive ear.
" That is Rollánd's horn !" Carle cried, " which ne'er yet
Was, save in battle, blown !"   But Ganelon
Replies : " No fight is there ! you, sire, are old,
Your hair and beard are all bestrewn with gray,
And as a child your speech.  Well do you know
Rollánd's great pride.  'T is marvellous God bears
With him so long.  Already took he Noble
Without your leave.  The pagans left their walls
And fought Rollánd, your brave knight, in the field ;
With his good blade he slew them all, and then
Washed all the plain with water, that no trace
Of blood was left — yea, oftentimes he runs
After a hare all day and blows his horn.
Doubtless he takes his sport now with his peers ;
And who 'neath Heav'n would dare attack Rollánd?
None, as I deem.  Nay, sire, ride on apace ;
Why do you halt?  Still far is the Great Land."

                                        Aoi.

Rollánd with bleeding mouth and temples burst,
Still, in his anguish, blows his olifant ;
Carle hears it, and his Franks.  The king exclaims:
" That horn has a long breath !"  Duke Naimes replies:
" Rollánd it is, and in a sore distress,
Upon my faith a battle rages there !
A traitor he who would deceive you now.
To arms !  Your war-cry shout, your kinsman save !
Plainly enough you hear his call for help."

                                        Aoi.

Carle orders all the trumpeters to sound
The march.   The French alight.   They arm themselves
With helmets, hauberks and gold-hilted swords,
Bright bucklers, long sharp spears, with pennons white
And red and blue.   The barons of the host
Leap on their steeds, all spurring on ; while through
The pass they march, each to the other says :
"Could we but reach Rollánd before he dies,
What deadly blows, with his, our swords would strike ! "
But what avails ?   Too late they will arrive.

Aoi.

The ev'n is clear, the sun its radiant beams
Reflects upon the marching legions, spears,
Hauberks and helms, shields painted with bright flowers,
Gold pennons all ablaze with glitt'ring hues.
Burning with wrath the emperor rides on ;
The French with sad and angered looks.   None there
But weeps aloud.   All tremble for Rollánd.

.     .     .     .     .     .     .

The king commands Count Ganelon be seized
And given to the scullions of his house.
Their chief, named Bègue, he calls and bids : " Guard well
This man as one who all my kin betrayed."
Him Bègue received, and set upon the count
One hundred of his kitchen comrades — best
And worst ; they pluck his beard on lip and cheek ;
Each deals him with his fist four blows, and falls
On him with lash and stick ; they chain his neck
As they would chain a bear, and he is thrown
For more dishonor on a sumpter mule,
There guarded so until to Carle brought back.

Aoi.

High are the mountains, gloomy, terrible,
The valleys deep, and swift the rushing streams.
In van, in rear, the brazen trumpets blow,
Answering the olifant.   With angry look
Rides on the emp'ror ; filled with wrath and grief,
Follow the French, each sobbing, each in tears,
Praying that God may guard Rollánd, until
They reach the battle-field.   With him what blows
Will they not strike !   Alas ? what boots it now ?
Too late they are and cannot come in time.

Aoi.

Carle in great anger rides — his snow-white beard
O'erspreads his breast-plate.   Hard the barons spur,
For never one but inwardly doth rage

That he is far from their great chief, Rollánd,
Who combats now the Saracens of Spain :
If wounded he, will one of his survive ?
O God ! What knights those sixty left by him !
Nor king nor captain better ever had. . . .

Aoi.

*Rabillon's Translation.*

## ROLAND'S DEATH.

WHEN all the French lay dead upon the field except Roland
and the Archbishop Turpin, Roland gathered together the
bodies of his dead comrades, the peers, that they might receive
the archbishop's blessing. He then fell fainting from grief,
and aroused himself to find the archbishop dead also.

Rollánd now feels his death is drawing nigh :
From both his ears the brain is oozing fast.
For all his peers he prays that God may call
Their souls to him ; to the Angel Gabriel
He recommends his spirit. In one hand
He takes the olifant, that no reproach
May rest upon him ; in the other grasps
Durendal, his good sword. Forward he goes,
Far as an arblast sends a shaft, across
A new-tilled ground and toward the land of Spain.
Upon a hill, beneath two lofty trees,
Four terraces of marble spread ; — he falls
Prone fainting on the green, for death draws near.

Aoi.

High are the mounts, and lofty are the trees.
Four terraces are there, of marble bright :
There Count Rollánd lies senseless on the grass.
Him at this moment spies a Saracen
Who lies among the corpses, feigning death,
His face and body all besmeared with blood.
Sudden he rises to his feet, and bounds
Upon the baron. Handsome, brave, and strong
He was, but from his pride sprang mortal rage.
He seized the body of Rollánd, and grasped
His arms, exclaiming thus : " Here vanquished Carle's
Great nephew lies ! This sword to Araby
I 'll bear." He drew it ; this aroused the count.

Aoi.

Rollánd perceived an alien hand would rob
Him of his sword; his eyes he oped; one word
He spoke: " I trow, not one of us art thou!"
Then with his olifant from which he parts
Never, he smites the golden studded helm,
Crushing the steel, the head, the bones; both eyes
Are from their sockets beaten out — o'erthrown
Dead at the baron's feet he falls; — " O wretch,"
He cries, " how durst thou, or for good or ill,
Lay hands upon Rollánd? Who hears of this
Will call thee fool. Mine olifant is cleft,
Its gems and gold all scattered by the blow."

Aoi.

Now feels Rollánd that death is near at hand
And struggles up with all his force; his face
Grows livid; Durendal, his naked sword,
He holds ; beside him rises a gray rock
On which he strikes ten mighty blows through grief
And rage. The steel but grinds; it breaks not, nor
Is notched; then cried the count: Saint Mary, help!
O Durendal! Good sword! ill starred art thou!
Though we two part, I care not less for thee.
What victories together thou and I
Have gained, what kingdoms conquered, which now holds
White-bearded Carle! No coward's hand shall grasp
Thy hilt: a valiant knight has borne thee long,
Such as none shall e'er bear in France the Free!"

Aoi.

Rollánd smites hard the rock of Sardonix;
The steel but grinds, it breaks not, nor grows blunt;
Then seeing that he cannot break his sword,
Thus to himself he mourns for Durendal:
"O good my sword, how bright and pure! Against
The sun what flashing light thy blade reflects!
When Carle passed through the valley of Moriane,
The God of Heaven by his Angel sent
Command that he should give thee to a count,
A valiant captain; it was then the great
And gentle king did gird thee to my side.
With thee I won for him Anjou — Bretaigne;
For him with thee I won Poitou, le Maine
And Normandie the free ; I won Provence
And Aquitaine, and Lumbardie, and all
The Romanie ; I won for him Baviere,
All Flandre — Buguerie — all Puillanie,
Costentinnoble which allegiance paid,
And Saxonie submitted to his power ;
For him I won Escoce and Galle, Irlande

14

And Engleterre he made his royal seat;
With thee I conquered all the lands and realms
Which Carle, the hoary-bearded monarch, rules.
Now for this sword I mourn. . . . Far better die
Than in the hands of pagans let it fall!
May God, Our Father, save sweet France this shame!"

Aoi.

Upon the gray rock mightily he smites,
Shattering it more than I can tell; the sword
But grinds.   It breaks not — nor receives a notch,
And upward springs more dazzling in the air.
When sees the Count Rollánd his sword can never break,
Softly within himself its fate he mourns:
" O Durendal, how fair and holy thou!
In thy gold-hilt are relics rare; a tooth
Of great Saint Pierre — some blood of Saint Basile,
A lock of hair of Monseigneur Saint Denis,
A fragment of the robe of Sainte-Marie.
It is not right that pagans should own thee;
By Christian hand alone be held.   Vast realms
I shall have conquered once that now are ruled
By Carle, the king with beard all blossom-white,
And by them made great emperor and lord."
May thou ne'er fall into a cowardly hand."

Aoi.

The Count Rollánd feels through his limbs the grasp
Of death, and from his head ev'n to his heart
A mortal chill descends.   Unto a pine
He hastens, and falls stretched upon the grass.
Beneath him lie his sword and olifant,
And toward the Heathen land he turns his head,
That Carle and all his knightly host may say:
" The gentle count a conqueror has died. . . ."
Then asking pardon for his sins, or great
Or small, he offers up his glove to God.

Aoi.

The Count Rollánd feels now his end approach.
Against a pointed rock, and facing Spain,
He lies.   Three times he beats his breast, and says:
"Mea culpa!   Oh, my God, may through thy grace,
Be pardoned all my sins, or great or small,
Until this hour committed since my birth!"
Then his right glove he offers up to God,
And toward him angels from high Heav'n descend.

Aoi.

Beneath a pine Rollánd doth lie, and looks
Toward Spain.   He broods on many things of yore:
On all the lands he conquered, on sweet France,
On all his kinsmen, on great Carle his lord
Who nurtured him ; — he sighs, nor can restrain
His tears, but cannot yet himself forget ;
Recalls his sins, and for the grace of God
He prays : " Our Father, never yet untrue,
Who Saint-Lazare raised from the dead, and saved
Thy Daniel from the lions' claws, — oh, free
My soul from peril, from my whole life's sins ! "
His right hand glove he offered up to God ;
Saint Gabriel took the glove. — With head reclined
Upon his arm, with hands devoutly joined
He breathed his last.   God sent his cherubim,
Saint-Raphael, *Saint Michiel del Peril.*
Together with them Gabriel came.   All bring
The soul of Count Rollánd to Paradise.
                    Aoi.
                        *Rabillon's Translation.*

# THE SHAH-NAMEH.

THE monarchs of ancient Persia made several attempts to collect the historic annals of their country, but both people and traditions were scattered by the Arabian conquest. The manuscript annals were carried to Abyssinia, thence to India, and were taken back to Persia just when the weakness of the conquerors was beginning to show itself. The various members of the Persian line, who had declared themselves independent of their conquerors, determined to rouse the patriotism of their countrymen by the recital of the stirring deeds of the warriors of old Persia.

The fame of Abul Kasin Mansur, born at Thus, in Khorasan, A. D. 920, reached Mahmoud of Ghaznin, who was searching for a poet to re-cast the annals of Persia. He called the poet to his court, and, on hearing him improvise, called him Firdusi (the paradisiacal). The poet was intrusted with the preparation of the Shah-Nameh, or Epic of Kings, for every one thousand distichs of which he was to receive a thousand pieces of gold. It had been the dream of the poet's life to build a bridge and otherwise improve his native town. He therefore asked that the payment be deferred until the completion of his work, that he might apply the entire sum to these improvements. But when the poem was completed, after thirty years' labor, the king, instigated by the slanders of the jealous prime minister, sent to the poet sixty thousand silver instead of gold dirhems. The enraged poet threw the silver to his attendants and fled from the country, leaving behind him an insulting poem to the sultan. He spent the remainder of his life at Mazinderan and Bagdad, where he was received with honor, and in his old age returned to Thus to die. Tradition relates that Mahmoud at last discovered the villainy of his minister, and sent the gold to Thus. But the old poet was dead, and his daughter indignantly refused the money. Mahmoud then applied the sum to the improvements of the town so long desired by Firdusi.

The Shah-Nameh is written in the pure old Persian, that Mohammed declared would be the language of Paradise. In its sixty thousand couplets are related the deeds of the Persian kings from the foundation of the world to the invasion by the Mohammedans; but it is of very little value as a historical record, the facts it purports to relate being almost lost among the Oriental exaggerations of the deeds of its heroes.

The only complete translation in a foreign language is the elaborate French translation of Julius Mohl.

The Shah-Nameh is still popular in Persia, where it is said that even the camel drivers are able to repeat long portions of it. Firdusi is sometimes called the Homer of the East, because he describes rude heroic times and men, as did Homer; but he is also compared to Ariosto, because of his wealth of imagery. His heroes are very different from those to whom we have been wont to pay our allegiance; but they fight for the same principles and worship as lovely maids, to judge from the hyperbole employed in their description. The condensation of the Shah-Nameh reads like a dry chronicle; but in its entirety it reminds one of nothing so much as a gorgeous Persian web, so light and varied, so brightened is it by its wealth of episode.

BIBLIOGRAPHY AND CRITICISM, THE SHAH-NAMEH. Samuel Johnson's The Shah-Nameh, or Book of Kings (in his Oriental Religion, Persia, 1885, pp. 711–782); E. B. Cowell's Persian Literature, Firdusi (in Oxford Essays, 1885, pp. 164–166); Elizabeth A. Reed's Persian Literature, Ancient and Modern, 1893, pp. 214–283.

STANDARD ENGLISH TRANSLATIONS, THE SHAH-NAMEH. The Shah-Nameh, Tr. and abridged in prose and verse with notes and illustrations, by James Atkinson, 1832; Abbreviated version taken from a Persian abridgment, half prose, half verse; The Epic of Kings, Stories re-told from Firdusi, by Helen Zimmern, 1882.

# THE STORY OF THE SHAH-NAMEH.

KAIUMERS was the first King of Persia, and against him Ahriman, the evil, through jealousy of his greatness, sent forth a mighty Deev to conquer him. By this Deev, Saiamuk, the son of Kaiumers, was slain, and the king himself died of grief at the loss of his son.

Husheng, his grandson, who succeeded Kaiumers, was a great and wise king, who gave fire to his people, taught them irrigation, instructed them how to till and sow, and gave names to the beasts. His son and successor, Tahumers, taught his people the arts of spinning, weaving, and writing, and when he died left his throne to his son Jemschid.

Jemschid was a mighty monarch, who divided men into classes, and the years into periods, and builded mighty walls and cities; but his heart grew proud at the thought of his power, and he was driven away from his land by his people, who called Zohak to the throne of Iran.

Zohak, who came from the deserts of Arabia, was a good and wise young man who had fallen into the power of a Deev. This Deev, in the guise of a skillful servant, asked permission one day to kiss his monarch between the shoulders, as a reward for an unusually fine bit of cookery. From the spot he kissed sprang two black serpents, whose only nourishment was the brains of the king's subjects.

The serpent king, as Zohak was now called, was much feared by his subjects, who saw their numbers daily lessen by the demands of the serpents. But when the children of the blacksmith Kawah were demanded as food for the serpents, the blacksmith defied Zohak, and raising his leathern apron as a standard, — a banner ever since honored in Persia, — he called the people to him, and set off in search of Feridoun, an heir of Jemschid. Under the young leader the oppressed people defeated the tyrant, and placed Feridoun on the throne.

Feridoun had three sons, Irij, Tur, and Silim. Having tested their bravery, he divided the kingdom among them, giving to Irij the kingdom of Iran. Although the other brothers had received equal shares of the kingdom, they were enraged because Iran was not their portion, and when their complaints to their father were not heeded, they slew their brother. Irij left a son, a babe named Minuchihr, who was reared carefully by Feridoun. In time he avenged his father, by defeating the armies of his uncles and slaying them both. Soon after this, Feridoun died, intrusting his grandson to Saum, his favorite pehliva, or vassal, who ruled over Seistan.

Saum was a childless monarch, and when at last a son was born to him he was very happy until he learned that while the child was perfect in every other way, it had the silver hair of an old man. Fearing the talk of his enemies, Saum exposed the child on a mountain top to die. There it was found by the Simurgh, a remarkable animal, part bird, part human, that, touched by the cries of the helpless infant, carried him to her great nest of aloes and sandal-wood, and reared him with her little ones.

Saum, who had lived to regret his foolish and wicked act, was told in a dream that his son still lived, and was being cared for by the Simurgh. He accordingly sought the nest, and carried his son away with great thanksgiving. The Simurgh parted tenderly with the little Zal, and presented him with a feather from her wing, telling him that whenever he was in danger, he had only to throw it on the fire and she would instantly come to his aid.

Saum first presented his son at the court of Minuchihr, and then took him home to Zaboulistan, where he was carefully instructed in every art and science.

At one time, while his father was invading a neighboring province, Zal travelled over the kingdom and stopped at the court of Mihrab, a tributary of Saum, who ruled at Kabul. Though a descendant of the serpent king, Mihrab was good, just, and wise, and he received the young warrior with hospitality. Zal had not been long in Kabul before he heard of the beauties of Rudabeh, the daughter of Mihrab, and she, in turn, of the great exploits of Zal. By an artifice of the princess they met and vowed to love one another forever, though they knew their love would meet with opposition. Saum and Zal both pleaded Zal's cause before Minuchihr, who relented when he heard from the astrologers that a good and mighty warrior would come of the union. Rudabeh's mother won the consent of Mihrab, so that the young people were soon married with great pomp. To them a son was born named Rustem, who, when one day old, was as large as a year-old child. When three years old he could ride a horse, and at eight years was as powerful as any hero of the time.

Nauder succeeded the good Minuchihr, and under him Persia was defeated by the Turanians, and Afrasiyab occupied the Persian throne. But Zal, whose father, Saum, had died, overthrew him and placed Zew upon the throne. Zew's reign was short, and Garshasp, his son, succeeded him. When he was threatened by the Turanians, his people went for aid to Zal, who, because he was growing old, referred them to Rustem, yet of tender age. Rustem responded gladly, and his father commanded that all the horses from Zaboulistan to Kabul be brought forth that his son might select a steed therefrom. Every horse bent beneath his grasp until he came to the colt Rakush, which responded to Rustem's voice, and suffered him to mount it. From that day to his death, this steed was his faithful companion and preserver.

Garshasp was too weak to rule over the kingdom, and Zal despatched Rustem to Mt. Alberz, where he had been told in a dream a youth dwelt called Kai-Kobad, descended from Feridoun. Kai-Kobad welcomed Rustem, and the two, with the noblest of the kingdom, defeated the power of Turan.

After a reign of a hundred years, the wise Kai-Kobad died, and was succeeded by his son, the foolish Kai-Kaus, who, not satisfied with the wealth and extent of his kingdom, determined to conquer the kingdom of Mazinderan, ruled by the Deevs. Zal's remonstrances were of no avail: the headstrong Kai-Kaus marched into Mazinderan, and, together with his whole army, was conquered, imprisoned, and blinded by the power of the White Deev.

When the news of the monarch's misfortune came to Iran, Rustem immediately saddled Rakush, and, choosing the shortest and most peril-beset route, set forth, unaccompanied, for Mazinderan. If he survived the dangers that lurked by the way, he would reach Mazinderan in seven days.

While sleeping in a forest, after his first day's journey, he was saved from a fierce lion by Rakush, who stood at his head.

On the second day, just as he believed himself perishing of thirst, he was saved by a sheep that he followed to a fountain of water; on the third night, Rakush, whom he had angrily forbidden to attack any animal without waking him, twice warned him of the approach of a dragon. The first time the dragon disappeared when Rustem awoke, and he spoke severely to his faithful horse. The second time he slew the dragon, and morning having dawned, proceeded through a desert, where he was offered food and wine by a sorceress. Not recognizing her, and grateful for the food, he offered her a cup of wine in the name of God, and she was immediately converted into a black fiend, whom he slew.

He was next opposed by Aulad, whom he defeated, and promised to make ruler of Mazinderan if he would guide him to the caves of the White Deev. A stony desert and a wide stream lay between him and the demon; but the undaunted Rustem passed over them, and choosing the middle of the day, at which time Aulad told him the Deevs slept, he slew the guards, entered the cavern, and after a terrible struggle, overcame and slew the great Deev.

He then released Kai-Kaus and his army, and restored their sight by touching their eyes with the blood from the Deev's heart.

Kai-Kaus, not satisfied with this adventure, committed

many other follies, from which it taxed his warrior sorely to rescue him.

Once he was imprisoned by the King of Hamaveran after he had espoused his daughter; again he followed the advice of a wicked Deev, and tried to search the heavens in a flying-machine, that descended and left him in a desert waste. It was only after this last humiliation that he humbled himself, lay in the dust many days, and at last became worthy of the throne of his fathers.

At one time Rustem was hunting near the borders of Turan, and, falling asleep, left Rakush to graze in the forest, where he was espied by the men of Turan and at once captured. When Rustem awoke he followed his steed by the traces of its hoofs, until he came to the city of Samengan. The king received him kindly, and promised to restore the horse if it could be found. While his messengers went in search of it, he feasted his guest, and led him for the night to a perfumed couch.

In the middle of the night Rustem awoke, to see a beautiful young woman enter the room, accompanied by a maid. She proved to be the princess, who had fallen in love with Rustem. She pleaded with him to return her love, promising, if he did so, to restore his cherished horse. Rustem longed for his steed; moreover, the maiden was irresistibly beautiful. He accordingly yielded to her proposals, and the two were wedded the next day, the king having given his consent.

After tarrying some time in Samengan, Rustem was forced to return to Iran. Bidding his bride an affectionate farewell, he presented her with a bracelet.

"If thou art given a daughter, place this amulet in her hair to guard her from harm. If a son, bind it on his arm, that he may possess the valor of Nariman."

In the course of time, the princess bore a boy, who was like his father in beauty and boldness, whom she christened Sohrab. But for fear that she would be deprived of him, she wrote to Rustem that a daughter had been born to her. To her son she declared the secret of his birth, and urged him to be like his father in all things; but she warned him not to disclose the secret, for she feared that if it came to the ears of Afrasiyab, he would destroy him because of his hatred of Rustem.

Sohrab, who had already cherished dreams of conquest, was elated at the knowledge of his parentage. "Mother," exclaimed he, "I shall gather an army of Turks, conquer Iran, dethrone Kai-Kaus, and place my father on the throne; then both of us will conquer Afrasiyab, and I will mount the throne of Turan."

The mother, pleased with her son's valor, gave him for a horse a foal sprung from Rakush, and fondly watched his preparations for war.

The wicked Afrasiyab well knew that Sohrab was the son of Rustem. He was also aware that it was very dangerous to have two such mighty warriors alive, since if they became known to each other, they would form an alliance. He planned, therefore, to aid Sohrab in the war, keeping him in ignorance of his father, and to manage in some way to have the two meet in battle, that one or both might be slain.

The armies met and the great battle began. Sohrab asked to have Rustem pointed out to him, but the soldiers on his side were all instructed to keep him in ignorance. By some strange mischance the two men whom his mother had sent to enlighten him, were both slain. Rustem was moved at the sight of the brave young warrior, but remembering that Tahmineh's offspring was a daughter, thought nothing more of the thrill he felt at sight of him. At last Sohrab and Rustem met in single combat. Sohrab was moved with tenderness for his unknown opponent, and besought him to tell him if he was Rustem, but Rustem declared that he was only a servant of that chief. For three days they fought bitterly, and on the fourth day Rustem overthrew his son. When Sohrab felt that the end had come he threatened his unknown opponent. "Whoever thou art, know that I came not out for empty glory but to find my father, and that though I have found him not, when he hears that thou hast slain his son he will search thee out and avenge me, no

matter where thou hidest thyself.    For my father is the great
Rustem."

Rustem fell down in agony when he heard his son's words,
and realized that his guile had prevented him from being
made known the day before.    He examined the onyx bracelet on Sohrab's arm ; it was the same he had given Tahmineh.
Bethinking himself of a magic ointment possessed by Kai-
Kaus, he sent for it that he might heal his dying son ; but
the foolish king, jealous of his prowess, refused to send it,
and Sohrab expired in the arms of his father.

Rustem's heart was broken.    He heaped up his armor,
his tent, his trappings, his treasures, and flung them into a
great fire.    The house of Zal was filled with mourning, and
when the news was conveyed to Samengan, he tore his garments, and his daughter grieved herself to death before a
year had passed away.

To Kai-Kaus and a wife of the race of Feridoun was born
a son called Saiawush, who was beautiful, noble, and virtuous.
But his foolish father allowed himself to be prejudiced against
the youth by slanderous tongues, so that Saiawush fled from
the court and sought shelter with Afrasiyab in Turan.    There
he speedily became popular, and took unto himself for a wife
the daughter of Afrasiyab.    But when he and Ferandis his
wife built a beautiful city, the hatred and jealousy of Gersi-
waz was aroused, so that he lied to Afrasiyab and said that
Saiawush was puffed up with pride, and at last induced
Afrasiyab to slay his son-in-law.

Saiawush had a son, Kai-Khosrau, who was saved by
Piran, a kind-hearted nobleman, and given into the care of
a goatherd.    When Afrasiyab learned of his existence he
summoned him to his presence, but the youth, instructed by
Piran, assumed the manners of an imbecile, and was accordingly freed by Afrasiyab, who feared no harm from him.

When the news of the death of Saiawush was conveyed
to Iran there was great mourning, and war was immediately
declared against Turan.    For seven years the contest was
carried on, always without success, and at the end of that
time Gudarz dreamed that a son of Saiawush was living

called Kai-Khosrau, and that until he was sought out and placed at the head of the army, deliverance could not come to Iran. Kai-Khosrau was discovered, and led the armies on to victory; and when Kai-Kaus found that his grandson was not only a great warrior, skilled in magic, but also possessed wisdom beyond his years, he resigned the throne and made Kai-Khosrau ruler over Iran.

Kai-Khosrau ruled many long years, in which time he brought peace and happiness to his kingdom, avenged the murder of his father, and compassed the death of the wicked Afrasiyab. Then, fearing that he might become puffed up with pride like Jemschid, he longed to depart from this world, and prayed Ormuzd to take him to his bosom.

The king, after many prayers to Ormuzd, dreamed that his wish would be granted if he set the affairs of his kingdom in order and appointed his successor. Rejoiced, he called his nobles together, divided his treasure among them, and appointed his successor, Lohurasp, whom he commanded to be the woof and warp of justice. Accompanied by a few of his faithful friends, he set out on the long journey to the crest of the mountains. At his entreaties, some of his friends turned back; those who stayed over night, in spite of his warnings, found on waking that they were covered by a heavy fall of snow, and were soon frozen. Afterwards their bodies were found and received a royal burial.

Lohurasp had a son Gushtasp who greatly desired to rule, and was a just monarch, when he succeeded to the throne. Gushtasp, however, was jealous of his son, Isfendiyar, who was a great warrior. When Gushtasp was about to be overcome by the forces of Turan, he promised Isfendiyar the throne, if he would destroy the enemy; but when the hosts were scattered, and Isfendiyar reminded his father of his promise, he was cast into a dungeon, there to remain until his services were again needed. When he had again gained a victory, he was told that the throne should be his when he had rescued his sisters from the brazen fortress of Arjasp, where they had been carried and imprisoned.

On his way to this tower Isfendiyar met with as many terrible foes as Rustem had encountered on his way to the White Deev, and as successfully overcame them. Wolves, lions, enchantresses, and dragons barred the way to the impregnable fortress, which rose three farsangs high and forty wide, and was constructed entirely of brass and iron. But Isfendiyar, assuming the guise of a merchant and concealing his warriors in chests, won his way into the castle, gained the favor of its inmates, and made them drunk with wine. This done, he freed his sisters, slew the guards, and struck down Arjasp.

Instead of keeping his promise, Gushtasp hastened to set his son another task. Rustem was his Pehliva, but it pleased him to send forth Isfendiyar against him, commanding him to bring home the mighty warrior in chains. Isfendiyar pleaded in vain with his father. Then he explained the situation to Rustem, and begged that he would accompany him home in peace to gratify his father. Rustem refused to go in chains, so the two heroes reluctantly began the hardest battle of their lives.

At the end of the first day, Rustem and Rakush were severely wounded, and on his return home Rustem happened to think of the Simurgh. Called by the burning of the feather, the kind bird healed the wounds of the hero and of Rakush, and instructed Rustem how to slay his foe. "Seek thou the tamarisk tree, and make thereof an arrow. Aim at his eye, and there thou canst blind and slay him."

Rustem followed the directions, and laid low the gallant youth. Isfendiyar died exclaiming, "My father has slain me, not thou, Rustem. I die, the victim of my father's hate; do thou keep for me and rear my son!"

Rustem, who had lived so long and accomplished such great deeds, died at last by the hand of his half-brother. This brother, Shugdad, stirred up the king of Kabul, in whose court he was reared, to slay Rustem because he exacted tribute from Kabul.

Rustem was called into Kabul by Shugdad, who claimed that the king mistreated him. When he arrived, the matter was settled amicably, and the brothers set out for a hunt with the king. The hunters were led to a spot where the false king had caused pits to be dug lined with sharp weapons. Rustem, pleased with his kind reception and suspecting no harm, beat Rakush severely when he paused and would go no further. Stung by the blows, the gallant horse sprang forward, and fell into the pit. As he rose from this, he fell into another, until, clambering from the seventh pit, he and Rustem fell swooning with pain.

"False brother!" cried Rustem; "what hast thou done? Was it for thee to slay thy father's son? Exult now; but thou wilt yet suffer for this crime!" Then altering his tone, he said gently: "But give me, I pray thee, my bow and arrows, that I may have it by my side to slay any wild beast that may try to devour me."

Shugdad gave him the bow; and when he saw the gleam in Rustem's eyes, concealed himself behind a tree. But the angry Rustem, grasping the bow with something of his former strength, sent the arrow through tree and man, transfixing both. Then thanking his Creator that he had been given the opportunity to slay his murderer, he breathed his last.

## SELECTIONS FROM THE SHAH-NAMEH.

### The Raja of India sends a Chessboard to Nushirvan.

"This account of the game of chess, written by Ferdusi more than eight hundred years ago, is curious as showing the antiquity of the game, its resemblance to it as now played, and the tradition that it was invented in India, and came originally from that country."

A Mubid related, how one day the king
Suspended his crown over the ivory throne,
All aloes-wood and ivory, and all ivory and aloes;
Every pavilion a court, and every court a royal one;
All the Hall of Audience crowned with soldiers;
Every pavilion filled with Mubids and Wardens of the Marches,
From Balkh, and Bokhara, and from every frontier —

For the King of the world had received advices
From his vigilant and active emissaries,
That an Ambassador had arrived from a King of India,
With the parasol, and elephants, and cavalry of Sind,
And, accompanied by a thousand laden camels,
Was on his way to visit the Great King.
When the circumspect Monarch heard this news,
Immediately he despatched an escort to receive him.
And when the illustrious and dignified Ambassador
Came into the presence of the Great King,
According to the manner of the great, he pronounced a benediction,
And uttered the praise of the Creator of the world.
Then he scattered before him abundance of jewels,
And presented the parasol, the elephants, and the ear-rings ;
The Indian parasol embroidered with gold,
And inwoven with all kinds of precious stones.
Then he opened the packages in the midst of the court,
And displayed each one, article by article, before the King.
Within the chest was much silver, and gold,
And musk, and amber, and fresh wood of aloes,
Of rubies, and diamonds, and Indian swords.
Each Indian sword was beautifully damascened ;
Everything which is produced in Kanuj and Mai
Hand and foot were busy to put in its place.
They placed the whole together in front of the throne,
And the Chief, the favored of wakeful Fortune,
Surveyed all that the Raja had painstakingly collected,
And then commanded that it should be sent to his treasury.
Then the Ambassador presented, written on silk,
The letter which the Raja had addressed to Nushirvan ;
And a chessboard, wrought with such exceeding labor,
That the pains bestowed upon it might have emptied a treasury.
And the Indian delivered a message from the Raja :
"So long as the heavens revolve, may thou be established in thy place !
All who have taken pains to excel in knowledge,
Command to place this chessboard before them,
And to exert their utmost ingenuity
To discover the secret of this noble game.
Let them learn the name of every piece,
Its proper position, and what is its movement.
Let them make out the foot-soldier of the army,
The elephant, the rook, and the horseman,
The march of the vizier and the procession of the King.
If they discover the science of this noble game,
They will have surpassed the most able in science.
Then the tribute and taxes which the King hath demanded
I will cheerfully send all to his court.
But if the congregated sages, men of Iran,
Should prove themselves completely at fault in this science,
Then, since they are not strong enough to compete with us in knowledge,

Neither should they desire taxes or tribute from this land and country:
Rather ought we to receive tribute from you,
Since knowledge hath a title beyond all else."

Khosru gave heart and ear to the speaker,
And impressed on his memory the words which he heard.
They placed the chessboard before the King,
Who gazed attentively at the pieces a considerable time.
Half the pieces on the board were of brilliant ivory,
The other half of finely imaged teak-wood.
The nicely-observant King questioned him much
About the figures of the pieces and the beautiful board.
The Indian said in answer: "O thou great Monarch,
All the modes and customs of war thou wilt see,
When thou shalt have found out the way to the game;
The plans, the marches, the array of the battle-field."
He replied: "I shall require the space of seven days;
On the eighth we will encounter thee with a glad mind."
They furnished forthwith a pleasant apartment,
And assigned it to the Ambassador as his dwelling.

Then the Mubid and the skilful to point out the way
Repaired with one purpose to the presence of the King.
They placed the chessboard before them,
And observed it attentively, time without measure.
They sought out and tried every method,
And played against one another in all possible ways.
One spoke and questioned, and another listened,
But no one succeeded in making out the game.
They departed, each one with wrinkles on his brow;
And Buzarchamahar went forthwith to the king.

He perceived that he was ruffled and stern about this matter,
And in its beginning foresaw an evil ending.
Then he said to Khosru: "O Sovereign,
Master of the world, vigilant, and worthy to command,
I will reduce to practice this noble game;
All my intelligence will I exert to point out the way."
Then the king said: "This affair is thine affair;
Go thou about it with a clear mind and a sound body,
Otherwise the Raja of Kanuj would say,
'He hath not one man who can search out the road,'
And this would bring foul disgrace on my Mubids,
On my court, on my throne, and on all my wise men."
Then Buzarchmahar made them place the chessboard before him,
And seated himself, full of thought, and expanded his countenance.
He sought out various ways, and moved the pieces to the right hand and
    to the left,
In order that he might discover the position of every piece.
When after a whole day and a whole night, he had found out the game,

He hurried from his own pavilion to that of the King,
And exclaimed: " O King, whom Fortune crowneth with victory,
At last I have made out these figures and this chessboard,
By a happy chance, and by the favor of the Ruler of the world,
The mystery of this game hath found its solution.
Call before thee the Ambassador and all who care about it;
But the King of kings ought to be the first to behold it.
You would say at once without hesitation,
It is the exact image of a battle-field."
The King was right glad to hear the news;
He pronounced him the Fortunate, and the bearer of good tidings.
He commanded that the Mubids, and other counsellors,
And all who were renowned for their wisdom should be assembled;
And ordered that the Ambassador should be summoned to the Presence,
And that he should be placed on a splendid throne.

Then Buzarchamahar, addressing him, said:
" O Mubid, bright in council as the sun,
Tell us, what said the King about these pieces,
So may intelligence be coupled with thee forever!"

And this was his answer: " My Master, prosperous in his undertakings,
When I was summoned and appeared before him,
Said to me: ' These pieces of teak and ivory
Place before the throne of him who weareth the crown,
And say to him: Assemble thy Mubids and counsellors,
And seat them, and place the pieces before them.
If they succeed in making out the noble game,
They will win applause and augment enjoyment:
Then slaves and money and tribute and taxes,
I will send to him as far as I have the means;
For a monarch is to be esteemed for his wisdom,
Not for his treasure, or his men, or his lofty throne.
But if the King and his counsellors are not able to do all this
And their minds are not bright enough to comprehend it,
He ought not to desire from us tribute or treasure,
And his wise soul, alas! must come to grief;
And when he seeth our minds and genius to be subtler than theirs,
Rather will he send them to us in greater abundance.' "

Then Buzarchamahar brought the chess-men and board,
And placed them before the throne of the watchful King,
And said to the Mubids and counsellors:
" O ye illustrious and pure-hearted sages,
Give ear all of you to the words he hath uttered,
And to the observations of his prudent chief."

Then the knowing-man arranged a battle-field,
Giving to the King the place in the centre;
Right and left he drew up the army,
Placing the foot-soldiers in front of the battle.

A prudent vizier he stationed beside the King,
To give him advice on the plan of the engagement ;
On each side he set the elephants of war [our bishops],
To support one another in the midst of the combat.
Further on he assigned their position to the war-steeds [our knights],
Placing upon each a horseman eager for battle.
Lastly, right and left, at the extremities of the field,
He stationed the heroes [the rooks] as rivals to each other.
When Buzarchamahar had thus drawn up the army,
The whole assembly was lost in astonishment ;
But the Indian Ambassador was exceedingly grieved,
And stood motionless at the sagacity of that Fortune-favored man ;
Stupefied with amazement, he looked upon him as a magician,
And his whole soul was absorbed in his reflections.
" For never hath he seen," he said, "a chessboard before,
Nor ever hath he heard about it from the experienced men of India.
I have told him nothing of the action of these pieces,
Not a word have I said about this arrangement and purpose.
How then hath the revelation come down upon him ?
No one in the world will ever take his place ! "

And Khosru was so proud of Buzarchamahar,
Thou mightest say that he was looking Fortune in the face.
He was gladdened at his heart, and loaded him with caresses,
And ordered him a more than ordinary dress of honor,
And commanded him to be given a royal cup
Filled to the brim with princely jewels,
And a quantity of money, and a charger and a saddle,
And dismissed him from the Presence overwhelmed with praises.

*Robinson's Translation.*


## ZAL AND RUDABEH.

" ZAL, recovered from the care of the Simurgh and arrived at manhood, is sent to govern the frontier province of Zabul ; the adjoining province of Kabul, though tributary to the Persian emperor, being governed by its own king, called Mihrab. This episode commences with a visit which Mihrab pays to Zal, who receives him with distinguished honor, entertains him at a sumptuous banquet, and they separate with mutual respect."

Then a chief of the great ones around him
Said : " O thou, the hero of the world,
This Mihrab hath a daughter behind the veil,
Whose face is more resplendent than the sun ;
From head to foot pure as ivory,
With a cheek like the spring, and in stature like the teak-tree.

" Upon her silver shoulders descend two musky tresses,
Which, like nooses, fetter the captive;
Her lip is like the pomegranate, and her cheek like its flower;
Her eyes resemble the narcissus in the garden;
Her eyelashes have borrowed the blackness of the raven;
Her eyebrows are arched like a fringed bow.
Wouldst thou behold the mild radiance of the moon? Look upon her
            countenance!
Wouldst thou inhale delightful odors? She is all fragrance!
She is altogether a paradise of sweets,
Decked with all grace, all music, all thou canst desire!
She would be fitting for thee, O warrior of the world;
She is as the heavens above to such as we are."

When Zal heard this description,
His love leaped to the lovely maiden:
His heart boiled over with the heat of passion,
So that understanding and rest departed from him.
Night came, but he sat groaning, and buried in thought,
And a prey to sorrow for the not-yet-seen.

*On returning from a second visit, Mihrab describes Zal to his wife and*
*        his daughter Rudabeh.*

" O beautiful silver-bosomed cypress,
In the wide world not one of the heroes
Will come up to the measure of Zal!
In the pictured palace men will never behold the image
Of a warrior so strong, or so firm in the saddle.
He hath the heart of a lion, the power of an elephant,
And the strength of his arm is as the rush of the Nile.
When he sitteth on the throne, he scattereth gold before him;
In the battle, the heads of his enemies.
His cheek is as ruddy as the flower of the arghavan;
Young in years, all alive, and the favorite of fortune;
And though his hair is white as though with age,
Yet in his bravery he could tear to pieces the water-serpent.

" He rageth in the conflict with the fury of the crocodile,
He fighteth in the saddle like a sharp-fanged dragon.
In his wrath he staineth the earth with blood,
As he wieldeth his bright scimitar around him.
And though his hair is as white as is a fawn's,
In vain would the fault-finder seek another defect!
Nay, the whiteness of his hair even becometh him;
Thou wouldst say that he is born to beguile all hearts!"

When Rudabeh heard this description,
Her heart was set on fire, and her cheek crimsoned like the pomegranate.
Her whole soul was filled with the love of Zal,
And food, and peace, and quietude were driven far from her.

*After a time Rudabeh resolves to reveal her passion to her attendants.*

Then she said to her prudent slaves:
" I will discover what I have hitherto concealed;
Ye are each of you the depositaries of my secrets,
My attendants, and the partners of my griefs.
I am agitated with love like the raging ocean,
Whose billows are heaved to the sky.
My once bright heart is filled with the love of Zal;
My sleep is broken with thoughts of him.
My soul is perpetually filled with my passion;
Night and day my thoughts dwell upon his countenance.

" Not one except yourselves knoweth my secret;
Ye, my affectionate and faithful servants,
What remedy can ye now devise for my ease?
What will ye do for me? What promise will ye give me?
Some remedy ye must devise,
To free my heart and soul from this unhappiness."

Astonishment seized the slaves,
That dishonor should come nigh the daughter of kings.
In the anxiety of their hearts they started from their seats,
And all gave answer with one voice:
" O crown of the ladies of the earth!
Maiden pre-eminent amongst the pre-eminent!
Whose praise is spread abroad from Hindustan to China;
The resplendent ring in the circle of the harem;
Whose stature surpasseth every cypress in the garden;
Whose cheek rivalleth the lustre of the Pleiades;
Whose picture is sent by the ruler of Kanuj
Even to the distant monarchs of the West —
Have you ceased to be modest in your own eyes?
Have you lost all reverence for your father,
That whom his own parent cast from his bosom,
Him will you receive into yours?
A man who was nurtured by a bird in the mountains!
A man who was a by-word amongst the people!
You — with your roseate countenance and musky tresses —
Seek a man whose hair is already white with age!
You — who have filled the world with admiration,
Whose portrait hangeth in every palace,
And whose beauty, and ringlets, and stature are such
That you might draw down a husband from the skies!"

*To this remonstrance she makes the following indignant answer:*

When Rudabeh heard their reply,
Her heart blazed up like fire before the wind.
She raised her voice in anger against them,
Her face flushed, but she cast down her eyes.

After a time, grief and anger mingled in her countenance,
And knitting her brows with passion, she exclaimed:
"O unadvised and worthless counsellors,
It was not becoming in me to ask your advice!
Were my eye dazzled by a star,
How could it rejoice to gaze even upon the moon?
He who is formed of worthless clay will not regard the rose,
Although the rose is in nature more estimable than clay!
I wish not for Cæsar, nor Emperor of China,
Nor for any one of the tiara-crowned monarchs of Iran;
The son of Saum, Zal, alone is my equal,
With his lion-like limbs, and arms, and shoulders.
You may call him, as you please, an old man, or a young;
To me, he is in the room of heart and of soul.
Except him never shall any one have a place in my heart;
Mention not to me any one except him.
Him hath my love chosen unseen,
Yea, hath chosen him only from description.
For him is my affection, not for face or hair;
And I have sought his love in the way of honor."

#### The slaves speak.

"May hundreds of thousands such as we are be a sacrifice for thee;
May the wisdom of the creation be thy worthy portion;
May thy dark narcissus-eye be ever full of modesty;
May thy cheek be ever tinged with bashfulness!
If it be necessary to learn the art of the magician,
To sew up the eyes with the bands of enchantment,
We will fly till we surpass the enchanter's bird,
We will run like the deer in search of a remedy.
Perchance we may draw the King nigh unto his moon,
And place him securely at thy side."

The vermil lip of Rudabeh was filled with smiles;
She turned her saffron-tinted countenance toward the slave, and said:
"If thou shalt bring this matter to a happy issue,
Thou hast planted for thyself a stately and fruitful tree,
Which every day shall bear rubies for its fruit,
And shall pour that fruit into thy lap."

#### The slaves arrange an interview between the lovers.

Then said the elegant cypress-formed lady to her maidens:
"Other than this were once your words and your counsel!
Is this then the Zal, the nursling of a bird?
This the old man, white-haired and withered?
Now his cheek is ruddy as the flower of the arghavan;
His stature is tall, his face beautiful, his presence lordly!
Ye have exalted my charms before him;

Ye have spoken and made me a bargain!"
She said, and her lips were full of smiles,
But her cheek crimsoned like the bloom of pomegranate.

*The interview takes place in a private pavilion of the princess.*

When from a distance the son of the valiant Saum
Became visible to the illustrious maiden,
She opened her gem-like lips, and exclaimed:
"Welcome, thou brave and happy youth!
The blessing of the Creator of the world be upon thee;
On him who is the father of a son like thee!
May destiny ever favor thy wishes!
May the vault of heaven be the ground thou walkest on!
The dark night is turned into day by thy countenance;
The world is soul-enlivened by the fragrance of thy presence!
Thou hast travelled hither on foot from thy palace;
Thou hast pained, to behold me, thy royal footsteps!"

When the hero heard the voice from the battlement,
He looked up and beheld a face resplendent as the sun,
Irradiating the terrace like a flashing jewel,
And brightening the ground like a flaming ruby.

Then he replied: "O thou who sheddest the mild radiance of the moon,
The blessing of Heaven, and mine, be upon thee!
How many nights hath cold Arcturus beholden me,
Uttering my cry to God, the Pure,
And beseeching the Lord of the universe,
That he would vouchsafe to unveil thy countenance before me!
Now I am made joyful in hearing thy voice,
In listening to thy rich and gracious accents.
But seek, I pray thee, some way to thy presence;
For what converse can we hold, I on the ground, and thou on the ter-
        race?"

The Peri-faced maiden heard the words of the hero;
Quickly she unbound her auburn locks,
Coil upon coil, and serpent upon serpent;
And she stooped and dropped down the tresses from the battlement,
And cried: "O hero, child of heroes,
Take now these tresses, they belong to thee,
And I have cherished them that they might prove an aid to my beloved."

And Zal gazed upward at the lovely maiden,
And stood amazed at the beauty of her hair and of her countenance;
He covered the musky ringlets with his kisses,
And his bride heard the kisses from above.
Then he exclaimed: "That would not be right —
May the bright sun never shine on such a day!
It were to lay my hand on the life of one already distracted."

It were to plunge the arrow-point into my own wounded bosom."
Then he took his noose from his boy, and made a running knot,
And threw it, and caught it on the battlement,
And held his breath, and at one bound
Sprang from the ground, and reached the summit.


As soon as the hero stood upon the terrace,
The Peri-faced maiden ran to greet him,
And took the hand of the hero in her own,
And they went like those who are overcome with wine.


Then he descended from the lofty gallery,
His hand in the hand of the tall princess,
And came to the door of the gold-painted pavilion,
And entered that royal assembly,
Which blazed with light like the bowers of Paradise;
And the slaves stood like houris before them:
And Zal gazed in astonishment
On her face, and her hair, and her stately form, and on all that splendor.


And Zal was seated in royal pomp
Opposite that mildly-radiant beauty;
And Rudabeh could not rest from looking towards him,
And gazing upon him with all her eyes;
On that arm, and shoulder, and that splendid figure,
On the brightness of that soul-enlightening countenance;
So that the more and more she looked
The more and more was her heart inflamed.


Then he kissed and embraced her, renewing his vows —
Can the lion help pursuing the wild ass? —
And said: "O sweet and graceful silver-bosomed maiden,
It may not be, that, both of noble lineage,
We should do aught unbecoming our birth;
For from Saum Nariman I received an admonition,
To do no unworthy deed, lest evil should come of it;
For better is the seemly than the unseemly,
That which is lawful than that which is forbidden.
And I fear that Manuchahar, when he shall hear of this affair,
Will not be inclined to give it his approval;
I fear, too, that Saum will exclaim against it,
And will boil over with passion, and lay his hand upon me.
Yet, though soul and body are precious to all men,
Life will I resign, and clothe myself with a shroud —
And this I swear by the righteous God —
Ere I will break the faith which I have pledged thee.
I will bow myself before Him, and offer my adoration,
And supplicate Him as those who worship Him in truth,
That He will cleanse the heart of Saum, king of the earth,

From opposition, and rage, and rancor.
Perhaps the Creator of the world may listen to my prayer,
And thou mayest yet be publicly proclaimed my wife."

And Rudabeh said: "And I also, in the presence of the righteous God,
Take the same pledge, and swear to thee my faith;
And He who created the world be witness to my words,
That no one but the hero of the world,
The throned, the crowned, the far-famed Zal,
Will I ever permit to be sovereign over me."

So their love every moment became greater;
Prudence was afar, and passion was predominant,
Till the gray dawn began to show itself,
And the drum to be heard from the royal pavilion.
Then Zal bade adieu to the fair one;
His soul was darkened, and his bosom on fire,
And the eyes of both were filled with tears;
And they lifted up their voices against the sun:
"O glory of the universe, why come so quick?
Couldst thou not wait one little moment?"

Then Zal cast his noose on a pinnacle,
And descended from those happy battlements,
As the sun was rising redly above the mountains,
And the bands of warriors were gathering in their ranks.

*Robinson's Translation.*

# THE POEM OF THE CID.

RODRIGO Ruy Diaz, El Cid Campeador, was born near Burgos, in Spain, about 1040. The name Cid was given him by the Moors, and means lord. Campeador means champion.

Ruy Diaz was the trusty lord of Sancho, King of Castile, who at his death divided his kingdom among his children. He then espoused the cause of the eldest son, Sancho, and assisted him in wresting their portion of the kingdom from his brothers Garcia and Alfonso. Sancho having been treacherously slain while besieging his sister Urraca's town of Zamora, the Cid attached himself to Alfonso, humiliating him, however, by making him and his chief lords swear that they had had no hand in Sancho's death. For this, Alfonso revenged himself by exiling the Cid on the slightest pretexts, recalling him only when his services were needed in the defence of the country.

This much, and the Cid's victories over the Moors, his occupation of Valencia, and his army's departure therefrom in 1102, led by his corpse seated on horseback, " clothed in his habit as he lived ", are historical facts.

A great mass of romances, among them the story of his slaying Count Don Gomez because he had insulted his father, Diego Laynez; of Don Gomez's daughter Ximena wooing and wedding him; of his assisting the leper and having his future success foretold by him, and of his embalmed body sitting many years in the cathedral at Toledo, are related in the " Chronicle of the Cid " and the " Ballads."

The Poem of the Cid narrates only a portion of his career, and "if it had been named," says Ormsby, "would have been called 'The Triumph of the Cid.'"

The Poem of the Cid was written about 1200 A. D. Its authorship is unknown.

It contains three thousand seven hundred and forty-five lines, and is divided into two cantares. The versification is careless; when rhyme hampered the poet he dropped it, and used instead the assonant rhyme.

The Poem of the Cid is of peculiar interest because it belongs to the very dawn of our modern literature, and because its hero was evidently a real personage, a portion of whose history was recorded in this epic not long after the events took place. The Cid is one of the most simple and natural of the epic heroes; he has all a man's weaknesses, and it is difficult to repress a smile at the perfectly natural manner in which, while he slaughters enough Moors to secure himself a place in the heavenly kingdom, he takes good care to lay up gold for the enjoyment of life on earth. The poem is told with the greatest simplicity, naturalness, and directness, as well as with much poetic fire.

BIBLIOGRAPHY AND CRITICISM, THE CID. Robert Southey's Chronicle of the Cid. . . . Appendix contains Poetry of the Cid by J. H. Frere, 1808, new ed., 1845; Matthew Arnold's Poem of the Cid, MacMillan, 1871, vol. xxiv., pp. 471–485; George Dennio's The Cid: A short Chronicle founded on the early Poetry of Spain, 1845; Butler Clarke's The Cid (in his Spanish Literature, 1893, pp. 46–53); E. E. Hale and Susan Hale's The Cid (in their Story of Spain, 1893, pp. 248–261); Stanley Lane Poole's The Cid (in his Story of the Moors in Spain, 1891, pp. 191–213); Sismondi's Poem of the Cid (in his Literature of the South of Europe, 1884, vol. ii., pp. 95–140); George Ticknor's Poem of the Cid (in his History of Spanish Literature, ed. 6, 1893, vol. i., pp. 12–26); W. T. Dobson's Classic Poets, 1879, pp. 35–138); J. G. von Herder's Der Cid, nach spanischen Romanzen besungen (in his works, 1852, vol. xiv.), translated.

Standard English Translations, the Poem of the Cid. The Poem of the Cid, Tr. by John Ormsby, 1879 ; Translations from the Poem of the Cid by John Hookam Frere (in his works, 1872, vol. ii., p. 409) ; Ballads of the Cid, Tr. by Lewis Gerard, 1883 ; Ancient Spanish Ballads, Tr. by John Gibson Lockhart, 1823.

## THE STORY OF THE POEM OF THE CID.

TEARS stood in the eyes of the Cid as he looked at his pillaged castle. The coffers were empty, even the falcons were gone from their perches. " Cruel wrong do I suffer from mine enemy ! " he exclaimed as they rode into Burgos. " Alvar Fanez, of a truth we are banished men."

From the windows of Burgos town the burghers and their dames looked down with tearful eyes upon the Cid and his sixty lances. " Would that his lord were worthy of him," said they.

He rode up to the gates of his house in Burgos ; the king's seal was upon them. " My lord," cried a damsel from an upper casement, " thy goods are forfeited to the king, and he has forbidden that we open door or shelter thee upon pain of forfeiture of our goods, yea, even of our sight ! "

Little hope then had the Cid of mercy from King Alfonso ; and sooner than bring suffering on his beloved people of Burgos he betook himself without the city and sat him down to think of what to do. " Martin Antolinez," said he, " I have no money with which to pay my troops. Thou must help me to get it, and if I live I will repay thee double."

Then the two together fashioned two stout chests covered with red leather and studded with gilt nails, and these they filled with sand. Then Martin Antolinez without delay sought out the money lenders, Rachel and Vidas, and bargained with them to lend the Cid six hundred marks, and take in pawn for them the two chests filled with treasure that he dared not at that time take away with him. For a year they were to keep the chests and pledge themselves not to look in them. Glad were the hearts of the money lenders as they lifted the heavy chests, and happy was the Cid when he saw the six hundred marks counted out before him.

Seeking the monastery of San Pedro de Cardeña, the Cid embraced his wife Ximena and his two daughters, and left them in the protection of the abbot, to whom he promised recompense. Hard was the pain of parting as when the finger nail is torn away from the flesh, but a banished man has no choice. And as they passed the night at Higeruela a sweet vision promising success comforted the Cid in his slumbers; and many from Castile, who heard of the departure of the hero, sought his banners to better their fortune.

Next day the Cid and his men took Castejon and sold the spoil to the Moors of Hita and Guadalajara, and then my Cid passed on and planted himself upon a lofty and strong hill opposite Alcocer, and levied tribute upon the neighboring peoples. When he had so besieged Alcocer for fifteen weeks he took it by stratagem, and Pero Bermuez, the slow of speech, planted his standard on the highest part. When the King of Valencia heard of this, he determined to capture my Cid, and accordingly sent three thousand Moors to lay siege to Alcocer.

When the water was cut off and bread became scarce, the six hundred Spanish men, acting upon the advice of Minaya, took the field against the three thousand Moors; and such was the valor of him that in a good hour was born, and of his standard bearer, Pero Bermuez, and of the good Minaya, that the Moors fell to the ground three hundred at a time, their shields shivered, their mail riven, their white pennons red with blood.

"Thanks be to God for victory!" said the Cid. In the Moorish king's camp was found great spoil, — shields, arms, and horses. Greatly the Christians rejoiced, for to them fell much spoil, and but fifteen of their men were missing. Even to the Moors my Cid gave some of his spoil, and from his share of one hundred horses he sent by Minaya thirty, saddled and bridled, with as many swords hung at the saddle bows, to King Alfonso. Also he sent by him a wallet of gold and silver for his wife and daughters, and to pay for a thousand Masses at Burgos.

Alfonso was well pleased to receive this token. "It is too soon to take him into favor, but I will accept his present, and I am glad he won the victory. Minaya, I pardon thee;

go to the Cid and say that I will permit any valiant man who so desires to follow him."

Upon the hill now called the hill of the Cid, he who girt on the sword in a good hour, took up his abode and levied tribute on the people for fifteen weeks. But when he saw that Minaya's return was delayed, he went even unto Saragossa, levying tribute and doing much damage, insomuch that the Count of Barcelona, Raymond de Berenger, was provoked into making an assault upon him in the Pine Wood of Bivar, where he was ingloriously defeated and taken prisoner. The count was the more shamed at this because my Cid had sent him a friendly message, saying that he did not want to fight him, since he owed him no grudge. When Count Raymond had given up his precious sword, the great Colada, the good one of Bivar endeavored to make friends with his prisoner, but to no avail. The count refused meat and drink, and was determined to die, until the Cid assured him that as soon as he ate a hearty meal he should go free. Then he departed joyfully from the camp, fearing even to the last lest the Cid should change his mind, a thing the perfect one never would have done.

Cheered by this conquest, the Cid turned to Valencia, and met a great Moorish army, which was speedily defeated, the Cid's numbers having been greatly increased by men who flocked to him from Spain. Two Moorish kings were slain, and the survivors were pursued even to Valencia. Then my Cid sat down before the city for nine months, and in the tenth month Valencia surrendered. The spoil — who could count it? All were rich who accompanied the Cid, and his fifth was thirty thousand marks in money, besides much other spoil. And my Cid's renown spread throughout Spain. Wonderful was he to look upon, for his beard had grown very long. For the love of King Alfonso, who had banished him, he said it should never be cut, nor a hair of it be plucked, and it should be famous among Moors and Christians. Then he again called Minaya to him, and to King Alfonso sent a hundred horses, with the request that his wife and daughters might be allowed to join him. Also he sent him word that he had been joined by a good bishop, Don Jerome, and had created for him a bishopric.

Now were the enemies of the good one of Bivar incensed in proportion as the king was pleased with this noble gift. And when the king silenced the envious ones, and ordered an escort for Ximena and her daughters, and treated Minaya with consideration, the Infantes of Carrion talked together, commenting on the growing importance of my Cid. " It would better our fortunes to marry his daughters, but they are below us in rank." And so saying they sent their salutations to the Cid.

The Cid met his wife and daughters on his new horse, Babieca, the wonder of all Spain, and great was his joy to clasp them again in his arms. And he took them up in the highest part of Valencia, and their bright eyes looked over the city and the sea, and they all thanked God for giving them so fair a prize.

When winter was past and spring had come, the King of Morocco crossed the sea to Valencia with fifty thousand men, and pitched his tents before the city. Then the Cid took his wife and daughters up in the Alcazar, and showed them the vast army. " They bring a gift for us, a dowry against the marriage of our daughters. Because ye are here, with God's help, I shall win the battle."

He went forth on the good Babieca; four thousand less thirty followed him to attack the fifty thousand Moors. The Cid's arms dripped with blood to the elbow; the Moors he slew could not be counted. King Yucef himself he smote three times, and only the swiftness of the horse he rode saved the king from death. All fled who were not slain, leaving the spoil behind. Three thousand marks of gold and silver were found there, and the other spoil was countless. Then my Cid ordered Minaya and Pero Bermuez to take to Alfonso the great tent of the King of Morocco, and two hundred horses. And the king was greatly pleased, and the Infantes of Carrion, counselling together, said, "The fame of the Cid grows greater; let us ask his daughters in marriage." And the king gave their request to Minaya and Bermuez, who were to bear it to the Cid.

Said my Cid, when he heard the proposal: "The Infantes of Carrion are haughty, and have a faction in court. I have no taste for the match; but since my king desires it, I will be silent."

When the king heard his answer, he appointed a meeting, and when he that in a good hour was born saw his king, he fell at his feet to pay him homage. But the king said: "Here do I pardon you, and grant you my love from this day forth."

The next day when the king presented to the Cid the offer of the Infantes, my Cid replied: "My daughters are not of marriageable age, but I and they are in your hands. Give them as it pleases you." Then the king commissioned Alvar Fanez to act for him and give the daughters of my Cid to the Infantes.

The Cid hastened home to prepare for the wedding. The palace was beautifully decorated with hangings of purple and samite. Rich were the garments of the Infantes, and meek their behavior in the presence of my Cid. The couples were wedded by the Bishop Don Jerome, and the wedding festivities lasted for fifteen days. And for wellnigh two years the Cid and his sons-in-law abode happily in Valencia.

One day while my Cid was lying asleep in his palace, a lion broke loose from its cage, and all the court were sore afraid. The Cid's followers gathered around his couch to protect him; but Ferran Gonzalez crept beneath the couch, crying from fear, and Diego ran into the court and threw himself across a wine-press beam, so that he soiled his mantle. The Cid, awakened by the noise, arose, took the lion by the mane, and dragged him to his cage, to the astonishment of all present. Then my Cid asked for his sons-in-law, and when they were found, pale and frightened, the whole court laughed at them until my Cid bade them cease. And the Infantes were deeply insulted.

While they were still sulking over their injuries, King Bucar of Morocco beleagured Valencia with fifty thousand tents. The Cid and his barons rejoiced at the thought of battle; but the Infantes were sore afraid, for they were cowards, and feared to be slain in battle. The Cid told them to remain in Valencia; but stung by shame they went forth with Bermuez, who reported that both had fleshed their swords in battle with the Moor.

Great was the slaughter of the Moors on that field. Alvar Fanez, Minaya, and the fighting bishop came back dripping with gore, and as for my Cid, he slew King Bucar himself, and brought home the famous sword, Tizon, worth full a thousand marks in gold.

The Infantes, still wrathful at their humiliation, talked apart: "Let us take our wealth and our wives and return to Carrion. Once away from the Campeador, we will punish his daughters, so that we shall hear no more of the affair of the lion. With the wealth we have gained from the Cid we can now wed whom we please."

Sore was the heart of the Cid when he heard of their determination; but he gave them rich gifts, and also the priceless swords Colada and Tizon. "I won them in knightly fashion," said he, "and I give them to you, for ye are my sons, since I gave you my daughters; in them ye take the core of my heart." He ordered Feliz Muñoz, his nephew, to accompany them as an escort, and sent them by way of Molina to salute his friend, Abengalvon the Moor.

The Moor received them in great state, and escorted them as far as the Salon; but when he overheard the Infantes plotting to destroy him, and seize his substance, he left them in anger. At night the Infantes pitched their tents in an oak forest full of tall trees, among which roamed fierce beasts. During the night they made a great show of love to their wives, and the next morning ordered the escort to go on, saying that they would follow alone. As soon as they were alone they stripped the daughters of the Cid of their garments, beat them with their saddle-girths and spurs, and left them for dead in the wild forest. "Now we are avenged for the dishonor of the lion," said they, as they departed for Carrion. But Feliz Muñoz, who had suspected the Infantes, had gone forward but a little way, and then crept back, so that from a thicket he perceived the sufferings of his cousins. Straightway he went to their rescue, found them clothes, and helped them home again.

When the Cid heard of this insult to himself and his daughters, he grasped his beard and swore a mighty oath that the Infantes would rue the day when they had thus offended him. All of the Cid's friends strove to comfort the ladies Elvira and Sol, and Abengalvon the Moor made them a rich supper for love of the Cid.

At the request of my Cid, King Alfonso summoned a Cortes at Toledo, to try the cause of the Cid and the Infantes. Thither went the Cid, richly clad, so that all men wondered at his rich garments, his long hair in a scarlet and gold coif, and his uncut beard bound up with cords. He and his hundred men wore bright hauberks under their ermines, and trenchant swords under their mantles, for they feared treachery.

The king appointed some of his counts as judges, and announced that he held this, the third Cortes of his reign, for the love of the Cid. Then my Cid stood forth.

"I am not dishonored because the Infantes deserted my daughters," said the Cid, "for the king gave them away, not I; but I demand my swords, Colada and Tizon. When my lords of Carrion gave up my daughters they relinquished all claims to my property."

The Infantes, well pleased that he demanded no more, returned the swords; and when the blades were unsheathed and placed in the hands of the king, the eyes of the court were dazzled by their brightness.

The Cid presented Tizon to his nephew and Colada to Martin Antolinez. "Now, my king, I have another grievance. I now demand that the Infantes restore the three thousand marks in gold and silver they carried from Valencia. When they ceased to be my sons-in-law they ceased to own my gold." Then the Infantes were troubled, for they had spent the money; but the judges gave them no relief, and they were forced to pay it out of their heritage of Carrion.

"So please your grace," said the Cid, "still another grievance, the greatest of all, I have yet to state. I hold myself dishonored by the Infantes. Redress by combat they must yield, for I will take no other."

The Count Garcia ridiculed the Cid's claim. "The noble lords of Carrion are of princely birth; your daughters are not fitting mates for them." Then, while his enemies were taunting him and the court broke into an uproar, the Cid called on Pero Bermuez, "Dumb Peter," to speak.

When Pero spoke he made himself clear. For the first time he told how like a craven Ferrando had demeaned himself in battle, and how he himself had slain the Moor on whom the prince had turned his back. He also reminded Ferrando of the affair of the lion. When Diego attempted to speak, he was silenced by Martin Antolinez, who told of the figure he cut when he clung to the wine-press beam in an agony of fear, on the day the lion came forth from its cage. Then the king, commanding silence, gave them permission to fight. Martin Antolinez engaged to meet Diego, Pero Bermuez was to combat with Ferrando, and Muño Gustioz challenged the brawler, Assur Gonzalez. It was agreed that the combat should be held at the end of three weeks in the vega of Carrion.

When all had been arranged to his satisfaction, the Cid took off his coif, and released his beard, and all the court wondered at him. Then he offered some of his wealth to all present, and, kissing the king's hand, besought him to take Babieca. But this the king refused to do: "Babieca is for the like of you to keep the Moors off with. If I took him he would not have so good a lord."

When the day for the combat arrived, the king himself went to Carrion to see that no treachery was used, and he said to the Infantes: "Ye have need to fight like men. If ye come out successful, ye will receive great honor. If ye are vanquished, the fault will be on your own heads. Seek to do no wrong; woe betide him who attempts it!"

Then the marshals placed the contestants in the lists and left them face to face. Each with his gaze fixed on the other, they rushed together and met midway of the lists.

At the thrust of Pero's lance, Ferrando fell from his horse and yielded, as he saw the dread Tizon held over him. At the same time Diego fled from the sword of Martin Antolinez, and Muño Gustioz's lance pierced Assur Gonzalez, who begged him to hold his hand, since the Infantes were vanquished.

Thus the battle was won, and Don Roderick's champions gained the victory. Great was the sorrow in the house of Carrion; but he who wrongs a noble lady deserves such suffering.

Rejoiced were they of Valencia when the champions brought home these tidings, and ere long, favored by Alfonso himself, the princes of Navarre and Aragon wooed my Cid's daughters, and were married to them with the most splendid nuptials. Now was the Cid happy, and happier still he grew as his honor increased, until upon the feast of Pentecost he passed away. The grace of Christ be upon him!

## SELECTIONS FROM THE POEM OF THE CID.

### Count Raymond and My Cid.

After one of the victories over the Moors won by the Cid after his banishment by King Alfonso, he despatched a messenger to the king with a gift of thirty horses, and while awaiting his return, encamped in the Pine-wood of Tebar and levied tribute on the surrounding country. This information was conveyed to the Count of Barcelona, Raymond Berenger, who prepared to march against the intruder.

> Great mustering there is of Moors and Christians through the land,
> A mighty host of men-at-arms he hath at his command.
> Two days, three nights, they march to seek the Good One of Bivar,
> To snare him where he harbors in the Pine-wood of Tebar;
> And such the speed of their advance, that, cumbered with his spoils,
> And unaware, my Cid wellnigh was taken in the toils.
> The tidings reached my Cid as down the sierra side he went,
> Then straightway to Count Raymond he a friendly message sent:

"Say to the count that he, meseems, to me no grudge doth owe:
Of him I take no spoil, with him in peace I fain would go."
"Nay," said the count, "for all his deeds he hath to make amends:
This outlaw must be made to know whose honor he offends."
With utmost speed the messenger Count Raymond's answer brought;
Then of a surety knew my Cid a battle must be fought.
"Now, cavaliers," quoth he, "make safe the booty we have won.
Look to your weapons, gentlemen; with speed your armor don.
On battle bent Count Raymond comes; a mighty host hath he
Of Moors and Christians; fight we must if hence we would go free.
Here let us fight our battle out, since fight we must perforce.
On with your harness, cavaliers, quick! saddle, and to horse!
Yonder they come, the linen breeks, all down the mountain side,
For saddles they have Moorish pads, with slackened girths they ride:
Our saddles are Galician make, our leggings tough and stout:
A hundred of us gentlemen should scatter such a rout.
Before they gain the level plain, home with the lance charge we,
And then, for every blow we strike, we empty saddles three.
Count Raymond Berenger shall know with whom he has to do;
And dearly in Tebar to-day his raid on me shall rue."
In serried squadron while he speaks they form around my Cid.
Each grasps his lance, and firm and square each sits upon his steed.
Over against them down the hill they watch the Franks descend,
On to the level ground below, where plain and mountain blend.
Then gives my Cid the word to charge — with a good will they go:
Fast ply the lances; some they pierce, and some they overthrow.
And he that in a good hour was born soon hath he won the field;
And the Count Raymond Berenger he hath compelled to yield;
And reaping honor for his beard a noble prize hath made:
A thousand marks of silver worth, the great Colada blade.

Unto his quarters under guard the captive count he sent,
While his men haste to gather in their spoils in high content.
Then for my Cid Don Roderick a banquet they prepare;
But little doth Count Raymond now for feast or banquet care.
They bring him meat and drink, but he repels them with disdain.
"No morsel will I touch," said he, "for all the wealth of Spain.
Let soul and body perish now; life why should I prolong,
Conquered and captive at the hands of such an ill-breeched throng?"
"Nay," said my Cid; "take bread and wine; eat, and thou goest free;
If not, thy realms in Christendom thou never more shalt see."
"Go thou, Don Roderick," said the Count, "eat if thou wilt, but I
Have no more lust for meat and drink: I only crave to die."
Three days, while they the booty share, for all that they entreat,
The Count his purpose holds unchanged, refusing still to eat.
Then said my Cid, "I pray thee, Count, take food and trust to me;
Thyself and two knights of thy train I promise to set free."
Glad was Count Raymond in his heart when he the promise heard —
"A marvel that will be, my Cid, if thou dost keep thy word."
"Then, Count, take food, and when I see thy hunger satisfied,
My word is pledged to let thee go, thyself and two beside.

But understand, one farthing's worth I render not again
Of what has been in battle lost and won on yonder plain.
I give not back the lawful spoils I fairly win in fight;
But for mine own and vassals' wants I hold them as my right.
My followers are needy men; I cannot if I would;
For spoil from thee and others won is all our livelihood.
And such, while God's good will it is, must be our daily life,
As outcasts forced to wander, with an angry king at strife."
With lighter heart Count Raymond called for water for his hands,
And then with his two gentlemen, sent by the Cid's commands,
He blithely sat him down to meat: God! with what gust ate he!
And glad was the Campeador such heartiness to see.
Quoth he, " Until thou eat thy fill we part not, Count, to-day."
" Nor loth am I," Count Raymond said, " such bidding to obey."
So he and his two cavaliers a hearty meal they made:
It pleased my Cid to watch his hands, how lustily they played.
" Now if thou wilt," Count Raymond said, " that we are satisfied,
Bid them to lead the horses forth, that we may mount and ride.
Never since I have been a Count have I yet broken fast
With such a relish; long shall I remember this repast."
Three palfreys with caparisons of costly sort they bring,
And on the saddles robes of fur and mantles rich they fling.
Thus, with a knight on either hand, away Count Raymond rides;
While to the outposts of the camp his guests the Champion guides.
" Now speed thee, Count; ride on," quoth he, " a free Frank as thou art.
For the brave spoil thou leavest me I thank thee from my heart;
And if to win it back again perchance thou hast a mind,
Come thou and seek me when thou wilt; I am not far to find.
But if it be not to thy taste to try another day,
Still, somewhat, be it mine or thine, thou carriest away."
" Nay! go in peace for me, my Cid: no more I seek of thee;
And thou, I think, for one year's space hast won enough of me."
He spurred his steed, but, as he rode, a backward glance he bent,
Still fearing to the last my Cid his promise would repent:
A thing, the world itself to win, my Cid would not have done:
No perfidy was ever found in him, the Perfect One.

*Ormsby's Translation.*

## MY CID'S TRIUMPH.

IN the Cortes called by the King of Spain to hear the cause
of the Cid, whose daughters had been shamefully treated and
deserted by their husbands, the Infantes of Carrion, Ferran and
Diego Gonzalez, the Cid demanded the restitution of his swords
and of three thousand marks of gold and silver he had given
the Infantes. These being granted, the Cid spoke again:—

" So please your grace ! once more upon your clemency I call ;
A grievance yet remains untold, the greatest grief of all.
And let the court give ear, and weigh the wrong that hath been done.
I hold myself dishonored by the lords of Carrion.
Redress by combat they must yield ; none other will I take.
How now, Infantes ! what excuse, what answer do ye make ?
Why have ye laid my heartstrings bare ?  In jest or earnest, say,
Have I offended you ? and I will make amends to-day.
My daughters in your hands I placed the day that forth ye went,
And rich in wealth and honors from Valencia were you sent.
Why did you carry with you brides ye loved not, treacherous curs ?
Why tear their flesh in Corpes wood with saddle-girths and spurs,
And leave them to the beasts of prey ?  Villains throughout were ye !
What answer ye can make to this 't is for the court to see."
The Count Garcia was the first that rose to make reply.
" So please ye, gracious king, of all the kings of Spain most high ;
Strange is the guise in which my Cid before you hath appeared ;
To grace your summoned court he comes, with that long straggling beard ;
With awe struck dumb, methinks, are some ; some look as though they
                                                         feared.
The noble lords of Carrion of princely race are born ;
To take the daughters of my Cid for lemans they should scorn ;
Much more for brides of equal birth :  in casting them aside —
We care not for his blustering talk — we hold them justified."
Upstood the Champion, stroked his beard, and grasped it in his hands.
" Thanks be to God above," he cried, " who heaven and earth commands,
A long and lordly growth it is, my pleasure and my pride ;
In this my beard, Garcia, say, what find you to deride ?
Its nurture since it graced my chin hath ever been my care ;
No son of woman born hath dared to lay a finger there ;
No son of Christian or of Moor hath ever plucked a hair.
Remember Cabra, Count ! of thine the same thou canst not say :
On both thy castle and thy beard I laid my hand that day :
Nay ! not a groom was there but he his handful plucked away.
Look, where my hand hath been, my lords, all ragged yet it grows ! "
With noisy protest breaking in Ferran Gonzalez rose :
" Cid, let there be an end of this ; your gifts you have again,
And now no pretext for dispute between us doth remain.
Princes of Carrion are we, with fitting brides we mate ;
Daughters of emperors or kings, not squires of low estate :
We brook not such alliances, and yours we rightly spurned."
My Cid, Ruy Diaz, at the word, quick to Bermuez turned.
" Now is the time, Dumb Peter, speak, O man that sittest mute !
My daughters' and thy cousins' name and fame are in dispute ;
To me they speak, to thee they look to answer every word.
If I am left to answer now, thou canst not draw thy sword."
Tongue-tied Bermuez stood, awhile he strove for words in vain,
But, look you, when he once began he made his meaning plain.
" Cid, first I have a word for you : you always are the same,
In Cortes ever jibing me, ' Dumb Peter ' is the name :

It never was a gift of mine, and that long since you knew ;
But have you found me fail in aught that fell to me to do ?
You lie, Ferrando ; lie in all you say upon that score.
The honor was to you, not him, the Cid Campeador ;
For I know something of your worth, and somewhat I can tell.
That day beneath Valencia wall — you recollect it well —
You prayed the Cid to place you in the forefront of the fray ;
You spied a Moor, and valiantly you went that Moor to slay ;
And then you turned and fled — for his approach, you would not stay.
Right soon he would have taught you 't was a sorry game to play,
Had I not been in battle there to take your place that day.
I slew him at the first onfall ; I gave his steed to you ;
To no man have I told the tale from that hour hitherto.
Before the Cid and all his men you got yourself a name,
How you in single combat slew a Moor — a deed of fame ;
And all believed in your exploit ; they wist not of your shame.
You are a craven at the core ; tall, handsome, as you stand :
How dare you talk as now you talk, you tongue without a hand ?
Again, Ferrando, call to mind — another tale for you —
That matter of the lion ; it was at Valencia too.
My Cid lay sleeping when you saw the unchained lion near ;
What did you do, Ferrando, then, in your agony of fear ?
Low did you crouch behind the couch whereon the Champion lay :
You did, Ferrando, and by that we rate your worth to-day.
We gathered round to guard our lord, Valencia's conqueror.
He rose, and to the lion went, the brave Campeador ;
The lion fawned before his feet and let him grasp its mane ;
He thrust it back into its cage ; he turned to us again :
His trusty vassals to a man he saw around him there :
Where were his sons-in-law ? he asked, and none could tell him where.
Now take thou my defiance as a traitor, trothless knight :
Upon this plea before our King Alfonso will I fight ;
The daughters of my lord are wronged, their wrong is mine to right.
That ye those ladies did desert, the baser are ye then ;
For what are they ? — weak women ; and what are ye ? — strong men.
On every count I deem their cause to be the holier,
And I will make thee own it when we meet in battle here.
Traitor thou shalt confess thyself, so help me God on high,
And all that I have said to-day my sword shall verify."
    Thus far these two.   Diego rose, and spoke as ye shall hear :
" Counts by our birth are we, of stain our lineage is clear.
In this alliance with my Cid there was no parity.
If we his daughters cast aside, no cause for shame we see.
And little need we care if they in mourning pass their lives,
Enduring the reproach that clings to scorned rejected wives.
In leaving them we but upheld our honor and our right,
And ready to the death am I, maintaining this, to fight."
Here Martin Antolinez sprang upon his feet :  " False hound !
Will you not silent keep that mouth where truth was never found ?
For you to boast ! the lion scare have you forgotten too ?

How through the open door you rushed, across the court-yard flew;
How sprawling in your terror on the wine-press beam you lay?
Ay! never more, I trow, you wore the mantle of that day.
There is no choice; the issue now the sword alone can try;
The daughters of my Cid ye spurned; that must ye justify.
On every count I here declare their cause the cause of right,
And thou shalt own the treachery the day we join in fight."
He ceased, and striding up the hall Assur Gonzalez passed;
His cheek was flushed with wine, for he had stayed to break his fast;
Ungirt his robe, and trailing low his ermine mantle hung;
Rude was his bearing to the court, and reckless was his tongue.
"What a to-do is here, my lords! was the like ever seen?
What talk is this about my Cid — him of Bivar, I mean?
To Riodouirna let him go to take his millers' rent,
And keep his mills agoing there, as once he was content.
He, forsooth, mate his daughters with the Counts of Carrion!"
Up started Muño Gustioz: "False, foul-mouthed knave, have done!
Thou glutton, wont to break thy fast without a thought of prayer,
Whose heart is plotting mischief when thy lips are speaking fair;
Whose plighted word to friend or lord hath ever proved a lie;
False always to thy fellow-man, falser to God on high.
No share in thy good will I seek; one only boon I pray,
The chance to make thee own thyself the villain that I say."
Then spoke the king: "Enough of words: ye have my leave to fight,
The challenged and the challengers; and God defend the right."

The marshals leave them face to face and from the lists are gone;
Here stand the champions of my Cid, there those of Carrion;
Each with his gaze intent and fixed upon his chosen foe,
Their bucklers braced before their breasts, their lances pointing low,
Their heads bent down, as each man leans above his saddle-bow.
Then with one impulse every spur is in the charger's side,
And earth itself is felt to shake beneath their furious stride;
Till, midway meeting, three with three, in struggle fierce they lock,
While all account them dead who hear the echo of the shock.
Ferrando and his challenger, Pero Bermuez, close;
Firm are the lances held, and fair the shields receive the blows.
Through Pero's shield Ferrando drove his lance, a bloodless stroke;
The point stopped short in empty space, the shaft in splinters broke.
But on Bermuez, firm of seat, the shock fell all in vain;
And while he took Ferrando's thrust he paid it back again.
The armored buckler shattering, right home his lance he pressed,
Driving the point through boss and plate against his foeman's breast.
Three folds of mail Ferrando wore, they stood him in good stead;
Two yielded to the lance's point, the third held fast the head.
But forced into the flesh it sank a hand's breadth deep or more,
Till bursting from the gasping lips in torrents gushed the gore.
Then, the girths breaking, o'er the croup borne rudely to the ground,
He lay, a dying man it seemed to all who stood around.
Bermuez cast his lance aside, and sword in hand came on;

Ferrando saw the blade he bore, he knew it was Tizon:
Quick ere the dreaded brand could fall, " I yield me," came the cry.
Vanquished the marshals granted him, and Pero let him lie.
   And Martin Antolinez and Diego — fair and true
Each struck upon the other's shield, and wide the splinters flew.
Then Antolinez seized his sword, and as he drew the blade,
A dazzling gleam of burnished steel across the meadow played;
And at Diego striking full, athwart the helmet's crown,
Sheer through the steel plates of the casque he drove the falchion down,
Through coif and scarf, till from the scalp the locks it razed away,
And half shorn off and half upheld the shattered head-piece lay.
Reeling beneath the blow that proved Colada's cruel might,
Diego saw no chance but one, no safety save in flight:
He wheeled and fled, but close behind him Antolinez drew;
With the flat blade a hasty blow he dealt him as he flew;
But idle was Diego's sword; he shrieked to Heaven for aid:
" O God of glory, give me help ! save me from yonder blade !"
Unreined, his good steed bore him safe and swept him past the bound,
And Martin Antolinez stood alone upon the ground.
" Come hither," said the king; " thus far the conquerors are ye."
And fairly fought and won the field the marshals both agree.
So much for these, and how they fought: remains to tell you yet
How meanwhile Muño Gustioz Assur Gonzalez met.
With a strong arm and steady aim each struck the other's shield,
And under Assur's sturdy thrusts the plates of Muño's yield;
But harmless passed the lance's point, and spent its force in air.
Not so Don Muño's; on the shield of Assur striking fair,
Through plate and boss and foeman's breast his pennoned lance he sent,
Till out between the shoulder blades a fathom's length it went.
Then, as the lance he plucked away, clear from the saddle swung,
With one strong wrench of Muño's wrist to earth was Assur flung;
And back it came, shaft, pennon, blade, all stained a gory red;
Nor was there one of all the crowd but counted Assur sped,
While o'er him Muño Gustioz stood with uplifted brand.
Then cried Gonzalo Assurez : " In God's name hold thy hand !
Already have ye won the field; no more is needed now."
And said the marshals, " It is just, and we the claim allow."
And then the King Alfonso gave command to clear the ground,
And gather in the relics of the battle strewed around.
And from the field in honor went Don Roderick's champions three.
Thanks be to God, the Lord of all, that gave the victory.
   But fearing treachery, that night upon their way they went,
As King Alfonso's honored guests in safety homeward sent,
And to Valencia city day and night they journeyed on,
To tell my Cid Campeador that his behest was done.
But in the lands of Carrion it was a day of woe,
And on the lords of Carrion it fell a heavy blow.
He who a noble lady wrongs and casts aside — may he
Meet like requital for his deeds, or worse, if worse there be.
But let us leave them where they lie — their meed is all men's scorn.

Turn we to speak of him that in a happy hour was born.
Valencia the Great was glad, rejoiced at heart to see
The honored champions of her lord return in victory :
And Ruy Diaz grasped his beard : " Thanks be to God,'' said he,
" Of part or lot in Carrion now are my daughters free ;
Now may I give them without shame whoe'er the suitors be."
And favored by the king himself, Alfonso of Leon,
Prosperous was the wooing of Navarre and Aragon,
The bridals of Elvira and of Sol in splendor passed ;
Stately the former nuptials were, but statelier far the last.
And he that in a good hour was born, behold how he hath sped !
His daughters now to higher rank and greater honor wed :
Sought by Navarre and Aragon for queens his daughters twain ;
And monarchs of his blood to-day upon the thrones of Spain.
And so his honor in the land grows greater day by day.
Upon the feast of Pentecost from life he passed away.
For him and all of us the Grace of Christ let us implore.
And here ye have the story of my Cid Campeador.

*Ormsby's Translation.*

# THE DIVINE COMEDY.

" This Poem of the earth and air,
This mediæval miracle of song."

DANTE ALIGHIERI was born at Florence, in May,
1265. His family belonged to the Guelph, or Papal
faction, and he early took part in the struggle between the
parties. In 1274 he first saw Beatrice Portinari, and he
says of this meeting in the " Vita Nuova," " I say that thenceforward Love swayed my soul, which was even then espoused
to him." Beatrice died in 1290, and Dante married Gemma
Donati, between 1291 and 1294. In 1295 he joined the
Art of Druggists, in order to become a member of the Ad-
ministrative Council. In 1300 he was made Prior, and in
1301, when the Neri entered Florence, he was exiled, his
property confiscated, and himself sentenced to be burned, if
found within the republic. After this he became a Ghi-
beline, and took up arms against the city with his fellow-
exiles, but withdrew from their council at last because of
disagreements, and separating from them, spent his time at
Verona, Padua, Sunigianda, and in the monastery of Gubbio.
In 1316 the government of Florence issued a decree allowing the exiles to return on payment of a fine ; but Dante
indignantly refused to acknowledge thus that he had been in
the wrong. He was in Ravenna in 1320, and died there
Sept. 14, 1321, on his return from an embassy to Venice.

The " Commedia " was written during Dante's nineteen
years of exile. The three parts, Hell, Purgatory, and Paradise, are emblematic of the threefold state of man, — sin,
grace, and beatitude. The thirty-three cantos into which each
part is divided, are in allusion to the years of the Saviour's
life, and the triple rhyme suggests the Trinity.

The Divine Comedy is written in the *terza rima*, which consists of three verses arranged in such a way that the middle line of each triplet rhymes with the first or third verse of the succeeding triplet.

The entire time occupied in the "Commedia" is eleven days, from March 25 to April 5, 1300.

Dante called the poem a comedy because of its prosperous ending. The prefix "divine" was given it later by its admirers.

The Divine Comedy is sometimes called the epic of mediævalism, and again, the epic of man. Dante himself said: "The subject of the whole work, then, taken literally, is the state of the soul after death, regarded as a matter of fact; for the action of the whole work deals with this and is about this. But if the work be taken allegorically, its subject is man, in so far as by merit or demerit in the exercise of free will, he is exposed to the rewards or punishment of justice."

For a time the Divine Comedy was neglected, and even in comparatively recent times the Inferno was the only portion read; but of late years there has been a re-awakening of interest in regard to the whole poem.

In no other of the epics has the author put so much of himself as Dante has in the "Commedia." It was he himself who saw this vision; he himself, proud, tortured, who carried the sense of his wrongs with him through Hell and Purgatory, even into Paradise. We learn the history of his times, all the crimes committed by men in high position, and we also learn the history of the unhappy Florentine, of whose poem it has been said, "none other in the world is so deeply and universally sorrowful."

BIBLIOGRAPHY AND CRITICISM, THE DIVINE COMEDY. J. Colomb de Batines's Bibliografia Dantesca, 2 vols., 1846; William Coolidge Lane's The Dante collections in the Harvard College and Boston Public Libraries (Bibliographical contributions of the library of Harvard University, 1885); William Coolidge Lane's Additions to the Dante collection

in the Harvard Library (see the Annual Reports of the
Dante Society of Cambridge, Mass., 1887) ; Brother Aza-
rius's Spiritual Sense of the Divina Commedia (in his Phases
of Thought and Criticism, 1892, pp. 125–182) ; Henry
Clark Barlow's Critical Contributions to the Study of the
Divine Comedy, 1865 ; Herbert Baynes's Dante and his
Ideal, 1891 : Vincenzo Botta's Introduction to the Study of
Dante, 1887 ; Oscar Browning's Dante, his Life and Writ-
ing, 1890, pp. 70–104 ; A. J. Butler's Dante, his Time and
Work, 1895 ; Richard William Church's Dante and Other
Essays, 1888, pp. 1–191 ; J. Farrazzi's Manuale Dantesco,
5 vols., 1865–77 ; William Torrey Harris's Spiritual Sense
of Dante's Divina Commedia, 1890 ; Francis Hettinger's
Dante's Divina Commedia, its Scope and Value, Tr. by H. S.
Bowden, 1887 (Roman Catholic standpoint) ; J. R. Lowell's
Essay on Dante (in his Among my Books, 1876) ; Lewis F.
Mott's Dante and Beatrice, an Essay on Interpretation,
1892 ; Giovanni Andrea Scartazzini's A Companion to
Dante, from the German, by A. J. Butler, 1892 ; Denton J.
Snider's Dante's Inferno : a Commentary, 1892 ; Augustus
Hopkins Strong's Dante and the Divine Comedy (in his
Philosophy and Religion, 1888, pp. 501–524) ; John Adding-
ton Symonds's An Introduction to the Study of Dante, Ed. 2,
1890 ; Paget Toynbee's Dictionary of the Divina Comme-
dia, 2 parts ; William Warren Vernon's Readings on the
Purgatorio of Dante, chiefly based on the Commentary of
Benvenuto da Imola ; Intro. by the Dean of St. Paul's, 2
vols., 1889 ; Dr. Edward Moore's Time References in the
Divina Commedia, London, 1887 ; Dr. E. Moore's Contributions to the Textual Criticism of the Divina Commedia,
Cambridge, 1889.

STANDARD ENGLISH TRANSLATIONS, THE DIVINE COMEDY.
The Divine Comedy, the Inferno, a literal prose translation
with the text of the original collated from the best editions,
with explanatory notes by J. A. Carlyle, Ed. 6, 1891 (contains valuable chapters on manuscripts, translations, etc.) ;
Divina Commedia, edited with translation and notes by

A. J. Butler, 1892 ; Vision of Hell, Purgatory, and Paradise, Tr. by H. F. Cary, 1888 ; The Divine Comedy, Tr. by H. W. Longfellow, 1887 ; The Divine Comedy, Tr. by C. E. Norton, 1891–92 (rhythmical prose translation) ; The Divine Comedy, Tr. of the Commedia and Lanzoniere, notes, essays, and biographical introduction by E. H. Plumptre, 1887 ; Divina Commedia, Tr. into English verse with notes and illustrations by J. A. Wilstach, 2 vols., 1888.

## THE DIVINE COMEDY.

### The Hell.

**The** Hell conceived by Dante was made by the falling of Lucifer to the centre of the earth. It was directly under Jerusalem. The earth, displaced by Lucifer's fall, made the Mount of Purgatory, which was the antipodes of Jerusalem.

The unbarred entrance gate, over which stands the inscription, " Leave hope behind, all ye who enter here," leads into a Vestibule, or Ante-Hell, a dark plain separated from Hell proper by the river Acheron. Hell proper then falls into three great divisions for the punishment of the sins of Incontinence, Bestiality, and Malice, which are punished in nine circles, each circle sub-divided. Circle One is the Limbo of the Unbaptized. Circles Two, Three, Four, and Five are reserved for the punishment of the sins of Incontinence, Lasciviousness, Gluttony, Avarice with Prodigality, and Anger with Melancholy. In Circle Six is punished the sin of Bestiality, under which fall Infidelity and Heresiarchy, Bestiality having here its Italian meaning of folly. In Circles Seven and Eight is punished Malice, subdivided into Violence and Fraud. There are three divisions of Violence, — the Violent against their neighbors (Tyrants, Murderers, etc.) ; the Violent against themselves (Suicides) ; and the violent against God (Blasphemers, etc.) ; and ten divisions of Circle Eight, — Fraud, *i. e.*, Seducers, Flatterers, Simoniacs, Soothsayers, Barrators, Hypocrites, Thieves, False Counsellors, Schismatics, and Forgers and Falsifiers. Below these ten pits yawns the well of the giants, above which the giants tower so that half their persons is visible. Within this well in Circle Nine is Cocytus, a lake of ice divided into four belts, — Caina, Antenora, Ptolemæa, and Judecca, where are punished, respectively, the Betrayers of their kindred, of their country, of their friends and guests, and of their benefactors. At the bottom of the pit is Lucifer, half above the ice and half below it, the centre of his body being the centre of gravity.

# THE STORY OF THE DIVINE COMEDY.

## The Hell.

THE poet Dante, in the thirty-fifth year of his life, this being the year 1300 A. D., on New Year's day of the old reckoning, lost his way in a rough and thorny forest, and when he attempted to regain it by mounting a hill that rose before him resplendent in sunshine, encountered a leopard, a lion, and a wolf. Driven back by these, and utterly despairing of rescue, he met one who declared himself to be that Vergil who had sung the fall of Troy and the flight of Æneas, and who promised to take him through the lower world and Purgatory, even unto Paradise. Dante questioned why it was permitted to him to take the journey denied to so many others, and was told that Vergil had been sent to his rescue by the beauteous Beatrice, long since in Paradise. When the poet, trembling with fear, heard that the shining eyes of Beatrice had wept over his danger in the forest, and that she had sought the gates of hell to effect his rescue, his strength was renewed, even as the flowers, chilled by the frosts of night, uplift themselves in the bright light of the morning sun ; and he entered without fear on the deep and savage way.

This allegory, being interpreted, probably means that the poet, entangled in the dark forest of political anarchy, was driven from the hill of civil order by the Leopard of Pleasure (Florence), the Lion of Ambition (France), and the Wolf of Avarice (Rome), and was by divine grace granted a vision of the three worlds that he might realize what comes after death, and be the more firmly established in the right political faith, — Ghibellinism.

" Through me is the way into the sorrowful city ; into eternal dole among the lost people. Justice incited my sublime Creator. Divine Omnipotence, the highest wisdom, and the Primal Love created me. Before me, there were no created things. Only eternal, and I eternal, last. Abandon hope, all ye who enter here ! "

Such was the inscription over the doorway, after the reading of which Dante's ears were assailed by words of agony and heart-rending cries. "This," said Vergil, "is the home of those melancholy souls who lived without infamy and without praise. Cowards and selfish in life, they are denied even entrance to hell." As they looked, a long train passed by, stung by gadflies and following a whirling standard.

Charon, about whose eyes were wheels of flame, endeavored to drive the poet and his guide away as they stood among the weary and naked souls that gathered shivering on the margin of Acheron ; but as a blast of wind and a burst of crimson light caused a deep sleep to fall on the poet, he was wafted across the river, and awaking he found himself in the Limbo of the Unbaptized, the first of the nine circles of hell, where were the souls of many men, women, and infants, whose only punishment was, without hope, to live on in desire. Here was no torment, only the sadness caused by the ever-unsatisfied longing for the ever-denied divine grace. This was Vergil's abode, and in the noble castles set among the green enamelled meadows dwelt Homer, Horace, and Ovid, Electra, Hector, and Camilla.

Passing down a narrow walk into a region of semi-darkness, they entered the second circle, where Minos stood, judging the sinners and girding himself with his tail as many times as was the number of the circle to which the spirit was to go. Here in darkness and storm were the carnal sinners, whose punishment was to be beaten hither and thither by the winds, — Semiramis, Dido, Cleopatra, Paris, Tristan, and all those who had sinned for love, and here Dante conversed with the spirit of Francesca da Rimini, whom he had known in life, and her lover Paolo, slain for their sin by her husband. Though there is no greater sorrow than to be mindful of the happy time in misery, she assured Dante that the sorrows of Hell were lightened by the presence of Paolo.

At the sight of Paolo's grief Dante fell swooning with pity, and awoke to find himself in the circle where a cold rain fell forever on the gluttons. Cerberus guarded the entrance, and now and again devoured the unhappy ones who lay prone on their faces in the murk and mire. Here Ciacco of Florence recognized and spoke with Dante, falling back in the mire as the poet passed on, to rise no more until the Day of Judgment.

Plutus guarded the fourth circle, where were confined the avaricious and prodigal, who, divided into two bands, rolled weights against each other, uttering wretched insults. Down the sloping banks to the marsh of the Styx the poets went, past the sullen and angry, who in life refused the comfort of the sweet air and gladdening sun, and were in consequence doomed forever to remain buried in the sullen mire. As Dante and Vergil passed over the Styx in the boat of the vile Phlegyás, Dante was saluted by the spirit of the once haughty and arrogant Philippo Argenti, whom he repulsed, and gladly saw set upon and torn by the people of the mire.

Then appeared to him the mosques of the city of Dis, within the valley, vermilion-hued from the fire eternal. Deep were the moats ; the walls appeared to be of iron. Upon the flaming summit sat the Furies, stained with blood, begirt with Hydras. Here even Vergil trembled as they waited the arrival of one sent from Heaven to open the gate and admit them.

Within, over the plain, were scattered sepulchres heated red hot, with uplifted coverings, from which issued forth dire laments from the Infidels and Heresiarchs tormented within. To Farinata degli Uberti, who rose from his tomb to ask the news of Florence, Dante spoke, observing in the mean time a shade that, on hearing the Tuscan tongue, rose next Uberti, questioning, " Where is my son, my Guido ? " Fancying from the poet's delay in answering, and his use of the past tense, that his beloved child no longer enjoyed the sweet light, Cavalcante fell back and appeared no more.

Leaving the dismal plain, whose countless tombs would remain open until the Judgment Day, the poets entered upon the next and seventh circle, composed of three smaller circles in which were punished the Violent against their neighbors, against nature, and against God. The steep banks of the ravine were guarded by the huge Minotaur, from which Dante and Vergil escaped only by running.

Within Phlegethon, the boiling river of blood, stood the tyrants, among whom were Dionysius, Azzolin, and Attila, uttering loud laments. If they ventured to stir from their place of torment they were pierced by the arrows of the Centaurs that guarded the banks. The Centaur Nessus conveyed Dante across the river into the second circle, the dolorous forest, where the Violent against nature, the Suicides, were transformed into closely set, twisted thorn-trees, infested with harpies that fed on their leaves, inflicting perpetual pain ; thence into the third circle, where the Violent against God, chief among whom was the arrogant Capaneus, dwelt in a sandy plain surrounded by the dolorous forest. Upon the naked souls, some of whom were lying supine, some crouching, others moving about continually, fell a perpetual shower of flakes of fire.

Picking their way along the edge of the forest, not daring to step on the sand waste, the poets came upon a little blood-red rivulet quenching the flames above it, Phlegethon again, formed by the rivers Acheron and Styx, whose source is the tears of Time. As they skirted the forest they saw a troop of spirits hastening past, one of whom, after a sharp look, grasped Dante's garment exclaiming, " What a wonder ! " The baked countenance, the ghastly face, was that of his old teacher Ser Brunetto, who not daring to stop for fear of increasing his punishment, followed him, questioning him on his appearance below, and comforting him by the assurance of his future greatness. Deep were the burns in the limbs of the other Florentines Dante met below, to whom he gave tidings of the state of affairs in their former home.

Mounting on the shoulders of the hideous monster Geryon, the poets were carried into a fearful abyss whose sides were Alp-like in steepness. This was the eighth circle, Malebolge, or Evil pits, consisting of ten concentric bolge, or ditches of stone with dikes between and rough bridges running across them to the centre.

In the first pit Jason and other deceivers of women were being lashed by horned demons. In pit two, a Florentine friend of Dante's was submerged with others in filth as a punishment for flattery. In pit three the Simoniacs were placed head down in purses in the earth, their projecting feet tortured with flames. The poets crossed the bridge, and Vergil carried Dante down the sloping bank so that he could speak to one who proved to be the unhappy Nicholas III., who accused Boniface for his evil deeds and expressed a longing for his arrival in this place of torture. From the next bridge-top Dante dimly perceived the slow procession of weeping soothsayers with heads reversed on their shoulders. There walked Amphiarus, Tiresias, Manto, and Michael Scott. So great was Dante's sorrow on beholding the misery of these men who had once been held in such great esteem, that he leaned against a crag and wept until reproved by Vergil as a reprobate for feeling compassion at the doom divine. Through the semi-darkness the poets looked down into pit five, where devils with fantastic names pitched barrators into a lake of boiling pitch and speared those who dared to raise their heads above the surface. From these Evil Claws Dante and Vergil escaped only by running into the sixth pit, where walked the hypocrites in richly gilded mantles. When Dante wondered at their weary faces and their tears, he was told by two of the Frati Gaudenti (Jolly Friars) of Florence who suffered here, that the cloaks and hoods were of heaviest lead, a load that grew more irksome with the ages. Caiaphas, Annas, and the members of the council that condemned Christ lay on the ground transfixed with stakes, and over their bodies passed the slow moving train of the hypocrites. The next bridge lay in ruins as a result of the earthquake at the Crucifixion, and Vergil experienced the utmost difficulty in conveying Dante up the crags to a point where he could look down into the dark dungeon of thieves, where the naked throng were entwined with serpents and at their bite changed from man to serpent and back again. Some burned and fell into ashes at the venomous bite, only to rise again and suffer new tortures. Here Dante spoke with Vanni Fucci of Pistoja, who robbed the sacristy of Florence, and whose face " was painted with a melancholy shame " at being seen in his misery. The eighth pit was brightly lighted by the flames that moved back and forth, each concealing within an evil counsellor. Ulysses and Diomed walked together in a flame cleft at the top, for the crime of robbing Deidamia of Achilles, of stealing the Palladium, and of fabricating the Trojan horse. As Dante looked into pit nine he saw a troop compelled to pass continually by a demon with a sharp sword who mutilated each one each time he made the round of the circle, so that the wounds never healed. These were the evil counsellors. Mahomet was there ; there too was Ali. But ghastliest of sights was that of a headless trunk walking through the grim plain, holding its severed head by the hair like a lantern, and exclaiming " O me ! " This was the notorious Bertrand de Born, the Troubadour, who had caused dissension between Henry II. of England and his son. Among this throng Dante recognized his kinsman Geri del Bello, who gave him a disdainful look because he had not yet avenged his death. From the tenth and last pit of Malebolge came a stench as great as though it came from all the hospitals of Valdichiana, Maremma, and Sardinia, between July and September. All the loathsome diseases were gathered into this moat to afflict the forgers and falsifiers. Here Dante saw Athamas, mad king of Thebes, the mad Gianni Schicchi, and Messer Adam of Brescia, the false coiner, who, distorted with dropsy, was perishing of thirst, and thinking constantly of the cool rivulets that descended from the verdant hills of Casentino.

As Dante and his guide turned their backs on the wretched valley and ascended the bank that surrounded it, the blare of a loud horn fell upon their ears, louder than Roland's blast at Roncesvalles. This came from the plain of the giants between Malebolge and the mouth of the infernal pit. All around the pit, or well, were set the giants with half their bodies fixed in earth. Nimrod, as a punishment for building the tower of Babel, could speak no language, but babbled some gibberish. Ephialtes, Briareus, and Antæus were here, all horrible in aspect; Antæus, less savage than the others, lifted the two poets, and stooping set them down in the pit below. This was the last and ninth circle, a dismal pit for the punishment of traitors, who were frozen in the vast lake that Cocytus formed here. In Caina were the brothers Alessandro and Napoleone degli Alberti, mutual fratricides, their heads frozen together. In Antenora was that Guelph Bocca who had caused his party's defeat; but the most horrible sight they encountered was in Ptolemæa, where Count Ugolino, who had been shut up with his sons and grandsons in a tower to starve by the Archbishop Ruggieri, was now revenging himself in their place of torture by continually gnawing the archbishop's head, frozen in the ice next his own. Farther down they walked among those who, when they shed tears over their woe had their teardrops frozen, so that even this solace was soon denied them. Dante promised to break the frozen veil from the eyes of one who prayed for aid, but when he learned that it was the Friar Alberigo, whose body was still on earth, and whose soul was already undergoing punishment, he refused, " for to be rude to him was courtesy."

In the fourth and last division of the ninth circle, the Judecca, a strong wind was blowing. Then Dante saw the emperor of the kingdom frozen in the ice, a mighty giant foul to look upon, with three faces, vermilion, white and yellow, and black. The waving of his two featherless wings caused the great winds that froze Cocytus. Teardrops fell from his six eyes ; in each mouth he was crunching a sinner, Judas Iscariot, Brutus, and Cassius.

Being warned by Vergil that it was time to depart, Dante clasped his guide around his neck, and Vergil began to climb down the huge monster until they reached his middle, the centre of gravity, where with much difficulty they turned and climbed upward along the subterranean course of Lethe, until they again beheld the stars.

## THE DIVINE COMEDY.

### THE PURGATORY.

THE Purgatory of Dante is situated on a mountain top on the opposite side of the earth from Jerusalem, and is surrounded by the western ocean. The souls of those who go there collect on the banks of the Tiber, and are taken to the mountain in a boat by an angel pilot. The shores of the island are covered with the reeds of humility. Around the base of the mount dwell the souls that, repenting late, must " expiate each year of deferred penitence with thirty years of deferred Purgatory " unless the time be shortened by the prayers of their friends on earth. There are three stages of this Ante-Purgatory : the first, for those who put off conversion through negligence ; the second, for those who died by violence and repented while dying ; the third, for those monarchs who were too much absorbed in earthly greatness to give much thought to the world to come. The ascent of the terraces, as also those of Purgatory proper, is very difficult, and is not allowed to be made after sunset. The gate of St. Peter separates Ante-Purgatory from Purgatory proper. Three steps, the first of polished white marble, the second of purple, rough and cracked, and the third of blood-red porphyry, signifying confession, contrition, and penance, lead to the gate where sits the angel clad in a penitential robe, with the gold and silver keys with which to unlock the outer and inner gates. Purgatory proper consists of seven terraces, in each of which one of the seven capital sins, Pride, Anger, Sloth, Avarice, Gluttony, and Lasciviousness are punished ; Pride first, because no other sin can be purged from the body until this deepest sin is eliminated. The soul, cleansed of these sins, mounts to the terrestrial paradise, which, above the sphere of air, crowns the Mount of Purgatory.

# THE STORY OF THE DIVINE COMEDY.

## The Purgatory.

As morning dawned and the poets slowly climbed out of the infernal region and stepped upon the isle from which the Mount of Purgatory rises, they were accosted by an old man with long white hair and beard, Cato of Utica, who demanded the reason of their coming, and only permitted them to remain when he heard that a lady from Heaven had given the command. Then he ordered Vergil to lave the smoke of Hell from Dante's face in the waves of the sea, and to gird him with the reed of humility. As the sun rose a radiant angel, guiding a boat laden with souls, appeared, and the poets fell on their knees until he departed.

As the newly-landed spirits questioned Vergil of the way up the mountain, Dante recognized among them his beloved friend Casella, the musician, and tried in vain to embrace his spirit body. At Dante's request, Casella began to sing, and the enchanted spirits were scattered only by the chiding voice of Cato.

Vergil surveyed the insurmountable height before them, and hastened with Dante to inquire the way of a troop of souls coming towards them. As they talked, Dante recognized one, blond and smiling, with a gash over one eyebrow and another over his heart. It was Manfredi, King of Apulia and Sicily, who was slain at Benevento by Charles of Anjou, and, being under excommunication, was not allowed Christian burial. He asked Dante to make him happy by telling his daughter that by faith he was saved from eternal destruction, but because of his sins he must spend thirty times the time that his presumption had endured at the foot of the mount, unless his time was shortened by the righteous prayers of his friends on earth.

It was with the greatest difficulty that the poets clambered up the steep and narrow path to the next terrace, and only the assurance that the ascent would grow easier as he neared the summit sustained Dante. As Vergil explained to him while resting on the next terrace that the sun appeared on his left because Purgatory and Jerusalem were in different hemispheres, some one spoke, and turning they saw a group of persons in an attitude of indolence, among them a Florentine acquaintance, Belacqua, a maker of musical instruments, who sat waiting the length of another lifetime for admission above because he had postponed conversion from time to time, through negligence.

Proceeding, the poets met a concourse of souls who had suffered violent death, chanting the Miserere, who perceiving Dante to be living, sent messages to their friends on earth. Among these were Giacopo del Cassero and Buonconte di Montefeltro, son of Dante's friend, Guido di Montefeltro, who fell in the battle of Campaldino, in which Dante had taken part. Wounded in the neck, he fell, and had just time to breathe a prayer to Mary, thus saving his soul from the Evil One, who was so incensed that, raising a great storm, he caused the rivers to overflow and sweep away the lifeless body, tearing from it the cross he had made with his arms in his last agony, and burying it in the mire of the Arno. The third shade bade him think of her when, returned home, he sang of his journey. She was Pia, born at Sienna, who died at Maremma, by the hand of her husband.

Dante at last managed to escape from these shades, who implored him to ask for prayers for them on earth, and moved on with Vergil until they met the haughty shade of Sordello, who clasped Vergil in his arms when he learned he was a Mantuan. Touched by this expression of love for his native land, Dante launched into an apostrophe to degenerate Italy, to that German Albert who refused to save the country groaning under oppression, and to lost Florence, torn by internecine wars.

When Sordello learned that the Mantuan shade was Vergil, he humbled himself before him, and paid him reverence, asking eagerly in what part of the underworld he dwelt. The sun was sinking, and as the poets could not ascend by night, he urged them to pass the night with him. Leading them to a vale carpeted with emerald grass and brilliant with flowers, he pointed out the shades singing "Salve Regina" as the Emperor Rudolph, — he who made an effort to heal sick Italy, — Philip III. of France, Charles I. of Naples, and Henry III. of England. As the hour of twilight approached, that hour in which the sailor thinks of home, and the pilgrim thrills at the sound of vesper bells, Dante beheld a shade arise, and lifting its palms begin to sing the vesper hymn. Soon two radiant angels clad in delicate green descended from Heaven, holding flaming swords. These, Sordello explained, were to keep off the serpent that threatened this fair vale at night.

As the hour of night approached in which the swallow laments its woes, Dante fell asleep on the grass and dreamed that he was Ganymede snatched from Mt. Ida by Jove's eagle. Awaking, he found himself alone with Vergil in a strange place, with the sun two hours high. Lucia, symbolical of the enlightening grace of Heaven, had conveyed him to the spot and pointed out to Vergil the gate of Purgatory. Cheered and confident, he rose, and they went together to the portal and mounted the three steps, the first of shining white marble, the second of purple stone, cracked and burnt, and the third of flaming red porphyry. There, on the diamond threshold, sat an angel with a naked sword, clad in a robe of ashen gray, whose face was too bright to look upon. When Dante fell on his knees and implored entrance, the angel imprinted on his forehead seven "P's" for the seven sins (Peccata), and opening the gate with the gold and silver keys, ushered them into the mighty portals. "From Peter I have these keys. Me he instructed to err rather in opening than in keeping shut. But see that ye look not behind, or ye will at once return."

With much difficulty the two poets ascended the steep and winding path, and paused to view the wonderful sculptures on the embankment, that would put Nature herself to shame, so natural were they. Many examples of Humility were there portrayed, — the Virgin Mary, the Holy Ark, drawn by oxen, the Psalmist dancing before the Lord, while

Michal looked forth in scorn from her palace window, and Trajan, yielding to the widow's prayer. As they stood there, the souls came in sight. "Reader, attend not to the fashion of the torment, but think of what follows." The unhappy ones crept around the terrace, bowed under a heavy burden of stones, and the most patient, as he bent under his burden, exclaimed, with tears, "I can do no more!" As they walked they repeated the Lord's Prayer, and kept their eyes fixed on the life-like sculptures on the floor of those who had suffered before them for the sins of pride: Lucifer, falling from Heaven; Briareus and Nimrod overcome by the bolts of Jove; Niobe, weeping among her dead children; Cyrus's head taunted by Tomyris; Troy humbled in ashes.

As Vergil approached the penitents to inquire the way to the next terrace, he and Dante were invited to join the procession and talk with one who could not lift his face enough to see them. This was Omberto, who had been slain by the Siennese for his unbearable pride. Dante also talked with his friend Oderigi, an illuminator of manuscript, who now humbly acknowledged that he was far surpassed by Franco Bolognese. "What is mundane glory?" he exclaimed, as he pointed out Provenzano Salvani, with whose fame Tuscany once rang, but who barely escaped Hell by his voluntary humiliation for a friend. "Lift up thy face!" commanded Vergil, as Dante walked with his head bowed, absorbed in the floor-sculptures; and as he looked, the white-robed angel whose face was like "a tremulous flame" approached, and struck Dante's forehead with his wings. Dante marvelled at the ease with which he mounted, until his master explained that the heaviest sin, the sin that underlies all others, had fallen from him when the angel struck the "P" from his forehead, and that the ascent would grow still lighter from terrace to terrace. "Blessed are the poor in spirit!" sung by sweet voices, greeted the mounting poets.

The second terrace was of livid stone unrelieved by any sculpture. The air was full of voices inculcating charity and self-denial, and others lamenting the sin of envy. Here envy was punished, and here the sharpest pain pierced Dante's heart as he saw the penitents sit shoulder to shoulder against the cliff, robed in sackcloth of the same livid color, their eyelids, through which bitter tears trickled, sewed together with wire. Sapia of Sienna first greeted Dante and entreated him to pray for her. When she had told how, after having been banished from her city, she had prayed that her townsman might be defeated by the Florentines, Dante passed on and spoke with Guido of Duca, who launched into an invective against Florence to his companion Rinieri. "The whole valley of the Arno is so vile that its very name should die. Wonder not at my tears, Tuscan, when I recall the great names of the past, and compare them with the curs who have fallen heir to them. Those counts are happiest who have left no families." Guido himself was punished on this terrace because of his envy of every joyous man, and the spirit with whom he talked was Rinieri, whose line had once been highly honored. "Go, Tuscan," exclaimed Guido, "better now I love my grief than speech." As the poets passed on, the air was filled with the lamentations of sinful but now repentant spirits.

Dazzled by the Angel's splendor, the poets passed up the stairs to the third terrace, Dante in the mean time asking an explanation of Guido's words on joint resolve and trust.

"The less one thinks of another's possessions," replied his guide, "and the more he speaks of 'our' instead of 'my,' the more of the Infinite Good flows towards him. If you thirst for further instruction, await the coming of Beatrice."

As they attained the next height, Dante, rapt in vision, saw the sweet Mother questioning her Son in the Temple, saw Pisistratus, his queen, and the martyred Stephen blessing his enemies in death. As he awoke, they passed on, to become involved in a thick cloud of smoke, through which it was impossible to distinguish any object, and whose purpose was to purge away anger, the sin-cloud that veils the mortal eye.

As they passed from the thick smoke into the sunset, Dante fell into a trance, and saw Itys, Haman, and other notable examples of unbridled anger, and as the visions faded away, was blinded by the splendor of the angel guide who directed them to the fourth terrace. As they waited for the dawn, Vergil answered Dante's eager questions. " Love," he said, " is the seed of every virtue, and also of every act for which God punished man. Natural love is without error ; but if it is bent on evil aims, if it lacks sufficiency, or if it overleaps its bounds and refuses to be governed by wise laws, it causes those sins that are punished on this mount. The defective love which manifests itself as slothfulness is punished on this terrace."

A troop of spirits rushed past them as morning broke, making up by their haste for the sloth that had marked their lives on earth. As they hurried on they urged themselves to diligence by cries of " In haste the mountains blessed Mary won !" " Caesar flew to Spain !" " Haste ! Grace grows best in those who ardor feel !" As the poet meditated on their words, he lapsed into a dream in which he saw the Siren who drew brave mariners from their courses ; and even as he listened to her melodious song, he beheld her exposed by a saint-like lady, Lucia, or Illuminating Grace. Day dawned, the Angel fanned the fourth " P " from his forehead, and the poet ascended to the fifth terrace, where lay the shades of the avaricious, prostrate on the earth, weeping over their sins. They who in life had resolutely turned their gaze from Heaven and fixed it on the things of the earth, must now grovel in the dust, denouncing avarice, and extolling the poor and liberal until the years have worn away their sin.

Bending over Pope Adrian the Fifth, Dante heard his confession that he was converted while he held the Roman shepherd's staff. Then he learned how false a dream was life, but too late, alas ! to escape this punishment. As Dante spoke with the shade of Capet the elder, a mighty trembling shook the mountain, which chilled his heart until he learned from the shade of Statius, whom they next met, that it was caused by the moving upward of a purified soul, his own, that had been undergoing purgation on this terrace five hundred years and more. " Statius was I," said the shade, "and my inspiration came from that bright fountain of heavenly fire, the Æneid ; it was my mother ; to it I owe my fame. Gladly would I have added a year to my banishment here, could I have known the Mantuan." Vergil's glance said " Be mute !" but Dante's smile betrayed the secret, and Statius fell at Vergil's feet adoring. Statius had suffered for the sin of prodigality, which was punished, together with avarice, on this terrace.

The three proceeded upward to the sixth terrace, the ascent growing easier on the disappearance of the " P " of avarice from Dante's forehead. Vergil and Statius moved on in loving conversation, Dante reverently following. " Your Pollio led me to Christianity," said Statius, " but my cowardice caused me long to conceal it. Prodigality brought me hither."

On the sixth terrace two trees stood in opposite parts of the pathway that the gluttons were compelled to tread, the first with branches broad at the top and tapering downward, so that it was impossible to mount it ; upon it fell a fount of limpid water. From its branches a voice cried, " Of this food ye shall have a scarcity. In the primal age, acorns furnished sweet food and each rivulet seemed nectar." Towards the next tree, grown from a twig of the tree of knowledge, the gluttons stretched eager hands, but a voice cried, " Pass on ; approach not ! " Such desire for food was excited by these tempting fruits, that the gluttons were emaciated beyond recognition. By his voice alone did Dante recognize his kinsman Forese, whose time in Purgatory had been shortened by the prayers of his wife Nella. Forese talked with Dante for a while on the affairs of Florence, and predicted the fall of his brother Corso Donati.

The dazzling splendor of the angel of the seventh terrace warned them of his approach, and, lightened of one more

"P," Dante and his companions climbed to where two bands of spirits, lascivious on earth, moved through paths of purifying flames, stopping as they passed to greet each other, and singing penitential hymns. Here, Statius explained to Dante why the shades of the sixth terrace were lean from want of food when they possessed no longer their physical bodies. "After death the soul keeps its memory, intelligence, and will more active than before, and as soon as it reaches either the banks of Acheron or the Tiber, a shade form is attached to it which acquires the soul's semblance, and has every sense given it, even that of sight."

Guido Guinicelli, from out the flame-furnace, explained to Dante the punishments of the terrace: "Thus are our base appetites burned out that we may enjoy future happiness," and Arnaud the Troubadour, hating his past follies, weeping and singing, implored Dante's prayers. It was only by telling him that the fire lay between him and Beatrice that Vergil prevailed on Dante to walk into the flames, which, though they tortured him by the intensity of their heat, did not consume even his garments. As they left the fire, the sun was setting, and they passed the night on the steps of the next terrace, Statius and Vergil watching Dante as the goatherds watch their flocks. In a dream the sleeping poet saw Leah, symbolical of the active life, in contrast to her sister Rachel, of contemplative life. On waking, Vergil told him that he would accompany him further, but not as a guide; henceforth his own free will must lead him. "Crowned, mitred, now thyself thou'lt rule aright."

Dense green were the heavenly woodlands of the terrestrial paradise; sweet were the bird songs, as sweet the songs of the whispering foliage; and on the pleasant mead, beyond the dimpling waters of a stream so small that three paces would span it, walked a beautiful lady, Matilda, gathering flowers and singing an enchanting melody. At Dante's request, she came nearer, and explained to him that God had created the terrestrial paradise from which man was banished by his fault alone. To vex him it was raised to this height. Its atmosphere was not that of the earth below, but given it from the free sphere of ether. Here every plant had its origin ; here each river had its virtue ; Lethe destroyed the memory of sin ; Eunoë restored to the mind the memory of things good.

As they talked, Hosannas were heard, and in the greatest splendor appeared the Car of the Church Triumphant. First came the seven golden candlesticks ; following them, many people in resplendent white garments ; next, the four and twenty elders, lily crowned — the twenty-four books of the Old Testament — singing to Beatrice " O blessed Thou ! " Then four six-winged, many-eyed living creatures described both by Ezekiel and John surrounded the massive car drawn by the Gryphon, emblem of our Lord in his divine and human nature, white, gold, and vermilion-hued, part lion, part eagle, whose wings pierced the heavens.

Three maidens, red, emerald, and white, the Theological Virtues, Faith, Hope, and Charity, danced at the right wheel of the car ; four clad in purple, Prudence, Justice, Fortitude, and Temperance, walked at the left wheel. With them came two old men, Luke and Paul ; then four together, James, Peter, John, and Jude, and last an aged man walking in slumber, Saint John, writer of the Revelation. These last were crowned with red roses and other tinted flowers. With a crash as of thunder, the car stopped before Dante, and a hundred angels, chanting, showered on it roses and lilies. In the midst of the shower, Beatrice descended, clad in a crimson robe, with a green mantle and a white veil, and crowned with an olive wreath. Thrilling with his ancient love, Dante turned to Vergil to sustain him, but Vergil was gone. As he looked again, her eyes, less severe from the veil that enveloped her, were fixed on him as she rebuked him, and he was sustained only by the compassion in the sweet voices of the angels, which soothed him until the tears rained down his cheeks.

After her death, when she had arisen from flesh to spirit, Beatrice complained that her influence was dimmed, and that he had sought such depths that she had been compelled to go to the gates of hell to implore Vergil to bring him hither that he might learn his future sufferings if he did not repent. As he answered her, blaming the things that had led him aside with joys deceitful, he tried to gaze into her eyes, but stung with penitential thorns, fell senseless to the ground. Matilda, who stood by, seized him and plunged him into the river Lethe, that he might forget his past sin. Dripping, he was given to the four lovely maidens, who led him before Beatrice that he might look into her eyes, fixed on the Gryphon. A thousand longings held him fast while, "weary from ten years' thirsting," he gazed upon her lovely eyes, now unveiled in their full splendor. Reproached at last by the seven virtues for his too intent gaze, Dante watched the car move on to the Tree of Knowledge, to which its pole was attached by the Gryphon. Dante, lulled to sleep by the hymn, was aroused by Matilda, who pointed out to him the radiant Beatrice, sitting under a tree surrounded by the bright forms of her attendants. The other attendants of the car had followed the Gryphon to the skies.

"Observe the car," said Beatrice, "and write what thou hast seen when thou returnest home." As she spoke, the car was attacked in turn by the eagle of persecution, the fox of heresy, and the dragon of Islamism; these driven away, it was disturbed by inward dissensions, the alliance between Boniface and Philip the Fair.

Rising, Beatrice called Dante, Statius, and Matilda to her, and as they walked upon that pleasant mead, she asked Dante the meaning of his continued silence. She explained the attacks on the chariot to him, but he declared that he could not understand her language. Then, at Beatrice's nod, Matilda called him and Statius, and plunged them into Eunoë, whence he rose regenerate, and prepared to mount to the stars.

# THE DIVINE COMEDY.

### The Paradise.

THE Paradise of Dante consists of nine heavens, each a revolving crystalline sphere, enclosed in another; without them, the boundless Empyrean. The first or innermost heaven, of the Moon, revolved by the angels, is the habitat of wills imperfect through instability. The second, of Mercury, revolved by the Archangels, is the abode of wills imperfect through love of fame. The third, of Venus, revolved by the Principalities, is the abode of wills imperfect through excess of human love. The fourth, of the Sun, revolved by the Powers, is the abode of the great intellectual lights, the doctors of the Church. The fifth heaven, of Mars, revolved by the Virtues, is the abode of the martyrs, warriors, and confessors, and is sacred to the Faith. The sixth, of Jupiter, revolved by the Dominations, is inhabited by just rulers. The seventh, of Saturn, revolved by the Thrones, is inhabited by monks and hermits. The eighth, of the Fixed Stars, revolved by the Cherubim, is inhabited by the apostles and saints. The ninth, or Primum Mobile, revolved by the Seraphim, is the abode of the moral philosophers. These abodes, however, are not real, but representative, to illustrate the differences in glory of the inhabitants of Paradise, for the real seat of each is in the Rose of the Blessed. In the heavens, the saints appear swathed in cocoons of light; in the Rose they are seen in their own forms. They know all because they behold God continually. In the Empyrean is the Rose of the Blessed, whose myriad leaves form the thrones of the spirits, and whose centre of light is the Father himself. Dividing the Rose horizontally, the lower thrones are held by those who died in infancy; among them are varying degrees of glory. Above it, are those who died adults. Supposing a vertical division, the thrones to the left are for those who looked forward to Christ's coming;

those to the right, not yet all occupied, by those who died after Christ's coming. Along the division lines are the holy women, the Virgin, Eve, Rachel, Beatrice, Sarah, Rebecca, Judith, and Ruth, Saint Anne and Saint Lucia, and the saints, John the Baptist, John the Evangelist, Adam, Moses, Saint Francis, Saint Benedict, Saint Augustine, Saint Peter, and in the midst, the Everlasting Glory of the Universe, whose light so fills the Rose that "naught can form an obstacle against it."

## THE STORY OF THE DIVINE COMEDY.

### The Paradise.

THE ascent to Paradise was accomplished by a fixed gaze into Beatrice's eyes, by which Dante, like Glaucus, was made divine, and by which he was lifted, with incredible swiftness, through the heavens. As soon as he had fixed his eyes on Beatrice's, who in turn looked towards heaven, they found themselves in the Heaven of the Moon, whose luminous yet pearl-like light enfolded them. While Beatrice was explaining to him that the spots on the moon were not caused by the varying degrees of atmospheric density, as he had supposed, but by the Divine Virtue infused in divine measure through the angelic dwellers in the first heaven, he met Piccarda, his sister-in-law, whose brother, Corso Donati, had torn her from her convent to wed her to Rosselin della Tosa, soon after which she died. Here also was Costanza, daughter of Roger I. of Sicily, grandmother of that Manfredi whom he had seen in Purgatory. Here Beatrice instructed Dante as to the imperfection of those wills that held not to their vows, but allowed violence to thwart them.

Another look into the smiling eyes, and the two were in the Heaven of Mercury, where those wills abide in whom love of fame partly extinguished love of God. One of the thousand splendors that advanced towards them was the soul of the Emperor Justinian, who reviewed the Empire, the Church, condemning severely the behavior of the Guelphs and Ghibellines, and told of the spirits who inhabited the little planet, whose lives were sweetened by living justice, and whose ears were gladdened by the sweetest harmonies.

Dante was unaware of his ascent into Venus, where dwelt those souls who were lovers on earth, until he perceived Beatrice's added beauty. Amid revolving lights Charles Martel of Hungary appeared, denounced his brother Robert of Sicily, and instructed Dante on the subjects of heredity and degeneracy ; that "sweet seed can come bitter" because the influence of the star under which the child is born can counteract that of the parent, and because his state is not always adapted to him by his parents and advisers.

In the sphere of the Sun, consecrated to the great doctors of divinity, Beatrice became still more beautiful ; but so absorbed was the poet in the love for the Eternal Source of all this splendor that for the first time he forgot her. Out of the whirling lights, shining like precious jewels, came Saint Thomas Aquinas, who pointed out to Dante his noted companions, Gratian, Peter Lombard, Solomon, Dionysius, Bœthius, and Bæda. Thomas then related the story of Saint Francis of Assisi and the founding of his order of the Franciscans, upon which Saint Bonaventura of the Franciscans, from the next flame garland, told of Saint Dominic and the Dominican order. Alas ! while both orders were great in the beginning, both narrators had to censure their present corruption.

The array of brilliant lights, dividing itself, formed into two disks which, revolving oppositely, sang the praises of the Trinity. The song of praise finished, Saint Thomas explained that Solomon was elevated to this sphere for his wisdom and his regal prudence, and warned Dante against the error of rash judgment.

The splendor of Mars was almost blinding ; it was ruddier than the others, and in it dwelt the souls of the crusaders and martyrs. While Dante's ears were ravished by exquisite music, his eyes were dazzled by the lights, which had arranged themselves in the form of a cross. From out the splendor, one star saluted Dante. It was the soul of his ancestor Cacciaguida, who had waited long for the coming of his descendant. He related to Dante the story of his life, commenting on the difference between the simple life of the Florentines of his day and the corrupt practices of Dante's time, and broke to the poet what had already been darkly hinted to him in Hell and Purgatory, — his banishment; how he must depart from Florence and learn how salt is the bread of charity, how wearisome the stairs in the abode of the stranger.

As Cacciaguida ceased and pointed out the other well-known dwellers in Mars, each one on the cross flashed as his name was called, — Joshua, Judas Maccabeus, Charlemagne and Roland, Godfrey of Bouillon, Robert Guiscard, and others.

In Jupiter, whose whiteness contrasted with the ruddiness of Mars, dwelt the souls of great rulers, certain of whom arranged themselves first to form the golden letters of *Diligite Justitiam qui judicatis terram* ("Love righteousness, ye that be judges of the earth"), and then formed themselves into the Roman eagle and sang of the justice and mercy that caused their elevation to this position, and of events about to occur in history.

Had Beatrice smiled as they ascended to Saturn, Dante would have perished as did Semele, from excess of light. In Saturn dwelt the spirits of the contemplative, the monks and hermits, and here was Jacob's ladder, up and down whose bars of gold sparkled the spirits of the saints, silent for the same reason that Beatrice smiled not. By divine election, Saint Peter Damian descended and spoke with Dante, accusing the churchmen of the time of worldliness and luxury. "Cephas and our Lord came on earth barefoot and poorly clad, but these men are covered with gorgeous raiment and ride upon sleek palfreys." As he closed, a thunder cry of approval went up from the other saints.

Up the wonderful ladder passed Dante and his lady into the eighth heaven of the Fixed Stars, and looking down saw the little earth and the starry heavens through which they had passed. Then, as Beatrice paused with her face all aflame, and her eyes full of ecstasy, down came the hosts of Christ's triumphal march, and within the living light, which dazzled Dante's eyes until he could not see, also appeared Mary, mother of God, crowned by Gabriel, rising into the Empyrean. Of those who remained behind, Beatrice asked that Dante be sprinkled with the waters of the living Fountain ; and while they gave their consent, Saint Peter appeared as a fire whirling ecstatically, and singing a divine song. He examined the trembling poet on faith, and his questions being answered satisfactorily, encircled him thrice with his light. Saint James, who next came forth, was likewise pleased with his response on Hope, and he was then blinded by the effulgence of John, so that for a time he could not see the face of his lady.

Of Love he spoke with John, and then talked with Adam. As he listened to the strains of richest melody, he noticed one of the lights — Saint Peter — change from white to red, and then, as silence fell, speak, enraged at the worldliness of the Holy See. " My cemetery has been made a sewer of blood and stench. When thou returnest to earth, reveal what thou hast heard. Do not thou conceal what I have not concealed."

Commanded by Beatrice, Dante looked back at earth once more, and as he looked, was carried up into the heaven of the Primum Mobile, where dwelt the moral philosophers. Here the angelic spirits circled round the point of intense light, the divine centre. The nearer God was the circle, the greater virtue it possessed. This order was inverse to that of the heavens, but Dante learned from Beatrice that the orbs revolved through narrow paths or wide according to the virtue of their parts, and that a strict agreement of harmony prevailed between the great and the small. The angel and the heavens were created simultaneously, and, as direct emanations from God, know no decay. Of this and many things concerning the Creation, did Beatrice enlighten Dante before the beauty of her smile told him that they were in the Empyrean. " Now shalt thou look upon the mighty hosts of Paradise."

The poet's dazzled eyes saw then a river of light from which issued living sparks sunk down into the flowers like rubies set in gold. Instructed by Beatrice he drank of the stream and the river changed into a lake; then he saw the Courts of Heaven made manifest, and the splendor of God. The ample Rose unfolded its leaves before him, breathing praise and perfume, and as he gazed into it Beatrice pointed out the radiant spirits and the thronged seats, one of which was reserved for the Emperor Henry of Luxembourg, from whom Dante expected so much, and who died before aught was accomplished. As Dante gazed, the hosts with wings of gold and faces of living flame, singing anthems, alternately sank into the Rose, like a swarm of bees sinking into summer flowers, and rose again to view the Divine splendor. Turning to question Beatrice again, Dante found in her place Saint Bernard of Clairvaux, an old man full of the tenderest pity, who pointed out to him Beatrice in her own place, the third round of the first rank. As from afar, Dante pleaded with the beautiful lady who had left her place in heaven to go even unto the gates of hell for his sake, to aid him still; she seemed to smile upon him before she again turned her gaze upon the Eternal Fountain of Light. Saint Bernard explained to the poet the divisions of the Rose and the seats of the saints, and then addressed a prayer to the Virgin, asking that Dante be permitted to look upon the Almighty Father. As he prayed, Beatrice and all the blessed ones clasped their hands to her who likes so well prayers of divine fervor. At a gesture from Bernard, the poet looked upward. Then what a radiant vision met his eyes! Three circles he saw of threefold color and one dimension. As he looked, one seemed to take our image, and again was lost in the infinite glory of the Light Divine. As he tried to describe it, imagination failed him, though his will remained, moving on with the even motion of the sun and stars.

## SELECTIONS FROM THE DIVINE COMEDY.

### Count Ugolino.

IN the frozen lake of Cocytus in the ninth circle of the Inferno, where were punished the traitors to kindred, country, friends, or benefactors, the poets beheld Count Ugolino, a Guelph, who, because of his treachery, was taken prisoner by the people with his sons and grandsons and thrust into a tower, where they were left to starve. Ugolino was frozen in the ice, where he forever gnawed the head of the Archbishop Ruggieri, his enemy. At the request of Dante he stopped to tell his story.

> " Thy will 'tis I renew
>     A desperate sorrow that doth crush my heart
>     Even before my lips its tale impart.
> But if my words may be a seed that, sowed,
>     Shall fruit of infamy to this traitor bear,
>     Then, though I weep, speech too shall be my care.
>
> " Who thou may'st be I know not, nor what mode
>     Hath brought thee here below, but then I glean,
>     From words of thine, thou art a Florentine.
> That I Count Ugolino was, know thou,
>     And this the Archbishop Ruggieri. Why
>     I will thee tell we are such neighbors nigh.
> Needs not to say that him I did allow
>     A friend's own trusts, but so his treachery wrought
>     That first my liberty, then my life, it sought.
>
> " But that which thou canst not have hitherto learned
>     That is, how cruel was my death, I thee
>     Will tell; judge thou if he offended me.
> Within the Mew, a tower which well hath earned
>     From me its name of Famine, and where wrath
>     Yet others waits, a narrow opening hath,
> Through which of several moons the broken light
>     Had strayed, when unto me in sleep was sent
>     A dream whereby the future's veil was rent.
>
> " This ill dream me this man set forth in might:
>     He wolf and whelps upon those mounts pursued
>     Which Pisa 'twixt and Lucca's domes obtrude.
> Hounds had he with him, lank and shrewd and keen,
>     And in their front Gualandi's sword had place,
>     Sismondi's lash and sour Lanfranchi's mace.

Father and sons' undoing soon was seen;
    Methought the sharp fangs on them closed, and tore
    Their flanks, which now the hue of crimson wore.

" Before the dawn I woke and heard my sons,
    The helpless children with me, in their sleep,
    Cry out for bread, cries pushed from sobbings deep.
Right cruel art thou, if not e'en now runs
    To tears thy grief at what my heart forbode,
    If tears of thine at misery's tale e'er flowed.
And then they woke, and came the hour around
    Which had been wont our scanty meal to bring;
    But from our dreams dumb terrors seemed to spring;

" When from below we heard the dreadful sound
    Of nails; the horrible tower was closed; all dumb
    I let my gaze into my sons' eyes come.
Weep I did not, like stone my feelings lay.
    They wept, and spoke my little Anselm: ' Pray
    Why lookest so?   Father, what ails thee, say?'
Shed I no tear, nor answered all that day
    Nor the next night, until another sun
    His journey through the wide world had begun.

" Then came a small ray into our sad, sad den,
    And when in their four faces I beheld
    That carking grief which mine own visage held,
Mine hands for grief I bit, and they, who then
    Deemed that I did it from desire to eat,
    Stood up each one at once upon his feet,
And said: ' Father, 't will give us much less pain
    If thou wilt eat of us: of thee was born
    This hapless flesh, and be it by thee torn.'

" Myself I calmed that they might not so grieve;
    Mute that day and the next we were; O thou
    Most cruel earth, that didst not open now!
When we the fourth day's agony did receive
    Stretched at my feet himself my Gaddo threw,
    And said: ' My father, canst thou nothing do?'
There died he, and, as now sees me thy sight,
    The three I saw fall one by one; first died
    One on the fifth; deaths two the sixth me tried.

* Then blind, I groped o'er them to left and right,
    And for three days called on their spirits dead;
    Then grief before the power of fasting fled."

              *Wilstach's Translation, Inferno. Canto XXXIII.*

## BUONCONTE DI MONTEFELTRO.

On the second terrace of the Ante-Purgatory, on the Purga-
torial Mount, were the spirits of those whose lives were ended
by violence.   Among those who here addressed Dante was
Buonconte di Montefeltro, who was slain in the battle of Campaldino, and whose body was never found.

> Another then : " Ah, be thy cherished aim
>     Attained that to the lofty Mount thee draws,
>     As thou with pity shalt advance my cause.
> Of Montefeltro I Buonconte am ;
>     Giovanna, and she only, for me cares ;
>     Hence among those am I whom waiting wears."
>
> " What violence or what chance led thee so wide
>     From Campaldino," I of him inquired,
>     " That 's still unknown thy burial-place retired ? "
> " Oh, Casentino's foot," he thus replied,
>     " Archiano's stream o'erflows, which hath its rise
>     Above the Hermitage under Apennine skies.
> There where its name is lost did I arrive,
>     Pierced through and through the throat, in flight,
>     Upon the plain made with my life-blood bright ;
>
> " There sight I lost, and did for speech long strive ;
>     At last I uttered Mary's name, and fell
>     A lifeless form, mine empty flesh a shell.
> Truth will I speak, below do thou it hymn ;
>     Took me God's Angel up, and he of Hell
>     Cried out : ' O thou from Heaven, thou doest well
> To rob from me the eternal part of him
>     For one poor tear, that me of him deprives ;
>     In other style I 'll deal with other lives ! '
>
> " Well know'st thou how in air is gathered dim
>     That humid vapor which to water turns
>     Soon as the cold its rising progress learns.
> The fiend that ill-will joined (which aye seeks ill)
>     To intellectual power, which mist and wind
>     Moved by control which faculties such can find,
> And afterwards, when the day was spent, did fill
>     The space from Protomagno to where tower
>     The Mounts with fog ; and high Heaven's covering power

The pregnant atmosphere moist to water changed.
　　Down fell the rain, and to the ditches fled,
　　Whate'er of it the soil's thirst had not sped;
And, as it with the mingling torrents ranged
　　Towards the royal river, so it flowed
　　That over every obstacle wild it rode.
The robust river found my stiffened frame
　　Near to its outlet, and it gave a toss
　　To Arno, loosening from my breast the cross

" I made of me when agony me o'ercame;
　　Along his banks and bottoms he me lapped,
　　Then in his muddy spoils he me enwrapped."

　　　　　　　*Wilstach's Translation, Purgatorio, Canto V.*


## BEATRICE DESCENDING FROM HEAVEN.

DANTE and Vergil mounted to the Terrestial Paradise, where, while they talked with Matilda, the Car of the Church Triumphant appeared in the greatest splendor. As it stopped before Dante it was enveloped in a shower of roses from the hands of a hundred angels.

I have beheld ere now, when dawn would pale,
　　The eastern hemisphere's tint of roseate sheen,
　　And all the opposite heaven one gem serene,
And the uprising sun, beneath such powers
　　Of vapory influence tempered, that the eye
　　For a long space its fiery shield could try:

E'en so, embosomed in a cloud of flowers,
　　Which from those hands angelical upward played,
　　And roseate all the car triumphal made,
And showered a snow-white veil with olive bound,
　　Appeared a Lady, green her mantle, name
　　Could not describe her robe unless 't were flame.
And mine own spirit, which the past had found
　　Often within her presence, free from awe,
　　And which could never from me trembling draw,
And sight no knowledge giving me at this time,
　　Through hidden virtue which from her came forth,
　　Of ancient love felt now the potent worth.
As soon as on my vision smote sublime
　　The heavenly influence that, ere boyhood's days
　　Had fled, had thrilled me and awoke my praise,

Unto the leftward turned I, with that trust
　　Wherewith a little child his mother seeks,
　　When fear his steps controls, and tear-stained cheeks,

To say to Vergil: " All my blood such gust
　　Of feeling moves as doth man's bravery tame;
　　I feel the traces of the ancient flame."

*Wilstach's Translation, Purgatorio, Canto XXX.*


## THE EXQUISITE BEAUTY OF BEATRICE.

WHILE Dante and Beatrice rose from the Heaven of Primal
Motion to the Empyrean, the poet turned his dazzled eyes from
the heavens, whose sight he could no longer bear, to the contemplation of Beatrice.

Wherefore my love, and loss of other view,
　　Me back to Beatrice and her homage drew.
If what of her hath been already said
　　Were in one single eulogy grouped, 't would ill
　　Her meed of merit at this moment fill.

The beauty which in her I now beheld
　　B'yond mortals goes; her Maker, I believe,
　　Hath power alone its fulness to receive.
Myself I own by obstacles stronger spelled
　　Than in his labored theme was ever bard
　　Whose verses, light or grave, brought problems hard;
For, as of eyes quelled by the sun's bright burst,
　　E'en so the exquisite memory of that smile
　　Doth me of words and forming mind beguile.

Not from that day when on this earth I first
　　Her face beheld, up to this moment, song
　　Have I e'er failed to strew her path along,
But now I own my limping numbers lame;
　　An artist sometimes finds his powers surpassed,
　　And mine succumbs to beauty's lance at last.
And I must leave her to a greater fame
　　Than any that my trumpet gives, which sounds,
　　Now, hastening notes, which mark this labor's bounds.

*Wilstach's Translation, Paradiso, Canto XXX*

# THE ORLANDO FURIOSO.

LUDOVICO ARIOSTO, author of the Orlando Furioso was born in Reggio, Italy, Sept. 8, 1474. In 1503 he was taken into the service of the Cardinal Hippolito d'Este, and soon after began the composition of the Orlando Furioso, which occupied him for eleven years. It was published in 1516, and brought him immediate fame. Ariosto was so unkindly treated by his patron that he left him and entered the service of the cardinal's brother, Alfonso, Duke of Ferrara. By him he was appointed governor of a province, in which position he repressed the banditti by whom it was infested, and after a successful administration of three years, returned to Ferrara to reside. The latter part of his life was spent in writing comedies and satires, and in revising the Orlando Furioso. He died in Ferrara, June 6, 1533.

The Orlando Furioso is a sequel to Boiardo's Orlando Innamorata, Ariosto taking up the story at the end of that poem. Its historical basis is the wars of Charlemagne with the Moors, which were probably confused with those of Charles Martel. As the Orlando of the poem is the same Roland whose fall at Roncesvalles in 778 is celebrated in the Song of Roland, its events must have occurred before that time.

Although the poem is called Orlando Furioso, Orlando's madness occupies a very small part of it, the principal threads of the story being Orlando's love for Angelica and his consequent madness, the wars of Charlemagne, and the loves of Bradamant and Rogero. From this Rogero the family of Este claimed to be derived, and for this reason Ariosto made Rogero the real hero of the poem, and took occasion to lavish the most extravagant praises upon his patron and his family.

With these principal threads are interwoven innumerable episodes which are not out of place in the epic, and lend variety to a story which would otherwise have become tiresome. The lightness of treatment, sometimes approaching ridicule, the rapidity of movement, the grace of style, and the clearness of language, the atmosphere created by the poet which so successfully harmonizes all his tales of magic and his occasional inconsistencies, and the excellent descriptions, have all contributed to the popularity of the poem, which is said to be the most widely read of the epics. These descriptions outweigh its faults, — the taking up the story of Boiardo without an explanation of the situation, the lack of unity, and the failure to depict character; for with the exception of Bradamant and Rogero, Ariosto's heroes and heroines are very much alike, and their conversation is exceedingly tiresome.

The Furioso is written in the octave stanza, and originally consisted of forty cantos, afterwards increased to forty-six.

The poem is the work of a practical poet, one who could govern a province. It is marred by an over-profusion of ornament, and contains no such lofty flights of fancy as are to be found in the Jerusalem Delivered. To this, no doubt, it owes, in part at least, its great popularity, for the poet's poem is never the people's poem.

BIBLIOGRAPHY AND CRITICISM, THE ORLANDO FURIOSO. Dublin University Magazine, 1845, xxvi., 187–201, 581–601, xxvii., 90–104; Retrospective Review, 1823, viii., 145–170, ix., 263–291; William T. Dobson's Classic Poets, 1879, pp. 186–238; Leigh Hunt's Stories from the Italian Poets, n. d. vol. ii., pp. 134–151; William Hickling Prescott's Italian Narrative Poetry. (See his Biographical and Critical Miscellanies, 1873, pp. 441–454); M. W. Shelley's Lives of the most eminent Literary and Scientific Men of Italy, Spain, and Portugal, 1835, pp. 239–255. (In Lardner's

Cabinet Cyclopedia, vol. i.) ; John Addington Symonds's Italian Literature, 1888, vol. i., pp. 493–522, vol. ii. pp. 1–50.

STANDARD ENGLISH TRANSLATIONS, THE ORLANDO FURIOSO. Orlando Furioso, Tr. from the Italian by Sir James Harrington, 1724 ; Orlando Furioso, Tr. by John Hoole, 1819 ; Orlando Furioso, Tr. into English verse by W. S. Rose, 2 vols., 1864–5.

## THE STORY OF THE ORLANDO FURIOSO.

THE Emperor Charlemagne was at war with the Moors and had camped near the Pyrenees with his host, determined to conquer their leaders, Marsilius of Spain and Agramant of Africa. To his camp came Orlando, the great paladin, with the beautiful Angelica, princess of Cathay, in search of whom he had roamed the world over. Orlando's cousin, Rinaldo, another of the great lords of Charlemagne, also loved Angelica, for he had seen her immediately after drinking of the Fountain of Love in the forest of Arden, and Charlemagne, fearing trouble between the cousins on her account, took Angelica from Orlando's tent and placed her in the care of Duke Namus of Bavaria.

Angelica did not like Orlando and she loathed Rinaldo, for he had been the first to meet her after she had tasted the waters of the Fountain of Hate. So when the Christian forces were one day routed in battle and the tents forsaken, she leaped on her palfrey and fled into the forest. Here the first person she met was the hated Rinaldo ; and fleeing from him she encountered the fierce Moor Ferrau, who, being also in love with her, drew his sword and attacked the pursuing paladin. But when the two discovered that Angelica had taken advantage of their duel to flee, they made peace and went in search of her.

As she fled, Angelica met Sacripant, an eastern lover who had followed her to France, and put herself under his protection. But when Sacripant was first defeated by Bradamant and then engaged in battle with the pursuing Rinaldo, she deemed herself safer without him and fled ; and presently a page appeared, a shade conjured there by a hermit magician whom Angelica had met, and announced to the warriors that Orlando had appeared and carried the maid to Paris.

Rinaldo immediately hastened to Paris, to find Orlando absent and Charlemagne, defeated by the Moors, entrenching himself in the city and preparing to send to England for aid. Rinaldo must be his ambassador, and that without a day's delay.

Frantic with jealousy, Rinaldo leaped into a ship in the midst of a storm, and hastened on his errand. Driven upon the coast of Scotland, he won the king's gratitude by saving his daughter Ginevra from shame and death, and secured from him a promise of all the horsemen and arms that could be spared. He was equally successful in England, and was soon reviewing the troops preparatory to their embarkation.

The warrior maid, Bradamant, sister of Rinaldo, after overthrowing Sacripant, pursued her way through the forest in search of Rogero the pagan. They had met once in battle and had loved, and since then she had ever roamed through the land in search of him. In the forest she found Pinabel, lamenting because his beloved lady had been snatched from him by a wizard on a winged steed, and carried to an impregnable castle. Thither he had seen many warriors conveyed, among them Rogero and Gradasso, conquered first by the lance and then thrown into profound slumber by the glare of a magic shield carried by the wizard.

Bradamant, anxious to save Rogero, offered to rescue Pinabel's lady if he would guide her to the castle. But when the treacherous knight learned that she was Bradamant, between whose house and his there was a deadly feud, he planned to slay her, and soon, by his treachery, managed to hurl her down a precipice.

Bradamant was only stunned by the fall, however, and soon awoke, to find herself at the entrance of a cave, which was the tomb of Merlin. Melissa, the prophetess maid, welcomed her, assured her that Rogero should be her spouse, and showed her their phantom descendants, brave princes and beautiful princesses of the house of Este. She then told her that Brunello, a knight of King Agramant, was hastening to the castle to release the prisoners by means of a magic ring, formerly the property of Angelica, which when put in the mouth would render one invisible, and, worn on the finger, made one proof against magic spells. Bradamant must overcome Brunello, wrest the ring from him, and herself free Rogero.

Following Melissa's advice, Bradamant overtook Brunello, seized the ring, and hastening to the castle, challenged Atlantes to battle. When he displayed the shield she pretended to become unconscious; but when he ran up to bind her she sprang up and seized him. He declared that he had imprisoned Rogero, his nephew, only to save him from the fate foretold by the stars, death by treachery at the hands of the Christians, and had brought the other knights and ladies there for his entertainment. Then Atlantes broke the spell and disappeared, together with the castle, and the prisoners trooped forth, Rogero among them.

Bradamant was happy, but alas! only for a moment; for as she and Rogero went down the mountain together he thoughtlessly leaped on the hippogrif, which alighted near him, and the winged steed, refusing his control, rose in the air, leaving the tearful Bradamant behind. The hippogrif flew rapidly over land and sea until it was directly above a small island, upon which it descended. Rogero sprang from its back, tied it to a myrtle tree, and, weary from his three thousand mile ride in heavy armor, prepared to drink from a rippling spring. The groves were of cedar, laurel, palm, and myrtle; roses and lilies filled the air with their perfume, and the wild stag and timid hare ran fearlessly through the groves. As he stooped to drink he heard a voice issuing from the myrtle to which he had tied the hippogrif. It was that of Astolpho, the English knight, who told him that the greater part of the island was under the control of Alcina the enchantress, who had left only a small portion to her sister Logistilla, to whom it all rightfully belonged. He himself had been enticed thither by Alcina, who had loved him for a few weeks, and then, serving him as she did all her lovers, had transformed him to a tree.

Rogero determined to profit by this advice; but when he was driven from the narrow path to Logistilla's domain and met Alcina he fell under the power of her beauty, and thought Astolpho a traducer. The days passed so gayly in her beautiful home that Rogero forgot the pagan cause, forgot his duty, forgot Bradamant, and was roused from his lethargy only by Melissa, to whom Bradamant had given the magic ring to enable her to find and rescue her lover. Melissa found the young knight when apart from Alcina, and gave him the ring that he might with it be enabled to see the enchantress in her true form. She then instructed him how to escape and seek the kingdom of Logistilla. Rogero was disgusted when the beautiful enchantress appeared as a hideous, wrinkled old woman, but concealing his change of feeling, waited until the opportunity presented itself to get his armor, take a steed, and pass by the warders of the gate. With great difficulty he reached a stream which separated Alcina's lands from those of Logistilla, and while ferrying across was overtaken by the boats of Alcina. With the help of Atlantes' shield, they were overcome, and Alcina was forced to depart, weeping, with only one boat, while Rogero entered the castle of the fairy Logistilla, from whom he learned many noble lessons.

Here came the other knights freed from Alcina's enchantment by Melissa, and Melissa herself with Astolpho, on the hippogrif, which she had learned to control. Astolpho was in his own armor and bore his wondrous spear, which had the power of overthrowing every one whom it so much as touched.

After a short rest among the pleasant gardens of Logistilla, Rogero departed on the hippogrif, and although anxious to see his Bradamant again, took the opportunity to pass over all the known world by this novel method of travel. He saw the troops in England gathering to go to the aid of Charlemagne, and rescued the beautiful Angelica, who had been taken by pirates and sold to the people of Ebuda, who chained her upon a rock as a victim for the orc. Rogero put the orc to sleep with his magic shield, giving Angelica the ring that the sight of the shield might not affect her as well. But when, charmed by the maid, he became too lover-like in his attentions, she put the ring in her mouth and disappeared. The angry Rogero turned, only to find that his hippogrif had broken its rein and was gone. Hastening through the forest, vexed with himself and the maiden, he fancied he saw Bradamant carried off by a giant, and following her, entered a magic castle of Atlantes, where he spent his days vainly trying to overtake his beloved and her captor.

Orlando could think only of his lost Angelica; and forgetful of the fact that his uncle Charlemagne was sorely pressed by the heathen, he stole from the camp one night in disguise, and went in search of her. Passing the isle of Ebuda he slew the orc, rescued Olympia, who was exposed as its victim, avenged her wrongs, and continued on his way until he reached the castle of Atlantes, and, fancying he saw Angelica, entered, and began the mad round of pursuit with many other Christian and pagan knights who were rendered unconscious of one another's presence by the magic of the wizard.

Hither came Angelica, invisible by means of the ring, to find a knight to protect her on her way to Cathay. Unfortunately as she showed herself to Sacripant, she was seen by Ferrau and Orlando, and all three pursued her from the castle. When they were sufficiently removed from it Angelica slipped the ring in her mouth and disappeared, and Ferrau and Orlando began to quarrel about Orlando's helmet, which the Moor was determined to win and wear. As Ferrau wore no helm until he could win Orlando's, that paladin hung his on a tree while they fought. Unseen by them, Angelica took it down, intending to restore it to Orlando later, and slipped away. When the knights discovered her absence they went in search of her, and Ferrau, coming upon her, took the helmet as she disappeared in fright. Orlando, assuming another crest, which he did not need, as his body was charmed and could not be hurt by any weapon, went forward, still in search of his love, and on the way encountered and almost totally destroyed two squadrons of Moors, and rescued from a robber's cave the beautiful Isabel, betrothed of Zerbino.

Melissa returned to Bradamant with the news that while Rogero was freed from the enchantment of Alcina, he was imprisoned in Atlantes' castle, from which she herself could rescue him by slaying the wizard, who would appear to her in the form of her lover. Bradamant resolved to do so; but when she saw the seeming Rogero set upon by two giants, she forgot her resolution, believed Melissa to be false, and spurring after him, became a prisoner in that wondrous castle, through which day and night she pursued her ever-fleeing lover.

When the Moors discovered the destruction of the two squadrons, Mandricardo, the Tartar king, determined to seek and do battle with the knight (unknown to him by name) who had wrought such destruction. The Tartar wore the arms of Hector save the sword, which was the property of Orlando, and until he gained it, he bore no weapon save the lance. With this, however, he stormed through the battle-field, striking terror to the hearts of all. With it alone, he destroyed a band of men conveying to Rodomont, the Saracen chief, his betrothed bride, Doralice, and won the maid for himself.

Outside Paris raged the infidel, chief among them the giant King Rodomont. Smiting those of his troops who hesitated to mount the scaling ladders, he waded through the wet moat, scaled the first wall, leaped the dry ditch, mounted the second wall, and ran alone through the city, spreading terror, death, and fire, while Charlemagne, ignorant of his presence, was busied in the defence of one of the gates against Agramant.

Now Rinaldo's army approached, unsuspected by the heathen, because of the aid of Silence, summoned by Saint Michael. Through these, welcomed by Charlemagne, Rodomont cut his way, hewing down fifteen or twenty foes at once, and, casting himself into the Seine, escaped, angry that he had not succeeded in destroying the city.

Discord, also summoned by Michael to the aid of the Christians, informed Rodomont on his return to the camp of the capture of Doralice, and the chief set forth raging, in search of Mandricardo, thoughtlessly abandoning King Agramant, struggling against the English re-inforcements. As night fell on a furious battle, the Moors were driven back, and Charlemagne pitched his tents without the city, opposite those of the Moors.

In the Moorish camp were two youths who loved one another with a love passing wonderful, Medoro and Cloridan. Both served Dardinello, and had crossed the sea with him. As they stood on guard that night they talked of their lord's death on the field that day, and Medoro suggested that they go in search of his body and bury it. Cloridan agreed, and they crept through the sleeping lines of the Christians, slaughtering many, found the body, and were hurrying into the forest when they heard the troops of Zerbino. Cloridan fled, fancying that Medoro would do the same, but on finding himself unaccompanied, retraced his footsteps, only to see his friend surrounded by a troop of horsemen. From his ambush he shot his arrows at the foe, until Zerbino in wrath seized Medoro by the throat, exclaiming, "Thou shalt die for this!" But when Medoro prayed to be allowed first to bury his lord, pity touched Zerbino, and he freed the youth, who fell, however, wounded by a thrust from a churlish horseman, in pursuit of whom Zerbino at once fled. Cloridan sprang in among the horsemen and fell dead by their thrusts at the side of the unconscious Medoro.

The bleeding youth was found by Angelica, who passed by, clad in rustic raiment; and the maid, struck with his beauty, recalled her knowledge of chirurgery and revived him. After Dardinello was buried, she and a shepherd assisted Medoro to a neighboring cottage, where she attended him until his wound was healed. But as he grew well, Angelica, who had scorned the suit of the proudest knights, fell sick of love for the humble youth, and resolved to take him with her to Cathay.

When Astolpho left the castle of Logistilla he carried with him as her gift a book from which he could learn to overcome all magic cheats, and a horn whose sound would put the boldest man to flight. Following her directions, he sailed past Scythia and India into the Persian Gulf, and there disembarking, passed through Arabia and along the Red Sea. There he overcame the giant Caligorantes, slew Orillo, who guarded the outlet of the Nile, and met there the brother knights Gryphon and Aquilant. Gryphon, led astray by an unworthy love, stole away from his brother, but was found again after many adventures, and the three, together with Sansonet and Marphisa, a warlike virgin, embarked for France. A great storm arose, and the vessel was forced to land in Syria. This was the land of the Amazons, and the troop escaped only by the warning and assistance of Guido, the savage, who was a bondsman in the land.

Astolpho became separated from the rest of the party and reached Europe alone. One day, while he was stooping to drink at a spring in the forest, a rustic sprang from a thicket, and leaping upon Rabican, rode him away. Astolpho, hastening after him, entered the enchanted castle of Atlantes, and soon recognized it as a house of magic. He broke the spell by the aid of his book, freed the captive knights, and finding the hippogrif, which he had learned to guide from Melissa, mounted it and rode away.

When the castle was destroyed, Rogero recognized Bradamant and clasped her in his arms, rejoicing to find her again. The maid, anxious to avoid further separation, promised to wed him if he would become a Christian, and demand her of her father, Duke Aymon. Rogero gladly promised to do so, and the two were hastening to Vallombrosa that he might be baptized when they encountered a maid, who prayed them to hasten to the relief of a youth doomed to death by fire. They hurried on, but paused to free Guido the savage, Gryphon, Aquilant, and Sansonet, who had been imprisoned by Pinabel, and Bradamant, pursuing Pinabel into the forest, slew him. But there, unfortunately, she lost her way, and while she was wandering about, Rogero, ignorant of her whereabouts, pushed on and freed the youth, who proved to be Bradamant's brother.

As Bradamant wandered through the forest she found Astolpho, who had just made a bridle for the hippogrif, and recognizing him, took his horse and spear in charge. A long time she wandered forlorn. She did not know the way to Vallombrosa; she did not know the whereabouts of Rogero. Her home was in sight, but if her mother saw her she would not again be suffered to depart. As she stood debating with herself, she was recognized by one of her brothers, and was forced to accompany him home. Thence she secretly sent her maid Hippalca to Vallombrosa with Rogero's horse Frontino, and a message explaining her absence.

After the capture of Doralice, Mandricardo hastened on, and overtook Orlando just as he had freed Zerbino and united him to Isabel. Recognizing Orlando by his crest as the chief who had destroyed the squadrons, the Tartar challenged him to combat. In courtesy to his foe, who would bear no sword until he could have Durindana, Orlando hung the blade on a tree, and the two knights spurred their steeds and broke their lances together. Then grappling, each endeavored to unhorse the other. The breaking of Orlando's saddle girth caused his fall just as he had slipped the bridle from the head of his enemy's horse, and the frightened steed, freed from its rein, ran madly through the wood, followed by Doralice.

Orlando told Zerbino to inform Mandricardo if he overtook him that he would wait in that spot three days for him to return and renew the combat, and bade the lovers farewell. As he wandered through the region while waiting, he found a peaceful little spot where a limpid rill rippled through a meadow dotted here and there with trees. Here the weary warrior sought repose; but as he looked about him he espied the name of Angelica carved on the trees, entwined with that of Medoro. Persuading himself that this was a fanciful name by which the maid intended to signify himself, he entered a little ivy-covered grotto, arching over a fountain, and there discovered on the rocky wall some verses in which

Medoro celebrated his union with Angelica. For a moment he stood as if turned to stone. Unable to weep, he again mounted his horse and sought a peasant's house to pass the night. There he heard the story of Angelica's infatuation, and saw the bracelet she had left them in return for their hospitality. The unhappy Orlando passed a sleepless night, weeping and groaning, and the next morning hastened to the forest that he might give way to his grief unobserved. There madness came upon him, and he uprooted the hateful trees, cut the solid stone of the grotto with his sword, making a desolation of the beautiful spot, and, casting off his armor, ran naked through the country, pillaging, burning, and slaying.

Zerbino and Isabel sought the spot in a few days to learn if Mandricardo had returned, found the scattered armor, and heard of Orlando's madness from a shepherd. Lamenting over their protector's misfortune, they gathered up the armor, hung it on a sapling, and wrote thereon Orlando's name. But while they were thus engaged, Mandricardo arrived, took the long coveted sword, and gave Zerbino, who attempted to prevent the theft, a mortal wound. The unhappy Isabel, intent on self-destruction, was comforted by a hermit, who promised to take her to a monastery near Marseilles.

Mandricardo had had but a few moments for repose after this combat with Zerbino, when the furious Rodomont overtook him and a terrible combat between the two began, the beautiful cause of it looking on with interest. But so strong were the champions that the struggle might have been prolonged indefinitely had not a messenger announced to the knights that they must postpone their private quarrels for a moment and hasten to the relief of King Agramant.

After Rogero had freed Richardetto, Bradamant's brother, and had attempted in vain to find Bradamant, he was troubled by the thought of King Agramant. He was determined to wed the warrior maid and become a Christian, but first came his vow to the pagan king. He therefore wrote her a note, saying that honor required his presence with Agra-

mant for at least fifteen or twenty days, but after that time he
would find means to justify himself with Agramant and
would meet her at Vallombrosa to be baptized.

He, with Richardetto, Aldigier, and Marphisa, whom they
met on her way to the pagan camp, rode on together, and
freed Vivian and Malagigi from the Moors and Manganese.
While they rested at a little fountain, Hippalca rode up, and
told them that she had just met Rodomont, who took Frontino from her. She also managed secretly to give Rogero
Bradamant's message and receive his letter in return.

While the party still remained at the fountain, Rodomont
came up with Mandricardo and Doralice, and all engaged in
a fierce battle, which was at last interrupted by Malagigi, who,
versed in wizard arts, conjured a demon into Doralice's
horse so that it ran away; and Rodomont and Mandricardo,
frightened by her screams, started in pursuit.

With the assistance of Rogero, Marphisa, Rodomont, and
Mandricardo, Agramant was enabled to drive Charlemagne
back into Paris, where he was saved only by the interposition
of Discord, who stirred up the old quarrels between Rodomont, Mandricardo, Rogero, and Gradasso over weapons,
bearings, and horses, until Agramant announced that they
should settle their difficulties by single combat, drawing lots
to see who should first engage in battle. But when they
were ready for the lists, fresh quarrels broke out, until the
king despaired of ever having peace in his ranks. Finally,
at his command, Doralice publicly declared Mandricardo
her choice, and the furious Rodomont fled from the camp.
On his way to Africa he found a little abandoned church between France and Spain, and decided to remain there instead of returning home. From this spot he saw Isabel on
her way to Marseilles, and falling in love with her, he slew
the hermit, dragged her to his retreat, and tried to win her.
But she, loathing him and faithful to Zerbino, caused him to
slay her, pretending that she was rendered invulnerable by
an ointment which she had prepared, and the secret of
which she would impart to him. The unhappy Rodomont
walled up the church to form her tomb, and threw a narrow

bridge across the stream. On this bridge he met every knight who came thither, and having overthrown him, took his arms to deck the tomb, on which he determined to hang a thousand such trophies. If the vanquished knight was a Moor he was set free without his arms; if a Christian he was imprisoned. Thither came the mad Orlando, and wrestled with Rodomont on the bridge until both fell into the stream. The madman then passed on through the country and met Medoro and Angelica on their way to India. They escaped with difficulty, Medoro's horse falling a victim to the madman, who continued to lay waste the land until he reached Zizera on the bay of Gibraltar, and, plunging into the sea, swam to Africa.

After Doralice had decided the quarrel between Mandricardo and Rodomont, Rogero and the Tartar met in the lists to decide their quarrel over their bearings. The battle was fearful, and when both fell to the ground it was supposed that Mandricardo was the victor. But when the crowd rushed to the lists they found the Tartar dead and Rogero only wounded. But the cheers of the crowd gave little pleasure to the hero, who grieved that he must lie on a sickbed instead of seeking Bradamant, according to his promise. Bradamant too, who had looked forward so eagerly to the day he had set, wept when it came without her lover. Soon she heard that Rogero's coming was prevented by his wounds; but when she also heard that he was attended by the warrior maid Marphisa, and that their names were frequently coupled in the pagan camp, she at once felt the pangs of jealousy. Unable to endure it longer, she armed herself, changing her usual vest for one whose colors denoted her desperation and desire to die, and set forth to meet and slay Marphisa, taking with her the spear left her by Astolpho, whose magic properties she did not know. With this she overthrew Rodomont and caused him to depart from his tomb and free his captives, and then, proceeding to Arles, challenged Rogero, who was sadly puzzled, not recognizing his challenger on account of her changed vest. Several knights attacked her before Rogero came

20

forth, only to be overthrown by the spear, and then Marphisa, who had rushed forth before Rogero could arm, met her, and the two women fought like tigers. When Rogero at last went forth he recognized Bradamant's voice, and suspecting the cause of her hostility, implored her to withdraw with him to a wood near by to hear his explanation. Marphisa followed them and attacked Bradamant so fiercely that Rogero was forced to her rescue, and lifting his sword would have struck the maid had he not been stopped by a voice from a tomb near by. It was that of Atlantes, who announced to Rogero and Marphisa that they were brother and sister, children of Rogero of Pisa and Galiciella; that Rogero had been treacherously slain and his town betrayed to Almontes, who cast Galiciella adrift on the sea. Atlantes rescued her, and took her children when she died; but Marphisa was stolen from him by a band of Arabs.

From this speech it was plainly the duty of Rogero and Marphisa to espouse the cause of Charlemagne and take arms against Agramant, who was their enemy. Bradamant and Marphisa then embraced, bade Rogero farewell, and proceeded to Charlemagne's camp, where Marphisa was received with honor and baptized, while Rogero promised to follow them as soon as he could find an excuse to leave Agramant.

When Astolpho left Bradamant in the forest, he quickly rose in the air and passed rapidly over the kingdoms of the world, Aragon, Navarre, Cadiz, Egypt, Morocco, Fez, over the sandy desert until he reached the kingdom of Nubia, whose king he rescued from the harpies by the sound of his magic horn. Then, mounted on his hippogrif again, he rose to the terrestrial Paradise, where he was welcomed by John, who informed him that he was sent thither by the grace of God that he might get instruction how to furnish aid to Charles and the Church, who were sorely in need of it. With John he rose in a chariot to the Heaven of the Moon, where, after seeing many strange things, he was given the wits of Orlando enclosed in a vial. They had been taken from him as a punishment for his loving a pagan, but were now to be restored to him that he might aid Charlemagne in conquering the Moors. Astolpho then descended to Nubia, restored sight to its king, and asking for his forces, went with them into Africa and attacked Biserta, the city of Agramant.

When these tidings were borne to Agramant he was greatly troubled, and desiring to end the war in Europe and hasten to his own country, he proposed to Charlemagne that the war be decided by single combat between two champions. Great was the agony of Rogero, the pagan champion, when he recognized in his opponent Rinaldo, the brother of Bradamant. He would never dare to slay him, so he parried the blows rained upon him, and struck back so feebly that the spectators, not understanding his motives, deemed him unable to cope with Rinaldo. But Melissa, determined that Merlin's prophecy should come true, appeared to Agramant in the guise of Rodomont, and urged him to break the compact and fall upon the Christians. Delighted to have the mighty king with him again, Agramant did not scruple to break his word, and rushed upon the Christian forces, breaking up the combat. After a sharp conflict, the Saracens were put to flight and Agramant hastened into Africa.

His people in Biserta, their strength drained by the long war, were unable to withstand the Christian foe, soon re-enforced by a powerful enemy. One day, as Astolpho and his friends were standing on the beach, a madman came raging towards them, whom Astolpho recognized as Orlando. The warriors attempted in vain to hold him until Astolpho ordered the ship's hawsers to be brought, and knotting them flung them at the count's limbs, and so threw him down and tied him. Then, after having had his body cleansed from mud and filth, he stopped his mouth with herbs so that he could breathe only through his nostrils, and holding the vial there, the lost senses were quickly inhaled, and Orlando was himself again, astonished and delighted to find himself with his friends.

With Orlando's help, Biserta was soon taken, and Agramant, who had met the Christian fleet under the leadership of Dudon and had barely escaped with his life, saw from afar the flames devouring his beloved city.

Landing with Sobrino upon a little isle, he found there King Sericane, who advised him to challenge the Christians to single combat in order to decide the outcome of the war, he, Gradasso, and Sobrino to stand in the lists against three Christian champions. Orlando agreed to do so, and selected for his companions in the fight Brandimart and Olivier. But the pagans were no match for Orlando, whom no weapon could injure, and Agramant and Gradasso soon fell, while Sobrino was wounded. But the joy over the Christian victory was not unalloyed by sorrow, for Olivier was severely wounded and the beloved Brandimart was slain.

The champions were now joined by Rinaldo, who after the breaking of the pact by Agramant, had set off for India in search of Angelica, whom he still madly loved. But Disdain guided his steps to the Fountain of Hate, one draught of which changed his love to loathing, so that he abandoned his undertaking and hastened to join the Christian forces in Africa.

Olivier's wound proved slow to heal, and when at last the warriors heard of a hermit on a lonely isle who could help him, they hastened to take their wounded comrade thither. There they found Rogero, who had been shipwrecked while sailing to Africa, and had been baptized by the hermit, who was warned in a dream of his coming. The Christian warriors gladly welcomed Rogero to their ranks, for they knew of his valor; and Rinaldo, who had learned how the young hero had saved the life of Richardetto and had preserved Vivian and Malagigi, embraced him, and at the suggestion of the hermit, plighted him to his sister. Before they left the isle, Sobrino was converted by the pious hermit, and Olivier's wound was healed.

The knights were received with the greatest honor by Charlemagne, especially Rogero, the new convert. But what unhappiness awaited him! In his absence Bradamant's father had promised the maid to Leo, the son of the Greek emperor, Constantine, in spite of her prayers and entreaties.

Although Bradamant declared that she would die sooner than wed another, the heart-broken Rogero hastily departed for Constantinople to slay his rival. In his absence, Bradamant besought Charlemagne not to compel her to marry Leo unless he could defeat her in single combat; and her angry parents, on learning of this, took her from the court and shut her up in the tower of Rocca Forte. Rogero, in the mean time, reached Leo's realms just as the Greeks engaged in battle with the Bulgarians. Because of his hatred for Leo, he fought with the Bulgarians, and when their king fell he rallied their scattered troops and put the Greeks to flight. Rogero then followed the fleeing Greeks unaccompanied, and being recognized, was taken captive that night as he slept in a hostelry. At the entreaty of a kinswoman whose son Rogero had slain that day, the emperor surrendered his captive to her, and he was thrust into a gloomy dungeon, where he suffered agonies from hunger and cold. But Leo, who had admired his valor in battle and had longed to know him, rescued him, recovered his horse and armor, and by his generosity compelled Rogero to admire him as much as he had before hated him. The news of Charlemagne's decree now reached Leo, and he, fearing to fight Bradamant, asked the unknown knight of the unicorn to take his place. Rogero's heart sank within him, but he dared not refuse. His life was Leo's, and he must sacrifice himself for him, must either slay Bradamant, or be slain by her for his deliverer's sake. He accompanied Leo to France, and feigning a cheerfulness he did not feel, changed armor and steed that he might not be known, and, while Leo remained in his tent outside the city, entered the lists and encountered Bradamant, who was determined to slay her hated suitor. Rogero was equally determined not to slay her nor to allow himself to be conquered. When twilight fell and king and court saw that while the young knight had not overcome the maid, he had not allowed himself to be overcome, they declared that the couple were well matched and that they should wed.

The hopeless Rogero hastened back to Leo's camp,

changed armor and steed, and during the night stole away from the hateful place to the greenwood that he might die there, since he could never possess his beloved. At the same time, Bradamant gave way to her grief in such a manner that Marphisa, already indignant at the treatment of her brother, appeared before the king in his behalf. She declared that Rogero and Bradamant had already exchanged all the vows of those who marry and therefore she was not free to wed another. She then suggested that since the matter had gone so far, Leo and Rogero should meet in the lists to decide to whom the lady belonged.

Leo at once set out in search of his knight of the unicorn, who he believed would defend him from all peril, and found him in the forest, almost fainting from fasting and sleeplessness. The Greek embraced Rogero tenderly and implored him to betray the cause of his grief, and so tender were his words and so gracious his manner that Rogero could not but unbosom himself. And when Leo learned that his unknown champion was no other than Rogero himself he declared that he would gladly forego Bradamant for him, and would rather have forfeited his life than caused such grief to such a faithful friend.

Joy filled the court when the story of Rogero's fidelity was made known, and the joy was increased when ambassadors came from Bulgaria, seeking the unknown knight of the unicorn that they might offer their throne to him. Duke Aymon and his wife were reconciled when they found that Rogero was to be a king, and the wedding was celebrated with the greatest splendor, Charlemagne providing for Bradamant as though she were his daughter.

In the midst of the celebrations Rodomont appeared to defy Rogero, and that knight, nothing loath, met him in the lists. The Moor fell under Rogero's blows, and all the Christian court rejoiced to see the last of the pagan knights fall by the hand of their champion.

## SELECTION FROM THE ORLANDO FURIOSO.

### The Death of Zerbino.

As Orlando talked with Zerbino, whose life he had saved and to whom he had given his lady Isabel, also rescued by him, Mandricardo the Tartar king came up and challenged Orlando to single combat. While they fought, Mandricardo's steed, from which Orlando had slipped the rein, became unmanageable, and fled with its rider. Orlando asked Zerbino and Isabel to tell Mandricardo, if they overtook him, that he would wait for him in that place for three days to renew the battle. But while waiting, Orlando learned of Angelica's love for Medoro, and losing his senses from grief, threw away his armor, and went wandering through France. Zerbino and Isabel returned to the place to see if Mandricardo had returned, and there learned of Orlando's condition.

> Far off, he [Zerbino] saw that something shining lay,
>   And spied Orlando's corselet on the ground;
>   And next his helm; but not that head-piece gay
>   Which whilom African Almontes crowned:
>   He in the thicket heard a courser neigh,
>   And, lifting up his visage at the sound,
>   Saw Brigliadoro the green herbage browse,
>   With rein yet hanging at his saddle-bows.

> For Durindane, he sought the greenwood, round,
>   Which separate from the scabbard met his view;
>   And next the surcoat, but in tatters, found;
>   That, in a hundred rags, the champaign strew.
>   Zerbino and Isabel, in grief profound,
>   Stood looking on, nor what to think they knew:
>   They of all matters else might think, besides
>   The fury which the wretched count misguides.

> Had but the lovers seen a drop of blood,
>   They might have well believed Orlando dead:
>   This while the pair, beside the neighboring flood,
>   Beheld a shepherd coming, pale with dread.
>   He just before, as on a rock he stood,
>   Had seen the wretch's fury; how he shed
>   His arms about the forest, tore his clothes,
>   Slew hinds, and caused a thousand other woes.

Questioned by good Zerbino, him the swain
  Of all which there had chanced, informed aright.
  Zerbino marvelled, and believed with pain,
  Although the proofs were clear : This as it might,
  He from his horse dismounted on the plain,
  Full of compassion, in afflicted plight ;
  And went about, collecting from the ground
  The various relics which were scattered round.

Isabel lights as well ; and, where they lie
  Dispersed, the various arms uniting goes.

.    .    .    .    .    .    .

Here Prince Zerbino all the arms unites,
  And hangs like a fair trophy, on a pine.
  And, to preserve them safe from errant knights,
  Natives or foreigners, in one short line
  Upon the sapling's verdant surface writes,
  ORLANDO'S ARMS, KING CHARLES'S PALADINE.
  As he would say, " Let none this harness move,
  Who cannot with its lord his prowess prove ! "

Zerbino having done the pious deed,
  Is bowning him to climb his horse ; when, lo !
  The Tartar king arrives upon the mead.
  He at the trophied pine-tree's gorgeous show,
  Beseeches him the cause of this to read ;
  Who lets him (as rehearsed) the story know.
  When, without further pause, the paynim lord
  Hastes gladly to the pine, and takes the sword.

" None can (he said) the action reprehend,
  Nor first I make the faulchion mine to-day ;
  And to its just possession I pretend
  Where'er I find it, be it where it may.
  Orlando, this not daring to defend,
  Has feigned him mad, and cast the sword away ;
  But if the champion so excuse his shame,
  This is no cause I should forego my claim."

" Take it not thence," to him Zerbino cried,
  " Nor think to make it thine without a fight :
  If so thou tookest Hector's arms of pride,
  By theft thou hadst them, rather than by right."
  Without more parley spurred upon each side,
  Well matched in soul and valor, either knight.
  Already echoed are a thousand blows ;
  Nor yet well entered are the encountering foes.

In 'scaping Durindane, a flame in show
  (He shifts so swiftly), is the Scottish lord.
He leaps about his courser like a doe,
  Where'er the road best footing does afford.
And well it is that he should not forego
  An inch of vantage; who, if once that sword
Smite him, will join the enamored ghosts, which rove
Amid the mazes of the myrtle grove.

As the swift-footed dog, who does espy
  Swine severed from his fellows, hunts him hard,
And circles round about; but *he* lies by
  Till once the restless foe neglect his guard;
So, while the sword descends, or hangs on high,
  Zerbino stands, attentive how to ward,
How to save life and honor from surprise;
And keeps a wary eye, and smites and flies.

On the other side, where'er the foe is seen
  To threaten stroke in vain, or make it good,
He seems an Alpine wind, two hills between,
  That in the month of March shakes leafy wood;
Which to the ground now bends the forest green,
  Now whirls the broken boughs, at random strewed.
Although the prince wards many, in the end
One mighty stroke he cannot 'scape or fend.

In the end he cannot 'scape one downright blow,
  Which enters, between sword and shield, his breast.
As perfect was the plate and corselet, so
  Thick was the steel wherein his paunch was drest:
But the destructive weapon, falling low,
  Equally opened either iron vest;
And cleft whate'er it swept in its descent,
And to the saddle-bow, through cuirass, went.

And, but that somewhat short the blow descends
  It would Zerbino like a cane divide;
But him so little in the quick offends,
  This scarce beyond the skin is scarified.
More than a span in length the wound extends;
  Of little depth: of blood a tepid tide
To his feet descending, with a crimson line,
Stains the bright arms which on the warrior shine.

'T is so, I sometimes have been wont to view
  A hand more white than alabaster, part
The silver cloth with ribbon red of hue;
  A hand I often feel divide my heart.

Here little vantage young Zerbino drew
From strength and greater daring, and from art;
For in the temper of his arms and might,
Too much the Tartar king excelled the knight.

The fearful stroke was mightier in show,
Than in effect, by which the prince was prest;
So that poor Isabel, distraught with woe,
Felt her heart severed in her frozen breast.
The Scottish prince, all over in a glow,
With anger and resentment was possest,
And putting all his strength in either hand,
Smote full the Tartar's helmet with his brand.

Almost on his steed's neck the Tartar fell,
Bent by the weighty blow Zerbino sped;
And, had the helmet been unfenced by spell
The biting faulchion would have cleft his head.
The king, without delay, avenged him well,
" Nor I for you till other season," said,
" Will keep this gift;" and levelled at his crest,
Hoping to part Zerbino to the chest.

Zerbino, on the watch, whose eager eye
Waits on his wit, wheels quickly to the right;
But not withal so quickly, as to fly
The trenchant sword, which smote the shield outright,
And cleft from top to bottom equally;
Shearing the sleeve beneath it, and the knight
Smote on his arm; and next the harness rended,
And even to the champion's thigh descended.

Zerbino, here and there, seeks every way
By which to wound, nor yet his end obtains;
For, while he smites upon that armor gay,
Not even a feeble dint the coat retains.
On the other hand, the Tartar in the fray
Such vantage o'er the Scottish prince obtains,
Him he has wounded in seven parts or eight,
And reft his shield and half his helmet's plate.

He ever wastes his blood; his energies
Fail, though he feels it not, as 't would appear;
Unharmed, the vigorous heart new force supplies
To the weak body of the cavalier.
His lady, during this, whose crimson dyes
Were chased by dread, to Doralice drew near,
And for the love of Heaven, the damsel wooed
To stop that evil and disastrous feud.

Doralice, who as courteous was as fair,
    And ill-assured withal, how it would end,
    Willingly granted Isabella's prayer,
    And straight to truce and peace disposed her friend.
    As well Zerbino, by the other's care,
    Was brought his vengeful anger to suspend;
    And, wending where she willed, the Scottish lord,
    Left unachieved the adventure of the sword.

.     .     .     .     .     .     .

For to leave Durindana such misdeed
    To him appeared, it past all other woes;
    Though he could hardly sit upon his steed,
    Through mighty loss of life-blood, which yet flows.
    Now, when his anger and his heat secede,
    After short interval, his anguish grows;
    His anguish grows, with such impetuous pains,
    He feels that life is ebbing from his veins.

For weakness can the prince no further hie,
    And so beside a fount is forced to stay:
    Him to assist the pitying maid would try,
    But knows not what to do, nor what to say.
    For lack of comfort she beholds him die;
    Since every city is too far away,
    Where in this need she could resort to leech,
    Whose succor she might purchase or beseech.

She, blaming fortune, and the cruel sky,
    Can only utter fond complaints and vain.
    " Why sank I not in ocean," (was her cry),
    " When first I reared my sail upon the main?"
    Zerbino, who on her his languid eye
    Had fixt, as she bemoaned her, felt more pain
    Than that enduring and strong anguish bred,
    Through which the suffering youth was well-nigh dead.

" So be thou pleased, my heart," (Zerbino cried),
    " To love me yet, when I am dead and gone,
    As to abandon thee without a guide,
    And not to die, distresses me alone.
    For did it me in place secure betide
    To end my days, this earthly journey done,
    I cheerful, and content, and fully blest
    Would die, since I should die upon thy breast

" But since to abandon thee, to whom a prize
    I know not, my sad fate compels, I swear,
    My Isabella, by that mouth, those eyes,
    By what enchained me first, that lovely hair;

My spirit, troubled and despairing, hies
Into hell's deep and gloomy bottom; where
To think, thou wert abandoned so by me,
Of all its woes the heaviest pain will be."


At this the sorrowing Isabel, declining
Her mournful face, which with her tears o'erflows,
Towards the sufferer, and her mouth conjoining
To her Zerbino's, languid as a rose;
Rose gathered out of season, and which, pining
Fades where it on the shadowy hedgerow grows,
Exclaims, " Without me think not so, my heart,
On this your last, long journey to depart.


" Of this, my heart, conceive not any fear.
For I will follow thee to heaven or hell;
It fits our souls together quit this sphere,
Together go, for aye together dwell.
No sooner closed thine eyelids shall appear,
Than either me internal grief will quell,
Or, has it not such power, I here protest,
I with this sword to-day will pierce my breast.


" I of our bodies cherish hope not light,
That they shall have a happier fate when dead:
Together to entomb them, may some wight,
Haply by pity moved, be hither led."
She the poor remnants of his vital sprite
Went on collecting, as these words she said;
And while yet aught remains, with mournful lips,
The last faint breath of life devoutly sips.


'T was here his feeble voice Zerbino manned,
Crying, " My deity, I beg and pray,
By that love witnessed, when thy father's land
Thou quittedst for my sake; and, if I may
In anything command thee, I command,
That, with God's pleasure, thou live-out thy day;
Nor ever banish from thy memory,
That, well as man can love, have I loved thee.


" God haply will provide thee with good aid,
To free thee from each churlish deed I fear;
As when in the dark cavern thou wast stayed,
He sent, to rescue thee, Anglante's peer;
So he (grammercy!) succored thee dismayed
At sea, and from the wicked Biscayneer.
And, if thou must choose death, in place of worse,
Then only choose it as a lesser curse."

I think not these last words of Scotland's knight
  Were so exprest, that he was understood:
With these, he finished, like a feeble light,
  Which needs supply of wax, or other food.
— Who is there, that has power to tell aright
  The gentle Isabella's doleful mood?
When stiff, her loved Zerbino, with pale face,
And cold as ice, remained in her embrace.

On the ensanguined corse, in sorrow drowned,
  The damsel throws herself, in her despair,
And shrieks so loud that wood and plain resound
  For many miles about; nor does she spare
Bosom or cheek; but still, with cruel wound,
  One and the other smites the afflicted fair;
And wrongs her curling locks of golden grain,
Aye calling on the well-loved youth in vain.

She with such rage, such fury, was possest,
  That, in her transport, she Zerbino's glaive
Would easily have turned against her breast,
  Ill keeping the command her lover gave;
But that a hermit, from his neighboring rest,
  Accustomed oft to seek the fountain-wave,
His flagon at the cooling stream to fill,
Opposed him to the damsel's evil will.

The reverend father, who with natural sense
  Abundant goodness happily combined,
And, with ensamples fraught and eloquence,
  Was full of charity towards mankind,
With efficacious reasons her did fence,
  And to endurance Isabel inclined;
Placing, from ancient Testament and new,
Women, as in a mirror, for her view.

The holy man next made the damsel see,
  That save in God there was no true content,
And proved all other hope was transitory,
  Fleeting, of little worth, and quickly spent;
And urged withal so earnestly his plea,
  He changed her ill and obstinate intent;
And made her, for the rest of life, desire
To live devoted to her heavenly sire.

Not that she would her mighty love forbear
  For her dead lord, nor yet his relics slight;
These, did she halt or journey, everywhere
  Would Isabel have with her, day and night.

The hermit therefore seconding her care,
Who, for his age, was sound and full of might,
They on his mournful horse Zerbino placed,
And traversed many a day that woodland waste.

.    .    .    .    .    .    .

He thought to bear her to Provence, where, near
The city of Marseilles, a borough stood,
Which had a sumptuous monastery; here
Of ladies was a holy sisterhood.

.    .    .    .    .    .    .

*Rose's Translation, Canto XXIV.*

# THE LUSIAD.

The discovery of Mozambique, of Melinda, and of Calcutta has been sung by Camoens, whose poem has something of the charm of the Odyssey and of the magnificence of the Æneid.

MONTESQUIEU.

THE Portuguese epic, the Lusiad, so-called from Lusitania, the Latin name for Portugal, was written by Luis de Camoens.

He was born in Lisbon in 1524, lost his father by shipwreck in infancy, and was educated by his mother at the University of Coimbra. On leaving the university he appeared at court, where his graces of person and mind soon rendered him a favorite. Here a love affair with the Donna Catarina de Atayde, whom the king also loved, caused his banishment to Santarem. At this place he began the Lusiad, and continued it on the expedition against the Moors in Africa sent out by John III., an expedition on which he displayed much valor and lost an eye. He was recalled to court, but jealousies soon drove him thence to India, whither he sailed in 1553, exclaiming, "Ungrateful country, thou shalt not possess my bones." In India his bravery and accomplishments won him friends, but his imprudences soon caused his exile to China, where he accumulated a small fortune and finished his poem. Happier circumstances permitted him to return to Goa; but on the way the ship laden with his fortune sank, and he escaped, saving only his poem. After sixteen years of misfortune abroad, Camoens returned to Lisbon in 1569. The pestilence that was then raging delayed the publication of the Lusiad until 1572. The poem received little attention; a small pension was bestowed on the poet, but was soon withdrawn, and the unfortunate Camoens was left to die in an almshouse. On his death-bed he deplored the impending fate of his country, which he

alone could see. " I have loved my country. I have returned not only to die on her bosom, but to die with her."

The Lusiad tells the story of the voyage of Vasco da
Gama. The sailors of Prince Henry of Portugal, commander
of the Portuguese forces in Africa, had passed Cape Nam
and discovered the Cape of Storms, which the prince re-
named the Cape of Good Hope. His successor Emmanuel,
determined to carry out the work of his predecessor by
sending out da Gama to undertake the discovery of the
southern passage to India. The Portuguese were generally
hostile to the undertaking, but da Gama, his brother, and his
friend Coello gathered a company, part of which consisted
of malefactors whose sentence of death was reversed on condition that they undertake the voyage, and reached India.

The Lusiad is divided into ten cantos, containing one
thousand one hundred and two stanzas. Its metre is the
heroic iambic, in rhymed octave stanzas.

The Lusiad is marred by its mythological allusions in imitation of Homer and Virgil, but these are forgotten when the
poet sings in impassioned strains of his country's past glory.

The Lusiad is simple in style ; its subject is prosaic ; it is
a constant wonder that out of such unpromising materials
Camoens could construct a poem of such interest. He
could not have done so had he not been so great a poet,
so impassioned a patriot.

Camoens was in one sense of the word a practical man,
like Ariosto ; he had governed a province, and governed
it successfully. But he had also taken up arms for his country, and after suffering all the slights that could be put upon
him by an ungrateful and forgetful monarch, still loved his
native land, loved it the more, perhaps, that he had suffered
for it and was by it neglected. He foresaw, also, as did no
one else, the future ruin of his country, and loved it the more
intensely, as a parent lavishes the fondest, most despairing
affection on a child he knows doomed to early death.

The Lusiad is sometimes called the epic of commerce ;
it could be called far more appropriately the epic of
patriotism.

BIBLIOGRAPHY AND CRITICISM, THE LUSIAD. J. Adamson's Memoirs of Life and Writing of Camoens, 2 vols., 1820 (vol. 2, account of works of Camoens in Portuguese and other languages, and of the works founded on his life or suggested by his writings) ; R. F. Burton's Camoens, his Life and his Lusiad, 2 vols., 1881 ; M. W. Shelley's Lives of the most Eminent Literary and Scientific Men of Italy, Spain, and Portugal, vol. 3 ; F. Bouterwek's History of Spanish and Portuguese Literature, 1823 (Tr. by T. Ross) ; Chambers's Repository, no. 32, Spirit of Camoens's Lusiad ; W. T. Dobson's Classic Poets, pp. 240–278 ; Montgomery's Men of Italy, iii., 295 ; Sismondi's Literature of the South of Europe, ii., 475–528 ; Southey's Sketch of Portuguese Literature in vol. i. of Quarterly Review, 1809 ; Fortnightly Review, i., 184 ; Quarterly, i., 235 ; Monthly Review, clx., 505 ; Edinburgh Review, 1805, vi., 43 ; New England Magazine, liii., 542 ; Revue de Deux Mondes, 1832, vi., 145.

STANDARD ENGLISH TRANSLATIONS, THE LUSIAD. The Lusiad, Tr. by J. J. Aubertin, 2 vols., 1881 (Portuguese text and English Tr., in verse) ; The Lusiad, Englished by R. F. Burton, 2 vols., 1881 ; The Lusiad, Tr. into Spenserian verse by R. F. Duff, 1880 ; The Lusiad, Tr. by Sir Richard Fanshawe, 1655 ; The Lusiad, Tr. by W. J. Mickle, 3 vols., Ed. 5, 1807 ; The Lusiad, Tr. by T. M. Musgrave (blank verse), 1826 ; The Lusiad, Tr. by Edward Quillinan, with notes by John Adamson, 1853.

## THE STORY OF THE LUSIAD.

WHEN Jupiter, looking down from Olympus, saw the Lusitanian fleet sailing over the heretofore untravelled seas, he called the gods together, and reviewing the past glory of the Portuguese, their victories over the Castilians, their stand against the Romans, under their shepherd-hero Viriatus, and their conquest of Africa, he foretold their future glories and their discovery and conquest of India.

Bacchus, who had long since made conquests in India, fearful lest his ancient honors should be forgotten, bitterly opposed the scheme of the Portuguese; Venus, however, was favorable to them, and Mars interceded, counselling Jove not to heed Bacchus, but to permit the Lusitanians to reach India's shore in safety.

When the council of the gods was dismissed, Mercury was sent to guide the Armada, which made its first landing at Mozambique. Canoes with curious palm-leaf sails, laden with dark-skinned natives, swarmed round the ships and were hailed with joy by Gama and his men, who invited them on board. A feast was spread for them, and to them Gama declared his intention of seeking India. Among them was a Moor who had at first thought the Portuguese Moors, on account of their dark skins. Feigning cordiality while plotting their ruin, he offered them a pilot to Quiloa, where, he assured them, they would find a Christian colony. He and his friends also laid a plot to place some soldiers in ambush to attack Gama's men when they landed next day to get water; in this way many would be destroyed, and certain death awaited the survivors at Quiloa, whither the promised pilot would conduct them. But the Moors had not counted on the strength of the Portuguese. Gama's vengeance was swift and certain. The thunder of his guns terrified the Moors, and the regent implored his pardon, and with make-believe tears insisted on his receiving at his hands the promised pilot.

Many questions were asked by Gama concerning the spicy shores of India, of the African coasts, and of the island to the north. " Quiloa, that," replied the Moor, " where from ancient times, the natives have worshipped the blood-stained image of the Christ." He knew how the Moorish inhabitants hated the Christians, and was secretly delighted when Gama directed him to steer thither.

A storm swept the fleet past Quiloa, but the pilot, still determined on revenge, pointed out the island town of Mombaça, as a stronghold of the Christians, and steering the fleet thither, anchored just outside the bar. Bacchus, now intent on the destruction of the Lusitanians, assumed the character of a priest to deceive the heralds sent ashore by Gama, who assured their commander that they saw a Christian priest performing divine rites at an altar above which fluttered the banner of the Holy Ghost. In a few moments the Christian fleet would have been at the mercy of the Moors, but Cytherea, beholding from above the peril of her favorites, hastily descended, gathered together her nymphs, and formed an obstruction, past which the vessels strove in vain to pass. As Gama, standing high on the poop, saw the huge rock in the channel, he cried out, and the Moorish pilots, thinking their treason discovered, leaped into the waves.

Warned in a dream by Mercury that the Moors were preparing to cut his cables, De Gama roused his fleet and set sail for Melinda, whose monarch, Mercury had told him, was both powerful and good.

The fleet, decorated with purple streamers and gold and scarlet tapestry in honor of Ascension Day sailed with drums beating and trumpets sounding, into the harbor of Melinda, where they were welcomed by the kind and truthful people. The fame of the Lusitanians had reached Melinda, and the monarch gladly welcomed them to his land. His herald entreated them to remain with him, and brought them sheep, fowls, and the fruits of the earth, welcome gifts to the mariners. Gama had vowed not to leave the ship until he could step on Indian ground, so the next day the king and the commander, clad in their most splendid vestments, met in barges, and the monarch of Melinda asked Gama to tell him of the Lusian race, its origin and climate, and of all his adventures up to the time of his arrival at Melinda.

"O king," said Gama, "between the zones of endless winter and eternal summer lies beautiful Europe, surrounded by the sea. To the north are the bold Swede, the Prussian, and the Dane; on her south-eastern line dwelt the Grecian heroes, world-renowned, and farther south are the ruins of proud Rome. Among the beauteous landscapes of Italy lies proud Venice, queen of the sea, and north of her tower the lofty Alps. The olive groves and vineyards of fair Gallia next greet the eye, and then the valorous fields of Spain, Aragon, Granada, and — the pride of Spain — Castile. On the west, a crown to it, lies Lusitania, on whom last smiles the setting sun, — against whose shores roll the waves of the western sea.

"Noble are the heroes of my country. They were the first to rise against the Moors and expel them from the kingdom. The forces of Rome were routed by our shepherd-hero, Viriatus. After his death our country languished until Alonzo of Spain arose, whose renown spread far and wide because of his battles against the Moors.

"Alonzo rewarded generously the heroes who fought under him, and to Prince Henry of Hungaria he gave the fields through which the Tagus flows and the hand of his daughter. To them was born a son, Alfonso, the founder of the Lusian throne. After the death of his father Henry, Alfonso's mother became regent, and ere long wedded her minister Perez and plotted to deprive her young son of his inheritance. The eighteen year old son arose, won the nobility to his side, and defeated his guilty mother and her husband in the battle of Guimaraens. Forgetful of the reverence due to parents, he cruelly imprisoned his mother, whose father, the king of Spain, indignant at such treatment of his daughter, now marched against the young prince and defeated him. As he lay in prison, his faithful guardian Egas knelt before the king, and vowed that his master, if released, would pay homage to him. Well he knew that his master would never bow his proud head to pay homage to Castile. So when the day arrived, Egas, and all his family, clad in gowns of white like sentenced felons, with unshod feet, and with the halter around their necks, sought Castile. 'O king, take us as a sacrifice for my perjured honor. Turn in friendship to the prince thy grandson, and wreak thy vengeance on us alone.'

"Fortunately Alonzo was noble enough to release the self-sacrificing Egas, and to forgive his grandson.

"The young Alfonso, pardoned by his grandfather, proceeded to Ourique, whither marched five Moorish kings. Over his head appeared the sacred cross; but he prayed heaven to show it to his army instead, that they might be inspired with the hope of victory. Filled with joy at the token, the Portuguese defeated the Moors, and on the bloody battle-field Alfonso was proclaimed King of Portugal, and from that day placed on his hitherto unadorned buckler five azure shields, arranged as a cross. He continued the wars with the Moors until, wounded and taken prisoner at Badajoz, he resigned the throne to his son, Don Sancho, who in turn won many victories. Alfonso II., Sancho II., Alfonso III., and Alfonso the Brave succeeded him. At the court of the latter was a beautiful maiden, Inez de Castro, whom Alfonso's son Don Pedro had married secretly. The courtiers, fearful lest Pedro should show favor to the Castilians because Inez was the daughter of a Castilian, told the king of his son's amour. In the absence of Pedro, Inez was led before the king, bringing with her her children, to help her to plead for mercy. But the king was merciless, his counsellors, brutal, and at his signal they stabbed her. Pedro never recovered from the shock given him by the fate of his beautiful wife, and after his succession to the throne, as a partial atonement for her suffering, he had her body taken from the grave and crowned Queen of Portugal.

"The weak Fernando, who took his wife Eleanora from her lawful husband, succeeded Pedro, and their daughter

Beatrice not being recognized by the Portuguese, at his death Don John, a natural brother, came to the throne In the mean time a Spanish prince had married Beatrice and invaded Portugal, claiming it as his right. The Portuguese were divided until Nuño Alvarez Pereyra came forward. 'Has one weak reign so corrupted you?' he cried. 'Have you so soon forgotten our brave sires? Fernando was weak, but John, our godlike king, is strong. Come, follow him ! Or, if you stay, I myself will go alone ; never will I yield to a vassal's yoke ; my native land shall remain unconquered, and my monarch's foes, Castilian or Portuguese, shall heap the plain ! '

"Inspired by Nuño's eloquence the Lusians took the field and defeated the Spanish in the battle of Aljubarota. Still dissatisfied, Nuño pressed into Spain and dictated the terms of peace at Seville. Having established himself upon the throne of Portugal, John carried the war into Africa, which wars were continued after his death by his son Edward. While laying siege to Tangier, Edward and his brother Fernando were taken prisoners, and were allowed to return home only on promise to surrender Ceuta. Don Fernando remained as the hostage they demanded. The Portuguese would not agree to surrender Ceuta, and Don Fernando was forced to languish in captivity, since the Moors would accept no other ransom. He was a patriotic prince than whom were none greater in the annals of Lusitania.

"Alfonso V., victorious over the Moors, dreamed of conquering Castile, but was defeated, and on his death was succeeded by John II., who designed to gain immortal fame in a way tried by no other king. His sailors sought a path to India, but 'though enriched with knowledge' they perished at the mouth of the Indus. To his successor, Emmanuel, in a dream appeared the rivers Ganges and Indus, hoary fathers, rustic in aspect, yet with a majestic grace of bearing, their long, uncombed beards dripping with water, their heads wreathed with strange flowers, and proclaimed to him that their countries were ordained by fate to yield to him ; that the fight would be great, and the fields would stream

with blood, but that at last their shoulders would bend
beneath the yoke. Overjoyed at this dream, Emmanuel
proclaimed it to his people. I, O king, felt my bosom
burn, for long had I aspired to this work. Me the king
singled out, to me the dread toil he gave of seeking unknown
seas. Such zeal felt I and my youths as inspired the Mynian
youths when they ventured into unknown seas in the Argo,
in search of the golden fleece.

"On the shore was reared a sacred fane, and there at the
holy shrine my comrades and I knelt and joined in the
solemn rites. Prostrate we lay before the shrine until morning dawned; then, accompanied by the 'woful, weeping,
melancholy throng' that came pressing from the gates of
the city, we sought our ships.

"Then began the tears to flow; then the shrieks of mothers,
sisters, and wives rent the air, and as we waved farewell an
ancient man cried out to us on the thirst for honor and for
fame that led us to undertake such a voyage.

"Soon our native mountains mingled with the skies, and the
last dim speck of land having faded, we set our eyes to scan
the waste of sea before us. From Madeira's fair groves we
passed barren Masilia, the Cape of Green, the Happy Isles,
Jago, Jalofo, and vast Mandinga, the hated shore of the
Gorgades, the jutting cape called by us the Cape of Palms,
and southward sailed through the wild waves until the stars
changed and we saw Callisto's star no longer, but fixed our
eyes on another pole star that rises nightly over the waves.
The shining cross we beheld each night in the heavens was
to us a good omen.

"While thus struggling through the untried waves, and
battling with the tempests, now viewing with terror the
waterspouts, and the frightful lightnings, now comforted by
the sight of mysterious fire upon our masts, we came in sight
of land, and gave to the trembling negro who came to us
some brass and bells. Five days after this event, as we
sailed through the unknown seas, a sudden darkness o'er-
spread the sky, unlighted by moon or star. Questioning
what this portent might mean, I saw a mighty phantom rise

through the air. His aspect was sullen, his cheeks were pale, his withered hair stood erect, his yellow teeth gnashed; his whole aspect spoke of revenge and horror.

"'Bold are you,' cried he, 'to venture hither, but you shall suffer for it. The next proud fleet that comes this way shall perish on my coast, and he who first beheld me shall float on the tide a corpse. Often, O Lusus, shall your children mourn because of me!' 'Who art thou?' I cried. 'The Spirit of the Cape,' he replied, 'oft called the Cape of Tempests.'"

The king of Melinda interrupted Gama. He had often heard traditions among his people of the Spirit of the Cape. He was one of the race of Titans who loved Thetis, and was punished by Jove by being transformed into this promontory.

Gama continued: "Again we set forth, and stopped at a pleasant coast to clean our barks of the shell-fish. At this place we left behind many victims of the scurvy in their lonely graves. Of the treason we met with at Mozambique and the miracle that saved us at Quiloa and Mombas, you know already, as well as of your own bounty."

Charmed with the recital of Gama, the King of Melinda had forgotten how the hours passed away. After the story was told the company whiled away the hours with dance, song, the chase, and the banquet, until Gama declared that he must go on to India, and was furnished with a pilot by the friendly king.

Bacchus, enraged at seeing the voyage so nearly completed, descended to the palace of Neptune, with crystal towers, lofty turrets, roofs of gold, and beautiful pillars inwrought with pearls. The sculptured walls were adorned with old Chaos's troubled face, the four fair elements, and many scenes in the history of the earth. Roused by Bacchus, the gods of the sea consented to let loose the winds and the waves against the Portuguese.

During the night, the Lusians spent the time in relating stories of their country. As they talked, the storm came upon them, and the vessels rose upon the giant waves, so that the sailors saw the bottom of the sea swept almost bare by the violence of the storm. But the watchful Venus perceived the peril of her Lusians, and calling her nymphs together, beguiled the storm gods until the storm ceased. While the sailors congratulated themselves on the returning calm, the cry of " Land ! " was heard, and the pilot announced to Gama that Calicut was near.

Hail to the Lusian heroes who have won such honors, who have forced their way through untravelled seas to the shores of India ! Other nations of Europe have wasted their time in a vain search for luxury and fame instead of reclaiming to the faith its enemies ! Italy, how fallen, how lost art thou ! and England and Gaul, miscalled " most Christian ! " While ye have slept, the Lusians, though their realms are small, have crushed the Moslems and made their name resound throughout Africa, even to the shores of Asia.

At dawn Gama sent a herald to the monarch ; in the mean time, a friendly Moor, Monçaide, boarded the vessel, delighted to hear his own tongue once more. Born at Tangiers, he considered himself a neighbor of the Lusians ; well he knew their valorous deeds, and although a Moor, he now allied himself to them as a friend. He described India to the eager Gama : its religions, its idolaters, the Mohammedans, the Buddhists, the Brahmins. At Calicut, queen of India, lived the Zamorin, lord of India, to whom all subject kings paid their tribute.

His arrival having been announced, Gama, adorned in his most splendid garments, and accompanied by his train, also in bright array, entered the gilded barges and rowed to the shore, where stood the Catual, the Zamorin's minister. Monçaide acted as an interpreter. The company passed through a temple on their way to the palace, in which the Christians were horrified at the graven images there worshipped. On the palace walls were the most splendid pictures, relating the history of India. One wall, however, bore no sculptures ; the Brahmins had foretold that a foreign foe would at some time conquer India, and that space was reserved for scenes from those wars.

Into the splendid hall adorned with tapestries of cloth of

gold and carpets of velvet, Gama passed, and stood before the couch on which sat the mighty monarch. The room blazed with gems and gold; the monarch's mantle was of cloth of gold, and his turban shone with gems. His manner was majestic and dignified; he received Gama in silence, only nodding to him to tell his story.

Gama proclaimed that he came in friendship from a valorous nation that wished to unite its shores with his by commerce. The monarch responded that he and his council would weigh the proposal, and in the mean time Gama should remain and feast with them.

The next day the Indians visited the fleet, and after the banquet Gama displayed to his guests a series of banners on which were told the history of Portugal and her heroes. First came Lusus, the friend of Bacchus, the hero-shepherd Viriatus, the first Alonzo, the self-sacrificing Egas, the valiant Fuaz, every hero who had strengthened Lusitania and driven out her foes, down to the gallant Pedro and the glorious Henry.

Awed and wondering at the deeds of the mighty heroes, the Indians returned home. In the night Bacchus appeared to the king, warning him against the Lusians and urging him to destroy them while in his power. The Moors bought the Catual with their gold. They also told the king that they would leave his city as soon as he allied himself with the odious strangers. When Gama was next summoned before the king he was received with a frown.

"You are a pirate! Your first words were lies. Confess it; then you may stay with me and be my captain."

"I know the Moors," replied Gama. "I know their lies that have poisoned your ears. Am I mad that I should voluntarily leave my pleasant home and dare the terrors of an unknown sea? Ah, monarch, you know not the Lusian race! Bold, dauntless, the king commands, and we obey. Past the dread Cape of Storms have I ventured, bearing no gift save friendly peace, and that noblest gift of all, the friendship of my king. I have spoken the truth. Truth is everlasting!"

A day passed and still Gama was detained by the power of the Catual, who ordered him to call his fleets ashore if his voyage was really one of friendship.

"Never!" exclaimed Gama. "My fleet is free, though I am chained, and they shall carry to Lisbon the news of my discovery."

As he spoke, at a sign from the Catual, hostile ships were seen surrounding the Lusian vessels. "Not one shall tell on Lisbon's shores your fate."

Gama smiled scornfully, as the fleet swept on towards his vessels. Loud sounded the drums, shrill the trumpets. The next moment sudden lightning flashed from Gama's ships and the skies echoed with the thunder of the guns.

No word fell from Gama's lips as, the battle over, they saw the sea covered with the torn hulks and floating masts; but the populace raged around the palace gates, demanding justice to the strangers.

The troubled king sought to make peace with Gama.

"My orders have been given. To-day, when the sun reaches its meridian, India shall bleed and Calicut shall fall. The time is almost here. I make no terms. You have deceived me once."

The Moors fell fainting on the floor; the monarch trembled. "What can save us?" he cried.

"Convey me and my train to the fleet. Command at once; it is even now noon."

Once more safe within his ship, with him the faithful Monçaide, who had kept him informed of the treason of the Moors, his ships laden with cinnamon, cloves, pepper, and gems, proofs of his visit, Gama, rejoicing, set sail for home.

Venus saw the fleet setting out, and planned a resting-place for the weary sailors, a floating isle with golden sands, bowers of laurel and myrtle, beautiful flowers and luscious fruits. Here the sea nymphs gathered, Thetis, the most beautiful, being reserved for Gama, and here days were spent in joyance.

At the banquet the nymphs sang the future glories of the

Lusians, and taking Gama by the hand, led him and his men to a mountain height, whence they could look upon a wondrous globe, the universe. The crystal spheres whirled swiftly, making sweet music, and as they listened to this, they saw the sun go by, the stars, Apollo, the Queen of Love, Diana, and the " yellow earth, the centre of the whole." Asia and Africa were unrolled to their sight, and the future of India, conquered by the Lusians, Cochin China, China, Japan, Sumatra, — all these countries given to the world by their voyage around the terrible cape.

"Spread thy sails ! " cried the nymphs ; " the time has come to go ! "

The ships departed on their homeward way, and the heroes were received with the wildest welcome by the dwellers on Tago's bosom.

## SELECTIONS FROM THE LUSIAD.

### INEZ DE CASTRO.

DURING the reign of Alfonso the Brave, his son Don Pedro secretly wedded a beautiful maiden of the court, Inez de Castro. The courtiers, jealous because Inez was a Castilian, betrayed Pedro's secret to the king, who, in the absence of his son, had Inez brought before him and slain by hired ruffians.

> While glory, thus, Alonzo's name adorn'd,
> To Lisbon's shores the happy chief return'd,
> In glorious peace and well-deserv'd repose,
> His course of fame, and honor'd age to close.
> When now, O king, a damsel's fate severe,
> A fate which ever claims the woful tear,
> Disgraced his honors — On the nymph's 'lorn head
> Relentless rage its bitterest rancor shed :
> Yet, such the zeal her princely lover bore,
> Her breathless corse the crown of Lisbon wore.
> 'T was thou, O Love, whose dreaded shafts control
> The hind's rude heart, and tear the hero's soul ;
> Thou, ruthless power, with bloodshed never cloy'd,
> 'T was thou thy lovely votary destroy'd.
> Thy thirst still burning for a deeper woe,
> In vain to thee the tears of beauty flow ;

The breast that feels thy purest flames divine,
With spouting gore must bathe thy cruel shrine.
Such thy dire triumphs ! — Thou, O nymph, the while,
Prophetic of the god's unpitying guile,
In tender scenes by love-sick fancy wrought,
By fear oft shifted, as by fancy brought,
In sweet Mondego's ever-verdant bowers,
Languish'd away the slow and lonely hours :
While now, as terror wak'd thy boding fears,
The conscious stream receiv'd thy pearly tears;
And now, as hope reviv'd the brighter flame,
Each echo sigh'd thy princely lover's name.
Nor less could absence from thy prince remove
The dear remembrance of his distant love:
Thy looks, thy smiles, before him ever glow,
And o'er his melting heart endearing flow :
By night his slumbers bring thee to his arms,
By day his thoughts still wander o'er thy charms :
By night, by day, each thought thy loves employ,
Each thought the memory, or the hope, of joy.
Though fairest princely dames invok'd his love,
No princely dame his constant faith could move:
For thee, alone, his constant passion burn'd,
For thee the proffer'd royal maids he scorn'd.
Ah, hope of bliss too high — the princely dames
Refus'd, dread rage the father's breast inflames ;
He, with an old man's wintry eye, surveys
The youth's fond love, and coldly with it weighs
The people's murmurs of his son's delay
To bless the nation with his nuptial day.
(Alas, the nuptial day was past unknown,
Which, but when crown'd, the prince could dare to own.)
And, with the fair one's blood, the vengeful sire
Resolves to quench his Pedro's faithful fire.
Oh, thou dread sword, oft stain'd with heroes' gore,
Thou awful terror of the prostrate Moor,
What rage could aim thee at a female breast,
Unarm'd, by softness and by love possess'd !

Dragg'd from her bower, by murd'rous ruffian hands,
Before the frowning king fair Inez stands ;
Her tears of artless innocence, her air
So mild, so lovely, and her face so fair,
Mov'd the stern monarch ; when, with eager zeal,
Her fierce destroyers urg'd the public weal ;
Dread rage again the tyrant's soul possess'd,
And his dark brow his cruel thoughts confess'd ;
O'er her fair face a sudden paleness spread,
Her throbbing heart with gen'rous anguish bled,
Anguish to view her lover's hopeless woes,

And all the mother in her bosom rose.
Her beauteous eyes, in trembling tear-drops drown'd,
To heaven she lifted (for her hands were bound);
Then, on her infants turn'd the piteous glance,
The look of bleeding woe; the babes advance,
Smiling in innocence of infant age,
Unaw'd, unconscious of their grandsire's rage;
To whom, as bursting sorrow gave the flow,
The native heart-sprung eloquence of woe,
The lovely captive thus: — "O monarch, hear,
If e'er to thee the name of man was dear,
If prowling tigers, or the wolf's wild brood
(Inspired by nature with the lust of blood),
Have yet been mov'd the weeping babe to spare,
Nor left, but tended with a nurse's care,
As Rome's great founders to the world were given;
Shalt thou, who wear'st the sacred stamp of Heaven
The human form divine, shalt thou deny
That aid, that pity, which e'en beasts supply!
Oh, that thy heart were, as thy looks declare,
Of human mould, superfluous were my prayer;
Thou couldst not, then, a helpless damsel slay,
Whose sole offence in fond affection lay,
In faith to him who first his love confess'd,
Who first to love allur'd her virgin breast.
In these my babes shalt thou thine image see,
And, still tremendous, hurl thy rage on me?
Me, for their sakes, if yet thou wilt not spare,
Oh, let these infants prove thy pious care!
Yet, Pity's lenient current ever flows
From that brave breast where genuine valor glows;
That thou art brave, let vanquish'd Afric tell,
Then let thy pity o'er my anguish swell;
Ah, let my woes, unconscious of a crime,
Procure mine exile to some barb'rous clime:
Give me to wander o'er the burning plains
Of Libya's deserts, or the wild domains
Of Scythia's snow-clad rocks, and frozen shore;
There let me, hopeless of return, deplore:
Where ghastly horror fills the dreary vale,
Where shrieks and howlings die on every gale,
The lion's roaring, and the tiger's yell,
There with my infant race, consigned to dwell,
There let me try that piety to find,
In vain by me implor'd from human kind:
There, in some dreary cavern's rocky womb,
Amid the horrors of sepulchral gloom,
For him whose love I mourn, my love shall glow,
The sigh shall murmur, and the tear shall flow:
All my fond wish, and all my hope, to rear

These infant pledges of a love so dear,
Amidst my griefs a soothing glad employ,
Amidst my fears a woful, hopeless joy.''

In tears she utter'd — as the frozen snow
Touch'd by the spring's mild ray, begins to flow,
So just began to melt his stubborn soul,
As mild-ray'd Pity o'er the tyrant stole ;
But destiny forbade : with eager zeal
(Again pretended for the public weal),
Her fierce accusers urg'd her speedy doom ;
Again, dark rage diffus'd its horrid gloom
O'er stern Alonzo's brow : swift at the sign,
Their swords, unsheath'd, around her brandish'd shine.
O foul disgrace, of knighthood lasting stain,
By men of arms a helpless lady slain !

Thus Pyrrhus, burning with unmanly ire,
Fulfilled the mandate of his furious sire ;
Disdainful of the frantic matron's prayer,
On fair Polyxena, her last fond care,
He rush'd, his blade yet warm with Priam's gore,
And dash'd the daughter on the sacred floor ;
While mildly she her raving mother eyed,
Resigned her bosom to the sword, and died.
Thus Inez, while her eyes to heaven appeal,
Resigns her bosom to the murd'ring steel :
That snowy neck, whose matchless form sustain'd
The loveliest face, where all the graces reign'd,
Whose charms so long the gallant prince enflam'd,
That her pale corse was Lisbon's queen proclaim'd,
That snowy neck was stain'd with spouting gore,
Another sword her lovely bosom tore.
The flowers that glisten'd with her tears bedew'd,
Now shrunk and languish'd with her blood embru'd.
As when a rose ere-while of bloom so gay,
Thrown from the careless virgin's breast away,
Lies faded on the plain, the living red,
The snowy white, and all its fragrance fled ;
So from her cheeks the roses died away,
And pale in death the beauteous Inez lay :
With dreadful smiles, and crimson'd with her blood,
Round the wan victim the stern murd'rers stood,
Unmindful of the sure, though future hour,
Sacred to vengeance and her lover's power.

O Sun, couldst thou so foul a crime behold,
Nor veil thine head in darkness, as of old
A sudden night unwonted horror cast
O'er that dire banquet, where the sire's repast

The son's torn limbs supplied! — Yet you, ye vales!
Ye distant forests, and ye flow'ry dales!
When pale and sinking to the dreadful fall,
You heard her quiv'ring lips on Pedro call;
Your faithful echoes caught the parting sound,
And Pedro! Pedro! mournful, sigh'd around.
Nor less the wood-nymphs of Mondego's groves
Bewail'd the memory of her hapless loves:
Her griefs they wept, and, to a plaintive rill
Transform'd their tears, which weeps and murmurs still.
To give immortal pity to her woe
They taught the riv'let through her bowers to flow,
And still, through violet-beds, the fountain pours
Its plaintive wailing, and is named Amours.
Nor long her blood for vengeance cried in vain:
Her gallant lord begins his awful reign,
In vain her murderers for refuge fly,
Spain's wildest hills no place of rest supply.
The injur'd lover's and the monarch's ire,
And stern-brow'd Justice in their doom conspire:
In hissing flames they die, and yield their souls in fire.

*Mickle's Translation, Canto III.*

## THE SPIRIT OF THE CAPE.

VASCO DE GAMA relates the incidents of his voyage from
Portugal to the King of Melinda. The southern cross had appeared in the heavens and the fleet was approaching the southern point of Africa. While at anchor in a bay the Portuguese
aroused the hostility of the savages, and hastily set sail.

" Now, prosp'rous gales the bending canvas swell'd;
From these rude shores our fearless course we held:
Beneath the glist'ning wave the god of day
Had now five times withdrawn the parting ray,
When o'er the prow a sudden darkness spread,
And, slowly floating o'er the mast's tall head
A black cloud hover'd: nor appear'd from far
The moon's pale glimpse, nor faintly twinkling star;
So deep a gloom the low'ring vapor cast,
Transfix'd with awe the bravest stood aghast.
Meanwhile, a hollow bursting roar resounds,
As when hoarse surges lash their rocky mounds;
Nor had the black'ning wave nor frowning heav'n
The wonted signs of gath'ring tempest giv'n.
Amazed we stood. 'O thou, our fortune's guide,

Avert this omen, mighty God!'   I cried;
' Or, through forbidden climes adventurous stray'd,
Have we the secrets of the deep survey'd,
Which these wide solitudes of seas and sky
Were doom'd to hide from man's unhallow'd eye?
Whate'er this prodigy, it threatens more
Than midnight tempests, and the mingled roar,
When sea and sky combine to rock the marble shore.'

"I spoke, when rising through the darken'd air,
Appall'd, we saw a hideous phantom glare;
High and enormous o'er the flood he tower'd,
And 'thwart our way with sullen aspect lower'd:
An earthy paleness o'er his cheeks was spread,
Erect uprose his hairs of wither'd red;
Writhing to speak, his sable lips disclose,
Sharp and disjoin'd, his gnashing teeth's blue rows;
His haggard beard flow'd quiv'ring on the wind,
Revenge and horror in his mien combin'd;
His clouded front, by with'ring lightnings scar'd,
The inward anguish of his soul declar'd.
His red eyes, glowing from their dusky caves,
Shot livid fires: far echoing o'er the waves
His voice resounded, as the cavern'd shore
With hollow groan repeats the tempest's roar.
Cold gliding horrors thrill'd each hero's breast,
Our bristling hair and tott'ring knees confess'd
Wild dread, the while with visage ghastly wan,
His black lips trembling, thus the fiend began:—

"'O you, the boldest of the nations, fir'd
By daring pride, by lust of fame inspir'd,
Who, scornful of the bow'rs of sweet repose,
Through these my waves advance your fearless prows,
Regardless of the length'ning wat'ry way,
And all the storms that own my sov'reign sway,
Who, mid surrounding rocks and shelves explore
Where never hero brav'd my rage before;
Ye sons of Lusus, who with eyes profane
Have view'd the secrets of my awful reign,
Have passed the bounds which jealous Nature drew
To veil her secret shrine from mortal view;
Hear from my lips what direful woes attend,
And, bursting soon, shall o'er your race descend.

"'With every bounding keel that dares my rage,
Eternal war my rocks and storms shall wage,
The next proud fleet that through my drear domain,
With daring search shall hoist the streaming vane,
That gallant navy, by my whirlwinds toss'd,

22

And raging seas, shall perish on my coast:
Then he, who first my secret reign descried,
A naked corpse, wide floating o'er the tide,
Shall drive — Unless my heart's full raptures fail,
O Lusus! oft shalt thou thy children wail;
Each year thy shipwreck'd sons thou shalt deplore,
Each year thy sheeted masts shall strew my shore.

   " ' With trophies plum'd behold a hero come,
Ye dreary wilds, prepare his yawning tomb.
Though smiling fortune bless'd his youthful morn,
Though glory's rays his laurell'd brows adorn,
Full oft though he beheld with sparkling eye
The Turkish moons in wild confusion fly,
While he, proud victor, thunder'd in the rear,
All, all his mighty fame shall vanish here.
Quiloa's sons, and thine, Mombaz, shall see
Their conqueror bend his laurell'd head to me;
While, proudly mingling with the tempest's sound,
Their shouts of joy from every cliff rebound.

   " ' The howling blast, ye slumb'ring storms prepare,
A youthful lover and his beauteous fair
Triumphant sail from India's ravag'd land;
His evil angel leads him to my strand.
Through the torn hulk the dashing waves shall roar,
The shatter'd wrecks shall blacken all my shore.
Themselves escaped, despoil'd by savage hands,
Shall, naked, wander o'er the burning sands,
Spar'd by the waves far deeper woes to bear,
Woes, e'en by me, acknowledg'd with a tear.
Their infant race, the promis'd heirs of joy,
Shall now, no more, a hundred hands employ;
By cruel want, beneath the parents' eye,
In these wide wastes their infant race shall die;
Through dreary wilds, where never pilgrim trod
Where caverns yawn, and rocky fragments nod,
The hapless lover and his bride shall stray,
By night unshelter'd, and forlorn by day.
In vain the lover o'er the trackless plain
Shall dart his eyes, and cheer his spouse in vain.
Her tender limbs, and breast of mountain snow,
Where, ne'er before, intruding blast might blow,
Parch'd by the sun, and shrivell'd by the cold
Of dewy night, shall he, fond man, behold.
Thus, wand'ring wide, a thousand ills o'er past,
In fond embraces they shall sink at last;
While pitying tears their dying eyes o'erflow,
And the last sigh shall wail each other's woe.

" ' Some few, the sad companions of their fate,
Shall yet survive, protected by my hate,
On Tagus' banks the dismal tale to tell,
How, blasted by my frown, your heroes fell.'

" He paus'd, in act still further to disclose
A long, a dreary prophecy of woes:
When springing onward, loud my voice resounds,
And midst his rage the threat'ning shade confounds.

" ' What art thou, horrid form that rid'st the air?
By Heaven's eternal light, stern fiend, declare.'
His lips he writhes, his eyes far round he throws,
And, from his breast, deep hollow groans arose,
Sternly askance he stood: with wounded pride
And anguish torn, ' In me, behold,' he cried,
While dark-red sparkles from his eyeballs roll'd,
' In me the Spirit of the Cape behold,
That rock, by you the Cape of Tempests nam'd,
By Neptune's rage, in horrid earthquakes fram'd,
When Jove's red bolts o'er Titan's offspring flam'd.
With wide-stretch'd piles I guard the pathless strand,
And Afric's southern mound, unmov'd, I stand:
Nor Roman prow, nor daring Tyrian oar
Ere dash'd the white wave foaming to my shore;
Nor Greece nor Carthage ever spread the sail
On these my seas, to catch the trading gale.
You, you alone have dar'd to plough my main,
And with the human voice disturb my lonesome reign."

" He spoke, and deep a lengthen'd sigh he drew,
A doleful sound, and vanish'd from the view:
The frighten'd billows gave a rolling swell,
And, distant far, prolong'd the dismal yell,
Faint and more faint the howling echoes die,
And the black cloud dispersing, leaves the sky.
High to the angel-host, whose guardian care
Had ever round us watch'd, my hands I rear,
And Heaven's dread King implore: ' As o'er our head
The fiend dissolv'd, an empty shadow fled;
So may his curses, by the winds of heav'n,
Far o'er the deep, their idle sport, be driv'n!' "

With sacred horror thrill'd, Melinda's lord
Held up the eager hand, and caught the word.
" Oh, wondrous faith of ancient days," he cries,
" Concealed in mystic lore and dark disguise!
Taught by their sires, our hoary fathers tell,
On these rude shores a giant spectre fell,
What time from heaven the rebel band were thrown:

And oft the wand'ring swain has heard his moan.
While o'er the wave the clouded moon appears
To hide her weeping face, his voice he rears
O'er the wild storm.   Deep in the days of yore,
A holy pilgrim trod the nightly shore;
Stern groans he heard; by ghostly spells controll'd,
His fate, mysterious, thus the spectre told:

" ' By forceful Titan's warm embrace compress'd,
The rock-ribb'd mother, Earth, his love confess'd:
The hundred-handed giant at a birth,
And me, she bore, nor slept my hopes on earth;
My heart avow'd my sire's ethereal flame;
Great Adamastor, then, my dreaded name.
In my bold brother's glorious toils engaged,
Tremendous war against the gods I waged:
Yet, not to reach the throne of heaven I try,
With mountain pil'd on mountain to the sky;
To me the conquest of the seas befell,
In his green realm the second Jove to quell.
Nor did ambition all my passions hold,
'T was love that prompted an attempt so bold.
Ah me, one summer in the cool of day,
I saw the Nereids on the sandy bay,
With lovely Thetis from the wave advance
In mirthful frolic, and the naked dance.
In all her charms reveal'd the goddess trod,
With fiercest fires my struggling bosom glow'd;
Yet, yet I feel them burning in my heart,
And hopeless, languish with the raging smart.
For her, each goddess of the heavens I scorn'd,
For her alone my fervent ardor burn'd.
In vain I woo'd her to the lover's bed,
From my grim form, with horror, mute she fled.
Madd'ning with love, by force I ween to gain
The silver goddess of the blue domain;
To the hoar mother of the Nereid band
I tell my purpose, and her aid command:
By fear impell'd, old Doris tried to move,
And win the spouse of Peleus to my love.
The silver goddess with a smile replies,
'What nymph can yield her charms a giant's prize!
Yet, from the horrors of a war to save,
And guard in peace our empire of the wave,
Whate'er with honor he may hope to gain,
That, let him hope his wish shall soon attain.'
The promis'd grace infus'd a bolder fire,
And shook my mighty limbs with fierce desire.
But ah, what error spreads its dreadful night,
What phantoms hover o'er the lover's sight!

The war resign'd, my steps by Doris led,
While gentle eve her shadowy mantle spread,
Before my steps the snowy Thetis shone
In all her charms, all naked, and alone.
Swift as the wind with open arms I sprung,
And, round her waist with joy delirious clung:
In all the transports of the warm embrace,
A hundred kisses on her angel face,
On all its various charms my rage bestows,
And, on her cheek, my cheek enraptur'd glows.
When oh, what anguish while my shame I tell!
What fix'd despair, what rage my bosom swell!
Here was no goddess, here no heavenly charms,
A rugged mountain fill'd my eager arms,
Whose rocky top, o'erhung with matted brier,
Received the kisses of my am'rous fire.
Wak'd from my dream, cold horror freez'd my blood;
Fix'd as a rock, before the rock I stood;
' O fairest goddess of the ocean train,
Behold the triumph of thy proud disdain;
Yet why,' I cried, ' with all I wish'd decoy,
And, when exulting in the dream of joy,
A horrid mountain to mine arms convey?'
Madd'ning I spoke, and furious sprung away.
Far to the south I sought the world unknown,
Where I, unheard, unscorn'd, might wail alone,
My foul dishonor, and my tears to hide,
And shun the triumph of the goddess' pride.
My brothers, now, by Jove's red arm o'erthrown,
Beneath huge mountains pil'd on mountains groan;
And I, who taught each echo to deplore,
And tell my sorrows to the desert shore,
I felt the hand of Jove my crimes pursue,
My stiff'ning flesh to earthy ridges grew,
And my huge bones, no more by marrow warm'd,
To horrid piles, and ribs of rock transform'd,
Yon dark-brow'd cape of monstrous size became,
Where, round me still, in triumph o'er my shame,
The silv'ry Thetis bids her surges roar,
And waft my groans along the dreary shore.'"

*Mickle's Translation, Canto V.*

# THE JERUSALEM DELIVERED.

THE Gerusalemme Liberata, or Jerusalem Delivered, was written by Torquato Tasso, who was born at Sorrento, March 11, 1544. He was educated at Naples, Urbino, Rome, Venice, Padua, and Bologna. In 1572 he attached himself to the court of Ferrara, which he had visited in 1565 in the suite of the Cardinal d'Este, and by whose duke he had been treated with great consideration. Here his pastoral drama "Aminta" was written and performed, and here he began to write his epic. The duke, angry because of Tasso's affection for his sister Eleanora, and fearful lest the poet should dedicate his poem to the Medicis, whom he visited in 1575, and into whose service he was asked to enter, kept him under strict surveillance, and pretended to regard him as insane. Feigning sympathy and a desire to restore his mind, he had the unfortunate poet confined in a mad-house. Tasso escaped several times, but each time returned in the hope of a reconciliation with the duke. During his confinement his poem was published without his permission: first in 1580, a very imperfect version; in 1581, a genuine one. This at once brought him great fame; but while its publishers made a fortune, Tasso received nothing. Neither did the duke relent, although powerful influences were brought to bear on him. Tasso was not released until 1586, and then, broken in health, he passed the rest of his life in Rome and Naples, living on charity, though treated with great honor. He died in Rome, April 25, 1595, just before he was to have been crowned at the capitol.

The Jerusalem Delivered has for its subject the first Crusade, and the events recorded in its twenty cantos comprise the happenings in the camp of the Crusaders during forty days of the campaign of 1099. Its metre is the *ottava rima*, the eight lined rhymed stanza.

Tasso was not so successful in the delineation of character and in the description of actions as in the interpretation of feeling, being by nature a lyric rather than an epic poet. But his happy choice of subject, — for the Crusades were still fresh in the memory of the people, and chivalry was a thing of the present — his zeal for the Christian cause, his impassioned delineations of love, and his exquisitely poetical treatment of his whole theme, rendered his epic irresistible.

BIBLIOGRAPHY AND CRITICISM, THE JERUSALEM DELIVERED. J. Black's Life of Tasso (with a historical and critical account of his writings), 2 vols. 1810 ; E. J. Hasell's Tasso, 1882 ; Rev. Robert Milman's Life of Tasso, 2 vols. 1850 ; Dennistown's Memoirs of the Dukes of Urbino, 1851, iii., 292–316 ; Hallam's Introduction to the Literature of Europe in the 15th, 16th, and 17th Centuries, 1839, ii., 192–199 ; Leigh Hunt's Stories from Italian Poets, 1888, ii., 289–474 ; Longfellow's Poets and Poetry of Europe, 1845, pp. 568–577 ; Sismondi's Literature of the South of Europe, Ed. 2, 1846, i., 359–391 ; J. A. Symonds's Renaissance in Italy, 1886, vol. 2, chapters 7–8 ; Edin. Rev., Oct. 1850, xcii., 294–302 ; Blackwood, 1845, lvii., 401–414 ; Quarterly Review, Jan. 1857, ci., 59–68.

STANDARD ENGLISH TRANSLATIONS, THE JERUSALEM DELIVERED. Jerusalem Delivered, Tr. from the Italian by John Hoole. First American from Eighth London Edition, 2 vols., 1810 ; Jerusalem Delivered, Tr. into English Spenserian verse with life of the author by J. H. Wiffen. New ed., 1883 ; Jerusalem Delivered, Tr. by Sir John Kingston James, 2 vols., 1884 ; Jerusalem Delivered, Tr. into the metre of the original by C. L. Smith, 1876–79 ; Jerusalem Delivered, Tr. by Sir Edward Fairfax and edited by Prof. Henry Morley, 1889.

## THE STORY OF THE JERUSALEM DELIVERED.

THE Eternal Father looked down from His lofty throne upon the Christian powers in Syria. In the six years they had spent in the East they had taken Nice and Antioch. Now, while inactive in winter quarters, Bohemond was strengthening himself in Antioch, and the other chiefs were thinking of glory or love; but Godfrey, to whom renown was the meanest of glories, was burning to win Jerusalem and restore it to the faith. Inspired by Gabriel, despatched by the Eternal Father, Godfrey called a council, and with an eloquence and fire more than mortal, roused the Christians to action. "We came not here to raise empires; the period has come when all the world is waiting for our next step. Now is the propitious moment. If we delay longer, Egypt will step in to the aid of our Syrian foe!"

Godfrey was unanimously elected chief, and immediate arrangements were made for the setting out to Jerusalem. Godfrey first reviewed the army. A thousand men marched under the lilied banner of Clotharius; a thousand more from the Norman meads under Robert; from Orange and Puy, troops came under the priests William and Ademar. Baldwin led his own and Godfrey's bands, and Guelpho, allied to the house of Este, brought his strong Carinthians. Other troops of horse and foot were led by William of England. After him came the young Tancred, the flower of chivalry, blighted now, alas! by unrequited love. He had seen by chance the pagan maid Clorinda, the Amazon, drinking at a pool in the forest, and had forgot all else in his love for her. After him came the small Greek force under Tatine; next, the invincible Adventurers under Dudon, bravest of men. Following these were Otho, Edward and his sweet bride Gildippe, who, unwilling to be separated from her husband, fought at his side, and, excellent above all others, the

young Rinaldo, whose glorious deeds were yet but a promise
of his great future. While but a boy he had escaped from the
care of his foster mother, Queen Matilda, and hastened to
join the Crusaders. The review was closed by the array of
foot soldiers led by Raymond, Stephen of Amboise, Alcasto,
and Camillus. The pageant having passed by, Godfrey
despatched a messenger to summon Sweno the Dane, who
with his forces was still tarrying in Greece, and at once set
out for Jerusalem.

Swift rumor had conveyed the tidings of his approach to
Aladine, King of Jerusalem, a merciless tyrant, who, enraged,
immediately laid heavier taxes upon the unfortunate Christians in his city. Ismeno, a sorcerer, once a Christian, but
now a pagan who practised all black arts, penetrated to the
presence of the king and advised him to steal from the
temple of the Christians an image of the Virgin and put it in
his mosque, assuring him that he would thus render his city
impregnable. This was done, and Ismeno wrought his
spells about the image, but the next morning it had disappeared. After a fruitless search for the image and the
offender, the angry king sentenced all the Franks to death.
The beautiful maid Sophronia, determined to save her
people, assumed the guilt, and was sentenced to be burned.
As she stood chained to the stake, her lover, Olindo, to
whom she had ever been cold, saw her, and in agony at her
sacrifice, declared to the king that Sophronia had lied and
that he was the purloiner of the image. The cruel monarch
ordered him also to be tied to the stake, that they might die
together; and the flames had just been applied when the two
were saved by the Amazon Clorinda, who convinced the
king that the Christians were innocent and that Allah himself, incensed at the desecration, had snatched away the
image.

To the camp of Godfrey at Emmaus came two ambassadors from the king of Egypt, Alethes, a supple crafty
courtier of low lineage, and Argantes, a haughty and powerful warrior. But their efforts to keep Godfrey from Jerusalem, first by persuasion, and then by threats, were in vain.

They were dismissed from the camp, and the army proceeded on its way.

When the walls and towers of the city where Messias died came in sight, the Christian army, crying "All Hail, Jerusalem!" laid aside their casques, and, shedding tears, trod barefoot the consecrated way.

At sight of the Franks, the pagans hastened to strengthen the fortifications of their city, and Aladine from a lofty tower watched Clorinda attack a band of Franks returning from a foray. At his side was the lovely Erminia, daughter of the King of Antioch, who had sought Jerusalem after the downfall of her city.

Erminia instructed Aladine of the various crusaders, and when she pointed out the noble Tancred, who had treated her with such consideration in Antioch, she felt her love for him revive, though she pretended to the king to hate him for his cruelty. Tancred recognized among the leaders of the pagans Clorinda, bereft of her helmet, and for love of her, refused to fight her. The pagans, driven back by the Christians, were rallied by Argantes, but only to be met by the matchless Adventurers under Dudon. When Dudon fell, the troops under Rinaldo, burning for revenge, reluctantly obeyed Godfrey's summons to return.

The funeral rites over, the artificers were sent to the forest to fell the trees, that engines might be fabricated for the destruction of the city walls.

Angry at the success of the Franks, Satan stirred up the infernal regions, and set loose his friends to work destruction to the Christians. One he despatched to the wizard Idraotes, at Damascus, who conceived the scheme of sending his beautiful niece Armida to ensnare the Christians. In a few days Armida appeared among the white pavilions of the Franks, attracting the attention and winning the love of all who saw her. Her golden locks appeared through her veil as the sunshine gleams through the stormy skies; her charms were sufficiently hidden to make them the more alluring. So attired, modestly seeking the camp of Godfrey, she was met by Eustace, his young brother, and taken to the prince.

With many tears and sighs, she told her pitiful story. She had been driven from her kingdom, an orphan, by the envy and wickedness of her uncle, and had come to ask the Christians to aid her in regaining her rights. Unfortunately for her success, she and her uncle had not calculated on Godfrey's absorption in his divine undertaking. He was proof against her charms, and was determined not to be delayed longer in laying siege to the city. It required the utmost persuasion of Eustace to induce him to permit ten of the Adventurers to accompany her. Armida, though disappointed in Godfrey's lack of susceptibility, employed her time so well while in camp that when she departed with the ten Adventurers chosen by lot, she was followed secretly by Eustace and many others who had not been chosen, but who were madly in love with her.

Before his departure, Eustace, jealous of Rinaldo, whom he was fearful Armida might admire, had persuaded him to aspire to the place of Dudon, to whom a successor must be elected. Gernando of Norway desired the same place, and, angry that the popular Rinaldo should be his rival, scattered through the camp rumors disparaging to his character : Rinaldo was vain and arrogant ; Rinaldo was rash, not brave ; Rinaldo's virtues were all vices. At last, stung past endurance by his taunts and insinuations, Rinaldo gave the lie to his traducer, and slew him in fair fight. False reports were taken to Godfrey by Rinaldo's enemies, and the ruler determined to punish the youth severely ; but he, warned by his friends, escaped from camp and fled to Antioch. To Godfrey, deprived thus of Rinaldo and many of his brave Adventurers, was brought the tidings that the Egyptian expedition was on its way, and that a ship laden with provisions had been intercepted on its way to his camp.

The bold Argantes, weary of the restraint of the siege, sent a challenge to the Christians, saying he would meet any Frank, high-born or low, in single combat, the conditions being that the vanquished should serve the victor. A thousand knights burned to accept the challenge, but Godfrey named Tancred, who proudly buckled on his armor and called for his steed. As he approached the field, he saw among the pagan hosts, who stood around to view the combat, the fair face of Clorinda, and stood gazing at her, forgetful of all else. Otho, seeing his delay, spurred on his horse, and fought till vanquished. Then Tancred woke from his stupor, and, burning with shame, rushed forward. The battle raged until night fell, and the weary warriors ceased, pledging themselves to return on the morrow.

Erminia, shut up in Jerusalem, mourned over the wounds of Tancred. She knew many healing balms, by which, were she with him, she might heal him and make him ready for the morrow's fight; but she was forced to administer them to his enemy instead. Unable to endure the suspense longer, she put on her friend Clorinda's armor and fled to the Christian camp to find her beloved. The Franks, who spied her, supposed her Clorinda, and pursued her; but she succeeded in reaching a woodland retreat, where she determined to remain with the kind old shepherd and his wife who had fled from the disappointments of the court and had here sought and found peace in their humble home. When Tancred heard from his followers that they had driven Clorinda from the camps, he determined to pursue and speak with her. Rising from his bed he sought the forest only to fall into the wiles of Armida, and be lured into a castle, in whose dungeon he lay, consumed with shame at the thought of his unexplained absence from the morrow's combat.

When morning dawned and Tancred did not appear, the good old Count Raymond went forth to meet Argantes. When he was about to overcome his antagonist, an arrow shot from the pagan ranks brought on a general conflict, in which the Christians were successful until a storm, summoned by the powers of darkness, put an end to the battle. The next morning a knight came to the camp of Godfrey to tell of Sweno's defeat and slaughter. He, the sole survivor of the band, had been commissioned by some supernatural visitants to bring Sweno's sword to Rinaldo.

While Godfrey's heart was wrung by this disaster, the

camp of Italians, led to suppose by some bloody armor found in a wood that Rinaldo had been treacherously slain with the connivance of Godfrey, accused the chief and stirred up the camp to revolt; but Godfrey, praying to Heaven for strength to meet his enemies, walked through the camp firmly and unfalteringly, unarmed and with head bare, his face still bright with the heavenly light left there by spiritual communion, and silenced the tumult by a few well-chosen words. His arch-accuser Argillan he sentenced to death; the others crept back to their tents in shame.

The Soldan Solyman, driven from Nice at its capture, had joined the Turks, and, spurred on by hate and fury, made a night attack on the Frankish camp. The Franks, saved only by the interposition of the angel Michael, and by the troops just returned, released from Armida's enchantment, fought fiercely, and at dawn put Solyman to flight. By the arts of Ismeno he was conveyed to Jerusalem by a secret way, where he cheered the discouraged Aladine.

Before attempting to storm the city, the Christian troops, by the advice of Peter the Hermit, walked in a long procession to Mt. Olivet, filling the heavens with melody, and there partook of the communion administered by the warrior priests, William and Ademar. The next morning, Godfrey, in the light armor of a foot-soldier, appeared with his barons, prepared for the storm. The troops were arranged carefully, the huge engines were moved forward, and the Franks made a bold attempt against the walls, from the top of which Clorinda aimed her arrows, wounding and slaying many men. Godfrey himself was wounded, but was healed by divine aid, and immediately returned to the field to rally his troops. Night fell, and the contest was deferred until another day.

Clorinda, burning to distinguish herself, determined to fire the huge towers of the Christians. Her eunuch tried to dissuade her because he had been warned in a dream that she would this night meet her death. He told her her history. Her mother was a Christian who had been compelled to put her infant away from her. This eunuch had rescued her from death and brought her up, failing, however, to obey an angel's command to have her baptized a Christian.

Clorinda would not heed his caution, but went forth and fired the Frankish machines. She and the fleeing pagans were pursued by the Christians; and while her companions reached the city in safety, she was accidentally shut out and met Tancred in mortal combat. She refused to tell her name until she felt her death-wound, and then she prayed her enemy to baptize her, that she might die a Christian. The broken-hearted Tancred fell fainting on her corpse, and was found there the next morning by the Franks. Neither his comrades, nor Godfrey and Peter the Hermit, were able to rouse him from his melancholy.

Their machines destroyed, timbers were needed by the Franks to construct new ones. Knowing this, Ismeno laid spells on the forest, so that the warriors sent thither by Godfrey were frightened away by the sights they saw therein. Even Tancred was put to flight when one of the demons took the form of his beloved Clorinda. To add to the discomfort of the Franks, excessive heat overpowered them, and they suffered tortures from lack of water until the prayers of Godfrey moved the Ruler of the Earth with pity, and He sent down the longed-for showers.

Delighted with the piety of Godfrey, the Great King sent him a dream by which he might know the will of Heaven. Lifted through the whirling spheres, his ears charmed with their music, his eyes dazzled by the brilliancy of the stars, he saw Duke Hugo, who told him that Rinaldo must be sought out before the conquest of Jerusalem could be accomplished. The same Power influenced the princes in council so that by the will of all, two knights, one of them him to whom Sweno's sword had been given, were despatched to seek Rinaldo. Instructed by Peter the Hermit, they sought the sea-coast, and found a wizard, who, after showing them the splendor of his underground abode beneath the river's bed, revealed to them the way in which they were to overcome the wiles of Armida.

A beautiful maid with dove-like eyes and radiant smile received them in her small bark, and they were soon flying over the sea, marvelling at the rich cities and vast fleets by which they passed. Leaving rich Cadiz and the Pillars of Hercules, they sped out into the unknown sea, while the maiden told them of how some day Columbus would venture into unknown seas to find a new continent. On, on they flew, past the Happy Isles, the Fortunate, long the song of the poet; where the olive and honey made happy the land, and the rivers swept down from the mountains in silver streamlets; where every bird-song was heavenly music, a place so divine that there were placed of old the Elysian fields. To one of these islands the lady steered, and the knights disembarked, and started on their perilous journey up the mountain. Following the wizard's instructions, they waved the golden rod at the monstrous serpents hissing in their pathway, and they vanished; they steeled their hearts against the charms of the voluptuous maids bathing in the lake, and passed without tasting the fountain of laughter. Then the spacious palace met their eyes. Built round a garden, its marble courts and unnumbered galleries formed a trackless maze through which they could never have found their way without the aid of the wizard's map. As they trod the marble floors they paused many times to view the matchless carvings on the silver doors, which told anew the beautiful old stories of love triumphant.

Once through the winding ways, they entered the wonderful garden which art and nature combined to render the most beautiful spot on earth. The same trees bore ripe fruit, buds, and blossoms; the birds sang joyfully in the green bowers; and the faint breezes echoed their song. One bird sang a song of love, and when the tender melody was done the other birds took it up and sang until the forest rang with melody, and all was love, love, love. Then the knights saw Rinaldo, lying in the grove, his head in the lap of the enchantress. His sword was gone from his side, and in its place hung a mirror in which he sometimes gazed at Armida's reflection. When Armida left him alone for a few hours, the knights surprised Rinaldo, and turned the wizard's diamond shield upon him. For the first time he saw himself as others saw him, and, blushing with shame, announced himself ready to return with them to rescue Jerusalem. Tearing off his ornaments, he hastened down the mountain, but not soon enough to escape Armida. Tears, prayers, threats she used in vain. She had captured him when he fled from the camp, intending to slay him; but moved by his beauty, she had spared him, and falling in love with him, had reared this palace that they might in it revel in love's pleasures. Now, miserable, she saw him desert her, and destroying the beautiful haunt, she drove her swift chariot across the seas to the camp of the Egyptian king, who was hastening towards Jerusalem. Intent on the slaughter of Rinaldo, her love for whom had changed to bitter hate, she offered the warriors of the Egyptian king, all of whom had fallen victims to her charms, her hand as a reward to the slayer of Rinaldo.

When Rinaldo and his rescuers reached the abode of the wizard they found him waiting with new arms for the young hero. The sage reproached him gently for his dalliance, and then, seeing the blush of shame upon his countenance, showed him the shield, which bore the illustrious deeds of his ancestors of the house of Este. Great as were their past glories, still greater would be those of the family which he should found, greatest of whom would be the Duke Alphonso.

Rinaldo, having told his story to Godfrey, and confessed his wrong-doing to Peter the Hermit, proceeded to the enchanted forest; and though as beauteous scenes, and as voluptuous sirens displayed themselves to him as dwelt in Armida's garden, yea, though one tree took the semblance of Armida herself, he boldly hacked the trunk and broke the magic spell. Joyfully the Franks set to work to fell the huge trees and construct vaster, stronger engines than before, under the direction of a master mechanic. At the same time, Vafrino, a cunning squire of Tancred, was commissioned to go forth in disguise and inspect the camp of the coming Egyptian king. Even before he departed, a carrier pigeon, driven back by a hawk, fell into Godfrey's hands, bearing a message to Aladine from Egypt, saying that in four or five days he would be with him in Jerusalem.

Godfrey, determined to take the city before that day should come, made the utmost exertions to have the machines completed. In Jerusalem, also, great preparations were made, machines built, and a fearful fire concocted by Ismeno with which to drive the assaulters from the wall.

Shriven by the priests, the Christian army went forth to battle. Godfrey took his stand against the northern gate; Raymond was assigned to the steep sharp crags at the southwest walls, and Guelph and the two Roberts were stationed on the track to Gaza to watch for the Egyptians.

The pagans fought with great fury, bringing out new instruments to oppose the huge battering rams, raining down arrows, and throwing the suffocating fire. But Rinaldo, to whom all this work appeared too slow, urged on his bold Adventurers to form a tortoise, hastened to the wall, seized a scaling-ladder, and, unmoved by any missile, mounted the wall and assisted his followers, in spite of the multitudes who surrounded him, attempting to hurl him down. But as Godfrey advanced, Ismeno launched his terrible fire-balls, more horrible than the flames of Mt. Etna; they affected even the vast tower, swelling and drying the heavy skins that covered its sides until protecting Heaven sent a breeze that drove the flames back to the city. Ismeno, accompanied by two witches, hurried to the wall, but was crushed by a stone that ground his and their bones to powder. Godfrey, inspired by a vision of the slain soldiery fighting in his ranks, leaped upon the wall and planted the red-cross flag. Raymond was also successful, and the Christians rushed over the walls into the town, following Aladine, who hastened to shut himself up in the citadel.

While the battle was raging, but success was assured to the Christians, Tancred and the terrible Argantes met, and glad of an opportunity to settle their quarrel, withdrew to a glade in the forest. Tancred, stung by the taunts of cowardice for his former failure to keep his appointment, fought bitterly. He had not the sheer strength of his antagonist, but his sleight at last overcame, and Argantes fell. Weakened by pain and loss of blood, Tancred fell senseless, and was thus found by Erminia, who had met Vafrino the spy in the camp of the Egyptians and had fled with him. They revived Tancred, and carried him home to be nursed by the delighted Erminia.

Vafrino had seen Armida in the camp and had learned through Erminia not only the princes' designs on Rinaldo, but also that they meant to assume the signs of the red-cross knights and thus reach the neighborhood of Godfrey and slay him. On this intelligence Godfrey changed the signs of his men that they might recognize the Egyptians on the following day and put them to death.

Terrible to the Franks was the sight of the Egyptian army when they opened their eyes upon it next morning. Clouds of dust obscured all the heavens, hills, and valleys, so great was the coming host. But Godfrey, with an eloquence that fired each soul, told them of the helplessness of the enemy, of how many of them were slaves, scourged to the battle, and reminded them of the great undertaking before them, the saving of the Sepulchre, until fired with zeal, and burning to fight, they rushed into battle and dispersed the Egyptians. Many of the Christians fell by the sword of the terrible Soldan, among them Gildippe and her husband, united in death as in life. Rinaldo, hearing of their slaughter, speedily avenged it by laying the Soldan low on the battle-field.

One after another of Armida's champions attacked Rinaldo, determined to win the prize, but his good sword sent them to earth, and Armida was left alone and unprotected. Rinaldo, having seen her fly away over the plain and knowing the victory achieved, followed and found her ready to put herself to death in a lonely glade. He snatched the sword from her hand and speedily changed back her hate to love. She fell upon his breast, and with the promise to become a Christian and give her life to him, accompanied him back to the city.

During the battle, Aladine and those who were imprisoned in the citadel overpowered Count Raymond, and rushed out to battle, only to be overcome and slain. Prince Altamore, who, covered with blood, remained alone on the field, yielded himself to Godfrey, and was given his life and his kingdom.

Then, from the field covered with spoil and floating with blood, the conquering troops, clad in their bloody armor, marched in solemn cavalcade to the Temple and paid their vowed devotions at the sacred tomb.

# SELECTION FROM THE JERUSALEM DELIVERED.

### SOPHRONIA AND OLINDO.

AT the instigation of the wizard Ismeno, Aladine, king of Jerusalem, stole an image of the Virgin from the temple of the Christians and put it in his mosque in order to render the city impregnable. When morning dawned the image was gone, and no search could reveal any clue to the theft.

> In every temple, hermitage, and hall,
> A long and eager search the monarch made,
> And tortures or rewards decreed to all
> Who screened the guilty, or the guilt betrayed;
> Nor ceased the Sorcerer to employ in aid
> Of the inquiry all his arts, but still
> Without success; for whether Heaven conveyed
> The prize away, or power of human will,
> Heaven close the secret kept, and shamed his vaunted skill.

> But when the king found all expedients vain
> To trace th' offender, then, beyond disguise,
> Flamed forth his hatred to the Christians; then,
> Fed by wild jealousies and sharp surmise,
> Immoderate fury sparkled in his eyes;
> Follow what may, he will revenge the deed,
> And wreak his rage: "Our wrath shall not," he cries,
> "Fall void, but root up all th' accursed seed;
> Thus in the general doom the guilty yet shall bleed!

" So that he 'scapes not, let the guiltless die !
But wherefore thus of guiltlessness debate?
Each guilty is, nor 'mongst them all know I
One, well-affected to the faith and state;
And what if some be unparticipate
In this new crime, new punishment shall pay
For old misdeeds; why longer do ye wait,
My faithful Mussulmans? up! up! away!
Hence with the torch and sword: seize, fire, lay waste, and slay ! "

Thus to the crowd he spake, the mandate flew,
And in the bosoms of the Faithful shed
Astonishment and stupor; stupor threw
On every face the paleness of the dead;
None dared, none sought to make defence; none fled,
None used entreaty, none excuse; but there
They stood, like marble monuments of dread,
Irresolute, — but Heaven conceived their prayer,
And whence they least had hope, brought hope to their despair.

Of generous thoughts and principles sublime
Amongst them in the city lived a maid,
The flower of virgins in her ripest prime,
Supremely beautiful ! but that she made
Never her care, or beauty only weighed
In worth with virtue; and her worth acquired
A deeper charm from blooming in the shade;
Lovers she shunned, nor loved to be admired,
But from their praises turned, and lived a life retired.

Yet could not this coy secrecy prevent
Th' admiring gaze and warm desires of one
Tutored by Love, nor yet would Love consent
To hide such lustrous beauty from the sun;
Love ! that through every change delight'st to run,
The Proteus of the heart ! who now dost blind,
Now roll the Argus eyes that nought can shun !
Thou through a thousand guards unseen dost wind,
And to the chastest maids familiar access find.

Sophronia hers, Olindo was his name;
Born in one town, by one pure faith illumed;
Modest — as she was beautiful, his flame
Feared much, hoped little, and in nought presumed;
He could not, or he durst not speak, but doomed
To voiceless thought his passion; him she slighted,
Saw not, or would not see; thus he consumed
Beneath the vivid fire her beauty lighted;
Either not seen ill known, or, known, but ill requited.

And thus it was, when like an omen drear
That summoned all her kindred to the grave,
The cruel mandate reached Sophronia's ear,
Who, brave as bashful, yet discreet as brave,
Mused how her people she from death might save ;
Courage inspired, but virginal alarm
Repressed the thought, till maiden shyness gave
Place to resolve, or joined to share the harm ;
Boldness awoke her shame, shame made her boldness charm.

Alone amidst the crowd the maid proceeds,
Nor seeks to hide her beauty, nor display ;
Downcast her eyes, close veiled in simple weeds,
With coy and graceful steps she wins her way :
So negligently neat, one scarce can say
If she her charms disdains, or would improve, —
If chance or taste disposes her array ;
Neglects like hers, if artifices, prove
Arts of the friendly Heavens, of Nature, and of Love.

All, as she passed unheeding, all, admire
The noble maid ; before the king she stood ;
Not for his angry frown did she retire,
But his indignant aspect coolly viewed :
" To give," — she said, " but calm thy wrathful mood,
And check the tide of slaughter in its spring, —
To give account of that thou hast pursued
So long in vain, seek I thy face, O king !
The urged offence I own, the doomed offender bring ! "

The modest warmth, the unexpected light
Of high and holy beauty, for a space
O'erpowered him, — conquered of his fell despite,
He stood, and of all fierceness lost the trace.
Were his a spirit, or were hers a face
Of less severity, the sweet surprise
Had melted him to love ; but stubborn grace
Subdues not stubborn pride ; Love's potent ties
Are flattering fond regards, kind looks, and smiling eyes.

If 't were not Love that touched his flinty soul,
Desire it was, 't was wonder, 't was delight :
" Safe be thy race ! " he said, " reveal the whole,
And not a sword shall on thy people light."
Then she : " The guilty is before thy sight, —
The pious robbery was my deed ; these hands
Bore the blest Image from its cell by night ;
The criminal thou seek'st before thee stands, —
Justice from none but me her penalty demands."

Thus she prepares a public death to meet,
A people's ransom at a tyrant's shrine:
Oh glorious falsehood! beautiful deceit!
Can Truth's own light thy loveliness outshine?
To her bold speech misdoubting Aladine
With unaccustomed temper calm replied:
"If so it were, who planned the rash design,
Advised thee to it, or became thy guide?
Say, with thyself who else his ill-timed zeal allied?"

"Of this my glory not the slightest part
Would I," said she, "with one confederate share;
I needed no adviser; my full heart
Alone sufficed to counsel, guide and dare."
"If so," he cried, "then none but thou must bear
The weight of my resentment, and atone
For the misdeed." "Since it has been my care,"
She said, "the glory to enjoy alone,
'T is just none share the pain; it should be all mine own."

To this the tyrant, now incensed, returned,
"Where rests the Image?" and his face became
Dark with resentment: she replied, "I burned
The holy Image in the holy flame,
And deemed it glory; thus at least no shame
Can e'er again profane it — it is free
From farther violation: dost thou claim
The spoil or spoiler? this behold in me;
But that, whilst time rolls round, thou never more shalt see.

"Albeit no spoiler I; it was no wrong
To repossess what was by force obtained:"
At this the tyrant loosed his threatening tongue,
Long-stifled passion raging unrestrained:
No longer hope that pardon may be gained,
Beautiful face, high spirit, bashful heart!
Vainly would Love, since mercy is disdained,
And Anger flings his most envenomed dart,
In aid of you his else protecting shield impart!

Doomed in tormenting fire to die, they lay
Hands on the maid; her arms with rough cords twining,
Rudely her mantle chaste they tear away,
And the white veil that o'er her drooped declining:
This she endured in silence unrepining,
Yet her firm breast some virgin tremors shook;
And her warm cheek, Aurora's late outshining,
Waned into whiteness, and a color took,
Like that of the pale rose, or lily of the brook.

The crowd collect ; the sentence is divulged ;
With them Olindo comes, by pity swayed ;
It might be that the youth the thought indulged,
What if his own Sophronia were the maid !
There stand the busy officers arrayed
For the last act, here swift the flames arise ;
But when the pinioned beauty stands displayed
To the full gaze of his inquiring eyes, —
'*T is* she ! he bursts through all, the crowd before him flies.

Aloud he cries : " To her, oh not to her
The crime belongs, though frenzy may misplead !
She planned not, dared not, could not, king, incur
Sole and unskilled the guilt of such a deed !
How lull the guards, or by what process speed
The sacred Image from its vaulted cell ?
The theft was mine ! and 't is my right to bleed ! "
Alas for him ! how wildly and how well
He loved the unloving maid, let this avowal tell.

" I marked where your high Mosque receives the air
And light of heaven ; I climbed the dizzy steep ;
I reached a narrow opening ; entered there,
And stole the Saint whilst all were hushed in sleep :
Mine was the crime, and shall another reap
The pain and glory ?   Grant not her desire !
The chains are mine ; for me the guards may heap
Around the ready stake the penal fire ;
For me the flames ascend ; 't is mine, that funeral pyre ! "

Sophronia raised to him her face, — her eye
Was filled with pity and a starting tear :
She spoke — the soul of sad humanity
Was in her voice, " What frenzy brings thee here,
Unhappy innocent ! is death so dear,
Or am I so ill able to sustain
A mortal's wrath, that thou must needs appear ?
I have a heart, too, that can death disdain,
Nor ask for life's last hour companionship in pain."

Thus she appeals to him ; but scorning life,
His settled soul refuses to retreat :
Oh glorious scene, where in sublimest strife
High-minded Virtue and Affection meet !
Where death 's the prize of conquest, and defeat
Seals its own safety, yet remains unblest !
But indignation at their fond deceit,
And rage, the more inflames the tyrant's breast,
The more this constant pair the palm of guilt contest.

He deems his power despised, and that in scorn
Of him they spurn the punishment assigned :
" Let," he exclaimed, " the fitting palm adorn
The brows of both ! both pleas acceptance find ! "
Beckoning he bids the prompt tormentors bind
Their galling chains around the youth — 't is done ;
Both to one stake are, back to back, consigned,
Like sunflowers twisted from their worshipped sun,
Compelled the last fond looks of sympathy to shun.


Around them now the unctuous pyre was piled,
And the fanned flame was rising in the wind,
When, full of mournful thoughts, in accents wild,
The lover to his mate in death repined:
" Is this the bond, then, which I hoped should bind
Our lives in blissful marriage ? this the fire
Of bridal faith, commingling mind with mind,
Which, I believed, should in our hearts inspire
Like warmth of sacred zeal and delicate desire ?


" Far other flames Love promised to impart,
Than those our envious planets here prepare ;
Too, ah too long they kept our hands apart,
But harshly now they join them in despair !
Yet does it soothe, since by a mode so rare
Condemned to die, thy torments to partake,
Forbid by fate thy sweetnesses to share ;
If tears I shed, 't is but for thy dear sake,
Not mine, — with thee beside, I bless the burning stake !


" And oh ! this doom would be indeed most blest,
My sharpest sufferings blandishments divine,
Might I but be permitted, breast to breast,
On thy sweet lips my spirit to resign ;
If thou too, panting toward one common shrine,
Wouldst the next happy instant parting spend
Thy latest sighs in sympathy on mine ! "
Sorrowing he spake ; she, when his plaints had end,
Did thus his fond discourse most sweetly reprehend.


" Far other aspirations, other plaints
Than these, dear friend, the solemn hour should claim.
Think what reward God offers to his saints ;
Let meek repentance raise a loftier aim :
These torturing fires, if suffered in his name,
Will, bland as zephyrs, waft us to the blest ;
Regard the sun, how beautiful his flame !
How fine a sky invites him to the west !
These seem to soothe our pangs, and summon us to rest."

The Pagans lifting up their voices, wept;
  In stifled sorrow wept the Faithful too;
  E'en the stern king was touched, — a softness crept
O'er his fierce heart, ennobling, pure, and new;
  He felt, he scorned it, struggled to subdue,
  And lest his wavering firmness should relent,
  His eyes averted, and his steps withdrew :
Sophronia's spirit only was unbent;
She yet lamented not, for whom all else lament.


In midst of their distress, a knight behold,
  (So would it seem) of princely port! whose vest
  And arms of curious fashion, grained with gold,
Bespeak some foreign and distinguished guest;
  The silver tigress on the helm impressed,
  Which for a badge is borne, attracts all eyes, —
  A noted cognizance, th' accustomed crest
Used by Clorinda, whence conjectures rise,
Herself the stranger is, — nor false is their surmise.


All feminine attractions, aims, and parts,
  She from her childhood cared not to assume;
  Her haughty hand disdained all servile arts,
The needle, distaff, and Arachne's loom;
  Yet, though she left the gay and gilded room
  For the free camp, kept spotless as the light
  Her virgin fame, and proud of glory's plume,
With pride her aspect armed, she took delight
Stern to appear, and stern, she charmed the gazer's sight.


Whilst yet a girl, she with her little hand
  Lashed and reined in the rapid steed she raced,
  Tossed the huge javelin, wrestled on the sand,
And by gymnastic toils her sinews braced;
  Then through the devious wood and mountain-waste
  Tracked the struck lion to his entered den,
  Or in fierce wars a nobler quarry chased;
And thus in fighting field and forest glen,
A man to savage beasts, a savage seemed to men.


From Persia now she comes, with all her skill
  The Christians to resist, though oft has she
  Strewed with their blood the field, till scarce a rill
Remained, that ran not purple to the sea.
  Here now arrived, the dreadful pageantry
  Of death presents itself, — the crowd — the pyre —
  And the bound pair; solicitous to see,
And know what crime condemns them to the fire,
Forward she spurs her steed and hastens to inquire.

The throng falls back, and she awhile remains,
The fettered pair more closely to survey;
One she sees silent, one she sees complains,
The stronger spirit nerves the weaker prey:
She sees him mourn like one whom the sad sway
Of powerful pity doth to tears chastise,
Not grief, or grief not for himself; but aye
Mute kneels the maid, her blue beseeching eyes
So fixed on heaven, she seems in heaven ere yet she dies.

Clorinda melts, and with them both condoles;
Some tears she sheds, but greater tenderness
Feels for her grief who most her grief controls, —
The silence moves her much, the weeping less;
No longer now does she delay to press
For information; turning towards one
Of reverend years, she said with eagerness,
"Who are they? speak! and oh, what crime has won
This death? in Mercy's name, declare the deed they've done!"

Thus she entreats; a brief reply he gives,
But such as well explains the whole event:
Amazed she heard it, and as soon conceives
That they are both sincerely innocent;
Her heart is for them, she is wholly bent
To avert their fate, if either arms can aid,
Or earnest prayers secure the king's consent;
The fire she nears, commands it to be stayed,
That now approached them fast, and to th' attendants said:

"Let none of you presume to prosecute
Your barbarous office, till the king I see;
My word I pledge that at Clorinda's suit,
Your fault he will forgive, if fault it be."
Moved by her speech and queenlike dignity
The guards obey, and she departs in quest
Of the stern monarch, urgent of her plea:
Midway they met; the monarch she addressed
And in this skilful mode her generous purpose pressed.

"I am Clorinda; thou wilt know perchance
The name, from vague remembrance or renown;
And here I come to save with sword and lance
Our common Faith, and thy endangered crown,
Impose the labor, lay th' adventure down,
Sublime, I fear it not, nor low despise;
In open field or in the straitened town,
Prepared I stand for every enterprise,
Where'er the danger calls, where'er the labor lies!"

*          *          *          *          *          *

" 'T would be assuredly a thing most rare,
 If the reward the service should precede;
 But of thy bounty confident, I dare
 For future toils solicit, as my meed,
 Yon lovers' pardon; since the charge indeed
 Rests on no evidence, 't was hard to press
 The point at all, but this I waive, nor plead
 On those sure signs which, urged, thou must confess
Their hands quite free from crime, or own their guilt far less.

" Yet will I say, though here the common mind
 Condemns the Christians of the theft, for me,
 Sufficient reasons in mine own I find
 To doubt, dispute, disparage the decree;
 To set their idols in our sanctuary
 Was an irreverence to our laws, howe'er
 Urged by the sorcerer; should the Prophet see
 E'en idols of our own established there?
Much less then those of men whose lips his faith forswear:

" The Christian statue ravished from your sight
 To Allah therefore rather I impute,
 In sign that he will let no foreign rite
 Of superstition his pure place pollute:
 Spells and enchantments may Ismeno suit,
 Leave him to use such weapons at his will;
 But shall we warriors by a wand dispute?
 No! no! our talisman, our hope, our skill,
Lie in our swords alone, and they shall serve us still!"

 She ceased; and he, though mercy could with pain
 Subdue a heart so full of rage and pride,
 Relents, her reasons move, her prayers constrain. —
 Such intercessor must not be denied;
 Thus, though reluctant, he at length complied:
 " The plea for the fair pleader I receive;
 I can refuse thee nothing; this," he cried,
 " May justice be or mercy, — let them live;
Guiltless — I set them free, or guilty I forgive!"

 Restored to life and liberty, how blest,
 How truly blest was young Olindo's fate!
 For sweet Sophronia's blushes might attest,
 That Love at length has touched her delicate
 And generous bosom; from the stake in state
 They to the altar pass; severely tried,
 In doom and love, already made his mate,
 She now objects not to become his bride,
And grateful live with him who would for her have died.

                              *Wiffen's Translation, Canto I̦.*

# PARADISE LOST.

PARADISE LOST was written by John Milton, who was born in London, Dec. 9, 1608, and died Nov. 8, 1674. After leaving college, he spent five years in study at home, during which time he wrote L'Allegro, Il Penseroso, Arcades, Comus, and Lycidas. In 1638 he travelled on the continent and in Italy, where he met Galileo. He hastened home in 1639 on account of the political disturbances in England, and espousing the Puritan cause, devoted the next twenty years of his life to the writing of pamphlets in its defence. In 1649 he was appointed Latin Secretary under Cromwell. In 1652 he lost his sight in consequence of overwork. At the age of twenty-nine, Milton had decided to make an epic poem his life work, and had noted many historical subjects. By 1641 he had decided on a Biblical subject. He had probably conceived Paradise Lost at the age of thirty-two, although the poem was not composed until he was over fifty. It was written after his blindness and dictated in small portions to various persons, the work being collected and revised by Milton and Aubrey Phillips. It was completed, according to the authority of Phillips, in 1663, but on account of the Plague and the Great Fire, it was not published until 1667.

Paradise Lost is divided into twelve books and is written, to use Milton's own words, "In English heroic verse without rhyme, as that of Homer in Greek and of Virgil in Latin, rhyme being no necessary adjunct or true ornament of poem or good verse."

Paradise Lost was neglected until the time of the Whig supremacy in England. In 1688 Lord Somers, the Whig leader, published an *édition de luxe* of the poem ; Addison's papers on it, in 1712, increased its popularity, and through the influence of the Whigs a bust of the poet was placed in Westminster Abbey in 1737.

There is no better proof of the greatness of Paradise Lost than the way in which it has survived hostile criticism. It has been criticised for the lengthy conversations and "arguments" of its characters ; for its materialization of the Divine Being ; because of its subject ; because of Milton's vagueness of description of things awesome and terrible, in comparison with Dante's minute descriptions. But the earnest spirit in which it was conceived and written ; the subject, giving it a "higher argument" than any merely national epic, even though many of Milton's, and his age's, special beliefs are things of the past, and its lofty and poetical style, have rendered unassailable its rank among the noblest of the epics.

BIBLIOGRAPHY AND CRITICISM, PARADISE LOST. Joseph Addison's Notes upon the Twelve Books of Paradise Lost ; by Albert S. Cook, 1892. (In the Spectator from Dec. 31, 1711–May 3, 1712) ; Samuel Austin Allibone's Dictionary of Authors, 1891, vol. ii., pp. 1301–1311 ; Matthew Arnold's A French Critic on Milton (see his Mixed Essays, 1880, pp. 260–273) ; Walter Bagehot's Literary Studies, by Richard Holt Hutton, 1879, vol. i., 202–219 ; Richard Bentley's Emendations on the Twelve Books of Paradise Lost, 1732 ; E. H. Bickersteth's Milton's Paradise Lost, 1876. (St. James Lectures, 2d series. Another edition, 1877) ; Hugh Blair's Paradise Lost (see his Lectures on Rhetoric and Belles Lettres, 1783, vol. ii., 471–476) ; Miss Christian Cann's A Scriptural and Allegorical Glossary to Paradise Lost, 1828 ; Charles Dexter Cleveland's Complete Concordance to Milton's Poetical Works, 1867 ; Samuel Taylor Coleridge's Lectures and Notes on Shakespeare and other English Poets collected by T. Ashe, 1893, pp. 518–529 ; William T. Dobson's The Classic Poets, their lives and times etc., 1879 ; Charles Eyre's Fall of Adam, from Milton's Paradise Lost, 1852 ; George Gilfillan's Second Gallery of Literary Portraits, 1852, pp. 17–25 ; S. Humphreys Gurteen's The Epic of the Fall of Man ; a comparative Study of Caedmon, Dante, and Milton, 1896 ; William Hazlitt On the Character of Milton's Eve (see his Round Table ed. by W. Carew Hazlitt, 1889, pp. 150–158) ; William Hazlitt On Milton's Versification (see his Round Table, ed. by W. Carew Hazlitt, 1889, pp. 51–57) ; John A. Himes's Study of Milton's Paradise Lost, 1878 ; Samuel Johnson's Milton (see his Lives of the Poets ; ed. by Mrs. Alexander Napier, 1890, vol. i.) ; Thomas Keightley's Introduction to Paradise Lost (see his An account of the Life, Opinions, and Writings of John Milton, 1855, pp. 397–484) ; Walter Savage Landor's Imaginary Conversations, Southey and Landor, 1853, vol. ii., 57-74, 156–159 ; Thomas Babington Macaulay's Milton (see his Critical and Historical Essays, ed. 10, 1860, vol. i., pp. 1–61) ; William Massey's Remarks upon Milton's Paradise Lost, 1761 ; David Masson's Introduction to Paradise Lost (see his edition of Milton's Poetical Works, 1893, vol. ii., pp. 1–57) ; David Masson's Life of Milton, 1880, vol. vi., 505–558, 621–636 ; David Masson's Three Devils (Luther's, Goethe's, and Milton's), (see his Three Devils and other Essays, 1874) ; James Peterson's A complete Commentary on Paradise Lost, 1744 ; Jonathan Richardson's Explanatory Notes and Remarks on Paradise Lost, 1734 ; Edmond Scherer's Milton and Paradise Lost (see his essays on English Literature ; Tr. by George Saintsbury, 1891, pp. 134–149 ; John Robert Seeley's Milton (see his Roman Imperialism and other Lectures and Essays), 1871, pp. 142–152 ; First Edition of Paradise Lost, Book Lore, 1886, iii., 72–75 ; J. A. Himes's Cosmology of Paradise Lost, Lutheran Quarterly, 1876, vi., 187–204 ; J. A. Himes's Plan of Paradise Lost, New Englander, 1883, xlii., 196–211 ; Satan of Milton and the Lucifer of Byron compared, Knickerbocker, 1847, xxx., 150–155 ; Satan of Paradise Lost, Dublin University Magazine, 1876, lxxxviii., 707–714 ; Augustine Birrell's Obiter Dicta (2d series 1887, pp. 42–51) ; Isaac Disraeli's Curiosities of Literature, Bent-

ley's Milton, 1867, pp. 138–139; Henry Hallam's Literary
History of Europe, 1873, ed. 5, vol. iii., pp. 475–483;
Mark Pattison's John Milton, n. d. (English Men of Letters
Series); H. A. Taine's History of English Literature; Tr.
by H. Van Laun, 1877, vol. ii., pp. 106–124.

## THE STORY OF PARADISE LOST.

WHEN that bright spirit, afterwards known as Satan, rose in rebellion against the Almighty Ruler of the Universe, presumptuously thinking himself equal to him in strength and following, he was overthrown by the Great Power and cast with his followers out of Heaven down to his future dwelling, flaming Hell.

Nine days he and his horrid crew fell through Chaos into the flaming pit yawning to receive them, and there lay for nine days, — rendered still more miserable by the thought of their immortality and the eternal bliss they had forfeited. Then Satan, rousing himself from the stupor consequent upon the fall, half rose and addressed the next in power to himself, Beelzebub.

" Thou art the same, yet not the same," said he ; " changed, lost is some of thy former brightness. Yet why repine? While we live, while we have so large a following, all is not lost. Our hate still lives, and have we but strength enough, we may still revenge ourselves upon him who thrust us into this accursed place."

Rising from the lake, his great shield slung over his shoulders, the unconquered archangel walked over the burning marl to the beach of that fiery sea, and there with chiding words addressed the legions strewn around him. The great army rose hastily at the voice of its chief and passed before him, spirits whose heavenly names were now forever lost, who later became the gods of the idolaters. There was mighty Moloch, Chemos, those who later went by the general names of Baalim and Ashtaroth, —Thammuz, Dagon, Rimmon, Osiris, Isis, Orus and their train, Belial, and last of all, the Ionian gods.

His despair in part dissipated by the sight of this heroic array, their prince, towering high above all, addressed them. No one had foreseen the calamity that had overtaken them. Who could have guessed the power of the Almighty? But though overthrown they were not totally defeated. A rumor had long since been rife of the creation of another world with which they could interfere. At any rate, there must never be peace between them and the heavenly Powers. War there must be, war in secret, or war waged openly. As he ended, shield clashed against shield, and swords, quickly drawn, flashed before his eyes, and loud cries hurled defiance to Heaven.

The legions, led by Mammon, who in Heaven had been an honored architect, sought a hill near by, and quickly emptying it of its rich store of gold and jewels, built a massive structure. Like a temple in form was it, and round about it stood Doric columns overlaid with gold. No king of any future state could boast of a grander hall than this palace of Pandemonium which was so quickly reared upon a hill in Hell, and to which the heralds' trumpets now summoned all the host.

On the massive throne, blazing with jewels, sat the fallen spirit, and thus addressed his followers : " Our success is sure in whatever we undertake. We shall never be riven with internecine warfare, for surely no one will quarrel over precedence in Hell. Therefore, united, we can, sure of our success, debate of the way in which we shall take up our warfare with the powers that have overthrown us."

Moloch, Belial, Mammon, and Beelzebub spoke. Moloch was in favor of open war, since nothing could be worse than Hell, and continued assault against the Most High would, in annoying him, be a sweet revenge. Belial, who though timorous and slothful, was a persuasive orator, denounced Moloch's plan. Since the ruler of Heaven was all-powerful, and they immortal, no one knew to what greater misery he could push them ; perhaps he would bury them in boiling pitch to eternity, or inflict a thousand undreamed-of tortures. War, open and secret, he disliked, since it was impossible to conceal aught from the eye of the Most High. To make the best of Hell seemed all that was possible ; in time they might become inured to its flames and better days might come, if they but accepted their doom patiently.

Mammon also considered war impossible. They could never hope to overcome the Almighty; neither could they hope nor wish for a reconciliation, for how hateful would be an eternity spent in cringing to one whom they hated. The desert soil of Hell teemed with riches, they could find peaceful pursuits, and it was his advice to continue there in quiet, untroubled by any thoughts of revenge.

Amid the murmur of applause that followed Mammon's speech, Beelzebub, than whom none towered higher save Satan, arose, his face grave, his attitude majestic. "Would you, Thrones and Imperial Powers," he cried, "think to build up a kingdom here, secure from the arm of Heaven? Have you so soon forgotten that this is not a kingdom ceded to you by the Most High, but a dungeon in which he has shut you for your everlasting punishment? Never will he forget that you are his prisoners; your lot will not be peace, but custody and stripes. What return can we make, then, but to think out some slow but sure and sweet revenge? It is not necessary to attempt to scale the walls of Heaven. Other things remain. There is this new world, his plaything. It may lie exposed, and we can at least make the attempt to seize it and lay it waste, and thus vex him." As he saw their eyes sparkle, he continued : "We may in this attempt come near to the steps of our old abode and breathe again its delicious airs instead of these hellish flames. But first we must find some one, strong, wary, and watchful, to send in search of it."

Satan strode forth, his courage and his consciousness of it making his face shine with transcendent glory. "Long is the way and hard ; its dangers unknown and terrible, but I should be a poor sovereign did I hesitate in the attempt to seek it out. I do not refuse the sovereignty, for I fear not to accept as great a share of hazard as of honor. Stay here ; charm away your time, and I will seek deliverance abroad for all of us."

As he spoke he rose to depart, fearful lest others might now offer to go and share the glory with him.

The legions rose with a sound like thunder, bowed in

deepest reverence and went forth, some, to explore their dismal abode, others to amuse themselves at games, others to discuss Free Will and Fate, while their leader pursued his way toward the gate of Hell.

The nine-fold gates were of brass, iron, and adamantine rock, reaching high to the mighty roof, and most horrible were the Shapes that guarded it.

On one side sat a creature, woman to the waist, below, a serpent, surrounded by a crew of hell hounds, forever barking and then seeking refuge within her. On the other, a Shape, black, fierce, terrible, crowned with the likeness of a kingly crown, and shaking in its hands a dreadful dart. As he strode, Hell trembled. Satan, undaunted, met him with fierce words. As the two stood, their lances pointed at each other, the woman shrieked and ran between them.

" Father, rush not upon thy son! Son, raise not thy hand against thy father ! " She then explained that she was Satan's daughter, Sin, who had sprung from his head full grown, and that she later became by him the mother of the creature called Death who sat with her to guard the gates.

Satan at once unfolded to them his plan of seeking the new world and making a happy home for both Sin and Death, where they could forever find food to gratify their hideous cravings. Charmed by his highly-colored pictures, and forgetful of the commands from above, Sin opened the mighty doors, so that the flames of Hell spread far out into Chaos, but her strength failed her when she attempted to close them again.

For a moment Satan looked out into the mixture of Hot and Cold and Moist and Dry that formed Chaos, and then started forth, now rising, now falling, his wings heavy with the dense masses, now wading, now creeping, until at last he reached the spot where was fixed the throne of Chaos and of Night. Here Satan learned of the situation of the new world and soon caught a glimpse of it, hanging like a star, by a golden chain, from Heaven.

Sitting in Heaven, high throned above all, God, all-seeing, all-knowing, was conscious of Satan's escape from Hell and his approach to the new world. To his Son, sitting on his right hand, he pointed out the fallen spirit. " No prescribed bounds can shut our Adversary in; nor can the chains of hell hold him. To our new world he goes, and there, by no fault of mine, will pervert man, whom I have placed therein, with a free will; so to remain until he enthralls himself. Man will fall as did Satan, but as Satan was self-tempted, and man will be deceived by another, the latter shall find grace where his tempter did not."

Great was the joy of the Son when he learned that man would receive mercy for his transgression. " Pardon and mercy he shall receive," declared the Father, " but some one must be willing to expiate his sin for him; the just must die for the unjust. Who in Heaven is willing to make the sacrifice ? "

For a moment all the Heavenly quire stood mute; then the Son of God spoke and implored his Father to let his anger fall on him, since he could not wholly die, but could arise from death and subdue his vanquisher.

When his Father accepted the sacrifice, and named him Son of God and Man who should hereafter be Universal King, Ruler of Heaven and Earth, Heaven rang with the shouts of the Angels, who, casting down their amaranthine wreaths until the golden pavement was covered with the garlands, took their golden harps and sang the praises of the Father and the Son.

While they sang, Satan walked over the vast globe on which he had alighted, through what in after years, when the world was peopled, was to be the Paradise of Fools, the spot to which the spirits of all things transitory and vain, of those who had worked for their reward in life instead of in Heaven, would come. He walked around the dark globe until, directed by a gleam of light, he found the spot where a ladder led up to Heaven. Just below it, down through the spheres, was the seat of Paradise to which he was bending his way.

Down through the crystal spheres he bent his way toward the Sun, which attracted him by its superior splendor. Espying Uriel, the Angel of the Sun, he quickly took the form of a youthful Cherub, and, approaching Uriel, told him that having heard of the new world he had been seized by a longing to quit the bands of Cherubim and see for himself the wonderful work of the Creator.

Directed by the unsuspecting Uriel, Satan sped downward and standing upon the top of Niphates, surveyed Eden.

As he looked, his spirit was troubled. He had brought Hell with him, and his unhappy thoughts boiled and surged in his troubled mind. "Sun, I hate thee, because thy beams recall to me what I was and how I fell. The matchless King of Heaven deserved no such return from me. His service was easy. Had I only been created a lower Power! — But even then, might not some higher one have led me into temptation? What shall I do, whither shall I fly, to escape infinite wrath, and infinite despair? Hell is around me, I myself am Hell! There is no hope for me. Submission is the only way left, and I could not unsay what I have said; I could never bridge the gulf made by my revolt. Farewell to remorse! Good is forever lost to me, and I must now make Evil my good. I can at least divide the empire of the world with the King of Heaven."

As he realized how his bitter thoughts had dimmed his countenance he smoothed it over with outward calm, but not before Uriel, from the Sun, had noted and wondered over his strange gestures.

Leaping over the high natural walls of Paradise, Satan, in the form of a cormorant, perched himself on the Tree of Life. Beautiful was the scene before him. All the trees and plants were of the noblest kind. In the midst of them stood the Tree of Life with its golden fruit, and not far off the Tree of Knowledge. Southward through Eden ran a river, which, passing under a huge hill, emerged into four great streams wandering through many afterwards famous realms. Between the rows of trees stretched level lawns where grazed the happy flocks, and over the green mead were sprinkled flowers of every hue. No fairer scene ever met living eyes, and fairest of all were the two stately forms, in whose looks shone the divinity of their Maker. Hand in hand they passed through the garden, refreshed themselves with the delicious fruits, and were happy in each other.

As he gazed on them while the animals fell asleep and the sun sank below the horizon, Satan, still torn with conflicting emotions, ruminated over the unhappiness he was to bring the lovely pair. He admired them, he could love them; they had not harmed him, but he must bring unhappiness upon them because of their likeness to their Creator. Through them only could he obtain his longed-for revenge.

Anxious to learn where to attack them, he prowled about them, now as a lion, now as a tiger, listening to their conversation. They spoke of their garden, of the Tree of Life, and of the forbidden Tree of Knowledge. "In the day ye eat thereof, ye shall surely die," had been their warning. Eve recalled the day of her creation, when she had first fled from Adam, and then yielded to his embraces, and Satan, watching their caresses, envied and hardened his heart. "Live while ye may!" he muttered. "Soon will I return and offer you new woes for your present pleasures."

In the mean time, Gabriel, warned by Uriel, who suspected that an evil spirit had crept into Paradise, had set watches around the garden. Ithuriel and Zephon, sent to search for him, spied Satan in the form of a toad, sitting near the ear of Eve, tainting her dreams with foul whispers. Touched by Ithuriel's spear, he was forced to resume his own shape and was taken to Gabriel. The angry Satan attempted to use force, but warned by a sign from Heaven that his strength was insufficient, fled, murmuring, through the night.

When morning dawned on Eden, a morn of unimaginable beauty, Adam waked Eve from her restless slumbers, and heard her troubled dreams, in which she had been tempted to taste of the fruit of the Tree of Knowledge. He comforted her, and after their morning hymn, in which they glorified their Creator, they set about their pleasant work of pruning the too luxuriant vines of their Paradise. In the mean time, the Father above, knowing the design of Satan, and determined that man should not fall without warning, sent Raphael down to Adam to tell him that he was threatened by an enemy, and that, as a free agent, if he fell, his sin would be upon his own head.

Six-winged Raphael swept down through the spheres and stood in Paradise, welcomed by Adam. Eve hastened to set before their guest every delicacy that Eden knew, and while she was preparing these Adam listened to the Angel's warning.

To emphasize the sin of disobedience, Raphael related to the pair the story of Satan's conspiracy with the other powers because the Father had proclaimed the power of his Son. The Father, knowing Satan's confidence in himself, had allowed him for two days to fight an equal number of his legions of angels, among whom was Abdiel who had fled, indignant, from Satan's ranks, and on the third day, when the legions of evil lay crushed beneath the mountains which the shining angels had heaped upon them, the Son of God drove forth in his chariot, and single-handed, forced them before him, terror-stricken, until, Heaven's wall having opened, they fell downward for nine days, in horror and confusion into the depths of Hell. The Messiah, returning home in triumph in his chariot, was welcomed by the bright orders into the home of his Father.

Delighted by the recital of Raphael, Adam asked him to relate the story of the Creation, and explain to him the motion of the celestial bodies. He then told Raphael of his own creation; how he awoke as from a sleep and found the Sun above him and around him the pleasant groves of Paradise; how he named the animals as they passed before him, according to the will of God, and how he had pleaded with his Maker for a companion and equal, until the Creator, casting him into a sound sleep, took from his side a rib and formed from it his beauteous Eve. As Adam concluded, the setting sun warned Raphael to depart.

Satan, after fleeing from Gabriel, had hidden in the dark parts of the earth, so that he could creep in at night unseen of Uriel. After the eighth night, he crept in past the watchful Cherubim, and stealing into Paradise, wrapped in the mist rising over the river that, shooting underground, rose up as a fountain near the Tree of Life, he crept, though not without loathing, into the serpent, in which form he could best evade the watchful eyes of the heavenly guards and accomplish his purpose.

When morning dawned, Eve asked Adam for once to permit her to work alone, so that they might accomplish more. Adam, who constantly desired her presence, prayed her to remain, warning her of the enemy of whom Raphael had spoken, and telling her that they could resist temptation more easily together than when separated. But Eve was obdurate, and Adam finally consented that she should go alone to work.

As she moved among the groves, tying up the drooping flowers, like to Pomona in her prime, or to Ceres, the sight of so much beauty, goodness, and innocence moved even the serpent, as he approached, intent on the destruction of her happiness. But as he looked, the thought of her joy but tortured him the more, since happiness was no longer possible for him.

This was before the serpent had been compelled to crawl his whole length on the ground, and as he moved on, fold on fold, his head proudly reared, his scales brilliant in color, he was not an unpleasant object to look upon. He circled about Eve as though lost in admiration, until her attention was attracted, and then astounded her by addressing her in her own language. When she demanded by what means he had acquired speech, he told her by the plucking and eating of a certain tree in the garden, which he had no sooner tasted than he felt his inward powers to develop until he found himself capable of speech.

Eve at once asked him to take her to the tree, but when she recognized the forbidden Tree of Knowledge, she demurred, assuring the serpent that God had commanded them not to touch it, for if they ate of it, they should surely die. "Am I not alive?" asked her tempter, "and have I not eaten of it? Is it not a rank injustice that you should be forbidden to taste it and to lack the Knowledge of Good and Evil which it would give you? Where can the offence lie? It must be envy that causes such a prohibition."

His words, the sight of the fruit, and natural hunger all prevailed on Eve, and she plucked a branch from the tree and tasted the fruit. As she ate she saw Adam coming in search of her, holding a garland which he had been binding to crown her. To his reproaches, she replied with the arguments of her tempter, until Adam, in despair, determined to taste the apple that he might not lose Eve. Paradise without her would not be Paradise, and no new wife could make him forget her.

After the first exhilaration of the food was past they began to reproach each other, mindful of their destiny, of which they had been warned by Raphael, and, engaged in this fruitless chiding, they were found by the Son, who, informed of their transgression by the angels, sought them out in their place of concealment. Adam and Eve he sentenced to a life of sorrow and labor, the serpent to go despised and ever at enmity with man. Then, pitying the unhappy pair, he clad them in skins and re-ascended to Heaven.

While this was occurring in Eden, Sin and Death, feeling in some mysterious way the success of their parent, determined to leave Hell and seek their new home. Passing through Chaos, they pushed the heavy elements this way and that, cementing them with Death's mace until they constructed of them a bridge from the gates of Hell to the point on earth at which Satan had first alighted, and here met him, just returning, flushed with success, to Hell.

All the followers of Satan were gathered in Pandemonium to hear the news of his success, which he related, overjoyed at having wrought the ruin of mankind and revenged himself on God by so small a thing as the eating of an apple. As he concluded and stood waiting their applause, he heard a universal hiss, and saw himself surrounded by serpents, and himself changing into an enormous dragon. The great hall was filled with the monsters, scorpions, asps, hydras, and those who stood waiting without with applause for their leader were likewise changed into loathsome reptiles. Without the hall a grove sprang up, loaded with tempting fruit, but when, tortured with thirst, they tried to eat, it turned in their mouths to bitter ashes. After a time they were permitted to take again their own shapes, but were compelled to resume this serpent-form for a certain number of days each year, to crush their pride.

When God saw the entrance of Sin and Death into the world, he proclaimed to his Saints that their seeming victory was but temporary, and that eventually his Son would defeat Sin, Death, and the Grave, and seal up the mouth of Hell. Then, as the Halleluias rang out, he ordered the angels to make certain changes in the universe as a punishment to man. The Sun was so to move as to affect the earth alternately with a cold and heat almost unbearable ; to the Moon were assigned her motions ; the other planets were to join in various ways, often "unbenign." The winds were assigned their stations to torment the earth and sea, and the thunder was set to strike terror to the heart of man. The poles of the earth were pushed aslant, and soon the effects of the changes were felt in heat, cold, wind, and storm.

Adam, though absorbed in his own misery and momentarily expecting Death, saw the changes, and bemoaned his woes the more. How would his mysterious progeny despise him, since he was the cause of their being brought into the world of woe ! When Eve attempted to comfort him he drove her from him with harsh words, saying that in time to come women would be the unhappy cause of all man's misery, as she had been of his. At last, seeing the futility of his outcries Adam began to cheer his wife, recalling the promise that their offspring should crush the head of the serpent, and suggested to her that they go to their former place of prayer and pour forth to God their true contrition and repentance.

The glad Son, presenting these prayers at his Father's throne, interceded with him for them, since their contrition now was worth more than their worship in a state of innocence. His intercession was accepted, but since they had lost the two gifts of Happiness and Immortality, they must leave the garden lest they be tempted to taste next of the Tree of Life and make their woe eternal.

Michael was sent down to drive them from the garden, and if the pair seemed repentant and disconsolate he was ordered to comfort them with the promise of better days and to reveal to them somewhat of the future. In habit as a man Michael descended and declared to Adam and Eve that they could no longer abide in Paradise. When Adam, himself broken with grief, attempted to console the heart-broken Eve, the Angel comforted her also, and causing a sleep to fall upon her, led Adam to a hill-top, whence could be seen the hemisphere of the earth, soon to be covered by the seats of empires.

Touching Adam's eyes with three drops from the well of life, the Angel showed him a long panorama, beginning with the crime of Cain, and showing the building of the Ark and its landing on Ararat. When he perceived that Adam's eyes were weary, he recited to him the story of Abraham, of the deliverance from Egypt, the wandering in the Wilderness, of the royal stock of David from which would spring the seed so often promised Adam, who should ascend the hereditary throne, and whose glory should be universal.

Overjoyed, Adam inquired when would take place the final death stroke to Satan, the bruising with the Victor's heel. Michael responded that Satan was not to be destroyed, but his works in Adam and his seed, and that the sacrifice of the Son's life for man would forever crush the strength of Satan's progeny, Sin and Death. Then, to that Heaven to which he would reascend, the faithful would go when the time came for the world's dissolution, and there would be received into the bliss eternal.

Strengthened and sustained, Adam went down from the mount and met Eve, just awaking from comforting dreams.

The Cherubim descended, and, urged by the Angel, the two
took their way into the wide world that lay before them, and
looking back beheld the flaming swords of the Cherubim at
the gates of their lost Paradise.

## SELECTIONS FROM PARADISE LOST.

### SATAN.

AFTER having been thrown out of Heaven with his crew,
Satan lay nine days in the burning lake into which he fell.
Then, rousing himself, he rose from the liquid flames, flew
over the lake, and alighting upon the solid though burning
land, thus addressed Beelzebub, who had accompanied him.

> " Is this the region, this the soil, the clime,"
> Said then the lost Archangel, " this the seat
> That we must change for Heaven? — this mournful gloom
> For that celestial light?   Be it so, since He
> Who now is sovran can dispose and bid
> What shall be right: farthest from Him is best,
> Whom reason hath equalled, force hath made supreme
> Above his equals.   Farewell, happy fields,
> Where joy forever dwells!   Hail, horrors! hail,
> Infernal World! and thou, profoundest Hell,
> Receive thy new possessor — one who brings
> A mind not to be changed by place or time.
> The mind is its own place, and in itself
> Can make a Heaven of Hell, a Hell of Heaven.
> What matter where, if I be still the same,
> And what I should be, all but less than he
> Whom thunder hath made greater?   Here at least
> We shall be free; the Almighty hath not built
> Here for his envy, will not drive us hence :
> Here we may reign secure ; and, in my choice,
> To reign is worth ambition, though in Hell:
> Better to reign in Hell than serve in Heaven.
> But wherefore let we then our faithful friends,
> The associates and co-partners of our loss,
> Lie thus astonished on the oblivious pool,
> And call them not to share with us their part
> In this unhappy mansion, or once more
> With rallied arms to try what may be yet
> Regained in Heaven, or what more lost in Hell?"
> So Satan spake; and him Beëlzebub

Thus answered : — " Leader of those armies bright
Which, but the Omnipotent, none could have foiled !
If once they hear that voice, their liveliest pledge
Of hope in fears and dangers — heard so oft
In worst extremes, and on the perilous edge
Of battle, when it raged, in all assaults
Their surest signal — they will soon resume
New courage and revive, though now they lie
Grovelling and prostrate on yon lake of fire,
As we erewhile, astounded and amazed ;
No wonder, fallen from such pernicious highth ! "

   He scarce had ceased when the superior Fiend
Was moving toward the shore ; his ponderous shield,
Ethereal temper, massy, large, and round,
Behind him cast.   The broad circumference
Hung on his shoulders like the moon, whose orb
Through optic glass the Tuscan artist views
At evening, from the top of Fesolè,
Or in Valdarno, to descry new lands,
Rivers, or mountains, in her spotty globe.
His spear — to equal which the tallest pine
Hewn on Norwegian hills, to be the mast
Of some great ammiral, were but a wand —
He walked with, to support uneasy steps
Over the burning marle, not like those steps
On Heaven's azure ; and the torrid clime
Smote on him sore besides, vaulted with fire.
Nathless he so endured, till on the beach
Of that inflamèd sea he stood, and called
His legions — Angel Forms, who lay entranced
Thick as autumnal leaves that strow the brooks
In Vallombrosa, where the Etrurian shades
High over-arched embower ; or scattered sedge
Afloat, when the fierce winds Orion armed
Hath vexed the Red-Sea coast, whose waves o'erthrew
Busiris and his Memphian chivalry,
While with perfidious hatred they pursued
The sojourners of Goshen, who beheld
From the safe shore their floating carcases
And broken chariot wheels.   So thick bestrown,
Abject and lost, lay these, covering the flood,
Under amazement of their hideous change.
He called so loud that all the hollow deep
Of Hell resounded : — " Princes, Potentates,
Warriors, the Flower of Heaven — once yours ; now lost,
If such astonishment as this can seize
Eternal Spirits !   Or have ye chosen this place
After the toil of battle to repose
Your wearied virtue, for the ease you find
To slumber here, as in the vales of Heaven ?

Or in this abject posture have ye sworn
To adore the Conqueror, who now beholds
Cherub and Seraph rolling in the flood
With scattered arms and ensigns, till anon
His swift pursuers from Heaven-gates discern
The advantage, and descending, tread us down
Thus drooping, or with linkèd thunderbolts
Transfix us to the bottom of this gulf? —
Awake, arise, or be for ever fallen!"

*Book I., 240-330.*

## APOSTROPHE TO LIGHT.

THIS passage forms the beginning of Book III., in which the
poet visits the realms of light after having described Hell and
its inhabitants.

Hail, holy Light, offspring of Heaven first-born!
Or of the Eternal coeternal beam
May I express thee unblamed? since God is light,
And never but in unapproachèd light
Dwelt from eternity — dwelt then in thee,
Bright effluence of bright essence increate!
Or hear'st thou rather pure Ethereal stream,
Whose fountain who shall tell? Before the Sun,
Before the Heavens, thou wert, and at the voice
Of God, as with a mantle, didst invest
The rising World of waters dark and deep,
Won from the void and formless Infinite!
Thee I revisit now with bolder wing,
Escaped the Stygian Pool, though long detained
In that obscure sojourn, while in my flight,
Through utter and through middle Darkness borne,
With other notes than to the Orphean lyre
I sung of Chaos and eternal Night,
Taught by the Heavenly Muse to venture down
The dark descent, and up to re-ascend,
Though hard and rare. Thee I revisit safe,
And feel thy sovran vital lamp; but thou
Revisit'st not these eyes, that roll in vain
To find thy piercing ray, and find no dawn;
So thick a drop serene hath quenched their orbs,
Or dim suffusion veiled. Yet not the more
Cease I to wander where the Muses haunt
Clear spring, or shady grove, or sunny hill,
Smit with the love of sacred song; but chief
Thee, Sion, and the flowery brooks beneath,

That wash thy hallowed feet, and warbling flow,
Nightly I visit: nor sometimes forget
Those other two equalled with me in fate,
So were I equalled with them in renown,
Blind Thamyris and blind Mæonides,
And Tiresias and Phineus, prophets old:
Then feed on thoughts that voluntary move
Harmonious numbers; as the wakeful bird
Sings darkling, and, in shadiest covert hid,
Tunes her nocturnal note.   Thus with the year
Seasons return; but not to me returns
Day, or the sweet approach of even or morn,
Or sight of vernal bloom, or summer's rose,
Or flocks, or herds, or human face divine;
But cloud instead and ever-during dark
Surrounds me, from the cheerful ways of men
Cut off, and, for the book of knowledge fair,
Presented with a universal blank
Of Nature's works, to me expunged and rased,
And wisdom at one entrance quite shut out.
So much the rather thou, Celestial Light,
Shine inward, and the mind through all her powers
Irradiate; there plant eyes; all mist from thence
Purge and disperse, that I may see and tell
Of things invisible to mortal sight.

*Book III.,* 1-55.

# PARADISE REGAINED.

" A cold and noble epic." — TAINE.

PARADISE REGAINED was written by Milton, judging from a passage in the Autobiography of Thomas
Ellwood, in the winter of 1665–6, but was not published
until 1671. It was printed at Milton's expense in a small
volume together with Samson Agonistes.

Paradise Regained tells the story of Christ's temptation
in the Wilderness, and the material was taken from the
accounts of Matthew and Luke, which the poet, with great
skill, expanded without essentially deviating from them.

The title has been criticised on the ground that the poem
should have extended over the whole of Christ's life on
earth. But Paradise Regained was written as a sequel to
Paradise Lost, and, as in the first poem the poet showed
that Paradise was lost by the yielding of Adam and Eve to
Satan, so in the second, he wished to show that Paradise
was regained by the resistance of Christ to temptation,
Satan's defeat signifying the regaining of Paradise for men
by giving them the hope of Christ's second coming. Therefore the poem naturally ends with Satan's rebuff and his final
abandonment of the attempt on the pinnacle of the Temple.

The poem has been criticised for its shortness, some
scholars even affecting to believe it unfinished ; its lack of
variety, in that it has but two characters, its lack of action,
and the absence of figurative language.

But with all these faults, it has a charm of its own, entirely
different from that of Paradise Lost. Satan has degenerated
during his years of " roaming up and down the earth ; " he
is no longer the fallen angel of Paradise Lost, who struggled
with himself before making evil his good. He is openly

given over to evil practices, and makes little effort to play the hypocrite. His temptations are worked up from that of hunger to that of the vision of the kingdoms of the earth with a wonderful power of description which makes up for the lack of action and the few actors. The pathless, rock-bound desert, the old man, poorly clad, who accosts the Christ, the mountain-top from which all the earth was visible, the night of horror in the desert, and the sublime figure of the Savior, are all enduring pictures which compensate for any rigidity of treatment. If figurative language is omitted it is because the theme does not need it, and does not show that the poem is less carefully finished than Paradise Lost. Its lack of action and similarity of subject to the longer poem sufficiently account for its not meeting with popular favor. Johnson was correct when he said, " had this poem been written not by Milton, but by some imitator, it would have claimed and received universal praise."

BIBLIOGRAPHY AND CRITICISM, PARADISE REGAINED. H. C. Beeching, On the Prosody of Paradise Regained and Samson Agonistes, 1889 ; Charles Dexter Cleveland's Complete Concordance to Milton's Poetical Works, 1867 ; William T. Dobson's The Classic Poets, their Lives and Times etc., 1879 ; George Gilfillan's Second Gallery of Literary Portraits, 1852, pp. 15–16 ; Samuel Johnson's Milton (see his Lives of the Poets ; ed. by Mrs. Alexander Napier, 1890, vol. i.) ; Thomas Babington Macaulay's Milton (see his Critical and Historical Essays, ed. 10, 1860, vol. i.) ; David Masson's Introduction to Paradise Regained (see his ed. of Milton's Poetical works, 1893, vol. iii., pp. 1–14 ; David Masson's Life of Milton, 1880, vol. vi., 651–661 ; Richard Meadowcourt's Critique on Milton's Paradise Regained, 1732 ; A Critical Dissertation on Paradise Regained with Notes, 2d ed. 1748 ; John Robert Seeley's Milton (see his Roman Imperialism and other Lectures and Essays, 1871, pp. 152–157) ; Mark Pattison's John Milton (English Men of Letters Series), n. d. ; H. A. Taine's History of English Literature, Tr. by H. Van Laun, 1877, vol. ii.

## THE STORY OF PARADISE REGAINED.

AFTER the expulsion from Paradise of Adam and Eve, Satan and his followers did not return to Hell, but remained on earth, the fallen angels becoming the evil gods of various idolatrous nations and Satan engaging in every kind of evil-doing which he knew would vex the Powers of Heaven. All the time he was troubled by the thought of the heavenly foe who he had been told would one day appear on earth to crush him and his rebel angels.

Now John had come out of the wilderness, proclaiming his mission, and among those who came to him to be baptized was one who was deemed the son of Joseph of Nazareth. John recognized in the obscure carpenter's son the one "mightier than he" whose coming he was to proclaim, and this fact was further made clear to the multitude and the observant Satan by the opening of the Heavens and the descent therefrom on Christ's head of the Dove, while a voice was heard declaring, "This is my beloved Son."

Satan, enraged, fled to the council of the fiends to announce to them the presence on earth of their long-dreaded enemy. He was empowered by them to attempt his overthrow, and they were the more confident because of his success with Adam and Eve.

Satan's purpose was known to the Eternal Father, who smiled to see him unwittingly fulfilling the plan so long foreordained for his destruction.

After his baptism, the Father had sent his Son into the wilderness to gain strength for his struggle with Sin and Death, and there Satan, in the guise of an old, poorly clad rustic, found him. Although the Son of God had wandered through the rock-bound, pathless desert, among wild beasts, without food for forty days, he had no fear, believing that some impulse from above had guided him thither before he should go out among men to do his divinely appointed task.

Then, when hunger came upon him as he wandered, thinking of past events and those to come, he met the aged man and was addressed by him.

"Sir, how came you hither, where none who ventures alone escapes alive? I ask because you look not unlike the man I lately saw baptized by John and declared the Son of God."

"I need no guide," replied the Son. "The Power who brought me here will bring me forth."

"Not otherwise than by miracle. Here we subsist only upon dry roots and must often endure parching thirst. If thou art indeed the Son of God, save thyself and relieve us wretched people by changing these stones to bread."

"Men live not by bread alone," replied the Son, "but by the word of God. Moses in the Mount was without food and drink for forty days. Elijah also wandered fasting in the wilderness. Thou knowest who I am as I know who thou art; why shouldest thou suggest distrust to me?"

"'T is true that I am that unfortunate spirit who fell from Heaven, but I have been permitted to roam around the earth and have not been altogether excluded from Heaven. God allowed me to test Job and prove his worth and to draw Ahab into fraud. Though I have lost much of my original brightness I can still admire all that is illustrious and good. The sons of men should not regard me as an enemy, for I have oft given them aid by oracles, dreams, and portents. My loss was not through them, so their restoration does not grieve me; only that fallen man will be restored and not I."

"Thou deservest to grieve, tissue of lies that thou art!" exclaimed our Savior. "Thou boastest of being released from Hell and permitted to come into Heaven. No joy hast thou there! Thy own malice moved thee to torture Job. Brag not of thy lies, thy oracles for men. Henceforth oracles are dumb, since God has sent his living oracle into the world to teach the truth."

Satan, though angry, still dissembled.

"Accuse me, reprove me, if thou wilt. Fallen as I am, I still love to hear the truth fall from thy lips."

Unmoved by his false words the Savior of men declared that he neither forbade nor invited his presence, and Satan, bowing low, disappeared as night fell over the desert.

In the mean time, those at Bethabara who had rejoiced at the declaration of John and had talked with the Messiah, were deeply grieved to find him gone and with him their hope of deliverance. His mother, too, was troubled at his absence, but comforted herself with the thought of his former absences, afterwards explained.

Satan, hastening from the desert, sought his troop of evil spirits to warn them that his undertaking was no easy one, and to summon them to his assistance.

Night fell on the Son of God, still fasting, wondering what would be the end. In sleep he was visited by dreams of Elijah, raven-fed, and of the same prophet fed by the angel in the desert, and as he dreamed that he ate with them, the lark's song awoke him and he wandered into a pleasant grove. As he viewed it, charmed by its beauty, a man appeared before him, no rustic this time, but one attired in the apparel of city or court.

"I have returned, wondering that thou still remainest here, hungering. Hagar once wandered here; the children of Israel, and the Prophet, but all these were fed by the hand of Heaven. Thou alone art forgotten and goest tormented by hunger."

Though the Son of God declared that he had no need to eat, Satan invited his attention to a table, set under a spreading tree. Upon it was heaped every known delicacy; by it waited youths handsome as Ganymede, and among the trees tripped naiads and nymphs of Diana, with fruits and flowers. Exquisite music was heard, and the perfumes of Araby filled the air.

"Why not sit and eat?" continued Satan. "These foods are not forbidden, and all these gentle ministers are ready to do thee homage."

"What hast thou to do with my hunger?" demanded Jesus. "Should I receive as a gift from thee what I myself could command if I so desired? I too could bring a table here, and swift-winged angels to attend me. Thy gifts are but guiles."

"I am forever suspected," responded Satan, as the table vanished. "Hunger cannot move thee, set on high designs. But what canst thou, a lowly carpenter's son, accomplish without aid? Where wilt thou find authority, where followers? First get riches; hearken to me, for fortune is in my hand. Wealth will win, while virtue, valor, and wisdom sit and wait in vain."

"Yet what can wealth do without these?" replied Jesus patiently. "How can it gain dominion, and keep it when gained? Gideon, Jephtha, David, and among the heathen (for I am not ignorant of history) Quinctius, Fabricius, Curius, Regulus, all these have risen from the depths and achieved the highest deeds. Then, why may not I accomplish as much, even more, without wealth, which but cumbers the wise man, and slackens virtue, rather than prompts it to worthy deeds? Suppose I reject both riches and realms? Not because the regal diadem is a wreath of thorns and he who wears it bears each man's burden, for the king's chief praise is the manner in which he bears this burden for the public. But he who rules himself is greater than a king, and he who cannot do this should not aspire to royal power. But it is surely more kingly to lead nations blinded by error into the light of God's truth. This dominion is over the nobler part of man. And it has ever been thought greater and nobler to give a kingdom and to lay down authority than to assume it. Therefore thy riches are needless both in themselves, and to gain a kingdom which would better be missed than gained."

Satan, though for a moment struck dumb by this answer to his arguments, soon collected himself and suggested that while the Savior knew so well what was best to know, say, and do, that if known he would be regarded as an oracle, still he did wrong to despise glory and deprive earth of his great deeds, citing as examples of more active spirits accomplishing much when younger than he, the young Alexander, Scipio, Pompey, and Cæsar. But the Savior replied that the glory which consisted of the approval of the rabble was only to be despised. The true glory was that of the man who dared to be truly good, who though little known on earth, was famous in Heaven. Such men did not lay waste fields, sack, pillage, and slay, but by deeds of peace won the approval of the Father. Such was Job, oft tempted by Satan; such was Socrates, who suffered unjust death for teaching truth. And the Son of God had come upon earth not to win glory for himself as vain men do, but for Him who sent him.

"Thy Father does not despise glory," sneered Satan. "He demands it from his angels, from men, even from us, his foes."

"With reason," answered the Son, "since he created all things, though not for glory. And what slighter recompense could he expect from men who could return nothing else?"

Satan, remembering his own ambition and his fall, was silent for a moment, and then spoke to remind the Savior that he was born to the throne of David, but that it must be wrested from the Roman by force of arms. It was his duty to do this and save his people from oppression.

"All things in due time," replied the Savior. "If the Writ tells of my sufferings, my tribulations, of violence done unto me, it also tells of my reign without end. I can wait. He who suffers best, can do best; he who obeys first, reigns best; and why shouldest thou be so anxious to hasten my rule when it means thy destruction?"

"When hope is gone, what is there left to fear? My punishment will come whether thou reign or no. I could hope that thy reign would stand between me and the anger of thy Father. And if I haste to the worst that can be, why shouldest thou go so slowly to the best? Perhaps thou fearest the dangerous enterprise, thou who, pent up in Galilean towns, hast seen so little."

So saying, he took the Son up into a high mountain at the foot of which stretched a vast plain. Two rivers watered the fertile land. The hills were covered with flocks; vast cities could be seen, and here and there, so wide was the land, a barren desert. Then the Tempter pointed out the vast cities of Assyria, Nineveh, Babylon, Persepolis, Bactra, and the vast host of the Parthian king, even then marching against the Scythians. As they watched the great host of mailed warriors, accompanied by chariots, elephants, archers, engineers, Satan pursued his argument. Suppose the Son should take possession of his kingdom; how should he hope to keep it in peace between two such powerful enemies as the Parthians and the Romans? It would be better to conquer first the nearest, the Parthians, and this could be done with Satan's help. In doing this he would not only be able to occupy his throne but would deliver the offspring of the Ten Tribes of Israel, who, scattered among the Medes, still served as slaves.

But the Savior, in response, only questioned Satan as to why he had suddenly become so solicitous for the salvation of the Tribes when he himself had once tempted David to number Israel and had thus brought pestilence upon them. And as to the Ten Tribes, they had brought their punishment upon themselves, and must serve the enemy and their idols until the Father should see fit to release them.

Though embarrassed by the failure of his wiles, Satan could not yet yield. Turning to the western side of the mountain, he pointed out to the Savior a long, narrow plain, bordered on the south by the sea and protected from northern blasts by a mountain range. There, crowning the seven hills stood the imperial city adorned with porches, theatres, baths, aqueducts, and palaces. Satan pointed out the different objects of interest in splendid Rome, the Capitol, Mt. Palatine, crowned by the imperial palace, and the great gates, through which issued or entered a continuous stream of prætors, proconsuls, lictors, legions, embassies, on all the roads which led through the far-stretching empire, even to those of the Asian kings, and remote Britain. All the glory of the world, he argued, lay in Parthia and Rome, and Rome was greater. He who ruled her was indeed ruler of the world, and yet its present emperor was old, weak, lascivious, without heir, and lived at Capreæ, his public cares entrusted to his favorite. How easily could the Son of God force from him the power and lift the yoke from his people !

But the splendor of the scene allured neither the eye nor the mind of the Son. The gluttonies, the gorgeous feasts, the hollow compliments and lies of the people did not attract him. His mission, he told his Tempter, was not yet to free that people, once just and frugal, now debased by their insatiable ambition. When the time came for him to sit on David's throne, this with all other kingdoms of the earth would be shattered while his kingdom would be eternal.

"Though thou despisest my offers," cried Satan, "thou knowest that I esteem them highly, and will not part with them for nought. This is the condition ; Wilt thou fall down and worship me as thy superior lord ? "

" It is written, thou accursed one," responded the Savior in disdain, " that thou shouldst worship and serve the Lord thy God alone. Who gave thee the kingdoms of the earth if He did not ? And what gratitude thou showest ! Get thee behind me ! Truly thou art Satan ! "

Satan, abashed but not silenced, pointed southwest toward Athens. Since the Savior seemed to prefer a contemplative life, why should he not seek that seat of learning ? All wisdom was not contained in Moses' law and the writings of the prophets. Let him master the learning of the great Athenian teachers, philosophers and orators, and he would be a king within himself.

But the Savior assured Satan that, having received light from above, he knew how false and fallacious were the boasted philosophies of the Greeks. Their philosophers, ignorant of themselves and of God, and arrogating all glory to themselves and ascribing none to Him, were unable to impart wisdom to any one. From Hebrew psalm and hymn, and captive harps in Babylon, the Greeks derived their arts, and the results, the odious praises of their vicious gods, could not compare with the songs of Sion in praise of the Father. Their orators, too, were far below the Hebrew prophets.

"Stay in the wilderness, then," thundered Satan, wroth at this failure. "Since neither riches nor arms, nor power, nor yet the contemplative life please thee, it is for thee the fittest place! But the time will yet come when violence, stripes, and a cruel death will make thee long for me and my proffered power. Truly the stars promise thee a kingdom, but of what kind and when I cannot read."

As he disappeared, darkness fell, and the Son of God, still hungry and cold, sought rest under a sheltering tree. But Satan watched near, and forbade rest. Thunder and lightning shook the Heavens ; rain drenched the earth ; the fury of the winds was loosed, and in their path the sturdiest trees were uprooted. Ghosts, furies, raved around the holy one, but, unshaken by fear, he endured all calmly, and came forth, as the bright sun shone upon the earth, to meet again the Prince of Darkness.

Enraged that the terrors of the night had had no effect upon his enemy, Satan cried out that he still doubted that the wanderer in the wilderness was the Son of God in the true sense, and would therefore try him another way.

So speaking, he caught him up and bore him through the air unto Jerusalem, and setting him on the highest pinnacle of the glorious Temple, said scornfully : —

"Stand there, if thou canst ; I have placed thee highest in thy Father's house. Now show if thou art indeed the Son of God. Cast thyself down, for it is written that He will command his angels concerning thee, so that they in their hands shall uplift thee."

"It is also written," said Jesus, "'Tempt not the Lord thy God.'" And as he so spoke and stood, Satan, overcome with amazement, fell whence he had expected to see his conqueror fall, and, struck with dread and anguish at his certain defeat, fled to his rebel angels.

Straightway, a "fiery globe" of angels received the Son on their pinions, bore him from the pinnacle into a flowery vale, and there refreshed him with ambrosial food and water from the Fount of Life, while all around him the angelic choir sang his praises for the conquest of his enemy, and

encouraged him to go forth on his work of saving mankind.
Thence, rested and refreshed, he arose, and went, unobserved,
home to his mother's house.


## SELECTION FROM PARADISE REGAINED.

### THE TEMPTATION OF THE VISION OF THE KINGDOMS OF THE EARTH.

SATAN, meeting the Savior in the wilderness, tempted him
to change the stones to bread, and then, after endeavoring to
awake in him a longing for wealth and power, appealed to his
ambition by leading him to a mountain top, and displaying to
him the kingdoms of the earth.

> With that (such power was given him then), he [Satan] took
> The Son of God up to a mountain high.
> It was a mountain at whose verdant feet
> A spacious plain outstretched in circuit wide
> Lay pleasant; from his side two rivers flowed,
> The one winding, the other straight, and left between
> Fair champaign, with less rivers intervened,
> Then meeting joined their tribute to the sea.
> Fertile of corn the glebe, of oil, and wine;
> With herds the pasture thronged, with flocks the hills;
> Huge cities and high-towered, that well might seem
> The seats of mightiest monarchs; and so large
> The prospect was that here and there was room
> For barren desert, fountainless and dry.
> To this high mountain-top the Tempter brought
> Our Saviour, and new train of words began: —
>
> "Well have we speeded, and o'er hill and dale,
> Forest, and field, and flood, temples and towers,
> Cut shorter many a league. Here thou behold'st
> Assyria, and her empire's ancient bounds,
> Araxes and the Caspian lake; thence on
> As far as Indus east, Euphrates west,
> And oft beyond; to south the Persian bay,
> And, inaccessible, the Arabian drouth:
> Here, Nineveh, of length within her wall
> Several days' journey, built by Ninus old,
> Of that first golden monarchy the seat,
> And seat of Salmanassar, whose success
> Israel in long captivity still mourns;

There Babylon, the wonder of all tongues,
As ancient, but rebuilt by him who twice
Judah and all thy father David's house
Led captive, and Jerusalem laid waste,
Till Cyrus set them free; Persepolis,
His city, there thou seest, and Bactra there;
Ecbatana her structure vast there shows,
And Hecatompylos her hundred gates;
There Susa by Choaspes, amber stream,
The drink of none but kings; of later fame,
Built by Emathian or by Parthian hands,
The great Seleucia, Nisibis, and there
Artaxata, Teredon, Ctesiphon,
Turning with easy eye, thou may'st behold.
All these the Parthian (now some ages past
By great Arsaces led, who founded first
That empire) under his dominion holds,
From the luxurious kings of Antioch won.
And just in time thou com'st to have a view
Of his great power; for now the Parthian king
In Ctesiphon hath gathered all his host
Against the Scythian, whose incursions wild
Have wasted Sogdiana; to her aid
He marches now in haste. See though from far,
His thousands, in what martial equipage
They issue forth, steel bows and shafts their arms,
Of equal dread in flight or in pursuit —
All horsemen, in which fight they most excel;
See how in warlike muster they appear,
In rhombs, and wedges, and half-moons, and wings.'

He looked, and saw what numbers numberless
The city gates outpoured, light-armèd troops
In coats of mail and military pride.
In mail their horses clad, yet fleet and strong,
Prancing their riders bore, the flower and choice
Of many provinces from bound to bound —
From Arachosia, from Candaor east,
And Margiana, to the Hyrcanian cliffs
Of Caucasus, and dark Iberian dales;
From Atropatia, and the neighboring plains
Of Adiabene, Media, and the south
Of Susiana, to Balsara's haven.
He saw them in their forms of battle ranged,
How quick they wheeled, and flying behind them shot
Sharp sleet of arrowy showers against the face
Of their pursuers, and overcame by flight;
The field all iron cast a gleaming brown.
Nor wanted clouds of foot, nor, on each horn,
Cuirassiers all in steel for standing fight,
Chariots, or elephants indorsed with towers

Of archers; nor of labouring pioneers
A multitude, with spades and axes armed,
To lay hills plain, fell woods, or valleys fill,
Or where plain was raise hill, or overlay
With bridges rivers proud, as with a yoke:
Mules after these, camels and dromedaries,
And waggons fraught with utensils of war.
Such forces met not, nor so wide a camp,
When Agrican, with all his northern powers,
Besieged Albracca, as romances tell,
The city of Gallaphrone, from thence to win
The fairest of her sex, Angelica,
His daughter, sought by many prowest knights,
Both Paynim and the peers of Charlemain.
Such and so numerous was their chivalry.

*Book III.*

He brought our Saviour to the western side
Of that high mountain, whence he might behold
Another plain, long, but in breadth not wide,
Washed by the southern sea, and on the north
To equal length backed with a ridge of hills
That screened the fruits of the earth and seats of men
From cold Septentrion blasts; thence in the midst
Divided by a river, off whose banks
On each side an imperial city stood,
With towers and temples proudly elevate
On seven small hills, with palaces adorned,
Porches and theatres, baths, aqueducts,
Statues and trophies, and triumphal arcs,
Gardens and groves, presented to his eyes
Above the highth of mountains interposed —
By what strange parallax, or optic skill
Of vision, multiplied through air, or glass
Of telescope, were curious to inquire.
And now the Tempter thus his silence broke: —
  "The city which thou seest no other deem
Than great and glorious Rome  Queen of the Earth
So far renowned, and with the spoils enriched
Of nations.  There the Capitol thou seest,
Above the rest lifting his stately head
On the Tarpeian rock, her citadel
Impregnable; and there Mount Palatine,
The imperial palace, compass huge, and high
The structure, skill of noblest architects,
With gilded battlements, conspicuous far,
Turrets, and terraces, and glittering spires.
Many a fair edifice besides, more like
Houses of gods — so well have I disposed
My aery microscope — thou may'st behold,

Outside and inside both, pillars and roofs
Carved work, the hand of famed artificers
In cedar, marble, ivory, or gold.
Thence to the gates cast round thine eye, and see
What conflux issuing forth, or entering in:
Prætors, proconsuls to their provinces
Hasting, or on return, in robes of state ;
Lictors and rods, the ensigns of their power ;
Legions and cohorts, turms of horse and wings ;
Or embassies from regions far remote,
In various habits, on the Appian road,
Or on the Æmilian — some from farthest south,
Syene, and where the shadow both way falls,
Meroe, Nilotic isle, and, more to west,
The realm of Bocchus to the Blackmoor sea ;
From the Asian kings (and Parthian among these),
From India and the Golden Chersoness,
And utmost Indian isle Taprobane,
Dusk faces with white silken turbants wreathed ;
From Gallia, Gades, and the British west ;
Germans, and Scythians, and Sarmatians north
Beyond Danubius to the Tauric pool.
All nations now to Rome obedience pay —
To Rome's great Emperor, whose wide domain,
In ample territory, wealth and power,
Civility of manners, arts and arms,
And long renown, thou justly may'st prefer
Before the Parthian.   These two thrones except,
The rest are barbarous, and scarce worth the sight,
Shared among petty kings too far removed ;
These having shown thee, I have shown thee all
The kingdoms of the world, and all their glory.

*Book IV.*

THE END.